HAMMOND

THE WORLD ALMANAC®

WORLD FACT BOOK

A VIEW OF THE WORLD IN MAPS, PHOTOS & FACTS

The World Almanac® World Fact Book

© COPYRIGHT 2008 BY
HAMMOND WORLD ATLAS CORPORATION

Printed in Canada.

HAMMOND

THE WORLD ALMANAC

WORLD FACT BOOK

A VIEW OF THE WORLD IN MAPS, PHOTOS & FACTS

First Edition

CONTENTS

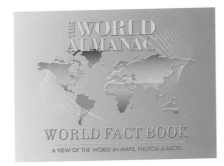

CONTENTS

THE WORLD ALMANAC® FACT BOOK ATLAS

Offering a broad range of features and functions, this atlas is more than a geographical reference work of superior quality and guide for virtual global exploration. It also includes a compendium of compelling facts and figures from *The World Almanac® and Book of Facts* that will enhance your understanding of the connections in the world around you. The information provided below will help you get the most enjoyment and benefit from its use.

KEY TO MAP SYMBOLS

▬ ▬ ▬	First Order (National) Boundary	Rome ★	National Capital
─────	Shoreline, River	**Athens**	National Capital (World Political)
⬭	Lake, Reservoir	Belfast ●	Major Town (Country Maps)
░	Glacier		
•‧• ⌁	Ruins	▲	Point Elevation
■	Antarctic Station (p.28)	⧌	Park

PRINCIPAL MAP ABBREVIATIONS

Arch.	Archipelago	L.	Lake	PN	Park
B.	Bay	Mt.	Mount		National
C.	Cape	Mtn.	Mountain	Prsv.	Preserve
Chan.	Channel	Mts.	Mountains	Pt.	Point
Cr.	Creek	Nat'l	National	R.	River
Dem.	Democratic	NP	National	Ra.	Range
Fk.	Fork		Park	Rep.	Republic
Ft.	Fort	Passg.	Passage	Res.	Reservoir
G.	Gulf	Pen.	Peninsula	Str.	Strait
I., Is.	Island(s)	Pk.	Peak	Terr.	Territory
Int'l	International	Plat.	Plateau		

INDEX

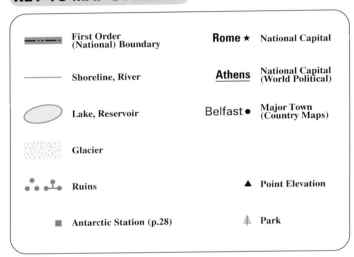

Master Index (p.237):
When you are looking for specific place or physical feature, your quickest rooute is the Master Index. This 3,800-entry alphabetical index lists the page for major places and features found on the country, state and province maps.

A Word About Names
Our source for all foreign names and physical names in the United States is the decision lists of the U.S. Board of Geographic Names, which contain hundreds of thousands of place names. If a place is not listed, the Atlas follows the name form appearing on official foreign maps or in official gazetteers of the country concerned. For rendering domestic city, town and village names, this atlas follows the forms and spelling of the U.S. Postal Service.

Boundary Policies
This atlas observes the boundary policies of the U.S. Department of State. Boundary disputes are customarily handled with a special symbol treatment, but de facto boundaries are favored if they seem to have any degree of permanence, in the belief that boundaries should reflect current geographic and political realities. The portrayal of independent nations in the atlas follows their recognition by the United Nations and/or the United States government.

COUNTRY PAGE

Page Number   Country Profile   Continent
Country Name   Locator   Flag
Photo

66   CANADA
NORTH AMERICA

Canada is the second-largest country in the world in area, occupying all of North America north of the United States except Alaska, Greenland and the French islands of Saint Pierre and Miquelon. The country consists of ten provinces and two large territories: Yukon and the Northwest Territories. Covering most of eastern and central Canada is the Shield (Laurentian Plateau), a rugged forested area of pre-Cambrian rock. To the north is the Arctic archipelago, stretching close to the North Pole. A vast prairie extends west of the Shield to the Canadian Rockies. Westernmost Canada is laced with towering mountain ranges and rich, productive forests. The Mackenzie, Yukon, Saint Lawrence, Nelson and the Churchill are the major rivers traversing the country. The climate varies from temperate in the south to subarctic and frigid arctic in the far north.

Canada's huge natural resources include nickel, zinc, copper, gold, lead, molybdenum, potash, fish, timber, coal, petroleum and natural gas. Wheat growing, dairy farming, livestock ranching and fruit farming are the major agricultural activities. Exports, primarily manufactured goods, flow to the United States, Japan and the United Kingdom.

A central feature of Canadian history and culture is the division between the two-thirds of the population who speak English and the French-speaking third who live largely in Québec. The indigenous Indians and Inuit (Eskimos) constitute less than 1 percent of the population. Canada's great cities are Toronto, Montréal, Vancouver, Ottawa (the capital), Edmonton, Calgary and Winnipeg. Nearly 90 percent of Canada's population is concentrated near the U.S.-Canadian border.

Historically, Canada's native population consisted largely of peoples of Algonquian stock. The Inuit, or Eskimos, still inhabit the Arctic archipelago and the northern reaches of the Canadian Shield. Although the Vikings are believed to have visited Canada about 1000 A.D., John Cabot in 1497 made the first recorded landing. In 1534 Jacques Cartier claimed the region for France. The intense rivalry that followed dominated Canadian history for more than two centuries. France lost control of Canada to Britain at the end of the French and Indian Wars in 1763. The British North America Act in 1817 established the Dominion of Canada, consisting of Nova Scotia, New Brunswick, Québec and Ontario. Other provinces were added in subsequent years, the last being Newfoundland in 1949. In 1931 the Statute of Westminster established the equality of the Canadian Parliament with that of Britain. The last decades of the twentieth century have seen Canadian political affairs dominated by the Québec independence movement. In 1995 the vote on Québec's separation was defeated by a slim margin.

Did you know? The Canada/U.S. boundary is the world's longest undefended border.

Toronto

AREA: 3,855,101 sq mi (9,984,670 sq km)
■ **CLIMATE:** The temperate south changes to subarctic and frigid arctic in the far north.
■ **PEOPLE:** Canadians are ethnically divided between English and French-speaking citizens. Indigenous Indians and Inuit (Eskimos) make up a small minority.
POPULATION: 33,098,932
LIFE EXPECTANCY AT BIRTH (YEARS): male, 76.6; female, 83.5
LITERACY RATE: 97%
ETHNIC GROUPS: British 28%, French 23%, other European 15%, Amerindian 2%
PRINCIPAL LANGUAGES: English, French (both official)
CHIEF RELIGIONS: Roman Catholic 46%, Protestant 36%, other 18%
■ **ECONOMY:** Natural resources include iron, nickel, zinc, copper, gold, lead, potash, diamonds, silver, fish, timber, coal and natural gas. Transportation equipment, primary metals, machinery and chemicals dominate the industrial sector.
MONETARY UNIT: Canadian dollar
GDP: $1,023 billion (2004 est.)
PER CAPITA GDP: $31,500
INDUSTRIES: transport equipment, chemicals, mining, food products, wood and paper products, fish products, petroleum and natural gas
CHIEF CROPS: wheat, barley, oilseed, tobacco, fruits, vegetables
MINERALS: iron ore, nickel, zinc, copper, gold, lead, molybdenum, potash, silver, coal, petroleum, natural gas
GOVERNMENT TYPE: confederation with parliamentary democracy
CAPITAL: Ottawa (pop., 1,093,000)
INDEPENDENCE DATE: July 1, 1867
WEBSITES: www.statcan.ca www.canada.gc.ca/main_c.html

Political Map   Physical Map
Fun Fact
Facts & Figures

ABOUT THE FACTS & FIGURES DATA (FROM THE WORLD ALMANAC):
Population figures for cities generally pertain to the entire metropolitan area. GDP (gross domestic product) estimates are based on so-called purchasing power parity calculations, which make use of weighted prices in order to take into account differences in price levels between countries. Please note that the addresses and content of websites are subject to change.

ABBREVIATIONS IN FACTS & FIGURES

est.	estimate(d)	ft	foot, feet
Gov.-Gen.	Governor-General	in	inch(es)
km	kilometer(s)	m	meter(s)
mi	mile(s)	NA	not available
pop.	population	Pres.	President
Prime Min.	Prime Minister	sq	square

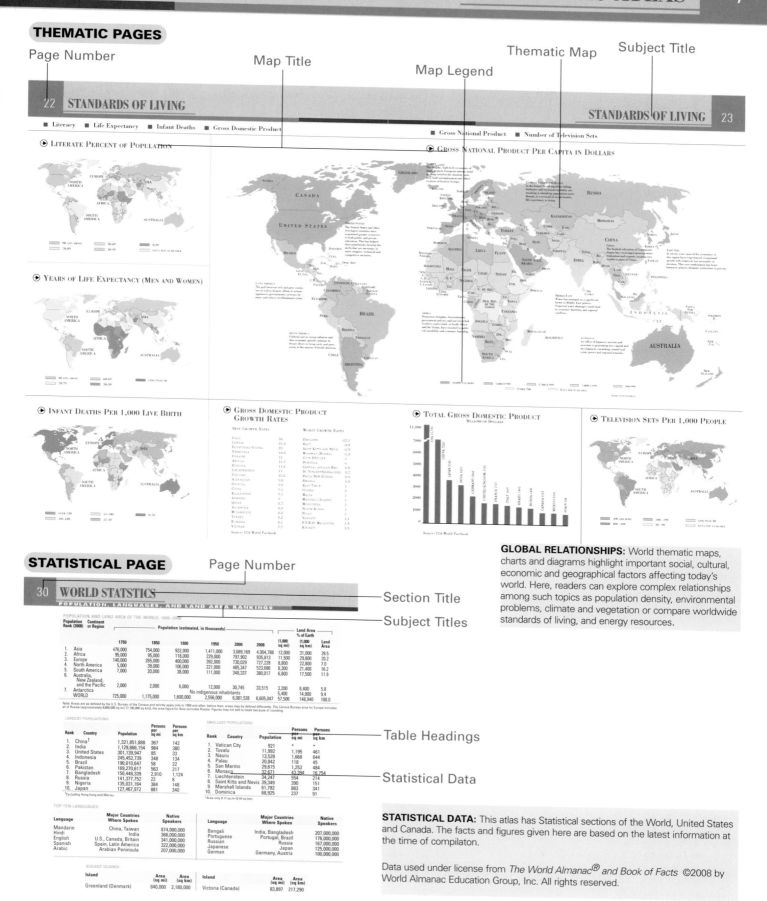

THEMATIC PAGES

Page Number · Map Title · Map Legend · Thematic Map · Subject Title

STATISTICAL PAGE

Page Number · Section Title · Subject Titles · Table Headings · Statistical Data

GLOBAL RELATIONSHIPS: World thematic maps, charts and diagrams highlight important social, cultural, economic and geographical factors affecting today's world. Here, readers can explore complex relationships among such topics as population density, environmental problems, climate and vegetation or compare worldwide standards of living, and energy resources.

STATISTICAL DATA: This atlas has Statistical sections of the World, United States and Canada. The facts and figures given here are based on the latest information at the time of compilaton.

Data used under license from *The World Almanac® and Book of Facts* ©2008 by World Almanac Education Group, Inc. All rights reserved.

Simply stated, the map-maker's challenge is to project the earth's curved surface onto a flat plane. To achieve this elusive goal, cartographers have developed map projections — equations which govern this conversion of geographic data. This section explores some of the most widely used projections.

GENERAL PRINCIPLES AND TERMS

The earth rotates around its axis once a day. Its end points are the North and South poles; the line circling the earth midway between the poles is the equator. The arc from the equator to either pole is divided into 90 degrees of latitude. The equator represents 0° latitude. Circles of equal latitude, called parallels, are traditionally shown at every fifth or tenth degree.

The equator is divided into 360 degrees. Lines circling the globe from pole to pole through the degree points on the equator are called meridians, or great circles. All meridians are equal in length, but by international agreement the meridian passing through the Greenwich Observatory near London has been chosen as the prime meridian or 0° longitude. The distance in degrees from the prime meridian to any point east or west is its longitude.

While meridians are all equal in length, parallels become shorter as they approach the poles. Whereas one degree of latitude represents approximately 69 miles (112 km.) anywhere on the globe, a degree of longitude varies from 69 miles (112 km.) at the equator to zero at the poles. Each degree of latitude and longitude is divided into 60 minutes. One minute of latitude equals one nautical mile (1.15 land miles or 1.85 km.).

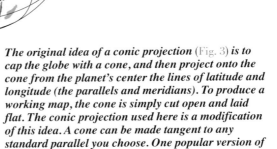

HOW TO FLATTEN A SPHERE: THE ART OF CONTROLLING DISTORTION

There is only one way to represent a sphere with absolute precision: on a globe. All attempts to project our planet's surface onto a plane unevenly stretch or tear the sphere as it flattens, inevitably distorting shapes, distances, area (sizes appear larger or smaller than actual size), angles or direction.

Since representing a sphere on a flat plane always creates distortion, only the parallels or the meridians (or some other set of lines) can maintain the same length as on a globe of corresponding scale. All other lines must be either too long or too short. Accordingly, the scale on a flat map cannot be true everywhere; there will always be different scales in different parts of a map. On world maps or very large areas, variations in scale may be extreme. Most maps seek to preserve either true area relationships (equal area projections) or true angles and shapes (conformal projections); some attempt to achieve overall balance.

PROJECTIONS: SELECTED EXAMPLES

Mercator (Fig. 1): This projection is especially useful because all compass directions appear as straight lines, making it a valuable navigational tool. Moreover, every small region conforms to its shape on a globe — hence the name conformal. But because its meridians are evenly-spaced vertical lines which never converge (unlike the globe), the horizontal parallels must be drawn farther and farther apart at higher latitudes to maintain a correct relationship.

Only the equator is true to scale, and the size of areas in the higher latitudes is dramatically distorted.

Robinson (Fig. 2): To create the two-page world map in the Maps of the World section, the Robinson projection was used. It combines elements of both conformal and equal area projections to show the whole earth with relatively true shapes and reasonably equal areas.

Conic (Fig. 3): This projection has been used frequently for air navigation charts and to create most of the national and regional maps in this atlas.

The original idea of a conic projection (Fig. 3) is to cap the globe with a cone, and then project onto the cone from the planet's center the lines of latitude and longitude (the parallels and meridians). To produce a working map, the cone is simply cut open and laid flat. The conic projection used here is a modification of this idea. A cone can be made tangent to any standard parallel you choose. One popular version of a conic projection, the Lambert Conformal Conic, uses two standard parallels near the top and bottom of the map to further reduce errors of scale.

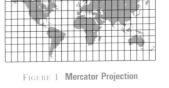

FIGURE 1 **Mercator Projection**

FIGURE 2 **Robinson Projection**

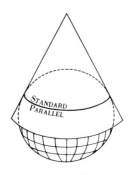

FIGURE 3 **Conic Projection**

Lambert Azimuthal Equal-Area Projection

(Fig. 4): Mathematically projected on a plane surface tangent to any point on the globe, this is the most common projection (also known as Zenithal Equal-Area) used for maps of Eastern and Western hemispheres. It is also a good projection for continents, as it shows correct areas with little distortion of shape.

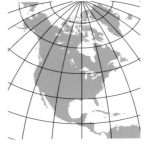

FIGURE 4
Lambert Azimuthal Equal-Area Projection

THEMATIC MAPS

■ Desertification and Acid Rain Damage   ■ Greenhouse Effect   ■ Main Tanker Routes and Major Oil Spills

➤ DESERTIFICATION AND ACID RAIN DAMAGE

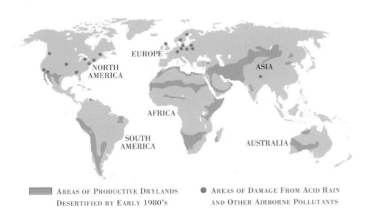

▓▓ AREAS OF PRODUCTIVE DRYLANDS
DESERTIFIED BY EARLY 1980's

● AREAS OF DAMAGE FROM ACID RAIN
AND OTHER AIRBORNE POLLUTANTS

➤ GREENHOUSE EFFECT

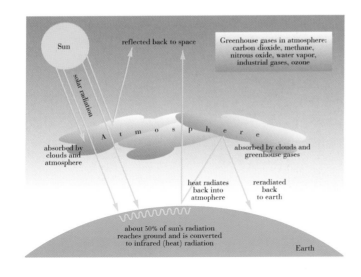

Sun

reflected back to space

Greenhouse gases in atmosphere:
carbon dioxide, methane,
nitrous oxide, water vapor,
industrial gases, ozone

solar radiation

Atmosphere

absorbed by
clouds and
atmosphere

absorbed by clouds and
greenhouse gases

heat radiates
back into
atmophere

reradiated
back
to earth

about 50% of sun's radiation
reaches ground and is converted
to infrared (heat) radiation

Earth

➤ MAIN TANKER ROUTES AND MAJOR OIL SPILLS

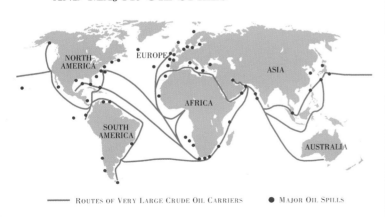

—— ROUTES OF VERY LARGE CRUDE OIL CARRIERS   ● MAJOR OIL SPILLS

GRIZZLY BEAR
Much of Pacific temperate rain forest
has been clear-cut. Remainder could
be gone in 35 years.

WOODLAND CARIBOU

HUMPBACK
WHALE

Hydroelectric power
projects and development
in Quebec are disrupting
wildlife habitats.

SPOTTED OWL

BLACK-FOOTED FERRET

CONDOR

Fragile barrier beaches of the
Atlantic coast have been damaged
by agricultural runoff, sewage and
overdevelopment.

WHOOPING CRANE

ATLANTIC RIDLEY
TURTLE

MANATEE

Ecological balance in coral reefs of
the Gulf and Caribbean area is being
upset by a booming tourist industry.

At the present rate of clearing, half
of Central America's rain forest will
disappear early in the 21st century.

One-third of Guinea's tropical
forest is expected to disappear
in the next decade.

HOWLER MONKEY

Erosion, the depletion of water
resources for irrigation, and overgraz-
ing have turned range and cropland
into desert.

GALÁPAGOS TORTOISE

BLACK CAIMAN

JAGUAR

VICUÑA

GOLDEN LION
TAMARIN

Every year over 5000 square miles
(13,000 sq km) of rain forest is
destroyed in Brazil's Amazon Basin.

CHINCHILLA

GIANT ARMADILLO

Southern Chile's rain forest is threatened by development.

The Atlantic waters
off Patagonia have
suffered from over-
fishing and oil spills.

BLUE WHALE

Acid Rain
Acid rain of nitric and
sulfuric acids has killed all
life in thousands of lakes,
and over 15 million acres
(6 million hectares) of
virgin forest in Europe and
North America are dead or
dying.

Deforestation
Each year, 50 million acres
(20 million hectares) of
tropical rainforests are
being felled by loggers. Trees
remove carbon dioxide from
the atmosphere and are
vital to the prevention of soil
erosion.

Vanishing Wilderness and Endangered Species

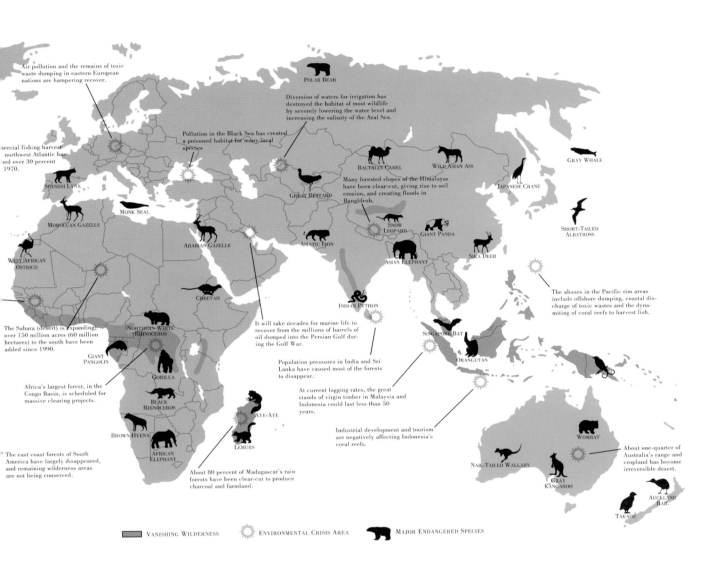

Air pollution and the remains of toxic waste dumping in eastern European nations are hampering recover.

POLAR BEAR

Diversion of waters for irrigation has destroyed the habitat of most wildlife by severely lowering the water level and increasing the salinity of the Aral Sea.

Pollution in the Black Sea has created a poisoned habitat for many local species

...mercial fishing harvest ...ed over 30 percent ...1970.

GRAY WHALE

SPANISH LYNX

BACTRIAN CAMEL   WILD ASIAN ASS

JAPANESE CRANE

MONK SEAL

GREAT BUSTARD

Many forested slopes of the Himalayas have been clear-cut, giving rise to soil erosion, and creating floods in Bangldesh.

MOROCCAN GAZELLE

SHORT-TAILED ALBATROSS

ARABIAN GAZELLE

ASIATIC LION

SNOW LEOPARD   GIANT PANDA

WEST AFRICAN OSTRICH

ASIAN ELEPHANT   SIKA DEER

CHEETAH

INDIAN PYTHON

The abuses in the Pacific rim areas include offshore dumping, coastal discharge of toxic wastes and the dynamiting of coral reefs to harvest fish.

The Sahara (desert) is expanding; over 150 million acres (60 million hectares) to the south have been added since 1990.

NORTHERN WHITE RHINOCEROS

It will take decades for marine life to recover from the millions of barrels of oil dumped into the Persian Gulf during the Gulf War.

SINGAPORE BAT

GIANT PANGOLIN

ORANGUTAN

Population pressures in India and Sri Lanka have caused most of the forests to disappear.

GORILLA

Africa's largest forest, in the Congo Basin, is scheduled for massive clearing projects.

At current logging rates, the great stands of virgin timber in Malaysia and Indonesia could last less than 50 years.

BLACK RHINOCEROS

AYE-AYE

Industrial development and tourism are negatively affecting Indonesia's coral reefs.

WOMBAT

BROWN HYENA

LEMURS

About one-quarter of Australia's range and cropland has become irreversible desert.

AFRICAN ELEPHANT

NAIL-TAILED WALLABY

* The east coast forests of South America have largely disappeared, and remaining wilderness areas are not being conserved.

About 80 percent of Madagascar's rain forests have been clear-cut to produce charcoal and farmland.

GRAY KANGAROO

AUCKLAND RAIL

TAKAHE

VANISHING WILDERNESS   ENVIRONMENTAL CRISIS AREA   MAJOR ENDANGERED SPECIES

Extinction

Biologists estimate that over 50,000 plant and animal species inhabiting the world's rain forests are disappearing each year due to pollution, unchecked hunting and the destruction of natural habitats.

Air Pollution

Billions of tons of industrial emissions and toxic pollutants are released into the air each year, depleting our ozone layer, killing our forests and lakes with acid rain and threatening our health.

Water Pollution

Only 3 percent of the earth's water is fresh. Pollution from cities, farms and factories has made much of it unfit to drink. In the developing world, most sewage flows untreated into lakes and rivers.

Ozone Depletion

The layer of ozone in the stratosphere shields earth from harmful ultraviolet radiation. But man-made gases are destroying this vital barrier, increasing the risk of skin cancer and eye disease.

■ **Climate Regions**   ■ **Average Temperatures**

⊙ CLIMATE REGIONS

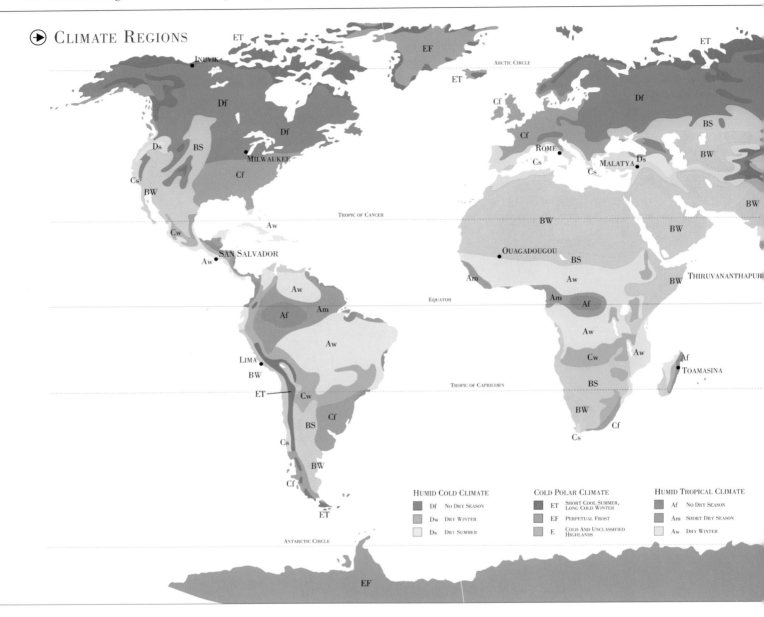

ET
EF
ARCTIC CIRCLE
INUVIK
ET
Df
Cf
Df
Cf
BS
Df
Ds
BS
Ds
BW
MILWAUKEE
ROME
MALATYA
Cs
Cf
Cs
BW
Cs
BW
TROPIC OF CANCER
Aw
BW
BW
Cw
BS
SAN SALVADOR
OUAGADOUGOU
Aw
Aw
THIRUVANANTHAPUR
BW
Am
Af
EQUATOR
Am
Af
Aw
Af
Aw
LIMA
Aw
BW
Cw
Af
ET
Cw
TROPIC OF CAPRICORN
TOAMASINA
BS
BS
Cf
BW
Cs
Cf
BW
Cf
ET

ANTARCTIC CIRCLE

EF

HUMID COLD CLIMATE
Df	No Dry Season
Dw	Dry Winter
Ds	Dry Summer

COLD POLAR CLIMATE
ET	Short Cool Summer, Long Cold Winter
EF	Perpetual Frost
E	Cold and Unclassified Highlands

HUMID TROPICAL CLIMATE
Af	No Dry Season
Am	Short Dry Season
Aw	Dry Winter

⊙ AVERAGE TEMPERATURES

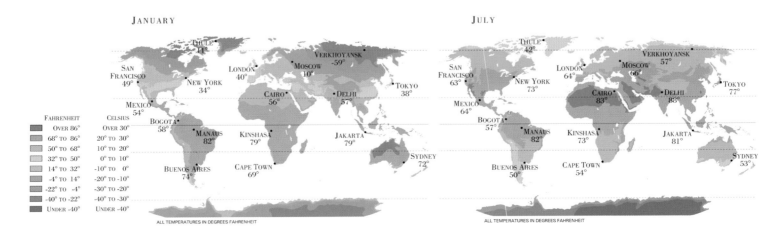

JANUARY

THULE
11°
SAN FRANCISCO 49°
NEW YORK 34°
LONDON 40°
MOSCOW 10°
VERKHOYANSK -59°
TOKYO 38°
MEXICO 54°
CAIRO 56°
DELHI 57°
BOGOTA 58°
MANAUS 82°
KINSHASA 79°
JAKARTA 79°
BUENOS AIRES 74°
CAPE TOWN 69°
SYDNEY 72°

FAHRENHEIT	CELSIUS
OVER 86°	OVER 30°
68° TO 86°	20° TO 30°
50° TO 68°	10° TO 20°
32° TO 50°	0° TO 10°
14° TO 32°	-10° TO 0°
-4° TO 14°	-20° TO -10°
-22° TO -4°	-30° TO -20°
-40° TO -22°	-40° TO -30°
UNDER -40°	UNDER -40°

ALL TEMPERATURES IN DEGREES FAHRENHEIT

JULY

THULE 42°
SAN FRANCISCO 63°
NEW YORK 73°
LONDON 64°
MOSCOW 66°
VERKHOYANSK 57°
TOKYO 77°
MEXICO 64°
CAIRO 83°
DELHI 88°
BOGOTA 57°
MANAUS 82°
KINSHASA 73°
JAKARTA 81°
BUENOS AIRES 50°
CAPE TOWN 54°
SYDNEY 53°

ALL TEMPERATURES IN DEGREES FAHRENHEIT

■ **Average Annual Rainfall**   ■ **Annual Temperature Range**   ■ **Selected Climate Stations**

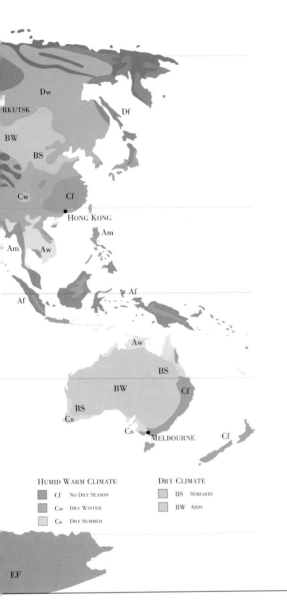

● AVERAGE ANNUAL RAINFALL

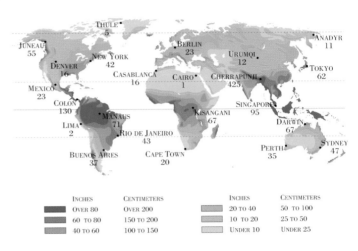

INCHES	CENTIMETERS		INCHES	CENTIMETERS
OVER 80	OVER 200		20 TO 40	50 TO 100
60 TO 80	150 TO 200		10 TO 20	25 TO 50
40 TO 60	100 TO 150		UNDER 10	UNDER 25

● ANNUAL TEMPERATURE RANGE

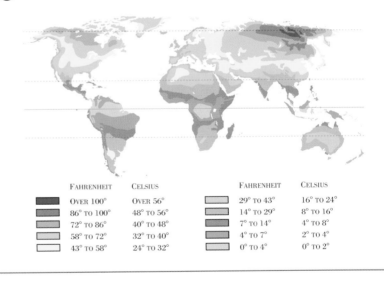

FAHRENHEIT	CELSIUS		FAHRENHEIT	CELSIUS
OVER 100°	OVER 56°		29° TO 43°	16° TO 24°
86° TO 100°	48° TO 56°		14° TO 29°	8° TO 16°
72° TO 86°	40° TO 48°		7° TO 14°	4° TO 8°
58° TO 72°	32° TO 40°		4° TO 7°	2° TO 4°
43° TO 58°	24° TO 32°		0° TO 4°	0° TO 2°

HUMID WARM CLIMATE
- Cf No Dry Season
- Cw Dry Winter
- Cs Dry Summer

DRY CLIMATE
- BS Semiarid
- BW Arid

● SELECTED CLIMATE STATIONS - TEMPERATURES AND RAINFALL

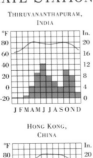

TOAMASINA, MADAGASCAR

THIRUVANANTHAPURAM, INDIA

SAN SALVADOR, EL SALVADOR

OUAGADOUGOU, BURKINA FASO

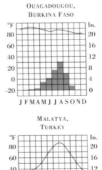

LIMA, PERU

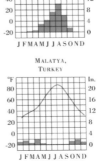

MELBOURNE, AUSTRALIA

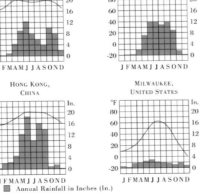

ROME, ITALY

HONG KONG, CHINA

MILWAUKEE, UNITED STATES

MALATYA, TURKEY

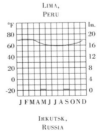

IRKUTSK, RUSSIA

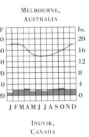

INUVIK, CANADA

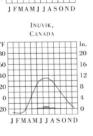

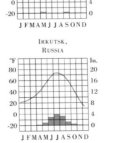

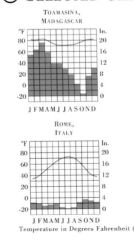

Temperature in Degrees Fahrenheit (°F)   ■ Annual Rainfall in Inches (In.)

■ Natural Vegetation

⊙ NATURAL VEGETATION

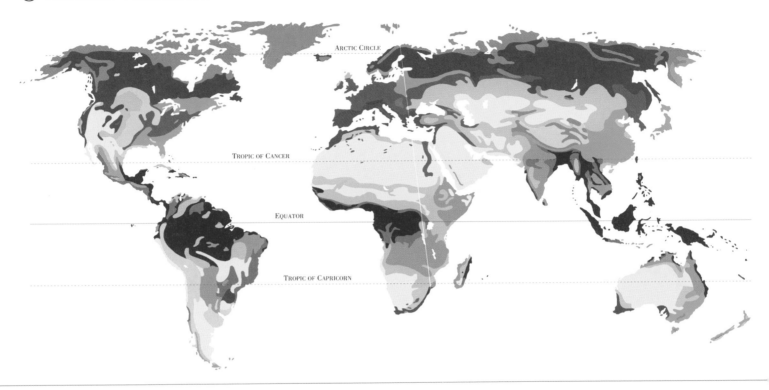

NEEDLELEAF FOREST
Found in higher latitudes with shorter growing seasons, and dominated by pure stands of softwood, evergreen conifers (cone-bearing trees) such as pine, fir and spruce. The light undergrowth consists of small shrubs, mosses, lichens and pine needles.

BROADLEAF FOREST
Found in the middle latitudes, this forest of deciduous (seasonal leaf-shedding) trees includes the hardwoods maple, hickory and oak. The forest floor is relatively barren, except for thick leaf cover during colder months.

MIXED NEEDLELEAF AND BROADLEAF FOREST
A transitional zone between northern softwoods and temperate hardwoods.

WOODLAND AND SHRUB (MEDITERRANEAN)
A mid-latitude area of broadleaf evergreens, dense growths of woody shrubs and open grassy woodland, characterized by pronounced dry summers and wet winters.

SHORT GRASS (STEPPE)
A mid-latitude, semi-arid area usually found on the fringe of desert regions, with continuous short-grass cover up to 8" (20 cm.) tall, used chiefly to graze livestock.

TALL GRASS (PRAIRIE)
Mid-latitude, semi-moist areas with continuous tall-grass cover up to 24" (61 cm.) in height, used for agricultural purposes. Rainfall is insufficient to support larger plants.

TROPICAL RAIN FOREST (SELVA)
A dense, evergreen forest of tall, varied hardwood trees with a thick broadleaf canopy and a dark, moist interior with minimal undergrowth.

LIGHT TROPICAL FOREST (TROPICAL SEMIDECIDUOUS OR MONSOON FOREST)
As above, with more widely spaced trees, heavier undergrowth, larger concentrations of single species. Dry season prevents most trees from remaining evergreen. Found in monsoon areas.

TROPICAL WOODLAND AND SHRUB (THORN FOREST)
Longer dry season results in low trees with thick bark and smaller leaves. Dense undergrowth of thorny plants, brambles and grasses. Transition belt between denser forests and grasslands.

TROPICAL GRASSLAND AND SHRUB (SAVANNA)
Stiff, sharp-edged grasses, from 2' to 12' (0.6 m. to 3.7 m.) high, with large areas of bare ground. Scattered shrubs and low trees in some areas.

WOODED SAVANNA
A transitional area where savanna joins a tropical or shrub forest, with low trees and shrubs dotting the grasslands.

DESERT AND DESERT SHRUB
Barren stretches of soft brown, yellow or red sand and rock wastes with isolated patches of short grass and stunted bushes, turning bright green when fed by infrequent precipitation.

RIVER VALLEY AND OASIS
River valleys are lush, fertile lands, with varied vegetation. An oasis is a fertile or verdant spot found in a desert near a natural spring or pool.

HEATH AND MOOR
A heath is open, uncultivated land covered with low, flowering evergreen shrubs such as heather. Moors are often high and poorly drained lands, with patches of heath and peat bogs.

TUNDRA AND ALPINE
An area of scarce moisture and short, cool summers where trees cannot survive. A permanently frozen subsoil supports low-growing lichens, mosses and stunted shrubs.

UNCLASSIFIED HIGHLANDS
Sequential bands or vertical zones of all vegetation types, which generally follow the warm-to-cold upward patterns found in corresponding areas of vegetation. (Map scale does not permit delineation of these areas.)

PERMANENT ICE COVER
Permanently ice and snow-covered terrain found in polar regions and atop high mountains.

■ Types of Soils ■ Types of Vegetation

⊕ TYPES OF SOILS

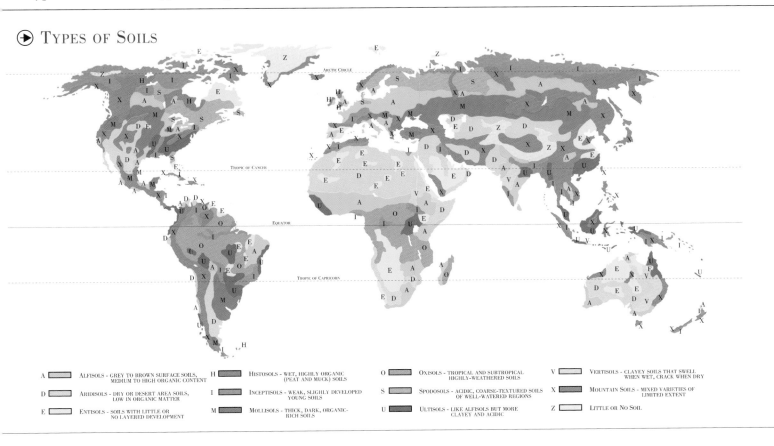

A ▭ ALFISOLS - GREY TO BROWN SURFACE SOILS, MEDIUM TO HIGH ORGANIC CONTENT

D ▭ ARIDISOLS - DRY OR DESERT AREA SOILS, LOW IN ORGANIC MATTER

E ▭ ENTISOLS - SOILS WITH LITTLE OR NO LAYERED DEVELOPMENT

H ▭ HISTOSOLS - WET, HIGHLY ORGANIC (PEAT AND MUCK) SOILS

I ▭ INCEPTISOLS - WEAK, SLIGHTLY DEVELOPED YOUNG SOILS

M ▭ MOLLISOLS - THICK, DARK, ORGANIC-RICH SOILS

O ▭ OXISOLS - TROPICAL AND SUBTROPICAL HIGHLY-WEATHERED SOILS

S ▭ SPODOSOLS - ACIDIC, COARSE-TEXTURED SOILS OF WELL-WATERED REGIONS

U ▭ ULTISOLS - LIKE ALFISOLS BUT MORE CLAYEY AND ACIDIC

V ▭ VERTISOLS - CLAYEY SOILS THAT SWELL WHEN WET, CRACK WHEN DRY

X ▭ MOUNTAIN SOILS - MIXED VARIETIES OF LIMITED EXTENT

Z ▭ LITTLE OR NO SOIL

⊕ TYPES OF VEGETATION

Needleleaf Forest
These typically coniferous softwood forests of Europe, Asia and North America cover about 9 percent of the earth's land.

Broadleaf Forest
Located in the most pleasant habitable climatic regions, temperate broadleaf forests have suffered the greatest destruction by people.

Mixed Forest
These hardwood and softwood forests, when added to the broadleaf forest area, are home to over half the world's population.

Prairie
Unique to the Americas, tall grass prairie lands have been successfully cultivated to become great grain fields of the world

Steppe
Slightly more moist than desert, steppe areas are sometimes cultivated but more often used for livestock ranching and herding.

Tropical Rain Forest
Teak, mahogany, balsawood, quinine, cocoa and rubber are some of the major products found in the world's tropical rain forest regions.

Savanna
A place of winter droughts and summer rainfall, these tropical grass and shrub areas are home to a wide variety of big-game animals.

Mediterranean
In addition to southern Europe and northern Africa, this vegetation also can be found in California, Chile, South Africa and Western Australia.

Desert Shrub
One-fifth of the world's land is desert and desert shrub, too dry for farming and ranching, and populated largely by nomads and oases-dwellers.

Tundra
Found along the Arctic fringe of North America and Eurasia, tundra is of little economic significance except for mineral exploitation.

■ **Population Distribution**　　■ **Population Density**

⊙ POPULATION DISTRIBUTION

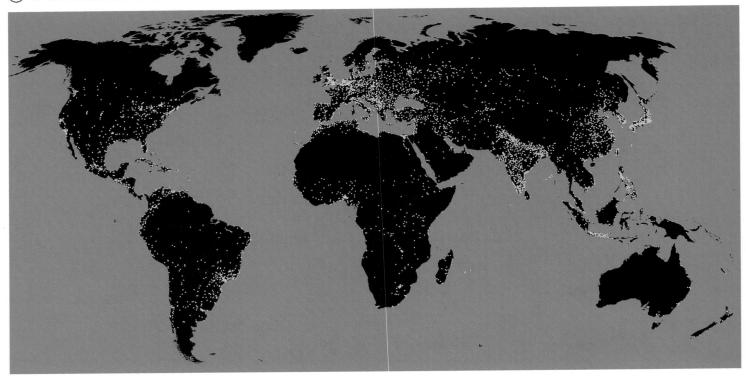

This map provides a dramatic perspective by illuminating populated areas with one point of light for each city over 50,000 residents. Over 675 million people live in cities with populations in excess of 500,000. According to the latest census data, there are 11,650 people per square mile (4,500 per sq km) in London. In New York, there are 32,250 (12,450). Hong Kong has over 18,000 people per square mile (7,000 per sq km), and the Tokyo-Yokohama agglomeration includes over 14,250 (5,500). During the last decade, the movement to the cities has accelerated dramatically, particularly in developing nations. In Lagos, Nigeria, where there are over 28,500 people per square mile (11,000 per sq km), most live in shantytowns. In São Paulo, Brazil, 2,000 buses arrive each day, bringing field hands, farm workers and their families in search of a better life. Tokyo, Mexico and Mumbai are the world's largest urban agglomerations. By 2015, the United Nations predicts that 30 of the 40 largest urban agglomerations will be located in less-industrialized nations.

⊙ POPULATION DENSITY PER SQUARE MILE (SQ. KM.)

1,000 - 5,000 (390 - 2,000)

500 - 1,000 (195 - 390)

100 - 500 (39 - 195)

30 - 100 (12 - 39)

UNDER 30 (UNDER 12)

Source: U.S. Bureau of the Census, International Database

■ Age Distribution ■ World's Largest Urban Areas ■ Population Increase

⊙ AGE DISTRIBUTION

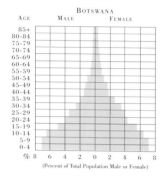

BOTSWANA

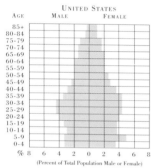

UNITED STATES

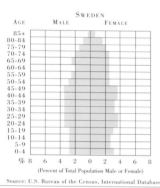

SWEDEN

Source: U.S. Bureau of the Census, International Database

⊙ URBAN & RURAL POPULATION COMPONENTS

WORLD'S LARGEST URBAN AREAS

MILLIONS OF INHABITANTS

Tokyo, Japan 26.5
Mexico, Mexico 18.1
Mumbai (Bombay), India 18.1
São Paulo, Brazil 17.7
New York, U.S. 16.6
Lagos, Nigeria 13.4
Los Angeles, U.S. 13.1
Kolkata, India 12.9
Shanghai, China 12.9
Buenos Aires, Argentina 12.5
Dhaka, Bangladesh 12.3
Jakarta, Indonesia 11.0
Osaka, Japan 11
Beijing, China 10.8
Rio de Janeiro, Brazil 10.5

URBAN & RURAL POPULATION COMPONENTS

SELECTED COUNTRIES
■ URBAN ■ RURAL

Uruguay 87% / 13%
Australia 85% / 15%
Japan 77% / 23%
United States 74% / 26%
Russia 73% / 27%
Hungary 62% / 38%
Iran 54% / 46%
Egypt 44% / 56%
Philippines 37% / 63%
Portugal 30% / 70%
China 26% / 74%
Maldives 20% / 80%
Bangladesh 15% / 85%
Nepal 6% / 94%

⊙ ANNUAL RATE OF POPULATION (NATURAL) INCREASE

3.5 percent or more
2.6 to 3.4 percent
1.8 to 2.5 percent
.09 to 1.7 percent
.01 to .08 percent
0.0 or decrease

Source: U.S. Bureau of the Census, International Database

■ Mineral Fuels   ■ Metals and Nonmetals   ■ Top Producers of Selected Mineral Commodities

➤ MINERAL FUELS

■ Oil Fields

■ Natural Gas Fields

● Major Coal Deposits

▲ Oil Sands

✦ Oil Shale

★ Major Uranium Deposits

■ Important Peat Deposits

➤ METALS AND NONMETALS

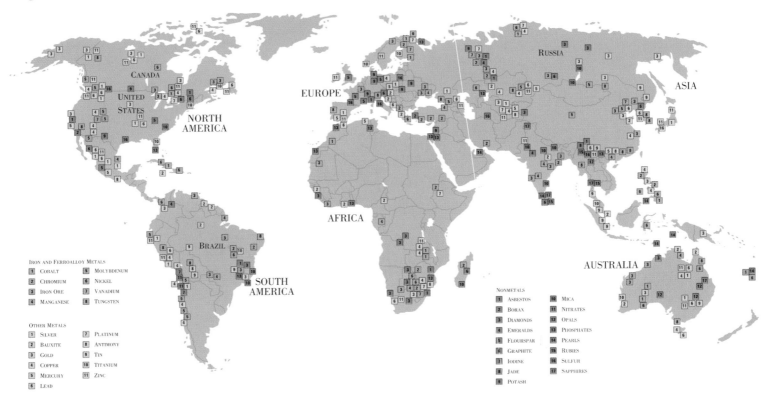

IRON AND FERROALLOY METALS

1 Cobalt
2 Chromium
3 Iron Ore
4 Manganese
5 Molybdenum
6 Nickel
7 Vanadium
8 Tungsten

OTHER METALS

1 Silver
2 Bauxite
3 Gold
4 Copper
5 Mercury
6 Lead
7 Platinum
8 Antimony
9 Tin
10 Titanium
11 Zinc

NONMETALS

1 Asbestos
2 Borax
3 Diamonds
4 Emeralds
5 Flourspar
6 Graphite
7 Iodine
8 Jade
9 Potash
10 Mica
11 Nitrates
12 Opals
13 Phosphates
14 Pearls
15 Rubies
16 Sulfur
17 Sapphires

■ **Energy Production/Consumption**　　■ **Nuclear Power Production**

◉ TOP FIVE WORLD PRODUCERS OF SELECTED MINERAL COMMODITIES

MINERAL FUELS	1	2	3	4	5
CRUDE OIL	SAUDI ARABIA	RUSSIA	UNITED STATES	IRAN	CHINA
GASOLINE	UNITED STATES	JAPAN	CHINA	CANADA	RUSSIA
NATURAL GAS	RUSSIA	UNITED STATES	CANADA	UNITED KINGDOM	NETHERLANDS
HARD COAL	CHINA	UNITED STATES	INDIA	AUSTRALIA	SOUTH AFRICA
URANIUM-BEARING ORES	CANADA	AUSTRALIA	NIGER	RUSSIA	KAZAKHSTAN

METALS	1	2	3	4	5
CHROMITE	SOUTH AFRICA	KAZAKHSTAN	INDIA	ZIMBABWE	TURKEY
IRON ORE	CHINA	BRAZIL	AUSTRALIA	RUSSIA	TURKEY
MANGANESE ORE	SOUTH AFRICA	GABON	AUSTRALIA	BRAZIL	INDIA
MINE NICKEL	RUSSIA	AUSTRALIA	CANADA	INDONESIA	CHINA
MINE SILVER	MEXICO	PERU	CHINA	AUSTRALIA	NEW CALEDONIA
BAUXITE	AUSTRALIA	GUINEA	BRAZIL	JAMAICA	CHINA
ALUMINUM	CHINA	RUSSIA	CANADA	UNITED STATES	AUSTRALIA
MINE GOLD	SOUTH AFRICA	AUSTRALIA	UNITED STATES	CHINA	RUSSIA
MINE COPPER	CHILE	INDONESIA	UNITED STATES	AUSTRALIA	RUSSIA
MINE LEAD	AUSTRALIA	CHINA	UNITED STATES	PERU	MEXICO
MINE TIN	CHINA	PERU	INDONESIA	BRAZIL	BOLIVIA
MINE ZINC	CHINA	AUSTRALIA	PERU	CANADA	UNITED STATES

NONMETALS	1	2	3	4	5
NATURAL DIAMOND	AUSTRALIA	DEM. REP. OF THE CONGO	RUSSIA	BOTSWANA	SOUTH AFRICA
POTASH	CANADA	RUSSIA	BELARUS	GERMANY	ISRAEL
PHOSPHATE ROCK	UNITED STATES	CHINA	MOROCCO	RUSSIA	TUNISIA
SULFUR (ALL FORMS)	UNITED STATES	CANADA	RUSSIA	CHINA	JAPAN

Names in Black Indicate More Than 10% of Total World Production

Source: U.S. Geological Survey, Mineral Commodity Summary; Handbook of International Economic Statistics

◉ COMMERCIAL ENERGY PRODUCTION/CONSUMPTION

PERCENTAGE OF WORLD TOTAL

■ PRODUCTION　■ CONSUMPTION

United States 15.9% / 22.5%

China 12.6% / 13.3%

Russia 11.7% / 6.7%

Saudi Arabia 5.5% / 1.4%

Canada 4.2% / 3.0%

Iran 2.7% / 1.4%

India 2.5% / 3.5%

Australia 2.4% / 1.2%

Norway 2.4% / 0.4%

Mexico 2.3% / 1.5%

United Kingdom 2.1% / 2.2%

Indonesia 2.0% / 1.0%

Venezuela 1.8% / 0.6%

Germany 1.4% / 3.3%

Source: U.S. Energy Information Administration

◉ NATIONS WITH HIGHEST PERCENTAGE OF NUCLEAR POWER PRODUCTION

■ NUCLEAR　■ THERMAL　■ HYDROELECTRIC

Belgium 98% / 1% / 1%

France 75% / 11% / 14%

South Korea 71% / 21% / 8%

Japan 65% / 9% / 26%

Finland 58% / 42%

Sweden 43% / 57%

Spain 41% / 40% / 19%

Switzerland 39% / 61%

Germany 26% / 71% / 3%

Hungary 22% / 78%

Ukraine 21% / 77% / 2%

Bulgaria 17% / 80% / 3%

United Kingdom 11% / 88% / 1%

United States 10% / 86% / 4%

■ Religions   ■ Language Families

▶ RELIGIONS

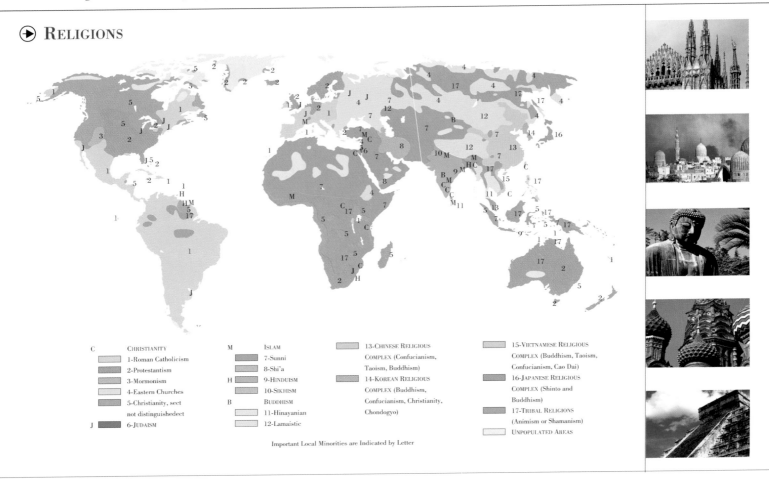

C	CHRISTIANITY	M	ISLAM		13-CHINESE RELIGIOUS		15-VIETNAMESE RELIGIOUS
	1-Roman Catholicism		7-Sunni		COMPLEX (Confucianism,		COMPLEX (Buddhism, Taoism,
	2-Protestantism		8-Shi'a		Taoism, Buddhism)		Confucianism, Cao Dai)
	3-Mormonism	H	9-Hinduism		14-KOREAN RELIGIOUS		16-JAPANESE RELIGIOUS
	4-Eastern Churches		10-Sikhism		COMPLEX (Buddhism,		COMPLEX (Shinto and
	5-Christianity, sect	B	BUDDHISM		Confucianism, Christianity,		Buddhism)
	not distinguishedect		11-Hinayanian		Chondogyo)		17-TRIBAL RELIGIONS
J	6-JUDAISM		12-Lamaistic				(Animism or Shamanism)
							UNPOPULATED AREAS

Important Local Minorities are Indicated by Letter

▶ LANGUAGE FAMILIES

■ The Indo-European Language Tree   ■ Langages of Europe

⊕ THE INDO-EUROPEAN LANGUAGE TREE

The most well-established family tree is Indo-European. Spoken by more than 2.5 billion people, it contains dozens of languages. Some linguists theorize that all people – and all languages – are descended from a tiny population that lived in Africa some 200,000 years ago.

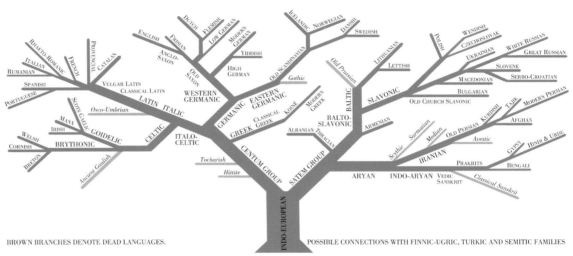

BROWN BRANCHES DENOTE DEAD LANGUAGES.

POSSIBLE CONNECTIONS WITH FINNIC-UGRIC, TURKIC AND SEMITIC FAMILIES

⊕ Pictures on the left:

1. Milan Cathedral, Italy
2. City of the Dead, Cairo, Egypt
3. Buddha Statue, Japan
4. St. Basil's Cathedral, Moscow
5. Temple, Mexico

1-INDO-EUROPEAN	9-URALIC
1A-GERMANIC	10-ALTAIC
1B-ROMANCE	11-PALEO-SIBERIAN
1C-SLAVIC	FAMILIES
1D-BALTIC	12-SINO-TIBETAN
1E-CELTIC	13-THAI-KADAI
1F-ALBANIAN	14-KOREAN
1G-GREEK	15-JAPANESE
1H-ARMENIAN	16-DRAVIDIAN
1J-IRANIAN	17-VIETNAMESE
1K-INDO-ARYAN	18-AUSTRO-ASIATIC
2-BASQUE	19-AUSTRONESIAN
3-CAUCASIAN FAMILIES	20-PAPUAN
4-BURUSHASKI	21-AUSTRALIAN
5-AFRO-ASIATIC	22-ESKIMO-ALEUT
(HAMITO-SEMITIC)	23-AMERICAN INDIAN
6-NILO-SAHARAN	FAMILIES
7-NIGER-CONGO	UNPOPULATED AREAS
8-KHOISAN	

NOTE: Names may vary, depending on source.

⊕ LANGUAGES OF EUROPE

INDO-EUROPEAN FAMILY

- GERMANIC SUBFAMILY
- ROMANCE SUBFAMILY
- CELTIC SUBFAMILY
- SLAVIC SUBFAMILY
- BALTIC SUBFAMILY
- GREEK
- ALBANIAN

URALIC FAMILY

- FINNIC SUBFAMILY
- UGRIC SUBFAMILY
- SAMOYED

ALTAIC FAMILY

- TURKIC SUBFAMILY

AFRO-ASIATIC FAMILY

- MALTESE
- BASQUE

■ Literacy   ■ Life Expectancy   ■ Infant Deaths   ■ Gross Domestic Product

⊕ LITERATE PERCENT OF POPULATION

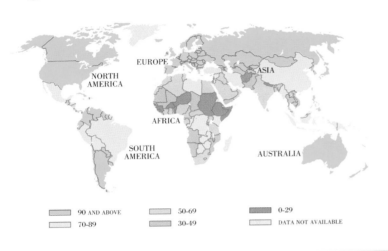

	90 AND ABOVE		50-69		0-29
	70-89		30-49		DATA NOT AVAILABLE

⊕ YEARS OF LIFE EXPECTANCY (MEN AND WOMEN)

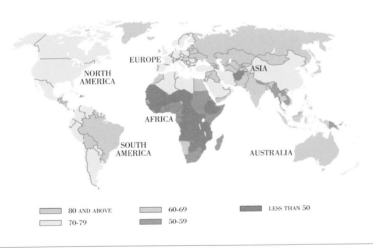

	80 AND ABOVE		60-69		LESS THAN 50
	70-79		50-59		

⊕ INFANT DEATHS PER 1,000 LIVE BIRTH

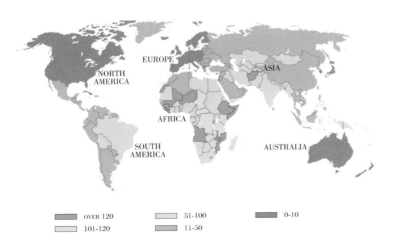

	OVER 120		51-100		0-10
	101-120		11-50		

UNITED STATES
The United States and other developed countries have committed greater resources to both public and private education. This has helped their populations develop the skills that are necessary in more complex, technical and competitive societies.

LATIN AMERICA
The gulf between rich and poor continues to widen, despite efforts to reform oppressive governments, increase literacy and relieve overburdened cities.

SOUTH AMERICA
Political unrest, rising inflation and slow economic growth continue to thwart efforts to bring unity and prosperity to the nations of South America.

⊕ GROSS DOMESTIC PRODUCT GROWTH RATES

BEST GROWTH RATES		WORST GROWTH RATES	
CHAD	38	ZIMBABWE	-12.1
LIBERIA	21.8	HAITI	-3.5
EQUATORIAL GUINEA	20	SAINT KITTS AND NEVIS	-1.9
VENEZUELA	16.8	MYANMAR (BURMA)	-1.3
UKRAINE	12	CÔTE D'IVOIRE	-1
ANGOLA	11.7	DOMINICA	-1
ETHIOPIA	11.6	CENTRAL AFRICAN REP.	0.5
LIECHTENSTEIN	11	ST. VINCENT/GRENADINES	0.7
URUGUAY	10.2	PAPUA NEW GUINEA	0.9
AZERBAIJAN	9.8	RWANDA	0.9
GEORGIA	9.5	EAST TIMOR	1
CHINA	9.1	GUINEA	1
KAZAKHSTAN	9.1	MALTA	1
ARMENIA	9	MARSHALL ISLANDS	1
QATAR	8.7	MICRONESIA	1
ARGENTINA	8.3	NORTH KOREA	1
MOZAMBIQUE	8.2	PALAU	1
TURKEY	8.2	VANUATU	1.1
ROMANIA	8.1	F.Y.R.O. MACEDONIA	1.3
VIETNAM	7.7	KIRIBATI	1.5

Source: CIA World Factbook

■ Gross National Product   ■ Number of Television Sets

◉ GROSS NATIONAL PRODUCT PER CAPITA IN DOLLARS

EUROPE
The healthy, high-tech economies of many western European nations stand in sharp relief to the obsolete factories, high unemployment and ethnic rivalries of Eastern Europe.

EASTERN EUROPE AND RUSSIA
In the former Soviet republics falling birthrates and increased mortality are resulting in shrinking populations even though, in a reversal of recent trends, life expectancy is rising.

CHINA
The limited relaxation of Communist dogma has encouraged growing industrialization and exports, creating new wealth in parts of China.

EAST ASIA
In recent years most of the economies of this region have experienced exceptional growth with relatively low inequality in incomes. This rare combination has been known to achieve dramatic reductions in poverty.

MIDDLE EAST
Water has emerged as a significant factor in Middle East politics. Projected water shortages could lead to economic hardship and regional conflicts.

AFRICA
Disastrous droughts, discriminatory government policies and ancient tribal rivalries, particularly in South Africa and the Sudan, have resulted in political instability and economic hardship.

AUSTRALIA
An influx of Japanese tourists and investors is generating new capital and development, escalating coastal real estate prices and regional tensions.

Legend:
- 10,000 AND MORE
- 5,000-9,999
- 2,500-4,999
- 1,000-2,499
- 700-999
- UNDER 700
- DATA NOT AVAILABLE

Source: CIA World Factbook

◉ TOTAL GROSS DOMESTIC PRODUCT
BILLIONS OF DOLLARS

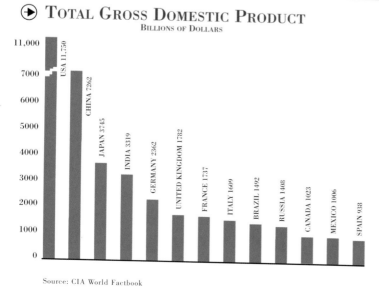

- USA 11,750
- CHINA 7262
- JAPAN 3745
- INDIA 3319
- GERMANY 2362
- UNITED KINGDOM 1782
- FRANCE 1737
- ITALY 1609
- BRAZIL 1492
- RUSSIA 1408
- CANADA 1023
- MEXICO 1006
- SPAIN 938

Source: CIA World Factbook

◉ TELEVISION SETS PER 1,000 PEOPLE

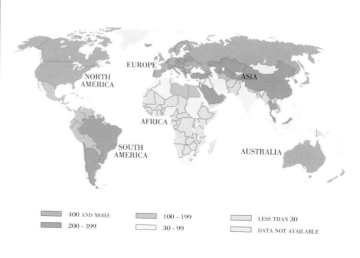

NORTH AMERICA · EUROPE · ASIA · AFRICA · SOUTH AMERICA · AUSTRALIA

Legend:
- 400 AND MORE
- 200 - 399
- 100 - 199
- 30 - 99
- LESS THAN 30
- DATA NOT AVAILABLE

■ **Top Producers of Agricultural Commodities**   ■ **Employment in Agriculture**

⊕ TOP FIVE WORLD PRODUCERS OF SELECTED AGRICULTURAL COMMODITIES

	1	2	3	4	5
WHEAT	CHINA	INDIA	UNITED STATES	RUSSIA	FRANCE
RICE	CHINA	INDIA	INDONESIA	BANGLADESH	VIETNAM
OATS	RUSSIA	CANADA	UNITED STATES	POLAND	FINLAND
CORN (MAIZE)	UNITED STATES	CHINA	BRAZIL	MEXICO	ARGENTINA
SOYBEANS	UNITED STATES	BRAZIL	ARGENTINA	CHINA	INDIA
POTATOES	CHINA	RUSSIA	INDIA	UKRAINE	UNITED STATES
COFFEE	BRAZIL	VIETNAM	INDONESIA	COLOMBIA	MEXICO
TEA	CHINA	INDIA	SRI LANKA	KENYA	TURKEY
TOBACCO	CHINA	BRAZIL	INDIA	UNITED STATES	INDONESIA
COTTON	CHINA	UNITED STATES	INDIA	PAKISTAN	BRAZIL
SUGAR	BRAZIL	INDIA	CHINA	THAILAND	PAKISTAN
CATTLE (STOCK)	BRAZIL	INDIA	CHINA	UNITED STATES	ARGENTINA
SHEEP (STOCK)	CHINA	AUSTRALIA	INDIA	IRAN	SUDAN
HOGS (STOCK)	CHINA	UNITED STATES	BRAZIL	GERMANY	SPAIN
COW'S MILK	UNITED STATES	INDIA	RUSSIA	GERMANY	FRANCE
HEN'S EGGS	CHINA	UNITED STATES	INDIA	JAPAN	RUSSIA
WOOL	AUSTRALIA	CHINA	NEW ZEALAND	IRAN	UNITED KINGDOM
ROUNDWOOD	UNITED STATES	CANADA	CHINA	BRAZIL	RUSSIA
NATURAL RUBBER	THAILAND	INDONESIA	MALAYSIA	INDIA	CHINA
FISH CATCHES	CHINA	PERU	JAPAN	INDIA	CHILE

Names in Black Indicate More Than 10% of Total World Production

Source: United Nations, Food and Agriculture Organization

Legend (right column, top)

- HERDING
- SHIFTING CROPS
- LIVESTOCK RANCHING
- LIGHT SUBSISTENCE CROPS
- RICE & INTENSIVE SUBSISTENCE CROPS
- INTENSIVE SUBSISTENCE CROPS
- PLANTATION CROPS
- LIVESTOCK, GRAINS & FRUIT
- HIGH-YIELD CROPS & LIVESTOCK
- LIVESTOCK & SUBSISTENCE CROPS
- HIGH-YIELD GRAIN CROPS
- SPECIALIZED CROPS
- DAIRY FARMING
- NON-AGRICULTURAL LAND

⊕ PERCENT OF TOTAL EMPLOYMENT IN AGRICULTURE, MANUFACTURING AND OTHER INDUSTRIES

- AGRICULTURE (INCLUDES FORESTRY AND FISHING)
- MANUFACTURING
- CONSTRUCTION
- TRADE AND COMMERCE
- FINANCE, INSURANCE REAL ESTATE
- SERVICES
- OTHER (INCLUDES MINING, UTILITIES, TRANSPORTATION)

0   20   40   60   80   100

India
China
Indonesia
Pakistan
Mexico
Brazil
Spain
Argentina
Italy
Japan
France
Canada
Australia
Germany
United States
United Kingdom

Legend (right column, bottom)

- ▲ AIRCRAFT
- △ MOTOR VEHICLES
- ▽ SHIPBUILDING
- ▼ TRANSPORTATION EQUIPMENT
- ■ IRON AND STEEL
- ▣ MACHINERY
- □ METALS AND METAL PRODUCTS
- ◪ ELECTRICAL PRODUCTS
- ⊡ OPTICAL INSTRUMENTS
- ● OIL REFINING
- ○ CHEMICALS
- △ TEXTILES
- ▲ CLOTHING
- ▼ RUBBER GOODS
- ▽ GLASS PRODUCTS
- ■ WOOD AND WOOD PRODUCTS
- □ PRINTING AND PUBLISHING

■ **Agricultural Regions**   ■ **Manufacturing Regions**

⊕ AGRICULTURAL REGIONS

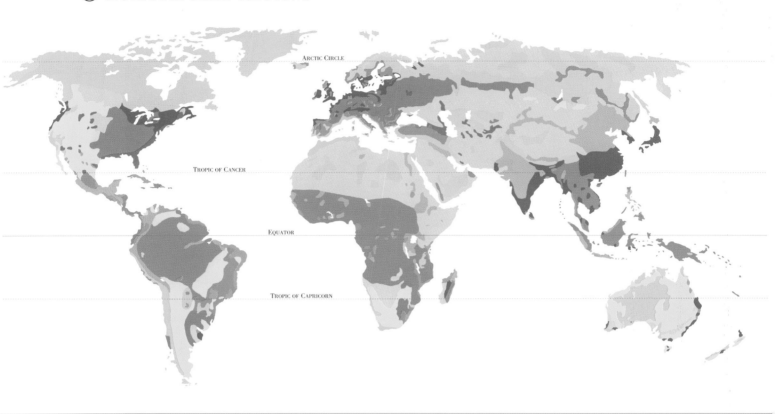

⊕ MANUFACTURING REGIONS

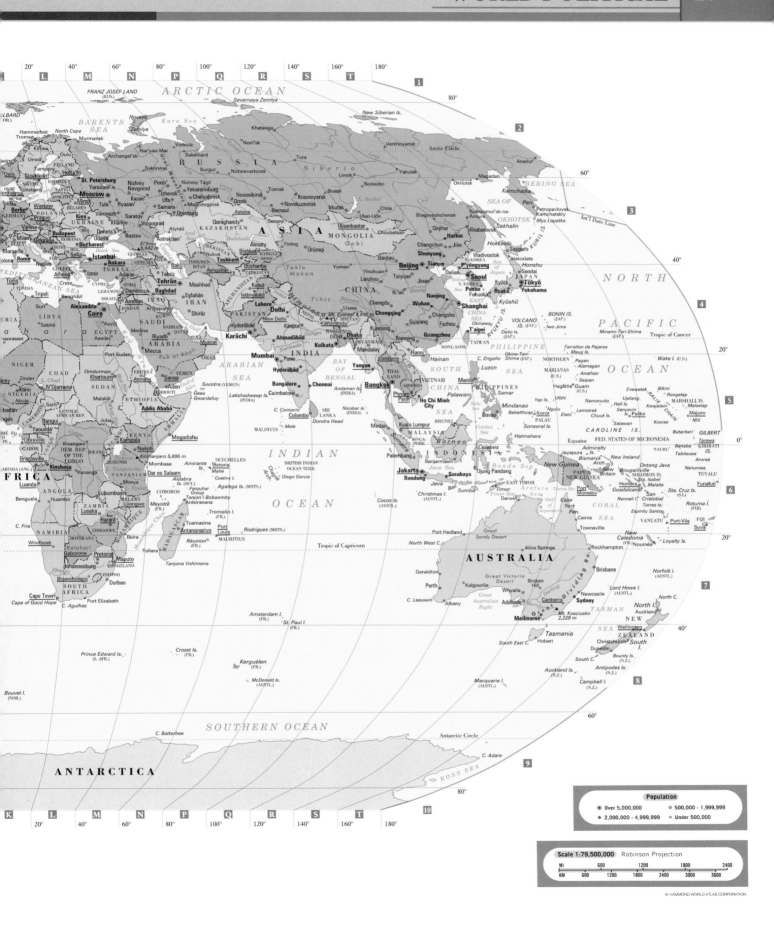

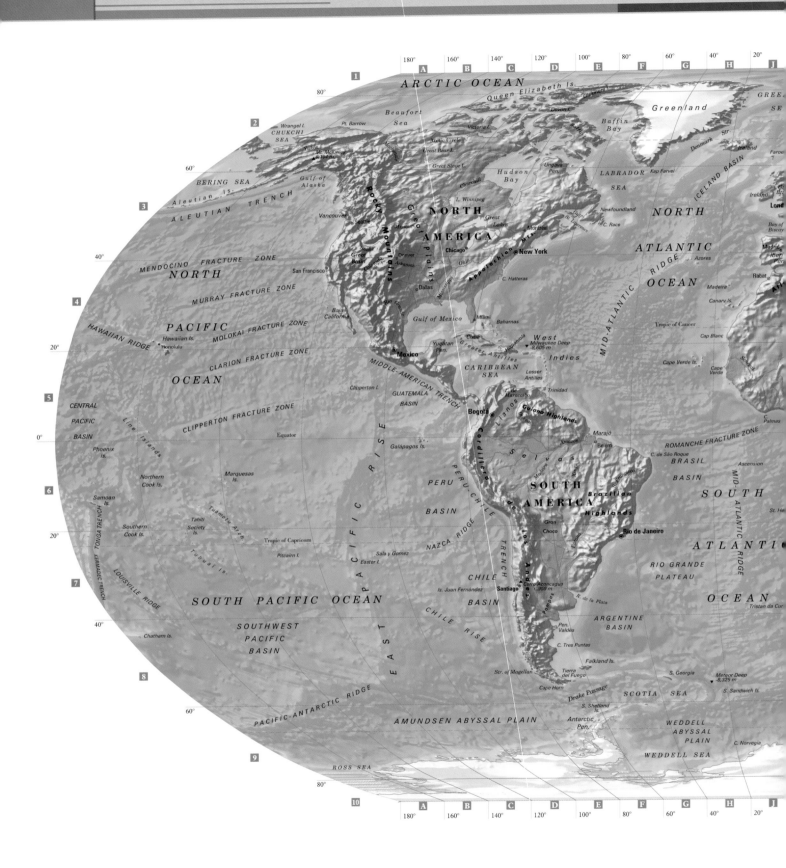

ARCTIC OCEAN

Queen Elizabeth Is.
Greenland
GREE
SE
Beaufort
Sea
Baffin
Bay
Denmark
Str.
Iceland
Faroe
Pt. Barrow
Victoria I.
CHUKCHI
SEA
Wrangel I.
Arctic Circle
Great Bear L.
Mt. McKinley
6,194 m
Great Slave L.
Hudson
Bay
Ungava
Pen.
LABRADOR
SEA
Kap Farvel
Ireland
Gr.
Bri.
ICELAND BASIN
Lon

BERING SEA
Gulf of
Alaska
L. Winnipeg
Churchill
NORTH
AMERICA
Newfoundland
NORTH
Bay of
Biscay
Aleutian Is.
ALEUTIAN TRENCH
Vancouver
Seattle
Rocky Mountains
Great Plains
Great Lakes
Montréal
St. Lawrence
C. Race
ATLANTIC
Madrid
Ibe
Pen

MENDOCINO FRACTURE ZONE
NORTH
Great Basin
Colorado
Arkansas
Ohio
Chicago
Appalachian Mts.
New York
MID-ATLANTIC
RIDGE
OCEAN
Azores
Rabat
Atl

San Francisco
Missouri
Mississippi
C. Hatteras

MURRAY FRACTURE ZONE
Dallas
Madeira
Tropic of Cancer
Cap Blanc

PACIFIC
Baja
California
Rio Grande
Gulf of Mexico
Miami
Bahamas
Cuba
Greater Antilles
Hispaniola
West
Indies
Milwaukee Deep
-8,605 m
Canary Is.
Cape Verde Is.
Cape
Verde

MOLOKAI FRACTURE ZONE
Hawaiian Is.
Honolulu
HAWAIIAN RIDGE

CLARION FRACTURE ZONE
Mexico
Yucatán
Pen.
CARIBBEAN
SEA
Lesser
Antilles
MIDDLE-AMERICAN TRENCH

OCEAN
Clipperton I.
GUATEMALA
BASIN
Trinidad
C.
Palmas

CLIPPERTON FRACTURE ZONE
Bogotá
L. de
Maracaibo
Guiana Highlands
ROMANCHE FRACTURE ZONE

CENTRAL
PACIFIC
BASIN
Line Islands
Equator
Galápagos Is.
Llanos
Amazon
Marajó
Belém
C. de São Roque
BRASIL
BASIN
Ascension

Phoenix
Is.
Cordillera
Selvas
SOUTH
AMERICA
Madeira
S
O
U
T
H

Northern
Cook Is.
Marquesas
Is.
PERU-CHILE
BASIN
Brazilian
Highlands
MID-
ATLANTIC
RIDGE

Samoan
Is.
Tahiti
Society
Is.
Tuamotu Arch.
PERU-CHILE TRENCH
São Francisco
St. He

Southern
Cook Is.
Tropic of Capricorn
Sala y Gómez
NAZCA RIDGE
Gran
Chaco
Paraná
Rio de Janeiro
RIO GRANDE
PLATEAU
ATLANTIC

Tubuai Is.
Pitcairn I.
Easter I.
Los Andes
Cerro Aconcagua
6,959 m
Santiago
Is. Juan Fernández
CHILE
BASIN
R. de la Plata
Pampas
ARGENTINE
BASIN
OCEAN
Tristan da Cur

TONGA TRENCH
KERMADEC TRENCH
LOUISVILLE RIDGE
EAST PACIFIC RISE
CHILE RISE
Pen.
Valdés
C. Tres Puntas

SOUTH PACIFIC OCEAN
Chatham Is.
SOUTHWEST
PACIFIC
BASIN
Str. of Magellan
Tierra
del Fuego
Falkland Is.
S. Georgia
Meteor Deep
-8,325 m

Cape Horn
Drake Passage
SCOTIA SEA
S. Sandwich Is.

PACIFIC-ANTARCTIC RIDGE
AMUNDSEN ABYSSAL PLAIN
Antarctic
Pen.
S. Shetland
Is.
WEDDELL
ABYSSAL
PLAIN
C. Norvegia

ROSS SEA
WEDDELL
SEA

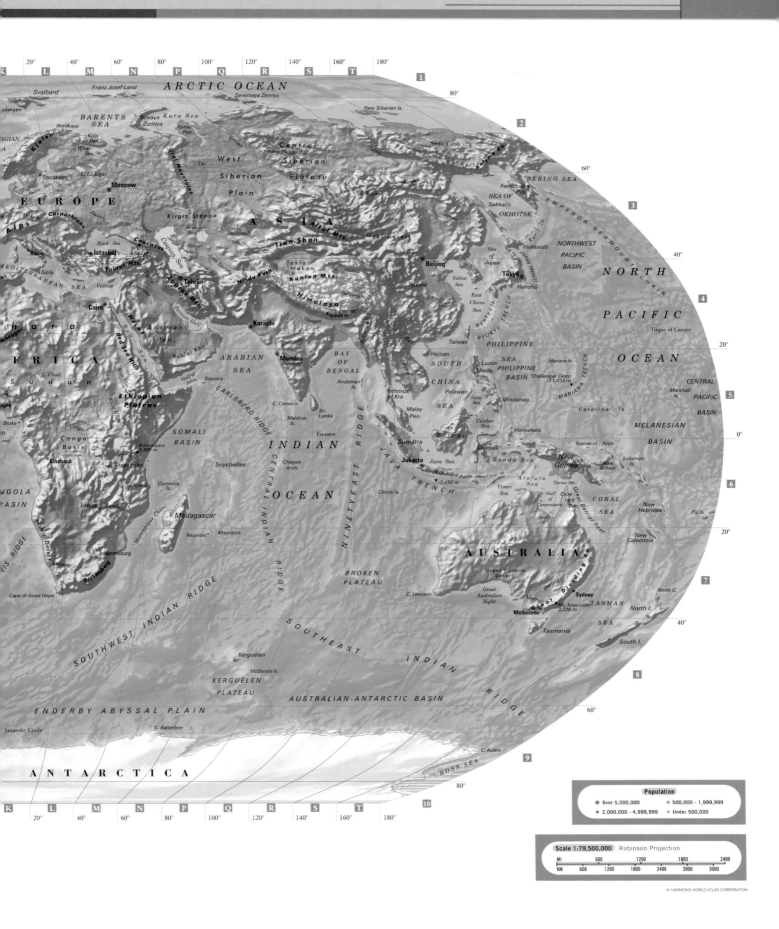

ARCTIC OCEAN

Svalbard
Franz Josef Land
Severnaya Zemlya
New Siberian Is.
80°

sbergen
Nordkapp
BARENTS SEA
Novaya Zemlya
Kara Sea
Yamal Pen.
Central Siberian Plateau
60°
BERING SEA
Kamchatka
SEA OF OKHOTSK
EMPEROR SEAMOUNT CHAIN

EGIAN
Kola Pen.
White Sea
Kielen
Nordkapp
Ural Mountains
Ob'
West Siberian Plain
Yenisey
Lena
Kolyma R.
Arctic Circle
40°
NORTHWEST PACIFIC BASIN
NORTH

Stockholm
L. Ladoga
Moscow
Kirgiz Steppe
Irtysh
A S I A
Altai Mts.
Gobi Desert
Amur
Hokkaidō
JAPAN TRENCH

EUROPE
Carpathians
Dnepr
Volga
Aral Sea
L. Balkhash
Tian Shan
Beijing
Sea of Japan
Tōkyō
PACIFIC BASIN
PACIFIC

LPS
Black Sea
Caucasus
Caspian Sea
Amu Darya
Takla Makan
Kunlun Mts.
Huang
Honshū
20°
Rome
Istanbul
El'brus 5,642 m
Tehrān
Hindu Kush
Yellow Sea
East China Sea
OCEAN
Tropic of Cancer

Sicily
Taurus Mts.
Zagros Mts.
Tigris
Himalaya
Mt. Everest 8,848 m
Taiwan
Ryukyu Is.
RYUKYU TRENCH

MEDITERRANEAN SEA
Cyprus
Euphrates
Indus
Ganges
Hainan
PHILIPPINE SEA
Mariana Is.
MARIANA TRENCH
CENTRAL PACIFIC BASIN
5

Cairo
Karachi
Normada
SOUTH CHINA SEA
Luzon
Manila
PHILIPPINE BASIN
Challenger Deep -11,033 m
Marshall Is.

hara
Red Sea Hills
Arabian Pen.
Persian Gulf
Gulf of Aden
ARABIAN SEA
Mumbai (Bombay)
BAY OF BENGAL
Andaman Is.
Palawan
Mindanao
Caroline Is.
MELANESIAN

FRICA
Sudan
Rub'al Khali
Socotra
CARLSBERG RIDGE
C. Comorin
Isthmus of Kra
Malay Pen.
Sulu Sea
Celebes Sea
Halmahera
BASIN

ahoggar
L. Chad
Blue Nile
Ethiopian Plateau
Maldive Is.
Sri Lanka
Equator
Sumátra
Borneo
Celebes
Bismarck Arch.
0°

Bioko
me
Congo
White Nile
SOMALI BASIN
Seychelles
INDIAN
Jakarta
Java Sea
New Guinea
New Britain
Solomon Is.

Kinshasa
Kilimanjaro 5,895 m
Chagos Arch.
OCEAN
Java -7,450 m
Banda Sea
Timor Sea
Arafura Sea
CORAL SEA
20°

NGOLA ASIN
Victoria
Comoros Is.
Lusaka
Zambezi
CENTRAL INDIAN RIDGE
Cocos Is.
JAVA TRENCH
Gulf of Carpentaria
Cape York Pen.
Great Barrier Reef
New Hebrides

vis Ridge
Namib Desert
Orange
Johannesburg
Madagascar
Mauritius
Réunion
NINETYEAST RIDGE
AUSTRALIA
Fiji Is.
New Caledonia

Drakensberg
Mozambique Chan.
Great Victoria Desert
Darling
Sydney
40°

Cape of Good Hope
SOUTHWEST INDIAN RIDGE
BROKEN PLATEAU
C. Leeuwin
Great Australian Bight
Murray
Mt. Kosciusko 2,228 m
Great Dividing Ra.
Melbourne
TASMAN SEA
North I.

SOUTHEAST INDIAN RIDGE
Tasmania
South I.

Kerguélen
McDonald Is.
KERGUÉLEN PLATEAU
AUSTRALIAN-ANTARCTIC BASIN
60°

ENDERBY ABYSSAL PLAIN

Antarctic Circle
C. Batterbee
ROSS SEA
80°

A N T A R C T I C A

Population	
● Over 5,000,000	◉ 500,000 - 1,999,999
● 2,000,000 - 4,999,999	○ Under 500,000

Scale 1:79,500,000 Robinson Projection

MI	600	1200	1800	2400
KM	600 1200	1800 2400	3000	3600

POPULATION AND LAND AREA OF THE WORLD, 1650–2008

Population Rank (2008)	Continent or Region	Population (estimated, in thousands)						Land Area		% of Earth
		1750	1850	1900	1950	2000	2008	(1,000 sq mi)	(1,000 sq km)	Land Area
1.	Asia	476,000	754,000	932,000	1,411,000	3,689,169	4,004,788	12,000	31,000	29.5
2.	Africa	95,000	95,000	118,000	229,000	797,902	935,813	11,500	29,800	20.2
3.	Europe	140,000	265,000	400,000	392,000	730,029	727,228	8,800	22,800	7.0
4.	North America	5,000	39,000	106,000	221,000	485,347	523,686	8,300	21,400	16.2
5.	South America	7,000	20,000	38,000	111,000	348,337	380,017	6,800	17,500	11.9
6.	Australia, New Zealand, and the Pacific	2,000	2,000	6,000	12,000	30,745	33,515	3,200	8,400	5.8
7.	Antarctica				No indigenous inhabitants			5,400	14,000	9.4
	WORLD	725,000	1,175,000	1,600,000	2,556,000	6,081,528	6,605,047	57,506	148,940	100.0

Note: Areas are as defined by the U.S. Bureau of the Census and strictly apply only to 1950 and after; before then, areas may be defined differently. The Census Bureau area for Europe includes all of Russia (approximately 6,600,000 sq mi [17,100,000 sq km]); the area figure for Asia excludes Russia. Figures may not add to totals because of rounding.

LARGEST POPULATIONS

Rank	Country	Population	Persons per sq mi	Persons per sq km
1.	China[1]	1,321,851,888	367	142
2.	India	1,129,866,154	984	380
3.	United States	301,139,947	85	33
4.	Indonesia	245,452,739	348	134
5.	Brazil	190,010,647	58	22
6.	Pakistan	169,270,617	563	217
7.	Bangladesh	150,448,339	2,910	1,124
8.	Russia	141,377,752	22	8
9.	Nigeria	135,031,164	384	148
10.	Japan	127,467,972	881	340

[1]Excluding Hong Kong and Macau.

SMALLEST POPULATIONS

Rank	Country	Population	Persons per sq mi	Persons per sq km
1.	Vatican City	921	*	*
2.	Tuvalu	11,992	1,195	461
3.	Nauru	13,528	1,668	644
4.	Palau	20,842	118	45
5.	San Marino	29,615	1,253	484
6.	Monaco	32,671	43,394	16,754
7.	Liechtenstein	34,247	554	214
8.	Saint Kitts and Nevis	39,349	390	151
9.	Marshall Islands	61,782	883	341
10.	Dominica	68,925	237	91

TOP TEN LANGUAGES

Language	Major Countries Where Spoken	Native Speakers	Language	Major Countries Where Spoken	Native Speakers
Mandarin	China, Taiwan	874,000,000	Bengali	India, Bangladesh	207,000,000
Hindi	India	366,000,000	Portuguese	Portugal, Brazil	176,000,000
English	U.S., Canada, Britain	341,000,000	Russian	Russia	167,000,000
Spanish	Spain, Latin America	322,000,000	Japanese	Japan	125,000,000
Arabic	Arabian Peninsula	207,000,000	German	Germany, Austria	100,000,000

BIGGEST ISLANDS

Island	Area (sq mi)	Area (sq km)	Island	Area (sq mi)	Area (sq km)
Greenland (Denmark)	840,000	2,180,000	Victoria (Canada)	83,897	217,290
New Guinea (Indonesia, Papua New Guinea)	306,000	793,000	Ellesmere (Canada)	75,767	196,240
Borneo (Indonesia, Malaysia, Brunei)	280,100	725,500	Celebes (Indonesia)	69,000	178,710
			South (New Zealand)	58,384	151,210
Madagascar	226,658	587,040	Java (Indonesia)	48,900	126,650
Baffin (Canada)	195,928	507,450	North (New Zealand)	44,204	114,490
Sumatra (Indonesia)	165,000	427,350	Cuba	42,804	110,860
Honshu (Japan)	87,805	227,410	Newfoundland (Canada)	42,031	108,860
Great Britain (United Kingdom)	84,200	218,080	Luzon (Philippines)	40,680	105,360

LARGEST LAND AREAS

Rank	Country	Land Area (sq mi)	Land Area (sq km)
1.	Russia	6,562,112	16,995,800
2.	China	3,600,946	9,326,410
3.	United States	3,537,437	9,161,923
4.	Canada	3,511,021	9,093,507
5.	Brazil	3,265,075	8,456,510
6.	Australia	2,941,298	7,617,930
7.	India	1,147,955	2,973,190
8.	Argentina	1,056,641	2,736,690
9.	Kazakhstan	1,030,815	2,669,800
10.	Algeria	919,595	2,381,740

SMALLEST LAND AREAS

Rank	Country	Land Area (sq mi)	Land Area (sq km)
1.	Vatican City	0.17	0.44
2.	Monaco	0.75	1.95
3.	Nauru	8	21
4.	Tuvalu	10	26
5.	San Marino	24	61
6.	Liechtenstein	62	160
7.	Marshall Islands	70	181
8.	Saint Kitts and Nevis	101	261
9.	Maldives	116	300
10.	Malta	122	316

AREAS AND AVERAGE DEPTHS OF OCEANS, SEAS, AND GULFS

Geographers and mapmakers recognize four major bodies of water: the Pacific, the Atlantic, the Indian, and the Arctic oceans. The Atlantic and Pacific oceans are considered divided at the equator into the North and South Atlantic and the North and South Pacific. The Arctic Ocean is the name for waters north of the continental landmasses in the region of the Arctic Circle.

	Area (sq mi)	Area (sq km)	Average Depth (ft)	Average Depth (m)
Pacific Ocean	64,186,300	166,241,800	12,925	3,940
Atlantic Ocean	33,420,000	86,557,400	11,730	3,575
Indian Ocean	28,350,500	73,427,500	12,598	3,840
Arctic Ocean	5,105,700	13,223,700	3,407	1,038
South China Sea	1,148,500	2,974,600	4,802	1,464
Caribbean Sea	971,400	2,515,900	8,448	2,575
Mediterranean Sea	969,100	2,510,000	4,926	1,501
Bering Sea	873,000	2,261,000	4,893	1,491
Gulf of Mexico	582,100	1,508,000	5,297	1,615
Sea of Okhotsk	537,500	1,392,000	3,192	973
Sea of Japan	391,100	1,013,000	5,468	1,667
Hudson Bay	281,900	730,100	305	93
East China Sea	256,600	664,600	620	189
Andaman Sea	218,100	564,900	3,667	1,118
Black Sea	196,100	507,900	3,906	1,191
Red Sea	174,900	453,000	1,764	538
North Sea	164,900	427,100	308	94
Baltic Sea	147,500	382,000	180	55
Yellow Sea	113,500	294,000	121	37
Persian Gulf	88,800	230,000	328	100
Gulf of California	59,100	153,000	2,375	724

PRINCIPAL OCEAN DEPTHS

Name of Area	Location (latitude)	Location (longitude)	Depth (m)	Depth (fathoms)	Depth (ft)
PACIFIC OCEAN					
Marianas Trench	11° 22′ N	142° 36′ E	10,924	5,973	35,840
Tonga Trench	23° 16′ S	174° 44′ W	10,800	5,906	35,433
Philippine Trench	10° 38′ N	126° 36′ E	10,057	5,499	32,995
Kermadec Trench	31° 53′ S	177° 21′ W	10,047	5,494	32,963
Bonin Trench	24° 30′ N	143° 24′ E	9,994	5,464	32,788
Kuril Trench	44° 15′ N	150° 34′ E	9,750	5,331	31,988
Izu Trench	31°05′ N	142°10′ E	9,695	5,301	31,808
New Britain Trench	06°19′ S	153°45′ E	8,940	4,888	29,331
Yap Trench	08°33′ N	138°02′ E	8,527	4,663	27,976
Japan Trench	36°08′ N	142°43′ E	8,412	4,600	27,599
Peru-Chile Trench	23°18′ S	71°14′ W	8,064	4,409	26,457
Palau Trench	07°52′ N	134°56′ E	8,054	4,404	26,424
Aleutian Trench	50°51′ N	177°11′ E	7,679	4,199	25,194
ATLANTIC OCEAN					
Puerto Rico Trench	19° 55′N	65°27′ W	8,605	4,705	28,232
South Sandwich Trench	55°42′S	25°56′ W	8,325	4,552	27,310
Romanche Gap	0°13′S	18°26′ W	7,728	4,226	25,354

AVERAGE GLOBAL TEMPERATURES, 1900–2000

Decade	Degrees Fahrenheit	Degree Celsius
1900-09	56.52	13.62
1910-19	56.57	13.65
1920-29	56.74	13.74
1930-39	57.00	13.89
1940-49	57.13	13.96
1950-59	57.06	13.92
1960-69	57.05	13.92
1970-79	57.04	13.91
1980-89	57.36	14.09
1990-99	57.64	14.24
2000	57.60	14.22

HIGHEST MEASURED TEMPERATURE

Continent or Region	Temperature (Fahrenheit)	Temperature (Celsius)	Place	Elevation (ft)	Elevation (m)	Date
Africa	136°	58°	El Azizia, Libya	367	112	Sept. 13, 1922
North America	134°	57°	Death Valley, California (Greenland Ranch)	−178	−54	July 10, 1913
Asia	129°	54°	Tirat Tsvi, Israel	−722	−220	June 21, 1942
Australia	128°	53°	Cloncurry, Queensland	622	190	Jan. 16, 1889
Europe	122°	50°	Seville, Spai	26	8	Aug. 4, 1881
South America	120°	49°	Rivadavia, Argentina	676	206	Dec. 11, 1905

LOWEST MEASURED TEMPERATURE

Continent or Region	Temperature (Fahrenheit)	Temperature (Celsius)	Place	Elevation (ft)	Elevation (m)	Date
Antarctica	−129.0°	−89°	Vostok	11,220	3,420	July 21, 1983
Asia	−90.0°	−68°	Oimekon, Russia	2,625	800	Feb. 6, 1933
Asia	−90.0°	−68°	Verkhoyansk, Russia	350	107	Feb. 7, 1892
Greenland	−87.0°	−66°	Northice	7,687	2,343	Jan. 9, 1954
North America	−81.4°	−63°	Snag, Yukon, Canada	2,120	646	Feb. 3, 1947
Europe	−67.0°	−55°	Ust-Shchugor, Russia	279	85	Jan.*
South America	−27.0°	−33°	Sarmiento, Argentina	879	268	June 1, 1907
Africa	−11.0°	−24°	Ifrane, Morocco	5,364	1,635	Feb. 11, 1935
Australia	−9.4°	−23°	Charlotte Pass, New South Wales	5,758	1,755	June 29, 1994
Oceania	14.0°	−10°	Haleakala Summit, Maui, Hawaii	9,750	2,972	Jan. 2, 1961

* Exact day and year unknown.

HIGHEST MOUNTAINS

Rank	Place	Peak	Height (ft)	Height (m)
1.	Everest	Nepal-Tibet	29,035	8,850
2.	K2 (Godwin Austen)	Kashmir	28,250	8,611
3.	Kanchenjunga	India-Nepal	28,208	8,598
4.	Lhotse I (Everest)	Nepal-Tibet	27,923	8,511
5.	Makalu I	Nepal-Tibet	27,824	8,481
6.	Lhotse II (Everest)	Nepal-Tibet	27,560	8,400
7.	Dhaulagiri	Nepal	26,810	8,172
8.	Manaslu I	Nepal	26,760	8,156
9.	Cho Oyu	Nepal-Tibet	26,750	8,153
10.	Nanga Parbat	Kashmir	26,660	8,126

LONGEST RIVER

River	Outflow	Length (mi)	Length (km)
AFRICA			
Congo	Atlantic Ocean	2,900	4,670
Niger	Gulf of Guinea	2,590	4,170
Nile	Mediterranean	4,160	6,690
Zambezi	Indian Ocean	1,700	2,740
ASIA			
Amur	Tatar Strait	1,780	2,860
Brahmaputra	Bay of Bengal	1,800	2,900
Chang	East China Sea	3,964	6,380
Euphrates	Shatt al-Arab	1,700	2,740
Huang	Yellow Sea	3,395	5,460
Indus	Arabian Sea	1,800	2,900
Lena	Laptev Sea	2,734	4,400
Mekong	South China Sea	2,700	4,350
Ob	Gulf of Ob	2,268	3,650
Ob-Irtysh	Gulf of Ob	3,362	5,410
Yenisey	Kara Seav	2,543	4,090
AUSTRALIA			
Murray-Darling	Indian Ocean	2,310	3,720
EUROPE			
Danube	Black Sea	1,776	2,860
Volga	Caspian Sea	2,290	3,690
NORTH AMERICA			
Mississippi	Gulf of Mexico	2,340	3,770
Mississippi-Missouri-Red Rock	Gulf of Mexico	3,710	5,970
Missouri	Mississippi River	2,315	3,730
Missouri-Red Rock	Mississippi River	2,540	4,090
Rio Grande	Gulf of Mexico	1,900	3,060
Yukon	Bering Sea	1,979	3,180
SOUTH AMERICA			
Amazon	Atlantic Ocean	4,000	6,440
Japura	Amazon River	1,750	2,820
Madeira	Amazon River	2,013	3,240
Parana	Rio de la Plata	2,485	4,000
Purus	Amazon River	2,100	3,380
Sao Francisco	Atlantic Ocean	1,988	3,200

WORLD'S HIGHEST DAMS

Rank	Name	Country	Height Above Lowest Formation (ft)	Height Above Lowest Formation (m)
*1.	Nurek	Tajikistan	984	300
2.	Grand Dixence	Switzerland	935	285
3.	Inguri	Georgia	892	272
4.	Vajont	Italy	860	262
5.	Manuel M. Torres	Mexico	856	261
6.	Alvaro Obregon	Mexico	853	260
7.	Mauvoisin	Switzerland	820	250
8.	Mica	Canada	797	243

* The Rogun, Tajikistan (under construction) will become the highest dam, 1,099 ft (335 m).

NOTABLE DESERTS OF THE WORLD

Arabian (Eastern), 70,000 sq mi (181,000 sq km) in Egypt between the Nile River and Red Sea, extending southward into Sudan

Chihuahuan, 140,000 sq mi (363,000 sq km) in Texas, New Mexico, Arizona, and Mexico

Gibson, 120,000 sq mi (311,000 sq km) in the interior of Western Australia

Gobi, 500,000 sq mi (1,295,000 sq km) in Mongolia and China

Great Sandy, 150,000 sq mi (388,000 sq km) in Western Australia

Great Victoria, 150,000 sq mi (388,000 sq km) in South and Western Australia

Kalahari, 225,000 sq mi (583,000 sq km) in southern Africa

Kara Kum, 120,000 sq mi (311,000 sq km) in Turkmenistan

Kyzyl Kum, 100,000 sq mi (259,000 sq km) in Kazakhstan and Uzbekistan

Libyan, 450,000 sq mi (1,165,000 sq km) in the Sahara, extending from Libya through southwestern Egypt into Sudan

Nubian, 100,000 sq mi (259,000 sq km) in the Sahara in northeastern Sudan

Patagonia, 300,000 sq mi (777,000 sq km) in southern Argentina

Rub al-Khali (Empty Quarter), 250,000 sq mi (648,000 sq km) in the southern Arabian Peninsula

Sahara, 3,500,000 sq mi (9,065,000 sq km) in northern Africa, extending westward to the Atlantic; largest desert in the world

Sonoran, 70,000 sq mi (181,000 sq km) in southwestern Arizona and southeastern California extending into northwestern Mexico

Syrian, 100,000 sq mi (259,000 sq km) arid wasteland extending over much of northern Saudi Arabia, eastern Jordan, southern Syria, and western Iraq

Taklimakan, 140,000 sq mi (363,000 sq km) in Xinjiang Province, China

Thar (Great Indian), 100,000 sq mi (259,000 sq km) arid area extending 400 mi (640 km) along the India-Pakistan border

NOTABLE WATERFALLS

Name (Location)	Height (ft)	Height (m)
AFRICA		
Tugela# (South Africa)	2,014	614
Victoria, Zambezi River* (Zimbabwe-Zambia)	343	105
AUSTRALIA, NEW ZEALAND		
Wallaman, Stony Creek# (Australia)	1,137	347
Wollomombi (Australia)	1,100	335
Sutherland, Arthur River# (New Zealand)	1,904	580
EUROPE		
Krimml# (Austria)	1,312	400
Gavarnie* (France)	1,385	422
Mardalsfossen (Northern) (Norway)	1,535	468
Mardalsfossen (Southern)# (Norway)	2,149	655
Skjeggedal, Nybuai River#** (Norway)	1,378	420
Trummelbach#(Switzerland)	1,312	400
NORTH AMERICA		
Della# (Canada)	1,443	440
Niagara: Horseshoe (Canada)	173	53
Takakkaw, Daly Glacier# (Canada)	1,200	366
Niagara: American (U.S.)	182	55
Ribbon** (U.S.)	1,612	491
Silver Strand, Meadow Brook** (U.S.)	1,170	357
Yosemite#** (U.S.)	2,425	739
SOUTH AMERICA		
Iguazu (Argentina-Brazil)	230	70
Glass (Brazil)	1,325	404
Patos-Maribondo, Grande River (Brazil)	115	35
Paulo Afonso, Sao Francisco River (Brazil)	275	84
Urubupunga, Parana River (Brazil)	39	12
Great, Kamarang River (Guyana)	1,600	488
Kaieteur, Potaro River (Guyana)	741	226
Angel#*(Venezuela)	3,212	979
Cuquenan (Venezuela)	2,000	610

Note: If the river name is not shown, it is the same as that of the falls. "Height" is the total drop in one or more leaps.
#Falls of more than one leap;
*falls that diminish greatly seasonally;
**falls that reduce to a trickle or are dry for part of each year.
The estimated mean annual flow, in cubic feet per second (cubic meters in parentheses), of major waterfalls is as follows: Niagara, 212,200 (6,000); Paulo Afonso, 100,000 (2,800); Urubupunga, 97,000 (2,700); Iguazu, 61,000 (1,700); Patos-Maribondo, 53,000 (1,500); Victoria, 35,400 (1,000); and Kaieteur, 23,400 (660).

MAJOR NATURAL LAKES

Name	Continent	Area (sq mi)	Area (sq km)	Maximum Depth (ft)	Maximum Depth (m)
Caspian Sea[1]	Asia-Europe	143,244	371,000	3,363	1,025
Superior	North America	31,700	82,100	1,330	405
Victoria	Africa	26,828	69,484	270	82
Huron	North America	23,000	59,600	750	229
Michigan	North America	22,300	57,800	923	281
Aral Sea[1]	Asia	13,000[2]	33,700[2]	220	67
Tanganyika	Africa	12,700	32,900	4,823	1,470
Baykal	Asia	12,162	31,500	5,315	1,620
Great Bear	North America	12,096	31,330	1,463	446
Nyasa (Malawi)	Africa	11,150	28,880	2,280	695
Great Slave	North America	11,031	28,570	2,015	614
Erie	North America	9,910	25,670	210	64
Winnipeg	North America	9,417	24,390	60	18
Ontario	North America	7,340	19,010	802	244
Balkhash[1]	Asia	7,115	18,430	85	26
Ladoga	Europe	6,835	17,700	738	225

Note: A lake is generally defined as a body of water surrounded by land.
[1]Salt lake.
[2]Approximate figure, could be less. The diversion of feeder rivers since the 1960s has devastated the Aral—once the world's fourth-largest lake (26,000 sq mi [67,000 sq km]). By 2000, the Aral had effectively become three lakes, with the total area shown.

LOWEST AVERAGE ANNUAL PRECIPITATION

Continent or Region	Precipitation (in)	Precipitation (mm)	Place	Elevation (ft)	Elevation (m)	Years of Data
South America	0.03	0.8	Arica, Chile	95	29	59
Africa	< 0.1	< 3	Wadi Halfa, Sudan	410	125	39
Antarctica	0.8[1]	20[1]	Amundsen-Scott South Pole Station	9,186	2,800	10
North America	1.2	30	Batagues, Mexico	16	5	14
Asia	1.8	46	Aden, Yemen	22	7	50
Australia	4.05	103	Mulka (Troudaninna), South Australia	1602	492	42
Europe	6.4	163	Astrakhan, Russia	45	14	25
Oceania	8.93	227	Puako, Hawaii	5	2	13

[1]The value given is the average amount of solid snow accumulating in one year as indicated by snow markers. The liquid content of the snow is undetermined.
[2]Approximate elevation.

HIGHEST AVERAGE ANNUAL PRECIPITATION

Continent or Region	Precipitation (in)	Precipitation (mm)	Place	Elevation (ft)	Elevation (m)	Years of Data
South America	523.6[1,2]	13,300[1,2]	Lloro, Colombia	520[3]	158[3]	29
Asia	467.4[1]	11,870[1]	Mawsynram, India	4,597	1,401	38
Oceania	460.0[1]	11,680[1]	Mt. Waialeale, Kauai, Hawaii	5,148	1,569	30
Africa	405.0	10,290	Debundscha, Cameroon	30	9	32
South America	354.0[2]	8,992[2]	Quibdo, Colombia	120	37	16
Australia	340.0	8,636	Bellenden Ker, Queensland	5,102	1,555	9
North America	256.0	6,502	Henderson Lake, British Columbia	12	4	14
Europe	183.0	4,648	Crkvica, Bosnia-Herzegovina	3,337	1,017	22

[1]The value given is continent's highest and possibly the world's depending on measurement practices, procedures, and period of record variations.
[2]The official greatest average annual precipitation for South America is 354 in (8,992 mm) at Quibdo, Colombia. The 523.6 in (13,300 mm) average at Lloro, Colombia (14 mi [23 km] SE and at a higher elevation than Quibdo) is an estimated amount.
[3]Approximate elevation.

WORLD AIR DISTANCES

Air Distances Between Major World Cities (in miles)	Anchorage	Beijing	Buenos Aires	Cairo	Cape Town	Caracas	Chicago	Hong Kong	Honolulu	London	Los Angeles	Madrid	Melbourne	Mexico	Montréal	Moscow	Mumbai	New Delhi	New York	Paris	Rio de Janeiro	Rome	San Francisco	Singapore	Tokyo
Amsterdam	4468	4890	7112	2015	5997	4883	4118	5772	7254	222	5558	921	10,286	5735	3426	1337	4255	3958	3654	271	5938	807	5465	6526	5788
Anchorage	—	3945	8320	6116	10,478	5353	2858	5073	2778	4491	2340	5181	7729	3776	3133	4364	6300	5709	3373	4697	8145	5263	2005	6678	3463
Athens	5500	4757	7265	671	4957	5815	5447	5316	8353	1488	6900	1474	9297	7021	4737	1387	3207	3120	4938	1305	6030	654	6792	5629	5924
Bangkok	6022	2027	0,490	4521	6301	10,558	8569	1076	6610	5929	7637	6334	4579	9793	8337	4394	1870	1812	8669	5877	9987	5493	7930	887	2865
Beijing	3997	—	1,994	4687	8034	8978	6625	1195	5084	5089	6255	5759	5632	7772	6541	3627	2953	2350	6867	5138	0,778	5076	5934	2754	1305
Buenos Aires	8320	11,994	—	7360	4285	3155	5582	11,478	7544	6907	6148	6236	7219	4580	5597	8369	9380	9823	5279	6857	1231	6925	6455	9940	11,411
Cairo	6116	4687	7360	—	4510	6337	6116	5057	8818	2158	7675	2069	8700	7677	5403	1770	2698	2752	5598	1973	6153	1305	7436	5152	5937
Cape Town	10,478	8034	4285	4510	—	6361	8489	7377	11,534	5988	9981	5306	6428	8516	7920	6277	5133	5769	7801	5782	3773	5231	10,248	6025	9155
Caracas	5353	8978	3155	6337	6361	—	2480	10,171	6024	4662	3610	4351	9703	2234	2443	6176	9034	8837	2124	4735	2805	5198	3908	11,408	8813
Chicago	2858	6625	5582	6116	8489	2480	—	7797	4256	3960	1741	4192	9667	1688	746	4984	8144	7486	714	4145	5288	4823	1860	9376	6313
Denver	2375	6385	5935	6846	9331	3078	920	7476	3346	4701	828	5028	8755	1438	1639	5501	8275	7730	1631	4900	5866	5887	953	9079	5815
Frankfurt	4656	4567	7137	1730	5944	5290	4460	5403	7341	628	5783	1193	9882	6127	3787	961	4076	3550	4028	589	6237	729	5709	6119	5533
Hong Kong	5073	1195	1,478	5057	7377	10,171	7797	—	5557	5986	7217	6556	4605	8789	7736	4443	2679	2339	8061	5992	11,002	5773	6904	1608	1792
Honolulu	2778	5084	7554	8818	11,534	6024	4256	5557	—	7241	2565	7874	5501	3791	4919	7049	8036	7413	4969	7452	8295	8040	2397	6728	3860
Houston	3256	7244	5072	7005	8608	2262	942	8349	3902	4860	1373	5014	8979	961	1605	5925	8875	8388	1419	5035	5015	5702	1648	9954	6685
Kinshasa	8875	7002	5130	2618	2047	5752	7085	6904	11,178	3951	8850	3305	8112	7915	6378	4328	4200	4692	6378	3742	4105	3186	8920	6132	8307
Lima	6385	10,365	1945	7725	6074	1699	3772	11,415	5944	6316	4170	5907	8052	2635	3967	7855	0,389	10,430	3635	6367	2351	6748	4516	11,689	9628
Lisbon	5110	6040	5976	2352	5301	4040	4001	6862	7835	989	5600	317	11,049	5396	3255	2433	4975	4844	3377	904	4777	1163	5679	7393	6943
London	4491	5089	6919	2158	5988	4662	3960	5986	7241	—	5454	786	10,508	5558	3256	1556	4526	2703	4680	1550	7162	1477	5884	6747	4663
Los Angeles	2340	6255	6148	7675	9981	3610	1750	7217	2565	5454	—	5852	7928	1566	2468	6036	8810	7015	2455	5661	6334	6336	349	8955	5476
Madrid	5181	5759	6236	2069	5306	4351	4192	6556	7874	786	5852	—	10,765	5642	3449	2140	4689	4528	3596	652	5045	849	5806	7079	6704
Melbourne	7729	5632	7219	8700	6428	9703	9667	4605	5501	10,508	7928	10,766	—	8420	10,390	8965	6101	6340	10,352	10,442	8218	9940	7850	3767	5070
Mexico	3776	7772	4580	7677	8516	2234	1688	8789	3791	5558	1566	5642	8420	—	2315	6671	9739	9119	2086	5723	4769	6374	1889	10,331	7036
Montréal	3113	6541	5597	5403	7920	2443	746	7736	4919	3256	2468	3449	10,390	2315	—	4397	7524	7012	333	3432	5082	4102	2544	9207	6470
Moscow	4364	3627	8369	1770	6277	6176	4984	4443	7049	1556	6036	2140	8965	6671	4397	—	3132	2703	4680	1550	7162	1477	5884	5236	4663
Mumbai	6300	2953	9380	2698	5133	9034	8144	2679	8172	4526	8810	4689	6140	9818	7582	3132	—	722	7875	4367	8438	3846	8523	2425	4247
Nairobi	8287	5720	6479	2217	2543	7179	8012	5447	10,740	4229	9600	3840	7159	9218	7267	3928	2811	3371	7365	4020	5556	3340	9598	4636	6996
New Delhi	5709	2350	9823	2752	5769	8837	7486	2339	7413	4178	7015	4528	6340	9119	7012	2703	722	—	7319	4103	8747	3684	7691	2574	3638
New York	3373	6867	5279	5598	7801	2124	714	8061	4969	3473	2455	3596	10,352	2086	333	4680	7811	7319	—	3638	4805	4293	2574	9539	6757
Panama	5000	8939	3319	7230	7090	867	2320	10,089	5254	5285	3025	5081	9027	1496	2542	6720	9832	9422	2213	5388	3296	5916	3326	11,692	8441
Paris	4697	5138	6857	1973	5782	4735	4145	5992	7452	215	5711	652	10,442	5723	3432	1550	4367	4103	3638	—	5681	668	5579	6676	6054
Rio de Janeiro	8145	10,778	1231	6153	3773	2805	5288	11,002	8295	5751	6334	5045	8218	4769	5082	7162	8334	8747	4805	5681	—	5704	6621	9776	11,535
Rome	5263	5076	6925	1305	5231	5198	4823	5773	8040	892	6336	849	9940	6374	4102	1477	3846	3684	4293	688	5704	—	6259	6231	6140
San Francisco	2005	5934	6455	7436	10,248	3908	1860	6904	2397	5369	349	5806	7850	1889	2544	5884	8406	7691	2574	5579	6621	6259	—	8449	5148
Seattle	1442	5432	6956	6809	10,205	4100	1737	6481	2681	4799	961	5303	8176	2340	2309	5217	7830	7046	2409	5012	6890	5680	679	8074	4793
Singapore	6678	2754	9870	5143	6007	11,408	9376	1608	6728	6747	8955	7079	3767	10,331	9207	5236	2427	2574	9539	6676	9776	6231	8449	—	3304
Stockholm	4102	4197	7799	2084	6422	5422	4288	5115	6873	892	5454	1613	9693	5965	3667	764	3880	3466	3939	964	6638	1229	5372	5993	5091
Tehran	5654	3496	8565	1220	5240	7322	6502	3844	8072	2739	7682	2974	7838	8182	5879	1534	1743	1584	6141	2624	7386	2126	7362	4106	4775
Tokyo	3463	1305	1,411	5937	9155	8813	6313	1792	3860	5956	5476	6704	5070	7036	6470	4663	4196	3638	6757	6054	1,535	6140	5148	3304	—
Washington, D.C.	3300	6965	5231	5800	7892	2051	594	8157	4839	3676	2295	3794	10,174	1883	490	4873	7900	7500	203	3841	4783	4496	2444	9667	6792

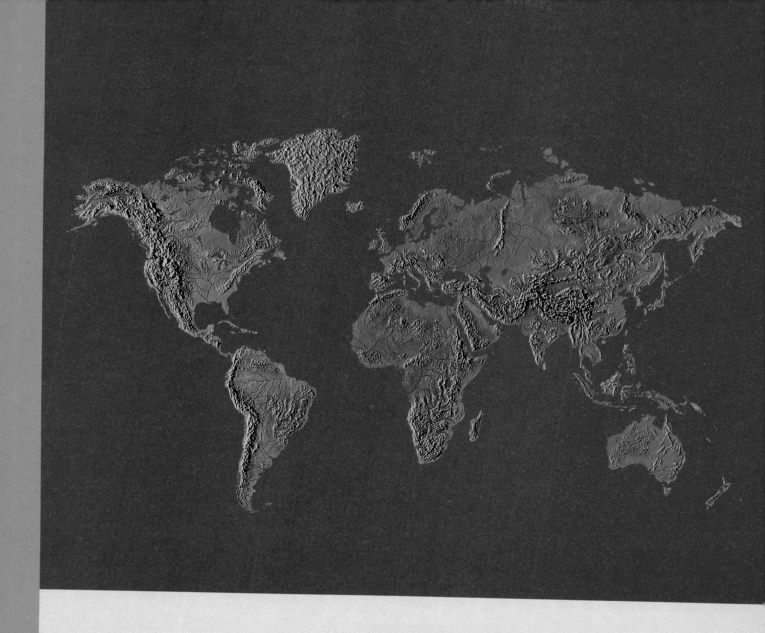

COUNTRY MAPS

Afghanistan, called "the roof of the world," is situated on extremely mountainous terrain that includes the towering peaks of the Hindu Kush in the northeast. The country experiences a range of climate zones, from the hot arid plains of the southwest, to the cold, wet mountains north and west of Kabul. Landlocked, it has few surface connections with the outside world. Because of its isolation, harsh environment and political turmoil, Afghanistan is an extremely poor country with a very low per capita income. Nomadic sheep herding, farming and traditional handcrafts have been seriously disrupted by political upheavals. Desperate farmers have turned to opium cash crops. Tribal loyalties make nationwide political stability difficult.

The Pashtuns (Pathans) are the majority ethnic group, but other Central Asian peoples - including Tajiks and Uzbeks - comprise large minorities. Pashto and Persian (Dari) are the main languages spoken. Most inhabitants are members of the Sunni branch of Islam. Kabul is the capital and chief city; also important are Qandahār (Kandahar) and Herāt.

The fabled Khyber Pass between Afghanistan and Pakistan served for centuries as a gate into India for invading hordes from Central Asia. Though isolated, the region was a crossroads between east and west. From the west came the Persian conquerors, Cyrus and Darius, in the sixth century B.C. Alexander the Great followed with his Greek armies in the late fourth century. Mongols and Turks coursed through mountain fastnesses during succeeding centuries. Islam penetrated the region in the seventh century A.D. During the nineteenth century the Afghan realm was the scene of the clash between Russian and British imperial ambitions in Asia. As a result, Afghanistan preserved its independence to serve as a buffer state between the armies of the Czar and the British Crown.

Following the Soviet invasion of 1979-80, millions of refugees fled the country, stripping Afghanistan of one-third of its population. In the mid 1990's the Taliban rose to power in reaction to anarchy and warlordism. After the September 11, 2001 terrorist attacks against the United States, coalition forces ousted the Taliban for sheltering Osama Bin Laden and other terrorists.

AREA: 250,001 sq mi (647,500 sq km)

■ **CLIMATE:** The country experiences a range of climate zones, from the hot arid plains of the southwest, to the cold, wet mountains north and west of Kabul.

■ **PEOPLE:** Though almost entirely Muslim, Afghanis are a mix of both Persian and Turkish backgrounds. Fierce tribal and ethnic loyalties have contributed to tensions over the years.

Northwestern Afghanistan

POPULATION: 31,056,997
LIFE EXPECTANCY AT BIRTH (YEARS): male, 42.3; female, 42.7
LITERACY RATE: 36%
ETHNIC GROUPS: Pashtun 44%, Tajik 25%, Hazara 10%, Uzbek 8%
PRINCIPAL LANGUAGES: Dari (Afghan Persian), Pashtu (both official); Turkic (including Uzbek, Turkmen); Balochi, Pashai, many others
CHIEF RELIGIONS: Muslim (official; Sunni 85%, Shi'a 15%)

■ **ECONOMY:** Nomadic sheep herding, farming and traditional handcrafts have been seriously disrupted by political upheavals. Desperate farmers have turned to opium cash crops.

> **Did you know?** Karsai won Afghanistan's first presidential election on October 9, 2004.

MONETARY UNIT: afghani
GDP: $21.5 billion (2003 est.)
PER CAPITA GDP: $800
INDUSTRIES: textiles, soap, furniture, shoes, fertilizer, cement handwoven carpets
CHIEF CROPS: wheat, fruits, nuts
MINERALS: natural gas, petroleum, coal, copper, chromite, talc, barites, sulfur, lead, zinc, iron ore, salt, precious and semiprecious stones
GOVERNMENT TYPE: transitional administration
CAPITAL: Kabul (pop., 2,956,000)
INDEPENDENCE DATE: August 19, 1919
WEBSITE: www.embassyofafghanistan.org

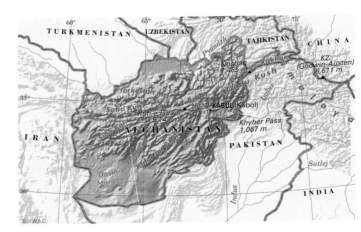

Albania, one of the smallest of the Balkan states, ranks as the poorest country in Europe. Located on the western coast of the Adriatic Sea, it is divided into a mountainous highland region in the north, east and south, and a western lowlands region which holds most of the country's agriculturally-productive land. A mild temperate climate with cool, cloudy, wet winters and hot clear dry summers. The interior is cooler and wetter. Natural resources include oil, gas, coal, iron, bauxite, copper and chrome ores. The chief agricultural products are wheat, corn, potatoes, fruits and vegetables, sugar beets, grapes, meat and dairy products. Industries include food processing, clothing and textiles, lumber, chemicals and hydropower. Exports of textiles and footware, metals and ores, crude oil, fruits, vegetables and tobacco go mainly to Italy, but also to Canada and Germany. An important part of the country's national income comes from remittances sent home by Albanians who work abroad.

Historically the Albanian people trace their origin to the ancient Illyrians. Albanian, a distinct Indo-European language, is spoken in two variations: Gheg in the north and Tosk in the south. A majority of the people are Muslims, with a large minority of Orthodox Christians. Tiranë is the capital and largest city, followed in size by Shkodër and the two port cities of Durrës and Vlorë.

By the 1500s, Albania came under Turkish rule and remained so until it gained independence in 1912. Italian influence and penetration were strong during the 1920s and 1930s. Following World War II, Albania fell under Communist control and remained so until 1991. During this period the country became a hermit nation, having practically no dealings with its European neighbors. In 1992, after the sweeping electoral victory of the Democratic Party, Sali Berisha became the first democratically elected President of Albania. In early 1997, unscrupulous investment companies collapsed, leaving thousands of people bankrupt, disillusioned, and angry. Armed revolts broke out across the country, leading to the near-total collapse of government authority. During the transitional period of 1997-2002, a series of short-lived Socialist-led governments succeeded one another. Alfred Moisiu, a consensus candidate of the ruling and opposition parties, was sworn in as President in July 2002.

> **Did you know?** The Roman Emperor Constantine came from Illyria, an ancient name for Albania.

AREA: 11,100 sq mi (28,748 sq km)

CLIMATE: A mild temperate climate with cool, cloudy, wet winters and hot clear dry summers. The interior is cooler and wetter.

Saranda-Blue Eye

PEOPLE: Mostly Muslim, with a large minority of Orthodox Christians, Albanians trace their origin to the ancient Illyrians. Albanian is spoken in two variations: Gheg in the north and Tosk in the south.

POPULATION: 3,581,655

LIFE EXPECTANCY AT BIRTH (YEARS): male, 74.4; female, 80.0

LITERACY RATE: 93%

ETHNIC GROUPS: Albanian 95%, Greek 3%

PRINCIPAL LANGUAGES: Albanian (Tosk is the official dialect), Greek

CHIEF RELIGIONS: Muslim 70%, Albanian Orthodox 20%, Roman Catholic 10%

ECONOMY: The poorest country in Europe, mineral exports and agriculture provide some income. Another important income source is from money sent home by Albanians abroad.

MONETARY UNIT: lek

GDP: $17.5 billion (2004 est.)

PER CAPITA GDP: $4,900

INDUSTRIES: food processing, textiles and clothing, lumber, oil, cement, chemicals, mining, basic metals, hydropower

MINERALS: petroleum, natural gas, coal, chromium, copper, timber, nickel

CHIEF CROPS: wheat, corn, potatoes, vegetables, fruits, sugar beets, grapes

GOVERNMENT TYPE: republic

CAPITAL: Tiranë (pop., 367,000)

INDEPENDENCE DATE: November 28, 1912

WEBSITE: www.albaniantourism.com

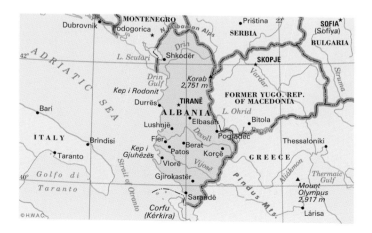

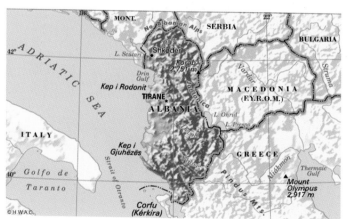

Algeria is physically divided into two parts. South of the Atlas Mountains lies the Sahara, a vast desert area romantically associated with wandering nomads and the famed Foreign Legion. Cool, wet winters and hot dry summers on the coast become colder and drier on the plateaus. The Sahara region has extremes of blistering hot days and chilly nights. The coastal region's climate, which is of a mild Mediterranean

Algiers

type, allows for the production of cereal crops, grapes and olives in the valley areas. Sheep and cattle are also raised. In pre-independence days the Sahara was thought to have little economic value, but during the post-World War II period huge oil and gas fields were discovered and exploited. In addition iron ore, phosphates, uranium, lead, and zinc are mined. petroleum, natural gas, and petroleum products are exported to the European Union, the United States, Canada and Brazil.

Despite government Arabization, Algerian culture remains a mix of Berber, French and Arab influences. Those who identify with their Berber heritage live mostly east of Algiers. Most of the nation's population resides north of the Atlas along the Mediterranean coast, where the capital city of Algiers is located, along with the important centers of Oran and Constantine. Most of the poulation is Sunni Muslim, and Arabic is the official language, although French and Berber are also spoken.

In 1830 France began the takeover of Algeria by deposing the Bey of Algiers. During the colonial period thousands of Frenchmen settled in Algeria, establishing vineyards and supplying metropolitan France with inexpensive wine. Over a century later with the rise of civil unrest, from 1954 to 1961, war between the French and the native Muslim population raged with great ferocity. With the establishment of independence in 1962, most of the French and other European settlers left Algeria, producing widespread economic disaster. Since then, the exploitation of hydrocarbons has resulted in a moderate recovery.

The Council of the Revolution, headed by Minister of Defense Col.

Houari Boumediene took over after a non-violent coup in 1965. Boumediene led the country as Head of State until he was formally elected in December, 1976. Boumediene, who died in 1978, is credited with building "modern Algeria."

In the 1980's economic stagnation and a rising Islamic movement led to a decade of violence which, in 1999, was somewhat tempered by an amnesty program for the rebels. In 2001, a Berber uprising resulted in the recognition of their language, Tamazight, as a national, if not official, language. Violence gradually abated, and the elections of 2004 were considered the fairest seen in Algeria.

AREA: 919,595 sq mi (2,381,740 sq km)

CLIMATE: Cool, wet winters and hot dry summers on the coast become colder and drier on the plateaus. The Sahara region has extremes of hot days and chilly nights.

Did you know? Algiers was a stronghold for Barbary pirates for 300 years.

PEOPLE: Despite government Arabization, Algerian culture remains a mix of Berber, French and Arab influences. Those who identify with their Berber heritage live mostly east of Algiers.

POPULATION: 32,930,091

LIFE EXPECTANCY AT BIRTH (YEARS): male, 69.1; female, 72.0

LITERACY RATE: 61.6%

ETHNIC GROUPS: Arab-Berber 99%

PRINCIPAL LANGUAGES: Arabic (official), French, Berber dialects

CHIEF RELIGION: Sunni Muslim (official) 99%

ECONOMY: Hydrocarbons are the country's major exports. Citrus, olives, dates and wine are important agricultural products, though religion forbids the consumption of alcohol.

MONETARY UNIT: dinar

GDP: $212.3 billion (2004 est.)

PER CAPITA GDP: $6,600

INDUSTRIES: petroleum, natural gas, light industries, mining, electrical, petrochemical, food processing

MINERALS: petroleum, natural gas, iron ore, phosphates, uranium, lead, zinc

CHIEF CROPS: wheat, barley, oats, grapes, olives, citrus, fruits

GOVERNMENT TYPE: republic

CAPITAL: Algiers (pop., 3,060,000)

INDEPENDENCE DATE: July 5, 1962

WEBSITE: www.algeria-us.org

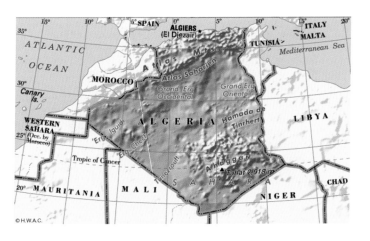

The landlocked Principality of Andorra is only two and a half times larger in area than Washington, D.C. Nestled in the rugged mountain terrain of the Pyrenees, the principality lies between France on the north and Spain on the south. The climate is temperate with cold, snowy winters and warm, dry summers. Natural resources include hydroelectric power, mineral water, timber, iron ore and lead. Cereal crops, vegetables and tobacco are the primary agricultural commodities. Sheep are raised.

Tourism dominates the economy, attracted by Andorra's duty-free status and by the summer and winter resorts. The banking sector is also important. Exports of furniture and tobacco products go to Spain and France.

Andorrans are a minority in their own country; Spanish, French, and Portuguese residents make up two thirds of the population. Catalan is the official language, though Spanish and French are also spoken. Roman Catholicism is the chief religion.

Andorra is the last independent survivor of the buffer states created by Charlemagne to keep the Muslim Moors from advancing into Christian France. An edict in 1607 established the head of the French state and the Bishop of Urgell as co-princes of Andorra. They exercise joint sovereignty over Andorra to this day. Governmental power rests with an executive council and a legislative general council.

Andorra has existed outside the mainstream of history, with few ties to countries other than France and Spain. In recent times, however, its thriving tourist industry along with developments in transportation and communications have removed the country from its isolation.

Did you know? Tiny Andorra is a major ski area in the Pyrennees.

AREA: 181 sq mi (468 sq km)

■ **CLIMATE:** The climate is temperate with cold, snowy winters and warm, dry summers.

■ **PEOPLE:** Andorra's people are mainly Spanish and Andorran. Ethnic minorities include Portuguese and French.

POPULATION: 71,201

LIFE EXPECTANCY AT BIRTH (YEARS): male, 80.6; female, 86.6

LITERACY RATE: 100%

ETHNIC GROUPS: Spanish 43%, Andorran 33%, Portuguese 11%, French 7%

Andorra la Vella-Caldea

PRINCIPAL LANGUAGES: Catalan (official), Castilian Spanish, French

CHIEF RELIGION: predominantly Roman Catholic

■ **ECONOMY:** Tourism dominates the economy, attracted by Andorra's duty-free status and by the summer and winter resorts. The banking sector is also important.

MONETARY UNIT: euro

GDP: $1.9 billion (2003 est.)

PER CAPITA GDP: $26,800

INDUSTRIES: tourism, cattle raising, timber, tobacco, banking

CHIEF CROPS: tobacco, rye, wheat, barley, oats, vegetables

MINERALS: iron ore, lead

GOVERNMENT TYPE: parliamentary co-principality

CAPITAL: Andorra la Vella (pop., 21,000)

INDEPENDENCE DATE: 1278

WEBSITE: www.andorra.ad/ang/home/index.htm

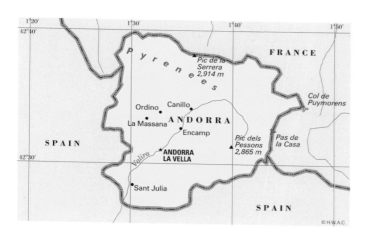

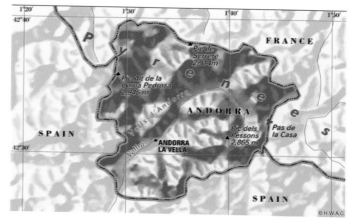

Angola is one of Africa's largest nations, extending from the Democratic Republic of the Congo in the north to Namibia in the south. The Angolan exclave of Cabinda lies on the Atlantic coast north of the Congo River mouth. A vast interior plateau comprises most of the country. The north has a cool dry season and hot rainy season, while the south, and the region along the coast to the capital, is semi-arid. Angola possesses considerable wealth. Oil, iron ore, copper, feldspar, diamonds and phosphates comprise important natural resources.

Luanda

The principal cash crops include bananas, sugarcane, coffee, sisal, corn, cotton, manioc, tobacco, vegetables and plantains. Livestock, forest products and fisheries contribute to the economy. Exports of petroleum products, diamonds and coffee go to the United States, China, France and South Korea.

Ovimbundu, Kimbundu, Bakongo and a few mixed European/African peoples make up the bulk of Angola's native population. Roman Catholics make up more than two thirds of the poulation, various Protestant and indigenous beliefs make up the remainder. Portuguese is the official language. Others include Ovimbundu, Kimbundu and Bakongo .

Starting in the 1500s, Portugal established its presence along the Atlantic coast of Angola. The capital, Luanda, was founded in 1575. Portugal exploited the African realm as a prime source of the slave trade. In the early twentieth century a serious effort at colonization settled more than 300,000 Portuguese in Angola by 1960. In 1961 rebellion against Portugal broke out, beginning a 15-year violent struggle for independence. During this period most of the Portuguese settlers left, stripping the country of skilled technicians and artisans.

As Marxist and pro-Western forces struggled for power, South Africa supported the pro-Western armies, while Cuba came to the aid of the Marxist government. Though a cease-fire came into being in 1991, fighting resumed in 1992. In May 1995, Angola's president met with the opposition leader in Zambia's capital of Lusaka. The resulting Lusaka Protocols, endorsed by the United Nations, called for a ceasefire and a subsequent power-sharing arrangement.

This agreement, too, collapsed into renewed conflict, and the UN Security Council voted in1997 to impose sanctions. The Angolan military launched a massive offensive in 1999, which destroyed the dominant party's conventional capacity and recaptured all major cities previously held by their forces. Civil war continued until the Popular Movement for the Liberation of Angola emerged victorious in February 2002. Angola's economy is slowly recovering, with the help of oil revenue, from this 27-year-long civil war.

AREA: 481,353 sq mi (1,246,700 sq km)

CLIMATE: Semi-arid in the south and along the coast to the capital. The north has a cool dry season and hot rainy season.

PEOPLE: Ovimbundu, Kimbundu, Bakongo and a few mixed European/African peoples make up the bulk of Angola's native population.

POPULATION: 12,127,071

LIFE EXPECTANCY AT BIRTH (YEARS): male, 36.1; female, 37.6

ETHNIC GROUPS: Ovimbundu 37%, Kimbundu 25%, Bakongo 13%

LITERACY RATE: 42%

PRINCIPAL LANGUAGES: Portuguese (official), Bantu and other African languages

CHIEF RELIGIONS: indigenous beliefs 47%, Roman Catholic 38%, Protestant 15%

ECONOMY: Oil, iron ore, gold, diamonds and phosphates contribute to Angola's wealth. Principal cash crops are coffee, sugarcane, sisal, tobacco, cotton and forest products.

MONETARY UNIT: New Kwanza (AON)

GDP: $23.2 billion (2004 est.)

PER CAPITA GDP: $2,100

INDUSTRIES: petroleum, mining, cement, basic metal products, fish processing, food processing

CHIEF CROPS: bananas, sugarcane, coffee, sisal, corn, cotton, manioc, tobacco, vegetables, plantains

MINERALS: petroleum, diamonds, iron ore, phosphates, copper, feldspar, gold, bauxite, uranium

GOVERNMENT TYPE: republic

CAPITAL: Luanda (pop., 2,623,000)

INDEPENDENCE DATE: November 11, 1975

WEBSITE: www.angola.org

> **Did you know?** In the 1400s, the Portuguese began trading slaves in Angola.

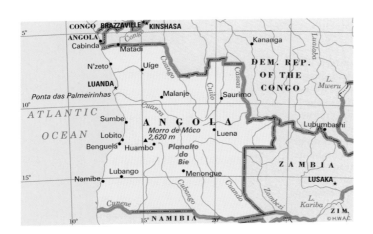

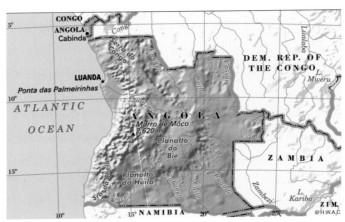

This West Indian nation is formed by three islands. Antigua, the largest in area and most populous, has a rolling terrain and a deeply indented coastline; Barbuda is a flat coral island; Redonda, to the west, is tiny and uninhabited. The islands share a tropical maritime climate with little seasonal temperature variation. The country's climate is occasionally marred by hurricanes and tropical storms from July to October.

Tourism is the mainstay of Antigua's economy as the island is noted for its delightful climate and beautiful beaches. Agriculture includes cotton, livestock, vegetables, and pineapples. Fishing also contributes to the economy. An oil refinery, which opened in 1982, contributes to a major portion of the islands' export income. Other exports include machinery and transport equipment, food and live animals. Exports go to the European Union, the United States and nearby Caribbean countries.

People of African descent now constitute the majority of the population. Other groups include British, Portuguese, Lebanese and Syrian. English is the official and universal language. Christianity is the main religion, with the majority of the Anglican Protestant faith. There are also evangelical Protestant and Roman Catholic minorities. The capital is at Saint John's on Antigua.

The British settled Antigua in 1632, Barbuda in 1661. African slaves were brought in to work the sugar cane, tobacco and sea-island cotton plantations. Cotton is still raised. English Harbour, near Falmouth on the south coast, was the Royal Navy's main base in the West Indies from 1725 to 1854. The dockyard, used by Admiral Nelson in the Napoleonic wars, has been restored as part museum, part marketplace and is now a prime tourist attraction. Antigua and Barbuda gained its independence in 1981 and joined the British Commonwealth that same year.

> **Did you know?** Most of the people of the islands trace their roots to West Africa.

AREA: 171 sq mi (443 sq km)

■ **CLIMATE:** Tropical maritime climate with little seasonal temperature variation is occasionally marred by hurricanes and tropical storms from July to October.

■ **PEOPLE:** People of African descent constitute the majority of the population. Other groups include British, Portuguese, Lebanese and Syrian.

Saint John's

POPULATION: 69,108

LIFE EXPECTANCY AT BIRTH (YEARS): male, 69.3; female, 74.1

LITERACY RATE: 89%

ETHNIC GROUPS: black, British, Portuguese, Lebanese, Syrian

PRINCIPAL LANGUAGES: English (official), local dialects

CHIEF RELIGIONS: predominantly Protestant, some Roman Catholic

■ **ECONOMY:** Tourism is the mainstay of Antigua's economy, while an oil refinery contributes to a major portion of the islands' export income.

MONETARY UNIT: East Caribbean dollar

GDP: $750 million (2002 est.)

PER CAPITA GDP: $11,000

INDUSTRIES: tourism, construction, light manufacturing

CHIEF CROPS: cotton, fruits, vegetables, bananas, coconuts, cucumbers, mangoes, sugarcane

CAPITAL: Saint John's (pop., 28,000)

INDEPENDENCE DATE: November 1, 1981

GOVERNMENT TYPE: constitutional monarchy with British-style parliament

WEBSITE: www.antigua-barbuda.com

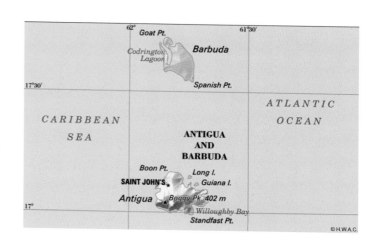

Exceeded in area only by Brazil, Argentina, home of the gaucho and the tango, is the second-largest country in South America. Argentina extends 2300 miles from the border with Bolivia in the north to Ushuaia on the island of Tierra del Fuego in the south. Argentina claims a sector of the frozen continent of Antarctica all the way to the South Pole. In addition, the Argentine claim to the Falkland Islands (Islas Malvinas), South Georgia and the South Sandwich Islands has exacerbated relations with the United Kingdom, once to the point of open warfare. Some of the richest topsoil in the world is found in the fertile temperate plains area known as the Pampas. The plains, the heartland of Argentina, fan out nearly 500 miles from Buenos Aires on the Río de la Plata. Northern Argentina consists of semitropical lowlands while the south comprises the dry Patagonian steppe and rainy Tierra del Fuego. Mineral resources include lead, zinc, tin, copper, iron, manganese, oil and uranium. Patagonia is home to Argentina's oil and natural gas reserves, which supply domestic needs. Sheep and cattle are important resources, as is wheat, cotton, tobacco, lemons, tobacco, soybeans and corn. Food processing, motor vehicles, textiles, chemicals and steel are major industries. Exports of oilseed by-products, cars, vegetable oils, fuels and grains go to Brazil, chile, the United States, China and Spain.

Argentinians are primarily of Spanish and Italian descent, with small groups of mixed white and Amerindian ancestry. Predominantly Roman Catholic, there are also small Protestant, Muslim and Jewish minorities. Spanish is the official language. The nation's political, cultural and economic life is centered on the great port city and capital of Buenos Aires. Córdoba and Rosario are large regional centers.

Spanish authority was first established during the 1500s. Independence from Spain was proclaimed in 1816. The late nineteenth and early twentieth centuries saw the spread of the agricultural frontier and the tremendous growth of the Argentine economy. Heavy immigration brought many Italians and Spaniards to the Pampas and Buenos Aires. A string of military coups brought the Peróns to power in 1945. Since then, Argentina has experienced hyper-inflation, economic recessions and political turmoil.

Did you know? Mt. Aconcagua (22,834 ft [6,960 m]) is the tallest peak in the western hemisphere.

Conditions were worsened by massive bank failures and plummeting consumer and investor confidence, followed by the ill-fated seizure of the Falkland Islands from Britain in April 1982. Economic conditions have improved in the 21st century with the introduction of anti-inflationary measures.

Salta-Valles Calchaquies

AREA: 1,068,302 sq mi (2,766,890 sq km)

CLIMATE: A mostly temperate climate that is arid in the southeast and subantarctic in the southwest.

PEOPLE: Argentinians are primarily of Spanish and Italian descent, with small groups of mixed white and Amerindian ancestry.
POPULATION: 39,921,833
LIFE EXPECTANCY AT BIRTH (YEARS): male, 72.0; female, 79.7
LITERACY RATE: 96.2%
ETHNIC GROUPS: European 97%, Amerindian 3%
PRINCIPAL LANGUAGES: Spanish (official), English, Italian, German, French
CHIEF RELIGION: Roman Catholic 92% (official)

ECONOMY: Exports include meat, wheat, wool, hides and vegetable oils from livestock ranches and grain farms of the Pampas. Patagonia's oil and gas reserves supply domestic needs.
MONETARY UNIT: peso
GDP: $483.5 billion (2004 est.)
PER CAPITA GDP: $12,400
INDUSTRIES: food processing, motor vehicles, consumer durables, textiles, chemicals and petrochemicals, printing, metallurgy, steel
MINERALS: lead, zinc, tin, copper, iron ore, manganese, petroleum, uranium
CHIEF CROPS: sunflower seeds, lemons, soybeans, grapes, corn, tobacco, peanuts, tea, wheat
GOVERNMENT TYPE: republic
CAPITAL: Buenos Aires (pop., 13,047,000)
INDEPENDENCE DATE: July 9, 1816
WEBSITE: www. turismo.gov.ar/eng/menu.htm

ASIA

The smallest of the now-defunct Soviet Union's republics, Armenia lies landlocked in the southern reaches of the Kavkaz (Caucasus) and is surrounded by Georgia, Azerbaijan, Iran and Turkey. This high plateau country has hot summers and cold winters. Its earthquake-prone terrain is very mountainous, with agriculture restricted to the Aras river valley. Fruits and vegetables are grown there, and vineyards produce brandy and other liqueurs. Small amounts of gold, copper, molybdenum, zinc and alumina are mined.

Industries include machinery, microelectronics, electric motors, tires, textiles and footwear, chemicals, trucks and jewelry. Exports include diamonds, scrap metal, machinery and equipment, copper ore and brandy, which go to Belgium, Israel, Russia and the United States.

The population is almost entirely Armenian. Ethnic minorities include Yezidis, Russians and Greeks. Yejmiadzin is the headquarters of the Armenian Orthodox Church, to which over 95 percent of the populace belong. Armenian is the official language. Yerevan is Armenia's capital and chief center of population.

The Armenians were the first to adopt Christianity as a national religion. The ancient Armenian civilization dates back to the kingdom of Armenia in the first millennium B.C. At various times the Armenians have been under the yoke of Persia, Greece and Rome. When it enjoyed freedom as an independent kingdom, Armenia embraced a much larger area than that of the present republic. Armenia fell under Ottoman Turkish control in the early 1500s. The Armenian people suffered a series of massacres in the Ottoman-controlled areas, resulting in over one million deaths during the late nineteenth and early twentieth centuries. Tsarist Russia annexed the present Armenian area in 1828; it became a Soviet republic in 1920.

After 71 years of subordination, Armenia became an independent country in 1991. Economic progress is still being hindered by the effects of the 1988 earthquake, which killed more than 25,000 people and made 500,000 homeless. Also the conflict with Azerbaijan over Nagorno-Karabakh has not been resolved, although a cease-fire has held since 1994.

Did you know? Armenia was the first nation to officially adopt Christianity (around 300 AD).

AREA: 11,506 sq mi (29,800 sq km)

CLIMATE: This mountainous, high plateau country has hot summers and cold winters.

PEOPLE: The capital is the chief center of the country's population, which is mostly Armenian. Ethnic minorities include Yezidis, Russians and Greeks.

Lake Sevan — Apostles Church (left)
Holy Bearer-of-God Church (Right)

POPULATION: 2,976,372

LIFE EXPECTANCY AT BIRTH (YEARS): male, 67.7; female, 75.4

LITERACY RATE: 99%

ETHNIC GROUPS: Armenian 93%, Russian 2%

PRINCIPAL LANGUAGES: Armenian (official), Russian

CHIEF RELIGIONS: Armenian Apostolic 94%, other Christian 4%, Yezidi 2%

ECONOMY: Agriculture is restricted to the Aras River valley, where fruits and vegetables are grown. Vineyards produce brandy and other liqueurs. Industry includes machinery and electric motors.

MONETARY UNIT: dram

GDP: $13.7 billion (2004 est.)

PER CAPITA GDP: $4,600

INDUSTRIES: machine tools, forging-pressing machines, electric motors, tires, knitted wear, footwear, silk fabric, chemicals, trucks, instruments, microelectronics, jewelry, software development, food processing

CHIEF CROPS: grapes, vegetables

MINERALS: gold, copper, molybdenum, zinc, alumina

GOVERNMENT TYPE: republic

CAPITAL: Yerevan (pop., 1,079,000)

INDEPENDENCE DATE: September 21, 1991

WEBSITE: www.gov.am/

Australia, least populous of the inhabited continents and smallest in area, is roughly a low, irregular plateau with a flat, arid center. The central desert area of the Northern Territory is famous as the site of Uluru, or Ayers Rock, the unique formation consisting of a single solid rock mass. The temperate southeastern quarter of the continent is a huge, fertile plain that produces much of the nation's agricultural wealth and is home to most of its people. The Murray and Darling rivers drain this rich quadrant. Relatively low mountains lie close to the southeast coast. Offshore lies the island state of Tasmania. The northern area of Australia is hot, and produces tropical crops. Off the northeastern coast lies the Great Barrier Reef, the most extensive coral reef in the world. The prevalent life forms of Australia, the marsupials — non-placental mammals typified by the platypus, kangaroo and koala — are unique.

The population is mainly of British origin, and English is practically the universal language. There are approximately 227,000 aboriginals. Over three-quarters of the nation's population is urban. Sydney and Melbourne are the great metropolitan centers. Other major cities are Brisbane, Adelaide, Perth and Canberra, the commonwealth capital.

Australia supplies more than three-quarters of the world's tantalum mineral concentrate. Other natural resources are bauxite, coal, gold and iron ore, which along with the riches of its agricultural sector — beef, wool, mutton, wheat, sugar cane and fruit — fuel the booming export trade. Vineyards in New South Wales, Victoria and South Australia produce wines that are world-famous. Its trading partners are primarily countries of the Pacific Rim — Japan, the United States, South Korea, New Zealand, Taiwan and Singapore. Manufacturing industries are important, with food industries, metallurgy, automobiles and machinery heading the list.

Did you know? Australia was founded as a British penal colony.

The original aboriginal inhabitants entered the continent from Southeast Asia possibly as long ago as 50,000 years before the present. Europeans first sighted the continent in the seventeenth century. In 1770 Captain James Cook explored the east coast and claimed it for Britain. First serving as a British penal colony, Australia drew thousands of new immigrants following gold discoveries in Victoria and New South Wales in 1851. Six self-governing colonies were subsequently settled and organized. In 1901 the six states of Queensland, New South Wales, Victoria, Tasmania, South Australia and Western Australia formed the Commonwealth of Australia.

AREA: 2,967,908 sq mi (7,686,850 sq km)

The Twelve Apostles

CLIMATE: Roughly a low, irregular plateau, flat and arid in the center, temperate in the southeast, hot and tropical in the north.

PEOPLE: The population is mainly of British origin, with small Asian and native aboriginal minorities. Over three-quarters of the nation's people live in urban areas.
POPULATION: 20,264,082
LIFE EXPECTANCY AT BIRTH (YEARS): male, 77.4; female, 83.3
LITERACY RATE: 100%
ETHNIC GROUPS: white 92%, Asian 7%, Aborigine and other 1%
PRINCIPAL LANGUAGES: English (official), aboriginal languages
ECONOMY: Bauxite, coal, gold and iron ore, along with beef, wool, mutton, wheat, sugar cane, fruit and world-famous wines fuel the booming export trade. Other industries include metallurgy, automobiles and machinery.
CHIEF RELIGIONS: Anglican 26%, Roman Catholic 26%, other Christian 24%
MONETARY UNIT: Australian dollar
GDP: $611.7 billion (2004 est.)
PER CAPITA GDP: $30,700
INDUSTRIES: mining, industrial and transport equipment, food processing, chemicals,
MINERALS: bauxite, coal, iron ore, copper, tin, silver, uranium, nickel, tungsten, mineral sands, lead, zinc, diamonds, natural gas, petroleum
CHIEF CROPS: wheat, barley, sugarcane, fruits
CAPITAL: Canberra (pop., 373,000)
INDEPENDENCE DATE: January 1, 1901
GOVERNMENT TYPE: democratic, federal state system
WEBSITE: www.australia.com

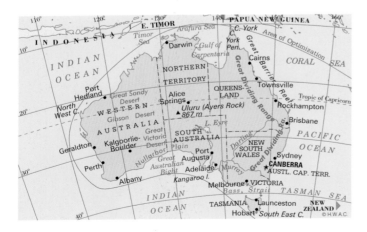

Once the core of the Hapsburg Empire that occupied much of Central and Southern Europe, Austria has been reduced by wars to a rather small landlocked state in the eastern Alps and along the western reaches of the Danube river. The country is 70 percent mountainous and possesses a continental temperate climate with cold winters and cool summers. Austria is strategically located at the crossroads of Central Europe and has many traversable Alpine passes and valleys. The population is concentrated in the eastern lowlands along the Danube and near the borders of Hungary and Slovenia.

Austria's few ethnic minorities include Slavs and Turks. German is the language of most of the populace. Roman Catholicism is the religion of 85 percent of the Austrian people. Vienna, the capital, is famed for its Baroque and nineteenth-century architecture and its historical position as the greatest music center of the Western world. Graz, Linz and Salzburg are the other centers.

Modern Austria boasts a prosperous and stable economy based on its plentiful raw materials, including iron ore and petroleum, and its technically skilled labor force. Steel, machinery, textiles and chemicals are important industrial products. Tourism and banking are also important. Austria is nearly self-sufficient in food production. Exports are primarily to Germany and other European countries.

Following the collapse of the Austro-Hungarian Empire of the Hapsburgs in 1918, the vastly truncated Republic of Austria led a precarious existence, hemmed in by Germany, Italy and the newly created successor states to the old empire. In 1938 Austria was annexed by Nazi Germany. Austrian independence was restored after World War II and it became a neutral buffer between the East and West superpowers. With the end of the Cold War Austria has benefited from increased trade with newly opened markets in Eastern Europe. Austria became a member of the EU on January 1, 1995.

Did you know? The Schottengymnasium, a school in Vienna, has been open since 1155.

AREA: 32,382 sq mi (83,870 sq km)

■ **CLIMATE:** Nearly three-quarters mountainous, the country has a continental temperate climate, with cold winters and cool summers.

■ **PEOPLE:** Austria's few ethnic minorities include Slavs and Turks. People live mostly in the eastern lowlands near the Danube, and along the borders of Hungary and Slovenia.

POPULATION: 8,192,880

Austrian Alps

LIFE EXPECTANCY AT BIRTH (YEARS): male, 75.0; female, 81.5

LITERACY RATE: 98%

ETHNIC GROUPS: German 88%

PRINCIPAL LANGUAGES: German (official), Serbo-Croatian, Slovenian

CHIEF RELIGIONS: Roman Catholic 78%, Protestant 5%

■ **ECONOMY:** Its strong economy is based on plentiful raw materials and a strong industrial base. Exports go primarily to Germany and other European countries. Tourism and banking are also important.

MONETARY UNIT: euro

GDP: $255.9 billion (2004 est.)

PER CAPITA GDP: $31,300

INDUSTRIES: construction, machinery, vehicles and parts, food, chemicals, lumber and wood processing, paper and paperboard, commercial equipment, tourism

MINERALS: iron ore, oil, timber, magnesite, lead, coal, copper

CHIEF CROPS: grains, potatoes, sugar beets, fruit

GOVERNMENT TYPE: federal republic

CAPITAL: Vienna (pop., 2,179,000)

INDEPENDENCE DATE: 1156

WEBSITE: www.austria.org

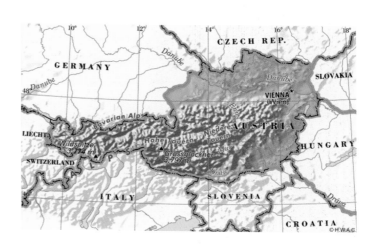

Azerbaijan is situated along the Caspian Sea and is bordered by Russia in the north, Georgia and Armenia on the west and Iran on the south. The terrain consists of lowlands along the Caspian Sea and upland foothills of the Kavkaz (Caucasus) range in the west. Baku, the capital city, lies on the Apsheron Peninsula that juts into the Caspian Sea. Sumgait and Gäncä (Gyandzhe) are other urban centers. The Naxçivan area is separated from the rest of Azerbaijan by intervening Armenia. The climate and vegetation are of the dry, semi-arid steppe type.

The Azerbaijani people (also called Azeri) are of Turkic extraction. There are small minorities of Dagestani, Russians and Armenians. Muslims constitute a majority of the population. Oil and natural gas dominate the economy. Iron ore, nonferrous metals and alumina are also mined. Cotton, rice and grain, fruit and vegetables, tea, tobacco and livestock are also important. Industries include petroleum and natural gas products, oilfield equipment, steel, iron ore, chemicals, petrochemicals and textiles. Exports of oil and gas, chemicals, oilfield equipment, textiles, cotton go to the European Union, Indonesia and Georgia.

Did you know?
Azerbaijan was once part of the Persian empire.

Azerbaijan became a Soviet Socialist Republic in 1920. With the collapse of the U.S.S.R., the independence of Azerbaijan was proclaimed in 1991. Following independence, warfare broke out with neighboring Armenia over the possession of the Armenian-inhabited enclave in the Nagorno-Karabakh within Azerbaijan.

AREA: 33,436 sq mi (86,600 sq km)
CLIMATE: Dry, semi-arid steppe type climate with hot summers and mild winters, and colder alpine conditions in the mountains.
PEOPLE: Azerbaijanis (also called Azeri) are of Turkic extraction, with small Dagestani, Russian and Armenian minorities.
POPULATION: 7,961,619
LIFE EXPECTANCY AT BIRTH (YEARS): male, 59.1; female, 67.6
LITERACY RATE: 97%
ETHNIC GROUPS: Azeri 90%, Dagestani 3%, Russian 3%, Armenian 2%
PRINCIPAL LANGUAGES: Azeri (official), Russian, Armenian

Traditional Azeri musicians

CHIEF RELIGIONS: Muslim 93%, Russian Orthodox 3%, Armenian Orthodox 2%
ECONOMY: Oil and natural gas dominate the economy, along with oil field equipment manufacturing. Cotton, rice and grain, fruit, vegetables and livestock are also important.
MONETARY UNIT: manat
GDP: $30.0 billion (2004 est.)
PER CAPITA GDP: $3,800
INDUSTRIES: petroleum products, oilfield equipment, steel, iron ore, cement, chemicals, textiles
MINERALS: petroleum, natural gas, iron ore, nonferrous metals, alumina
CHIEF CROPS: cotton, grain, rice, grapes, fruit, vegetables, tea, tobacco
GOVERNMENT TYPE: republic
CAPITAL: Baku (pop., 1,816,000)
INDEPENDENCE DATE: August 30, 1991
WEBSITE: www.president.az

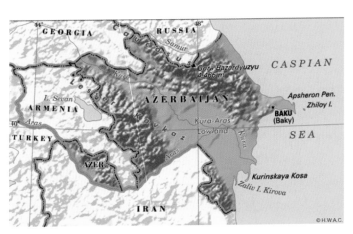

Consisting of 700 separate low, flat coral islands of which only thirty are inhabited, the Bahamas stretch more than 500 miles from off the southeast coast of Florida almost to Haiti. Splendid beaches and a pleasantly warm climate, moderated by the warm waters of the Gulf Stream, make this island country a tourist mecca. The islands of New Providence, on which is the capital of Nassau, and Grand Bahama, whose largest town is Freeport, are the main tourist centers. Other islands are developing resort facilities.

The country has a stable economy, dependent on tourism and related construction. The islands are also important as an offshore banking center. Salt, aragonite and timber are the chief natural resources. Fruits, vegetables and poultry are the primary agricultural commodities. Lobster and fish also contribute to the economy. Mineral products, fish, salt, rum, chemicals, fruits and vegetables go to the United States, the European Union and Canada.

The population is mostly of black African descent. Minorities include whites, Asians and Hispanics. English is the official and universal language. Christianity is the predominant religion; there are Baptist, Anglican, Methodist and Roman Catholic congregations.

> **Did you know?** Only about 40 of the Bahamas' 700-plus islands are inhabited.

It was on one Bahama island, San Salvador, in 1492 that Columbus made his first landing in the Western Hemisphere. Britain took possession of the islands in the 1600s, holding them for three centuries before they became independent in 1973.

AREA: 5,382 sq mi (13,940 sq km)

TOPOGRAPHY: Nearly 700 islands (29 inhabited) and over 2,000 islets in the western Atlantic Ocean extend 760 mi (1,220 km) northwest to southeast.

■ **CLIMATE:** A pleasant tropical marine climate is moderated by the warm waters of the Gulf Stream.

■ **PEOPLE:** The population is mostly black. Minorities include whites, Asians and Hispanics.

POPULATION: 303,770

LIFE EXPECTANCY AT BIRTH (YEARS): male, 62.2; female, 69.1

Nassau

LITERACY RATE: 98.2%

ETHNIC GROUPS: black 85%, white 12%

PRINCIPAL LANGUAGES: English, Creole (among Haitian immigrants)

CHIEF RELIGIONS: Baptist 32%, Anglican 20%, Roman Catholic 19%, other Christian 24%

■ **ECONOMY:** A stable economy, dependent on tourism and related construction. The islands are also important as an offshore banking center. Exports include mineral products, salt, rum, chemicals fruits and vegetables.

MONETARY UNIT: Bahamas dollar

GDP: $5.3 billion (2004 est.)

PER CAPITA GDP: $17,700

INDUSTRIES: tourism, banking, cement, oil refining and transshipment, pharmaceuticals, steel pipe

MINERALS: salt, aragonite

CHIEF CROPS: citrus, vegetables

GOVERNMENT TYPE: independent commonwealth

CAPITAL: Nassau (pop., 222,000)

INDEPENDENCE DATE: July 10, 1973

WEBSITE: www.bahamas.gov.bs

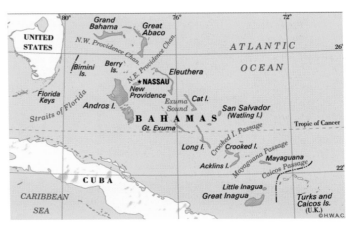

The Persian Gulf state of Bahrain, 15 miles offshore from Saudi Arabia, is formed by the main island, Bahrain, and ten smaller islands. Consisting mostly of low desert plains, the islands enjoy mild, pleasant winters, but summer brings hot, humid weather. Precipitation is low. Petroleum refining and the production of crude oil and natural gas are the most important economic resources. More than 50 percent of the oil refined is piped from Saudi Arabia. Declining oil reserves have forced Bahrain to turn to other industries, including aluminum and textiles. Services, dominated by banking, are of major economic importance.

The indigenous Bahraini and other Arabic peoples constitute two thirds of the population; Iranians, Indians, Pakistanis and Europeans make up the remaining third. Arabic is the official and chief language. Islam is the official religion, with Shiites outnumbering Sunnis by a significant majority; there is a small Christian minority. Manama is the capital and largest city.

Bahrain may have been "Dilmun," a trade center mentioned in Sumerian records, but little is known of its ancient history. The dynasty of the present Amir was founded in 1783. British protectorate status began in the nineteenth century. The country declared itself fully independent in 1971.

> **Did you know?** Only 1% of this island nation's land supports agriculture.

AREA: 257 sq mi (665 sq km)

CLIMATE: The arid climate features mild winters and hot, humid summers. The lack of fertile soil and sufficient land area has severely limited agriculture.

PEOPLE: A highly international economy reflects this diverse cosmopolitan community. Foreign-born residents and workers come largely from Asian and other Arab countries.

POPULATION: 698,585

LIFE EXPECTANCY AT BIRTH (YEARS): male, 71.5; female, 76.5

LITERACY RATE: 88.5%

ETHNIC GROUPS: Arab 73%, Asian 19%, Iranian 8%

Hoora-Exhibition Avenue

PRINCIPAL LANGUAGES: Arabic (official), English, Farsi, Urdu

CHIEF RELIGIONS: Muslim (official; Shi'a 70%, Sunni 30%)

ECONOMY: Petroleum products are the country's major exports. Other industries include aluminum and textiles. Services, dominated by banking, are of major economic importance.

MONETARY UNIT: dinar

GDP: $13.0 billion (2004 est.)

PER CAPITA GDP: $19,200

INDUSTRIES: petroleum processing and refining, aluminum smelting, offshore banking, ship repairing, tourism

MINERALS: oil, natural gas

CHIEF CROPS: fruit, vegetables

CAPITAL: Manama (pop., 139,000)

INDEPENDENCE DATE: August 15, 1971

GOVERNMENT TYPE: constitutional monarchy

WEBSITE: www.bahrain.gov.bh/english/index.asp

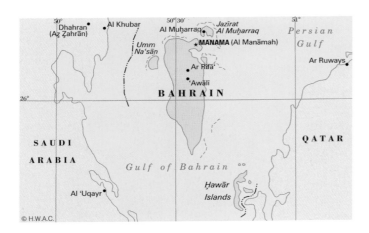

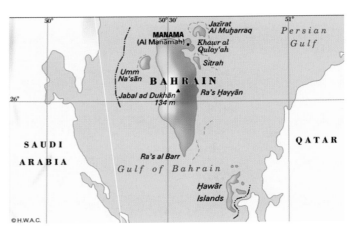

Bangladesh is located in the Ganges-Brahmaputra delta area, a subtropical alluvial plain bisected by many rivers and streams. Jute fields, rice paddies, tea plantations and tropical jungles are prominent features of the delta landscape. The climate is tropical with mild winters, hot, humid summers, and a warm, rainy monsoon season from June to October. The cyclones of the annual monsoon season frequently flood the delta area, taking the lives of thousands of its inhabitants.

The country is surrounded almost entirely by India, except for the extreme southeast corner that borders Burma (Myanmar). Parts of the border area with India contain the only highland areas of the country — the Sylhet region in the northeast and the extreme eastern tract inland from the port city of Chittagong.

The population is overwhelmingly Bengali. Most of the people are Muslim, the minority Hindu faith being the only other sizable religion. Bengali is the official and predominant language, but English is also widely used. Dhāka is the capital and largest city.

Bangladesh is one of the world's poorest, most densely populated and least developed countries. Its few exploited natural resources include coal and natural gas. The economy is overwhelmingly agricultural. The production of jute, used to manufacture rope, makes Bangladesh the world's leading exporter of that crop. Rice cultivation is the single most important economic activity. Tea, sugarcane, wheat and chillies are also grown. Fish and seafood contribute to the economy.

Industries include textiles, jute goods, frozen fish and seafood, fertilizers, sugar, tea, leather, ship-breaking for scrap, pharmaceuticals, ceramic tableware and newsprint. The United States and Western Europe are the main importers of Bangladeshi products.

Did you know? This low-lying country is plagued by flooding caused by monsoons.

During British rule, today's Bangladesh was part of the province of Bengal. With the departure of the British in 1947, East Bengal became a part of the new, mostly Muslim nation of Pakistan. East Pakistan, as Bangladesh was then called, was separated from the rest of Pakistan by a thousand miles and by differences in language and outlook. Though East Pakistan elected a majority of the seats in the Pakistan National Assembly, the Pakistan government prevented the meeting of the assembly. Riots ensued in East Pakistan in 1971 and Pakistani troops invaded the area. Indian intervention resulted in the defeat of the Pakistani forces. The independence of Bangladesh was proclaimed on December 16, 1971.

AREA: 55,599 sq mi (144,000 sq km)

■ **CLIMATE:** Tropical with mild winters and hot, humid summers, and a humid, warm, rainy monsoon season from June to October.

■ **PEOPLE:** The population is overwhelmingly Bengali. Over 85 percent of the people are Muslim, the minority Hindu faith being the only other sizable religion.

Dhāka-Lalbagh Fort

POPULATION: 147,365,352

LIFE EXPECTANCY AT BIRTH (YEARS): male, 61.8; female, 61.6

LITERACY RATE: 56%

ETHNIC GROUPS: Bengali 98%

PRINCIPAL LANGUAGES: Bangla (official, also known as Bengali), English

CHIEF RELIGIONS: Muslim (official) 83%, Hindu 16%

■ **ECONOMY:** One of the world's poorest countries. Overwhelmingly agricultural, it is the world's leading exporter of jute for making rope. Garments, leather, frozen fish and seafood are also important exports.

MONETARY UNIT: taka

GDP: $275.7 billion (2004 est.)

PER CAPITA GDP: $2,000

INDUSTRIES: cotton textiles, jute, garments, tea processing, paper newsprint, cement, chemical fertilizer, light engineering

CHIEF CROPS: rice, jute, tea, wheat, sugarcane, potatoes, tobacco, pulses, oilseeds, spices, fruit

MINERALS: natural gas, coal

GOVERNMENT TYPE: parliamentary democracy

CAPITAL: Dhaka (pop., 11,560,000)

INDEPENDENCE DATE: December 16, 1971

WEBSITE: www.bangladeshgov.org

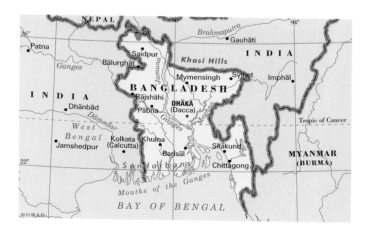

The easternmost island of the West Indies, Barbados is one of the most densely populated areas of the Western Hemisphere. Relatively flat, the terrain rises gently to a central highland region. The climate is tropical with a rainy season from June to October and infrequent hurricanes.

Natural resources include petroleum, fish, quarrying and natural gas. From the time of its colonization by the British, Barbados has been known for a dominant activity, the growing of sugarcane, and the distilling and exporting of rum. Its distinctly British atmosphere and a profusion of attractions in a vivid tropical setting have made tourism the greatest producer of income, supplanting sugar production. Offshore finance and data processing are also economically important. Light manufacturing includes food processing, rum, electronics, textiles, paper and chemicals. Exports of these goods go to the United States, the European Union, Trinidad and Tobago, St. Lucia and Jamaica.

The population is mostly black African. Minorities include whites, Asians and people of mixed descent. English Is the official and universal language. Christianity is the main religion, with Anglican and other Protestant denominations predominating. Bridgetown is the capital and main population center.

British rule, which began in 1627, ended in 1966, when Barbados became independent.

Did you know?
Barbados is named for its bearded fig trees (from the Spanish barbados, "bearded ones").

Bridgetown parliament building

AREA: 166 sq mi (431 sq km)

■ **CLIMATE:** Tropical with a rainy season from June to October and infrequent hurricanes.

■ **PEOPLE:** The population is mostly black. Minorities include whites, Asians and people of mixed descent. Barbados is one of the most densely populated areas of the Western Hemisphere.

POPULATION: 279,912

LIFE EXPECTANCY AT BIRTH (YEARS): male, 69.5; female, 73.8

LITERACY RATE: 97.4%

ETHNIC GROUPS: black 90%, white 4%

PRINCIPAL LANGUAGE: English

CHIEF RELIGIONS: Protestant 67%, Roman Catholic 4%

■ **ECONOMY:** Once dependent on sugarcane and rum, the economy is now driven by tourism. Light manufacturing and offshore finance are also economically important.

MONETARY UNIT: Barbados dollar

GDP: $4.6 billion (2004 est.)

PER CAPITA GDP: $16,400

INDUSTRIES: tourism, sugar, light manufacturing, component assembly for export

MINERALS: petroleum, natural gas

CHIEF CROPS: sugarcane, vegetables, cotton

GOVERNMENT TYPE: parliamentary democracy

CAPITAL: Bridgetown (pop., 140,000)

INDEPENDENCE DATE: November 30, 1966

WEBSITE: www.barbados.gov.bb

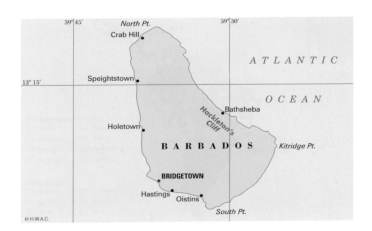

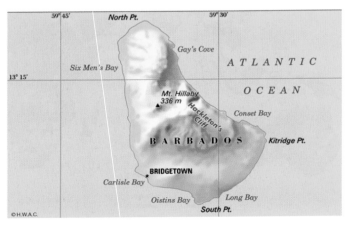

Landlocked Belarus sits at a crossroads in Eastern Europe between Poland on the west, Lithuania and Latvia on the north and Ukraine on the south. Generally flat glacial plains dominate the terrain. In the upper reaches of the Pripyat river in western Belarus are vast marshes. The transitional continental and maritime climate is typified by cold winters and cool, moist summers. The country's natural resources include timber, peat, potash, small amounts of oil and natural gas. Other mineral resources include granite, dolomite, marl, chalk, sand and gravel. Agriculturally, Belarus is a leading producer of meat, milk, eggs, grains, flax, sugar beets and vegetables. Belarus ranks among the most developed of the former Soviet states. Machinery, transport and construction equipment, electrical and electronic goods, textiles and chemical fibers are the leading industrial products. Exports of these products go to Russia and European Union countries.

Byelorussians make up most of the population, with Russians, Poles and Ukranians in the minority. Most profess the Orthodox Christian faith; there are Roman Catholic and Jewish minorities. Byelorussian and Russian are spoken. Minsk is the capital and largest city.

Belarus spent several centuries under Polish rule until Tsarist Russia conquered the area in the late 1700s. At the end of the Russian Revolution and Civil War, the western half of Belarus came again under Polish sovereignty but was regained by the U.S.S.R. in 1939. The central and eastern portion was established as the Byelorussian Soviet Socialist Republic of the Soviet Union. During World War II all of the Byelorussian S.S.R. was occupied by Nazi Germany from 1941 through 1944 and suffered much damage. With the collapse of the Soviet Union, Belarus proclaimed its independence on August 25, 1991. The country has been run by the country's first President, Alexander Lukashenko, since 1994.

> **Did you know?** "Bela Rusian" means "White Russian," a distinct ethnic group.

AREA: 80,155 sq mi (207,600 sq km)

■ **CLIMATE:** The transitional continental and maritime climate is typified by cold winters and cool, moist summers.

■ **PEOPLE:** Byelorussians make up most of the population, with Russians, Poles and Ukranians in the minority.

POPULATION: 10,293,011

LIFE EXPECTANCY AT BIRTH (YEARS): male, 62.8; female, 74.7

LITERACY RATE: 98%

Minsk-Victory Square

ETHNIC GROUPS: Belarusian 81%, Russian 11%

■ **ECONOMY:** Machinery, transport and construction equipment, and electronic goods are the leading industrial products. Agricultural products include, grain, potatoes, vegetables, flax, beef, milk and sugar beets.

MONETARY UNIT: ruble

GDP: $70.5 billion (2004 est.)

PER CAPITA GDP: $6,800

PRINCIPAL LANGUAGES: Belarusian, Russian

CHIEF RELIGIONS: Eastern Orthodox 80%, other 20%

INDUSTRIES: machine tools, tractors, trucks, earthmovers, motorcycles, domestic appliances, chemical fibers, fertilizer, textiles

MINERALS: oil and natural gas, granite, dolomitic limestone, marl, chalk, sand, gravel, clay

CHIEF CROPS: grain, potatoes, vegetables, sugar beets, flax

GOVERNMENT TYPE: republic

CAPITAL: Minsk (pop., 1,705,000)

INDEPENDENCE DATE: August 25, 1991

WEBSITE: www.belarusembassy.org

Located on the North Sea, two major rivers - the Schelde and the Meuse - traverse Belgium, while canals connect them with the Rhine in the Netherlands. While most of the country is generally flat and low-lying, it becomes increasingly hilly and forested toward the Ardennes region in the southeast. The country has a temperate climate, rainy, humid and cloudy, with mild winters and cool summers. Belgium is a key trading and manufacturing center. Coal and natural gas are the chief mineral and fuel resources. Livestock, milk, sugar beets and grain are the chief farm products. Machinery, cut diamonds, motor vehicles, steel, chemicals, food products and textiles are exported to the European Union and the United States. Despite this, services account for three quarters of the Gross Domestic Product.

Brussels is the capital, while Antwerp is the country's great port city. Gent, Charleroi and Liège are other chief urban centers. The country is split ethnically and linguistically in two parts; a northern half which is Flemish-speaking, and the southern half, which is Walloon in speech. Flemish is a form of Dutch, and Walloon is a French dialect. The capital city of Brussels is bilingual.

A small German-speaking minority inhabits the German border area. The split between the Flemings and Walloons is the dominant political problem of the country. The majority of the people are Roman Catholic, though there is a small Protestant minority.

Belgium's strategic location between France and Germany has been the stage for many military campaigns and major battles: Waterloo in 1815, Flanders in 1914 to 1918, the Ardennes during World War II. As nations go, Belgium is a young state; it did not become independent until 1831. Before that time the Belgian area had existed successively under Burgundian, Spanish Hapsburg and Austrian Hapsburg rule, Napoleonic France, and lastly the Kingdom of the Netherlands. Belgium is one of the founding members of the European Union.

> **Did you know?** Belgium has two main ethnic groups, Flemings and Walloons.

AREA: 11,786 sq mi (30,528 sq km)

CLIMATE: A temperate climate, rainy, humid and cloudy, with mild winters and cool summers.

PEOPLE: The country is politically split between a Flemish (Dutch speaking) northern half, and a Walloon (French speaking) southern half. A small German-speaking minority inhabits the German border area.

POPULATION: 10,379,067

LIFE EXPECTANCY AT BIRTH (YEARS): male, 75.3; female, 81.8

Antwerp-Grote Markt

LITERACY RATE: 98%

ETHNIC GROUPS: Fleming 58%, Walloon 31%

PRINCIPAL LANGUAGES: Dutch, French, German (all official); Flemish, Luxembourgish

CHIEF RELIGIONS: Roman Catholic 75%; Protestant, other 25%

ECONOMY: Machinery, textiles, chemicals, cut diamonds, glass and pharmaceuticals are important industries. Despite this, services account for three quarters of the GDP.

MONETARY UNIT: euro

GDP: $316.2 billion (2004 est.)

PER CAPITA GDP: $30,600

INDUSTRIES: engineering and metal products, motor vehicle assembly, processed food and beverages, chemicals, basic metals, textiles, glass, petroleum, coal

MINERALS: coal, natural gas

CHIEF CROPS: sugar beets, fresh vegetables, fruits, grain, tobacco

GOVERNMENT TYPE: parliamentary democracy under a constitutional monarch

CAPITAL: Brussels (pop., 998,000)

INDEPENDENCE DATE: October 4, 1830

WEBSITE: www.diplobel.us

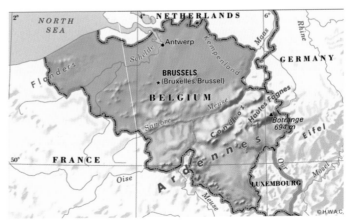

Located on the western edge of the Caribbean Sea, Belize is bounded by Mexico on the north and Guatemala on the south and west. It has a swampy coast that rises gradually toward the interior, which is dominated by tropical jungle.

The climate is hot and humid, with a rainy season from May to November and a dry season from February to May. Natural resources include timber, seafood and hydropower. Principal agricultural products include bananas, cocoa, citrus and sugarcane. Industries include textiles, fish and seafood processing and lumber. Exports of sugar, bananas, citrus, garments, fish products molasses and wood go to the United States and the United Kingdom. Tourism, particularly ecotourism, is a major source of foreign income.

Temple at Caraco

The country has a diverse population of mestizo (Spanish-Indian), Creole (Black African), Mayan Indian, Garifuna (black-Carib Indian), and others. English is the official language; Spanish and various Indian languages are also spoken. Christianity is the dominant religion, with Roman Catholicsm accounting for half and Protestantism for a third of believers. Belize City is the largest urban center. However, following a severe hurricane in 1961, the capital was moved to the inland city of Belmopan.

> **Did you know?** Belize is the only English-speaking nation in Central America.

The Mayan civilization flourished in the Belize area until about A.D. 1000. In the 1600s and 1700s English settlers exploited the mahogany forests, using African slaves as labor. In 1862 the Crown Colony of British Honduras was established. The colony was renamed Belize in 1973. In a dispute over the ownership of the area, Guatemala threatened to invade the colony in 1975. The threat was thwarted with the dispatch of British troops. Belize became independent in 1981.

AREA: 8,867 sq mi (22,966 sq km)

■ **CLIMATE:** Tropical, hot and humid, with a rainy season from May to November and a dry season from February to May.

■ **PEOPLE:** The country has a diverse population of mestizo (Spanish-Indian), Creole (black African), Mayan Indian, Garifuna (black-Carib Indian), and others.

POPULATION: 287,730

LIFE EXPECTANCY AT BIRTH (YEARS): male, 65.1; female, 69.9

LITERACY RATE: 70.3%

ETHNIC GROUPS: mestizo 49%, Creole 25%, Maya 11%, Garifuna 6%

PRINCIPAL LANGUAGES: English (official), Spanish, Mayan, Garifuna (Carib), Creole

CHIEF RELIGIONS: Roman Catholic 50%, Protestant 27%

■ **ECONOMY:** Tourism is the primary source of foreign income, followed by marine products, citrus, cane sugar, wood and bananas.

MONETARY UNIT: Belize dollar

GDP: $1.8 billion (2004 est.)

PER CAPITA GDP: $6,500

INDUSTRIES: garment production, food processing, tourism, construction

CHIEF CROPS: bananas, coca, citrus, sugarcane

GOVERNMENT TYPE: parliamentary democracy

CAPITAL: Belmopan (pop., 9,000)

INDEPENDENCE DATE: September 21, 1981represented by Gov.-Gen. Sir Colville Young

WEBSITE: www.belize.gov.bz

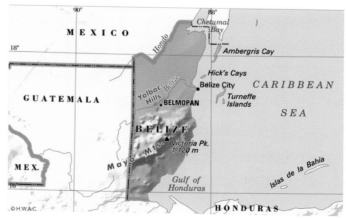

Though his small tropical West African nation takes its name from the Bight of Benin, on which it lies. Sandy beaches, unbroken by natural harbors, give way inland to a tropical hot and humid south followed by a flat, semi-arid region. Farther north lies a swampy depression area that in turn gives way to hills and then mountains. Hampered by unexploited natural resources of high quality marble limestone, and timber, and a poorly developed infrastructure, the economy is chiefly agricultural. Crops include sorghum, cassava, tapioca, yams, beans, rice, cotton, palm oil, cocoa and peanuts. Poultry and livestock are raised. Cotton is the major export, but palm oil products and crude oil are also produced and exported to China, France, Thailand and Côte d'Ivoire.

There are more than forty African ethnic groups. The largest, the Fon, are followed by the Adja, Yoruba and the Bariba. African languages are spoken by the people, but French is the official language. Indigenous (animist) beliefs are held by half the population. Christians and Muslims are significant minorities. Cotonou, the chief city, was once a French trading post. Porto-Novo is the capital.

Here the powerful Kingdom of Abomey held sway from the seventeenth century until the French took control in the mid-eighteenth century. The country gained independence from France in 1960 as Dahomey. Its name was changed to Benin in 1975.

> **Did you know?** Benin was the name of an African kingdom founded in the 12th century.

AREA: 43,483 sq mi (112,620 sq km)

■ **CLIMATE:** A semi-arid region in the north gives way to a tropical hot and humid south.

■ **PEOPLE:** There are more than forty African ethnic groups. The largest, the Fon, are followed by the Adja, Yoruba and the Bariba.

POPULATION: 7,862,944

LIFE EXPECTANCY AT BIRTH (YEARS): male, 50.3; female, 51.4

LITERACY RATE: 37.5%

ETHNIC GROUPS: 42 groups, including Fon, Adja, Yoruba, and Bariba

PRINCIPAL LANGUAGES: French (official), Fon, Yoruba, various tribal languages

Rural Benin

CHIEF RELIGIONS: indigenous beliefs 50%, Christian 30%, Muslim 20%

■ **ECONOMY:** Cotton is the chief export of an economy that relies on subsistence agriculture, but palm oil products, crude oil and cocoa are also produced and exported.

MONETARY UNIT: CFA franc

GDP: $8.3 billion (2004 est.)

PER CAPITA GDP: $1,200

INDUSTRIES: textiles, food processing, chemical production, construction materials

MINERALS: offshore oil, limestone, marble

CHIEF CROPS: cotton, corn, cassava, yams, beans, palm oil, peanuts

GOVERNMENT TYPE: republic

CAPITAL: Porto-Novo (pop., 238,000)

INDEPENDENCE DATE:
August 1, 1960

WEBSITE: www.beninembassyus.org

L ying landlocked between China and India, the Kingdom of Bhutan controls strategic mountain passes in the eastern Himalayas. Its climate varies from tropical in the southern plains to cool winters and hot summers in the central valleys, to severe winters and cool summers in the high mountains. Strongly linked to India through trade, the Bhutanese economy is mostly agricultural. Crops include rice, corn, root corps, citrus and food grains. Poultry and cattle are raised. Cardamom and other spices, and also precious stones are among its more exotic exports. Gypsum, cement, timber and handicrafts are also important. The country's main export partner is India. Industry is limited largely to the cottage variety. The country has strong potential resources in hydroelectric power and tourism. However, the Bhutanese government has limited the growth of tourism, wanting to control foreign influence and to preserve its unique culture and Buddhist religion.

While Bhote make up the bulk of the population, more than a third of Bhutan's people are Nepalese. There are also a small number of indigenous or migrant tribes. The people, related to the Tibetans to the north, are chiefly Buddhist in religion. A large Nepalese minority practices Hinduism. Dzongkha is the official language, but Nepali is widely spoken. Thimphu is the capital and chief city.

In the late nineteenth century Britain began the guidance of Bhutan's external affairs. The kingdom was established in 1909. When the British left in 1949, India assumed control of Bhutan's foreign relations. In 1971 Bhutan joined the United Nations.

Did you know? Bhutan has 770 species of birds, as well as tigers, elephants, and snow leopards.

AREA: 18,147 sq mi (47,000 sq km)

■ **CLIMATE:** Tropical in the southern plains, with cool winters and hot summers in the central valleys and severe winters and cool summers in the high mountains.

■ **PEOPLE:** While Bhote make up the bulk of the population, more than a third of Bhutan's people are Nepalese. There are also a small number of indigenous or migrant tribes.

POPULATION: 2,279,723

LIFE EXPECTANCY AT BIRTH (YEARS): male, 54.3; female, 53.7

LITERACY RATE: 42.2%

National dress

ETHNIC GROUPS: Bhote 50%, Nepalese 35%, indigenous tribes 15%

PRINCIPAL LANGUAGES: Dzongkha (official), Tibetan, Nepalese dialects

CHIEF RELIGIONS: Lamaistic Buddhist (official) 75%, Hindu 25%

■ **ECONOMY:** The economy is mostly agricultural with close trade ties to India. Cardamom and other spices, precious stones, gypsum, timber and handicrafts are important exports.

MONETARY UNIT: ngultrum

GDP: $2.9 billion (2003 est.)

PER CAPITA GDP: $1,400

INDUSTRIES: cement, wood products, processed fruits, alcoholic beverages

MINERALS: gypsum, calcium carbide

CHIEF CROPS: rice, corn, root crops, citrus, foodgrains

GOVERNMENT TYPE: monarchy

CAPITAL: Thimphu (pop., 35,000)

INDEPENDENCE DATE: August 8, 1949

WEBSITE: www.kingdomofbhutan.com

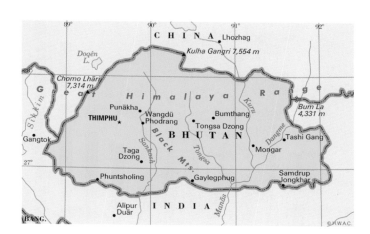

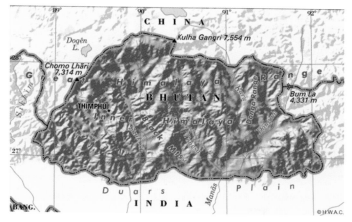

Bolivia's economic status as one of the poorest nations of the Western Hemisphere is traceable to its totally landlocked position high astride the Andes. Difficulty in transporting products to world markets has hindered development of Bolivia's resources and inhibited economic growth. The country is divided into three distinct regions: the Altiplano - one of the world's highest inhabited regions - a bleak mineral-rich plateau lying between two ranges of the Andes Mountains; the Yungas, an intermediate region containing the eastern mountain slopes and valleys; and the Llanos, the sparsely populated Chaco lowlands. The climate varies with altitude from humid and tropical to cold and semiarid. Mining is the most important economic activity: tin, silver, lead and zinc, iron, tungsten, antimony and gold are the chief minerals. Natural gas and petroleum exports are important. Soybeans, cotton, potatoes, corn, sugarcane, rice, wheat, coffee, beef and barley are the chief crops. Cultivation of the coca plant, the source of the illicit drug cocaine, takes place on a major scale. Major exports of natural gas, tin, zinc, coffee, silver, wood, gold, jewelry and soy products go to the United States, Brazil, Colombia and Argentina.

The population is composed of a majority of Amerindian peoples - the Quechua and Aymara constituting the largest groups - with mixed Indian-Spanish mestizos and those of European descent make up the rest of the populace. Spanish is the official language, but Quechua and Aymara are also widely spoken. Roman Catholicism is the faith of most of the people. La Paz is the administrative capital; Sucre is the legal and judicial capital. Other important cities are Santa Cruz and Cochabamba.

> **Did you know?** Lake Titicaca, which stretches across the Bolivia-Peru border, is the largest lake in South America (3,200 sq mi [8,300 sq km]).

The Bolivian Altiplano was a center of Indian life long before the days of the Incas, who conquered the region in the thirteenth century. The Spanish conquest began in the 1530s, and the Indians were virtually enslaved to work the rich silver mines of Upper Peru, as Bolivia was then called. In 1809, Upper Peru became one of the first Spanish colonies to revolt against Spain. Bolivian independence was proclaimed in 1825. From 1879 to 1884 Bolivia and Peru fought Chile in the War in the Pacific. Chile was victorious and Bolivia was forced to cede the province of Atacama, its only coastal territory. In 1903 Bolivia ceded the large rubber-tree area of Acre to Brazil. Discovery of oil at the foot of the Bolivian Andes precipitated the Chaco War of 1932-35 with Paraguay, which claimed the region. More than 100,000 lives were lost on both sides. A defeated Bolivia lost three-quarters of the Chaco to Paraguay. Until the 1952 revolution, contending ideologies and the demands of new groups convulsed Bolivian politics. A series of coups and countercoups ended in 1982 with democratic civilian rule.

AREA: 19,741 sq mi (51,129 sq km)

■ **CLIMATE:** The country has hot summers and cold winters, with mild, rainy winters near the coast, and short cool summers and severe winters in higher elevations.

■ **PEOPLE:** Bosniaks make up the bulk of the population followed by Serbs and Croats.

La Paz center

POPULATION: 4,498,976

LIFE EXPECTANCY AT BIRTH (YEARS): male, 69.8; female, 75.5

LITERACY RATE: NA

ETHNIC GROUPS: Bosniak 48%, Serbian 37%, Croatian 14%

PRINCIPAL LANGUAGES: Bosnian (official), Croatian, Serbian

CHIEF RELIGIONS: Muslim 40%, Orthodox 31%, Roman Catholic 15%, Protestant 4%

■ **ECONOMY:** Steel, textiles, vehicle assembly, tobacco products and wooden furniture are chief industries. Natural resources include coal, iron ore, timber, bauxite, lead and zinc.

MONETARY UNIT: converted marka (BAM)

GDP: $26.2 billion (2004 est.)

PER CAPITA GDP: $6,500

INDUSTRIES: steel, mining, vehicle assembly, textiles, tobacco products, wooden furniture, tank and aircraft assembly, domestic appliances, oil refining

CHIEF CROPS: wheat, corn, fruits, vegetables

MINERALS: coal, iron, bauxite, manganese, copper, chromium, lead, zinc

GOVERNMENT TYPE: federal republic

CAPITAL: Sarajevo (pop., 579,000)

INDEPENDENCE DATE: March 1, 1992

WEBSITE: www.bhembassy.org

Bosnia occupies most of the country's area. Herzegovina is a smaller area in the southern part of the country, centered on the city of Mostar. The land consists of mountains and valleys with a very small coastline on the Adriatic Sea. The chief rivers are the Sava and the Drina. Bosnia has hot summers and cold winters, with mild, rainy winters near the coast, and short cool summers and severe winters in higher elevations. Natural resources include timber, bauxite, coal, copper, iron ore, lead, zinc and manganese. Fruit, wine grapes, cereals and livestock are raised. Metals, vehicles, textile, furniture, tobacco products and armaments are the chief manufactures. Exports of metals, clothing and wood products go to European Union countries.

Bosnians make up the bulk of the population followed by Serbs and Croats. The Serbs are Orthodox Christians; the Croats are Roman Catholic Christians.

Serbo-Croatian is spoken by nearly all the population. Sarajevo is the official capital and largest city. Slavic tribes settled the region about 600 A.D. During the early Middle Ages, Bosnia was a vassal of Hungary except for a period during the 1300s. During the early 1400s, Herzegovina was independent. By 1528 the Ottoman Turks had conquered the region. During Ottoman rule, which lasted until 1878, many Bosnian Slavs were converted to Islam. At the Congress of Berlin in 1878, Austria-Hungary was given the right to occupy Bosnia and Herzegovina. The area was incorporated directly into the dual monarchy in 1908. It was in Sarajevo that the assassination of the Austrian archduke precipitated World War I. After that war Bosnia and Herzegovina became part of the Kingdom of Serbs, Croats and Slovenes, later renamed Yugoslavia. At the end of World War II, the area became a republic within the Socialist Federal Republic of Yugoslavia. In April 1992, the Western powers recognized the independence of Bosnia and Herzegovina. At that time civil war between Bosnian Serbs, Muslims and Croats broke out, and thousands of civilians were killed in the following years. During 1995 talks between the Croatian, Serbian (Yugoslav) and Bosnian governments resulted in an agreement to establish two governmental entities within the country: a Bosnian-Croat federation and a Serb republic, both under a central government.

> **Did you know?**
> Archduke Ferdinand's 1914 murder in Sarajevo sparked World War I.

AREA: 19,741 sq mi (51,129 sq km)

■ **CLIMATE:** The country has hot summers and cold winters, with mild, rainy winters near the coast, and short cool summers and severe winters in higher elevations.

Mostar

■ **PEOPLE:** Bosniaks make up the bulk of the population followed by Serbs and Croats.

POPULATION: 4,498,976

LIFE EXPECTANCY AT BIRTH (YEARS): male, 69.8; female, 75.5

LITERACY RATE: NA

ETHNIC GROUPS: Bosniak 48%, Serbian 37%, Croatian 14%

PRINCIPAL LANGUAGES: Bosnian (official), Croatian, Serbian

CHIEF RELIGIONS: Muslim 40%, Orthodox 31%, Roman Catholic 15%, Protestant 4%

■ **ECONOMY:** Steel, textiles, vehicle assembly, tobacco products and wooden furniture are chief industries. Natural resources include coal, iron ore, timber, bauxite, lead and zinc.

MONETARY UNIT: converted marka (BAM)

GDP: $26.2 billion (2004 est.)

PER CAPITA GDP: $6,500

INDUSTRIES: steel, mining, vehicle assembly, textiles, tobacco products, wooden furniture, tank and aircraft assembly, domestic appliances, oil refining

CHIEF CROPS: wheat, corn, fruits, vegetables

MINERALS: coal, iron, bauxite, manganese, copper, chromium, lead, zinc

GOVERNMENT TYPE: federal republic

CAPITAL: Sarajevo (pop., 579,000)

INDEPENDENCE DATE: March 1, 1992

WEBSITE: www.bhembassy.org

andlocked Botswana is bordered by Namibia, Zambia, Zimbabwe and South Africa. The nation is semiarid with warm winters and hot summers. The Kalahari, an arid tableland, dominates the southwestern part of the country. Elephants, ostriches, antelope, giraffes, leopards and lions roam the central steppe and eastern savanna. Botswana also contains the Okavango swamps, a great inland delta formed by the Okavango River.

Historically the economy depended on cattle raising and crops. Agriculture is still the chief employer, but the rapid growth of the economy in the 1970s and 80s is due to the mining industry. Diamonds are the chief export. The mining of copper, nickel and coal are also important, along with meat and textiles. Exports go to the European Union and nearby South African countries.

The original people of the area were Bushmen, who now comprise only five percent of the population. The majority is Tswana, a Bantu people who migrated from Central or East Africa before the nineteenth century. Others include Kalanga, Basarwa, Kgalagadi and white. Almost three fourths of the population is Christian. Gaborone is the capital and largest city.

Did you know? The Kalahari Desert covers most of southwestern Botswana.

The British occupied the territory as a protectorate in the nineteenth century, when it became known as Bechuanaland. In 1966 the country gained its independence and assumed its present name.

AREA: 231,804 sq mi (600,370 sq km)

■ **CLIMATE:** The nation is semiarid with warm winters and hot summers.

■ **PEOPLE:** The majority is Tswana, a Bantu people from Central or East Africa. Others include Kalanga, Basarwa, Kgalagadi and white.

POPULATION: 1,639,833

LIFE EXPECTANCY AT BIRTH (YEARS): male, 31.0; female, 30.5

LITERACY RATE: 69.8%

ETHNIC GROUPS: Tswana 79%, Kalanga 11%, Basarwa 3%

PRINCIPAL LANGUAGES: English (official), Setswana

CHIEF RELIGIONS: indigenous beliefs 85%, Christian 15%

Chobe National Park

■ **ECONOMY:** Diamonds are the chief export, while copper, nickel and coal mining are also important. Tourism, financial services, agriculture and cattle raising are key sectors.

MONETARY UNIT: pula

GDP: $15.1 billion (2004 est.)

PER CAPITA GDP: $9,200

INDUSTRIES: mining, livestock processing, textiles

MINERALS: diamonds, copper, nickel, salt, soda ash, potash, coal, iron ore, silver

CHIEF CROPS: sorghum, maize, millet, beans, sunflowers, groundnuts

CAPITAL: Gaborone (pop., 199,000)

INDEPENDENCE DATE: September 30, 1966

GOVERNMENT TYPE: parliamentary republic

WEBSITE: www.gov.bw

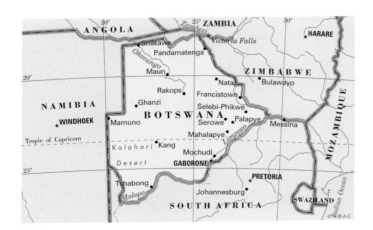

Brazil, the world's fifth-largest country in area and population, is a federal republic consisting of twenty-six states and one federal district. The country is divided into four distinct major regions. The Selvas is a vast rain forested region containing the Amazon, which flows more than 1,500 miles. Other major rivers are the São Francisco, Paraná and Uruguay. In the northeast is the semi-arid scrub land known as the Caatingas. In the east is the agricultural and mineral heartland of plains, plateaus and highlands. The climate is mostly tropical, with a dry season in the winter. However, the south enjoys a basically temperate climate. Brazil's flora and fauna have been put under strain by the advance of the frontier. New farmland and commercial logging in the Selvas rain forest has resulted in the destruction of vast areas of virgin forest. However, progress is being made in preserving remaining forests.

Brazil leads in the extraction of iron ore, tin, manganese and bauxite. Iron ore comes from the states of Minas Gerais and Pará. Dams on the Paraná and Tocantins rivers are among the world's largest hydroelectric facilities. Agriculturally, Brazil was once thought of only in terms of coffee-growing. While still the world's leading source of that beverage, Brazil has become a top producer of soybeans, oranges, cattle, corn, sugar and tobacco. Steel, textiles, consumer goods, motor vehicles, aircraft and chemicals are important industrial products. Iron ore, soybean bran, orange juice, coffee, footwear and motor vehicle parts are exported to the United States, Argentina, China and the Netherlands.

Did you know? Brazil, the world's 5th-largest country, spans nearly half of South America.

The Brazilian population is made up of many ethnic strains. Europeans are represented by the founding Portuguese group and by German and Italian descendants in Santa Catarina and Rio Grande do Sul. Japanese are present in São Paulo and Paraná. The people of African descent form an important part of Brazil's ethnic mix - perhaps as much as 50 percent or more. The Amerindians are a statistically small part of the population. Roman Catholicism is the predominant religion. Brazil is the only Portuguese-speaking country in Latin America. São Paulo is the nation's largest city and economic center, and the former capital, Rio de Janeiro, is a leading port city. Belo Horizonte, Salvador (Bahia), Belém and Manaus are also important. During the 1950s, the new capital city of Brasília was built in the interior.

In 1500 Pedro Alvares Cabral claimed the land for Portugal. In 1822 Brazil was declared independent by the son of Portugal's king, Dom Pedro, who assumed the title of emperor. In 1889 the monarchy was toppled, to be succeeded by a republic. After years of military intervention in the government, the military regime peacefully seceded power to civilian rule in 1985.

Rio de Janeiro from Sugarloaf Mountain

AREA: 3,286,487 sq mi (8,511,965 sq km)

■ **CLIMATE:** The northwest is a vast rain forested region, while the northeast is semi-arid scrub land. The east is mostly tropical, with a dry winter, and the south is basically temperate.

■ **PEOPLE:** Brazil is made up of many ethnic groups. Europeans make up the majority, while other groups include people of African descent, Japanese and Amerindians.

POPULATION: 188,078,227

LIFE EXPECTANCY AT BIRTH (YEARS): male, 67.5; female, 75.6

LITERACY RATE: 83.3%

ETHNIC GROUPS: European 55%, Creole 38%, African 6%

PRINCIPAL LANGUAGES: Portuguese (official), Spanish, English, French

CHIEF RELIGION: Roman Catholic (nominal) 80%

■ **ECONOMY:** Still a leading source of coffee and citrus products, Brazil has become a top producer of transport equipment, commercial aircraft and motor vehicles.

MONETARY UNIT: real

GDP: $1,492 billion (2004 est.)

PER CAPITA GDP: $8,100

INDUSTRIES: textiles, shoes, chemicals, cement, lumber, aircraft, motor vehicles and parts, other machinery and equipment

MINERALS: bauxite, gold, iron ore, manganese, nickel, phosphates, platinum, tin, uranium, petroleum

CHIEF CROPS: coffee, soybeans, wheat, rice, corn, sugarcane, cocoa

CAPITAL: Brasília (pop., 3,099,000)

INDEPENDENCE DATE: September 7, 1822

GOVERNMENT TYPE: federal republic

WEBSITE: www.brasilemb.org

Washed by the South China Sea and surrounded by Malaysia, the Sultanate of Brunei consists of two separate enclaves on the north coast of Borneo. The country has a hot, humid and rainy equatorial climate. The Sultan of Brunei is one of the world's richest men. His wealth derives from the country's oil and natural gas resources, which make Brunei among the richest states in Southeast Asia. Petroleum products are exported mostly to Japan, South Korea and Australia.

The population is more than two thirds Malay, who are mostly Muslim; Chinese are second in number, and there are also small groups of Dayaks. Malay is the official language, but English and Chinese are also spoken. The capital and largest city is Bandar Seri Begawan, formerly known as Brunei Town.

Brunei was a British protectorate from 1888 until it became independent on January 1, 1984. The same ruling family has governed for over six centuries.

AREA: 2,228 sq mi (5,770 sq km)

■ **CLIMATE:** The country has a hot, humid and rainy equatorial climate.

■ **PEOPLE:** The population is more than two thirds Malay, who are mostly Muslim; Chinese are second in number, and there are also small groups of Dayaks.

POPULATION: 379,444

LIFE EXPECTANCY AT BIRTH (YEARS): male, 71.9; female, 76.8

LITERACY RATE: 88.2%

ETHNIC GROUPS: Malay 67%, Chinese 15%, indigenous 6%

PRINCIPAL LANGUAGES: Malay (official), English, Chinese

CHIEF RELIGIONS: Muslim (official) 67%; Buddhist 13%; Christian 10%; indigenous beliefs, other 10%

■ **ECONOMY:** Among the richest states in Southeast Asia, Brunei's

> **Did you know?** Tiny Brunei once ruled over all of Borneo and part of the Philippines.

Sultan Omar Ali Saifuddin Mosque

wealth derives from the country's oil and natural gas resources.

MONETARY UNIT: Brunei dollar (BND)

GDP: $6.8 billion (2003 est.)

PER CAPITA GDP: $23,600

INDUSTRIES: petroleum, petroleum refining, liquefied natural gas, construction

MINERALS: petroleum, natural gas

CHIEF CROPS: rice, vegetables, fruits

CAPITAL: Bandar Seri Begawan (pop., 61,000)

INDEPENDENCE DATE: January 1, 1984

GOVERNMENT TYPE: independent sultanate

WEBSITE: www.gov.bn

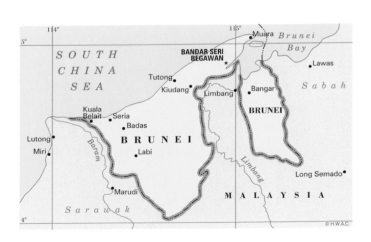

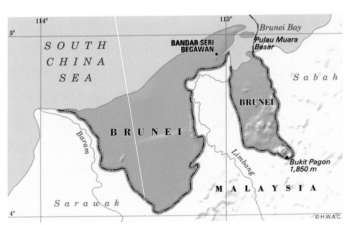

Bulgaria lies on the eastern side of the Balkan Peninsula in southeastern Europe. The country is divided into several roughly parallel east-west zones: the Danubian tableland in the north, the Balkan Mountains (Stara Planina) through the central part and the Thracian Plain and Rhodope Mountains in the south and southwest. Four major rivers - Danube, Maritsa, Iskŭr and Tundzha - traverse the country. The temperate climate features cold, damp winters and hot, dry summers. Bulgaria, the fourth-largest exporter of tobacco in the world, is also a surplus food producer, growing grain crops, oil seeds, fruits and vegetables. Bulgaria is one of the few sources of attar of roses, used in perfumes. Actively exploited mineral resources include manganese and iron ore. Industrial production consists of machine manufacturing, metal working and food processing, textile and chemical production. Bulgaria's trading partners are Italy, Germany, Turkey, Belgium, Greece, United States and France. The country's Black Sea coast has been developed as a summer resort area for tourists. The majority of the population is Bulgarian. There are small groups of Turks, Romas, Macedonians, Armenians and Tatars. The predominant language is Bulgarian. In religion, the majority are Bulgarian Orthodox; there is a Muslim minority. Sofia is the capital and chief city. Plovdiv and Varna are also sizable and important.

Slavs settled the area in the sixth century, and were conquered in turn by Turkic-speaking Bulgars in the seventh century. Over time the two groups merged. Ottoman Turks overran Bulgaria in the fourteenth century and remained in control for five centuries. In the late nineteenth century, Bulgaria gained a measure of autonomy under Ottoman rule, and in 1908 became a totally independent kingdom. After World War II, Bulgaria spent decades under Communist control. The monarchy was abolished in 1946. After 1989 a gradual process of democratization began. Bulgaria became a member of the North Atlantic Treaty Organization on March 29, 2004, and a member of the European Union on January 1, 2007.

Did you know? In the Middle Ages, Bulgaria became an important center of Slavic culture.

AREA: 42,823 sq mi (110,910 sq km)

▌ **CLIMATE:** The temperate continental climate features cold, damp winters and hot, dry summers.

▌ **PEOPLE:** The majority of the population is Bulgarian. There are small groups of Turks, Romas, Macedonians, Armenians and Tatars.

POPULATION: 7,385,367

LIFE EXPECTANCY AT BIRTH (YEARS): male, 68.1; female, 75.6

LITERACY RATE: 98%

Street in Old Plovdiv

ETHNIC GROUPS: Bulgarian 84%, Turk 10%, Roma 5%

PRINCIPAL LANGUAGES: Bulgarian (official), Turkish

CHIEF RELIGIONS: Bulgarian Orthodox 84%, Muslim 12%

▌ **ECONOMY:** Bulgaria is famous for its rose oil used in perfume. The Black Sea coast is a growing summer resort. Bulgaria's trading partners are Italy, Germany, Turkey, Belgium, Greece, United States and France.

MONETARY UNIT: lev

GDP: $61.6 billion (2004 est.)

PER CAPITA GDP: $8,200

INDUSTRIES: electricity, gas and water, food, beverages and tobacco, machinery and equipment, base metals, chemical products, coke, refined petroleum, nuclear fuel

MINERALS: bauxite, copper, lead, zinc, coal

CHIEF CROPS: vegetables, fruits, tobacco, wheat, barley, sunflowers, sugar beets

GOVERNMENT TYPE: republic

CAPITAL: Sofia (pop., 1,076,000)

INDEPENDENCE DATE: March 3, 1878

WEBSITE: www.government.bg/English

Landlocked Burkina Faso lies in the bulge of Western Africa and consists for the most part of a vast plateau drained by the Black, White and Red Volta rivers. The tropical climate has warm, dry winters and hot, wet summers. Burkina Faso is a land of hardworking farmers and cattle-raisers. Poor soils and variable rains make the task of rasing food and export crops a recurrent struggle. Among the poorest countries in the world, Burkina Faso also suffers from few natural resources, high population density and poor communications. Its cash crops are peanuts, shea nuts, cotton and sesame. Food crops include sorghum, millet, corn and rice. Burkina Faso is not self-sufficient in food grains. Industrial production is limited to cotton textile manufacturing, agricultural processing and gold mining. Exports of cotton, animal products and gold go to Singapore, China, Thailand, and the European Union. The country's link to the world is by a railroad running from Ouagadougou, the capital and largest city, through Côte d'Ivoire to the sea. Bobo Dioulasso is the country's second-largest city.

The population is more than two thirds Malay, who are mostly Muslim; Chinese are second in number, and there are also small groups of Dayaks. Islam is the religion for half the population, indigenous religions for about 40 percent, and Roman Catholicism for the remainder. French is the official language, but 90 percent speak African languages.

Burkina Faso occupies the site of the former Mossi empire, which lasted for about six centuries until 1896, when the French took control of much of West Africa. In 1919 the area was established as a separate colony under the name Upper Volta. The colony gained full independence in 1960. In 1984 the name was changed to Burkina Faso.

> **Did you know?** Burkina Faso means "land of incorruptible men."

Ouagadougou-Place Nations Unies

AREA: 105,869 sq mi (274,200 sq km)

■ **CLIMATE:** The tropical climate has warm, dry winters and hot, wet summers.

■ **PEOPLE:** The country is ethnically almost half Mossi. Other groups include Bobo, Mande, Lobi, Fulani, Gourounsi, and Senufo.

POPULATION: 13,902,972

LIFE EXPECTANCY AT BIRTH (YEARS): male, 42.6; female, 45.8

LITERACY RATE: 36%

ETHNIC GROUPS: Mossi (approximately 40%), Gurunsi, Senufo, Lobi, Bobo, Mande, Fulani

PRINCIPAL LANGUAGES: French (official), Sudanic languages

CHIEF RELIGIONS: Muslim 50%, indigenous beliefs 40%, Christian (mainly Roman Catholic) 10%

■ **ECONOMY:** Among the world's poorest countries, Burkina has few natural resources. Cash crops are cotton, peanuts, shea nuts, and sesame. Industry is limited to cotton textile manufacturing, agricultural processing and gold mining.

MONETARY UNIT: CFA franc

GDP: $15.7 billion (2004 est.)

PER CAPITA GDP: $1,200

INDUSTRIES: cotton lint, beverages, agricultural processing, soap, cigarettes, textiles, gold

MINERALS: manganese, limestone, marble, gold, antimony, copper, nickel, bauxite, lead, phosphates, zinc, silver

CHIEF CROPS: peanuts, shea nuts, sesame, cotton, sorghum, millet, corn, rice

GOVERNMENT TYPE: republic

CAPITAL: Ouagadougou (pop., 821,000)

INDEPENDENCE DATE: August 5, 1960

WEBSITE: www.burkinaembassy-usa.org

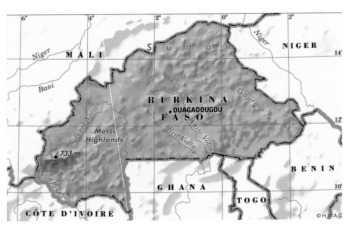

Small, landlocked Burundi is located in east central Africa. The Democratic Republic of the Congo borders it on the west, Rwanda on the north, Tanzania on the east and Lake Tanganyika on the south. Most of the country consists of grassy uplands and high plateaus. The Ruzizi river valley, which lies along the western boundary with the Democratic Republic of the Congo, constitutes part of the Great Rift Valley along with Lake Tanganyika. The climate is temperate and warm, with with two wet and dry seasons and occasional frost in the uplands. Alluvial gold, nickel, phosphates are mined. Coffee and tea are the main crops and account for most of the foreign exchange earnings. Sugar, cotton fabrics and hides are also exported. Exports go mainly to European Union countries and Pakistan.

The Hutu ethnic group constitutes most of the population, and the Tutsi make up a significant minority. There is a small Twa (pygmy) population. Kirundi and French are the official languages. Roman Catholics make up two-thirds of the religious adherents. Bujumbura is the capital and largest city.

Burundi's earliest inhabitants were the pygmies (Twa) and Hutu, a Bantu people. They were subjugated in the sixteenth century by the Tutsi, a tall warrior people who probably came from Ethiopia. In the late nineteenth century Burundi became part of German East Africa. After World War I, the area became part of the Belgian-mandated territory of Rwanda-Urundi, which in 1946 was made a United Nations trusteeship. After becoming independent in 1962, warfare between the dominant Tutsi and the Hutu farming class resulted in more than 100,000 deaths in 1972-73.

Did you know? Tutsi-Hutu ethnic violence killed 200,000 Burundis in the 1990s.

Internecine violence flared again in October 1993, when the first elected Hutu president was killed in a failed army coup. The resulting clashes between the Tutsi-led army and Hutu militias have left over 100,000 dead, with many more fleeing from the conflict to neighboring Democratic Republic of the Congo. By 1995, an estimated one million people in the region remained homeless. In 2003 an international agreement between the Tutsi-dominated government and the Hutu rebels led to an integrated defense force, established a new constitution and elected a majority Hutu government in 2005. The new government signed a ceasefire with the country's last rebel group in 2006 but still faces many challenges.

AREA: 10,745 sq mi (27,830 sq km)

Gitega Mushasha

■ **CLIMATE:** The country has an equatorial climate with two wet and two dry seasons. Temperatures vary with altitude.

■ **PEOPLE:** The majority is Hutu, a Bantu people. Others include Tutsi, a Hamitic people and a small Twa (pygmy) population.

POPULATION: 8,090,068

LIFE EXPECTANCY AT BIRTH (YEARS): male, 42.7; female, 44.0

LITERACY RATE: 35.3%

ETHNIC GROUPS: Hutu 85%, Tutsi 14%, Twa (Pygmy) 1%

PRINCIPAL LANGUAGES: Kirundi, French (both official); Swahili

CHIEF RELIGIONS: Roman Catholic 62%, indigenous beliefs 23%, Muslim 10%, Protestant 5%

■ **ECONOMY:** Coffee and tea are the main crops and account for most of the foreign exchange earnings. Sugar, cotton fabrics and hides are also exported. Alluvial gold, nickel, phosphates are mined.

MONETARY UNIT: franc

GDP: $4.0 billion (2004 est.)

PER CAPITA GDP: $600

INDUSTRIES: light consumer goods, assembly of imported components, public works construction, food processing

MINERALS: nickel, uranium, rare earth oxides, peat, cobalt, copper, platinum (not yet exploited), vanadium

CHIEF CROPS: coffee, cotton, tea, corn, sorghum, sweet potatoes, bananas, manioc

GOVERNMENT TYPE: in transition

CAPITAL: Bujumbura (pop., 378,000)

INDEPENDENCE DATE: July 1, 1962

WEBSITE: www.burundiembassy-usa.org

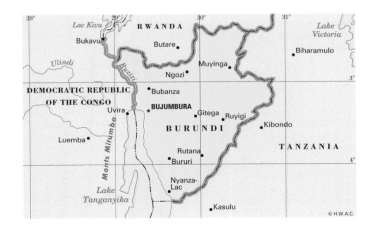

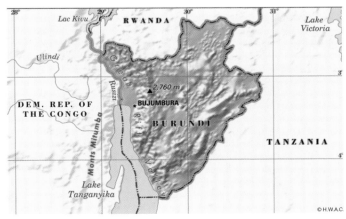

Cambodia is situated between Thailand, Laos and Vietnam. The country is formed largely by a saucer-shaped alluvial plain that contains the large lake of Tonle Sap in the west and is drained by the Mekong river. Summers are marked by a rainy monsoon season, and winters are dry in this tropical climate.

Mineral resources include iron ore, manganese and phosphates, gemstones and gold. Timber is another potentially important resource. Rubber plantations are an important export-directed activity. Rice and corn are the main subsistence commodities. Garments, shoes, cigarettes, natural rubber, rice and spices are chief exports. Exports go mainly to the United States, and European Union countries. The tourism industry is expanding.

The vast majority of the people are Khmer (Cambodian), and are Buddhist in religion. There are also small groups of Vietnamese and Chinese. Khmer is the official and predominant language. Phnom Penh is the capital and largest city.

Modern Cambodia is what remains of the great Khmer Empire, which by the 1200s, stretched across Southeast Asia. During this period the magnificent temple center of Angkor was built. French rule was established over the kingdom in 1863, lasting until Cambodia became an independent constitutional monarchy in 1954. In 1970, pro-Western General Lon Nol deposed neutralist Prince Norodom Sihanouk in a coup d'etat, declaring Cambodia a republic. That same year the country was drawn into the Vietnam Conflict when United States and South Vietnamese troops began their drive against North Vietnamese forces within Cambodia. The country suffered great turmoil during the nineteen-year period from 1970 to 1989. Khmer Rouge communist insurgents became increasingly powerful and took over the country in 1975 at the time of the collapse of South Vietnam. As many as a million people may have died or been killed in this period. Beginning in 1978, Vietnamese forces invaded the country and the Khmer Rouge retreated to the area near the Thai border. Vietnamese forces withdrew in 1989. Under United Nations guidance a new Cambodian government was established in 1993.

Did you know? The beautiful Angkor Wat temple ruins date from the 12th century.

AREA: 69,900 sq mi (181,040 sq km)

█ **CLIMATE:** A tropical monsoon climate with a rainy season from May to October and a dry season the rest of the year.

Phnom Penh

█ **PEOPLE:** The vast majority of the people are Khmer (Cambodian), and are Buddhist in religion. There are also small groups of Vietnamese and Chinese.

POPULATION: 13,881,427

LIFE EXPECTANCY AT BIRTH (YEARS): male, 55.7; female, 61.2

LITERACY RATE: 35%

ETHNIC GROUPS: Khmer 90%, Vietnamese 5%, Chinese 1%

PRINCIPAL LANGUAGES: Khmer (official), French, English

CHIEF RELIGION: Theravada Buddhist (official) 95%

█ **ECONOMY:** garments, shoes, cigarettes, natural rubber, rice and spices are chief exports. Natural resources include timber, gemstones, some iron ore, manganese and phosphates. Tourism is expanding.

MONETARY UNIT: riel

GDP: $27.0 billion (2004 est.)

PER CAPITA GDP: $2,000

INDUSTRIES: tourism, garments, rice milling, fishing, wood and wood products, rubber, cement, gem mining, textiles

MINERALS: gemstones, iron ore, manganese, phosphates

CHIEF CROPS: rice, rubber, corn, vegetables

CAPITAL: Phnom Penh (pop., 1,157,000)

INDEPENDENCE DATE: November 9, 1953

GOVERNMENT TYPE: constitutional monarchy

WEBSITE: www.cambodia.gov.kh

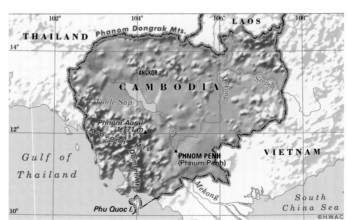

The name "Cameroon" derives from "Rio dos Comorões" (River of Shrimp). Fifteenth-century Portuguese were so impressed with the shrimp in a local river that they applied the name to the entire region. Cameroon extends nearly 800 miles from the Gulf of Guinea to Lake Chad. It is a cross section of Africa, beginning with the grassland in its semi-arid north, through a transitional savanna-clad plateau, to forested western mountains and southern equatorial rainforests. The climate varies from tropical to semi-arid. Favored with such tropical resources as timber, cocoa, coffee, rubber, palm oil and cotton, Cameroon enjoys a diversified primary commodity economy. Bauxite, iron ore and limestone are among its mineral resources. Exports of crude oil and petroleum products, lumber, cocoa beans, aluminum, coffee and cotton go to the European Union and the United States.

French and English are the official languages, but twenty-four diverse African languages reflect the many ethnic groups among the Cameroon Highlanders, Equatorial Bantu, Kirdi and Fulani peoples. About one-third of the people are Christian, a smaller percentage in the north is Muslim, and half follow indigenous beliefs. The capital is Yaoundé; the port of Douala is the largest city.

Historically, Cameroon was one of the main racial crossroads of Africa because of Bantu migrations from the east and links to the Sahara caravan trade routes to the north. It became a German colony late in the nineteenth century. The French and British divided the colony after World War I under League of Nations mandates. These mandates were later converted into United Nations Trusteeships. In 1960 French Cameroon became independent. In the year following, under a UN plebiscite, southern British Cameroon voted to join Cameroon, while the northern part joined Nigeria. The new Cameroon has generally enjoyed political and economic stability.

Did you know? Mt. Cameroon (13,350 ft [4,069 m]) is the highest mountain in West Africa.

AREA: 183,568 sq mi (475,440 sq km)

▮ **CLIMATE:** Varies with terrain and region from semi-arid in the north, to forested western mountains and southern equatorial rainforests, to tropical along the coast.

▮ **PEOPLE:** Numerous African languages reflect the many ethnic groups among the Cameroon Highlanders, Equatorial Bantu, Kirdi and Fulani peoples.

POPULATION: 17,340,702

Volcanic plugs near Rhumsik

LIFE EXPECTANCY AT BIRTH (YEARS): male, 47.1; female, 48.8

LITERACY RATE: 63.4%

ETHNIC GROUPS: Highlanders 31%, Equatorial Bantu 19%, Kirdi 11%, Fulani 10%, northwest Bantu 8%, east Nigritic 7%

PRINCIPAL LANGUAGES: English, French (both official); 24 African language groups

CHIEF RELIGIONS: indigenous beliefs 40%, Christian 40%, Muslim 20%

▮ **ECONOMY:** Resources such as crude oil and petroleum products, timber, cocoa, aluminium, coffee and cotton give Cameroon a diversified primary commodity economy.

MONETARY UNIT: CFA franc

GDP: $30.2 billion (2004 est.)

PER CAPITA GDP: $1,900

INDUSTRIES: petroleum production and refining, food processing, light consumer goods, textiles, lumber

MINERALS: petroleum, bauxite, iron ore

CHIEF CROPS: coffee, cocoa, cotton, rubber, bananas, oilseed, grains, root starches

GOVERNMENT TYPE: republic

CAPITAL: Yaoundé (pop., 1,616,000)

INDEPENDENCE DATE: January 1, 1960

WEBSITE: www.spm.gov.cm

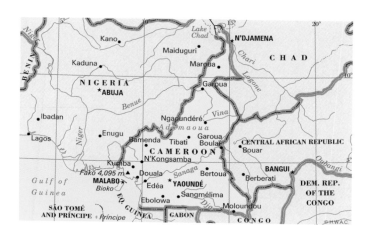

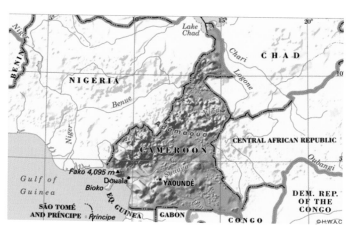

Canada is the second-largest country in the world in area, occupying all of North America north of the United States except Alaska, Greenland and the French islands of Saint Pierre and Miquelon. The country consists of ten provinces and two large territories: Yukon and the Northwest Territories. Covering most of eastern and central Canada is the Shield (Laurentian Plateau), a rugged forested area of pre-Cambrian rock. To the north is the Arctic archipelago, stretching close to the North Pole. A vast prairie extends west of the Shield to the Canadian Rockies. Westernmost Canada is laced with towering mountain ranges and rich, productive forests. The Mackenzie, Yukon, Saint Lawrence, Nelson and the Churchill are the major rivers traversing the country. The climate varies from temperate in the south to subarctic and frigid arctic in the far north.

Canada's huge natural resources include nickel, zinc, copper, gold, lead, molybdenum, potash, fish, timber, coal, petroleum and natural gas. Wheat growing, dairy farming, livestock ranching and fruit farming are the major agricultural activities. Wood and paper products, transportation equipment, processed food, primary metals, machinery and chemicals dominate the industrial sector. Exports, primarily manufactured goods, flow to the United States, Japan and the United Kingdom.

A central theme of Canadian history and culture is the division between the two-thirds of the population who speak English and the French-speaking third who live largely in Québec. The indigenous Indians and Inuit (Eskimos) constitute less than 1 percent of the population. Canada's great cities are Toronto, Montréal, Vancouver, Ottawa (the capital), Edmonton, Calgary and Winnipeg. Nearly 90 percent of Canada's population is concentrated near the U.S.-Canadian border.

Historically, Canada's native population consisted largely of peoples of Algonquian stock. The Inuit, or Eskimos, still inhabit the Arctic archipelago and the northern reaches of the Canadian Shield. Although the Vikings are believed to have visited Canada about 1000 A.D., John Cabot in 1497 made the first recorded landing. In 1534 Jacques Cartier claimed the region for France. The intense rivalry that followed dominated Canadian history for more than two centuries. France lost control of Canada to Britain at the end of the French and Indian Wars in 1763. The British North America Act in 1817 established the Dominion of Canada, consisting of Nova Scotia, New Brunswick, Québec and Ontario. Other provinces were added in subsequent years, the last being Newfoundland in 1949. In 1931 the Statute of Westminster established the equality of the Canadian Parliament with that of Britain. The last decades of the twentieth century have seen Canadian political affairs dominated by the Québec independence movement. In 1995 the vote on Québec's separation was defeated by a slim margin.

Did you know? The Canada/U.S. boundary is the world's longest undefended border.

Toronto

AREA: 3,855,101 sq mi (9,984,670 sq km)
■ **CLIMATE:** The temperate south changes to subarctic and frigid arctic in the far north.
■ **PEOPLE:** Canadians are ethnically divided between English and French-speaking citizens. Indigenous Indians and Inuit (Eskimos) make up a small minority.
POPULATION: 33,098,932
LIFE EXPECTANCY AT BIRTH (YEARS): male, 76.6; female, 83.5
LITERACY RATE: 97%
ETHNIC GROUPS: British 28%, French 23%, other European 15%, Amerindian 2%
PRINCIPAL LANGUAGES: English, French (both official)
CHIEF RELIGIONS: Roman Catholic 46%, Protestant 36%, other 18%
■ **ECONOMY:** Natural resources include iron, nickel, zinc, copper, gold, lead, potash, diamonds, silver, fish, timber, coal and natural gas. Transportation equipment, primary metals, machinery and chemicals dominate the industrial sector.
MONETARY UNIT: Canadian dollar
GDP: $1,023 billion (2004 est.)
PER CAPITA GDP: $31,500
INDUSTRIES: transport equipment, chemicals, mining, food products, wood and paper products, fish products, petroleum and natural gas
CHIEF CROPS: wheat, barley, oilseed, tobacco, fruits, vegetables
MINERALS: iron ore, nickel, zinc, copper, gold, lead, molybdenum, potash, silver, coal, petroleum, natural gas
GOVERNMENT TYPE: confederation with parliamentary democracy
CAPITAL: Ottawa (pop., 1,093,000)
INDEPENDENCE DATE: July 1, 1867
WEBSITES: www.statcan.ca www.canada.gc.ca/main_e.html

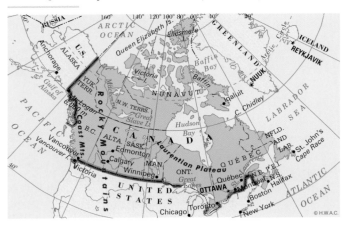

Situated nearly 400 miles west of Dakar, Cape Verde consists of ten main islands and five islets. Seven of the main islands are mountainous and of volcanic origin. The climate is temperate with warm dry summers. Precipitation is light and erratic. Poor soil and scanty rainfall, coupled with prolonged drought and a high birthrate make necessary the importation of foodstuffs. The economy is largely based on fish processing, the manufacture of clothing, ship repair and the production of construction materials. Exports include shoes, garments, fish and crustaceans, hides and skins which go to Portugal, the United States and the United Kingdom.

Most of the people are Creole - of mixed African and Portuguese descent - and Roman Catholic in religion. There is a significant African minority. The people speak Portuguese and Crioulo, a blend of West African and Portuguese. Praia, the capital, is situated on São Tiago, the largest and most populous island.

The islands were discovered by the Portuguese sailing for Prince Henry the Navigator in 1460 A.D. After 500 years of Portuguese rule, Cape Verde became independent in 1975. A one-party system ruled until 1990 when multi-party elections were held. The country continues to enjoy a stable democratic government.

Maio Island-Sea salt mine

AREA: 1,557 sq mi (4,033 sq km)

■ **CLIMATE:** The climate is temperate with warm dry summers. Precipitation is light and erratic.

Did you know? Pico do Cano is the only volcano still active on these volcanic islands.

■ **PEOPLE:** Most of the people are Creole of mixed African and Portuguese descent. There is a significant African minority.

POPULATION: 420,979

LIFE EXPECTANCY AT BIRTH (YEARS): male, 66.8; female, 73.5

LITERACY RATE: 71.6%

ETHNIC GROUPS: Creole 71%, African 28%, European 1%

PRINCIPAL LANGUAGES: Portuguese (official), Crioulo

CHIEF RELIGIONS: Roman Catholic (infused with indigenous beliefs), Protestant (mostly Church of the Nazarene)

■ **ECONOMY:** The economy is largely based on fish processing, clothing manufacturing, ship repair and the production of construction materials. Exports include shoes, garments, fish and crustaceans, hides and skins.

MONETARY UNIT: escudo

GDP: $600 million (2002 est.)

PER CAPITA GDP: $1,400

INDUSTRIES: food and beverages, fish processing, shoes and garments, salt mining, ship repair

MINERALS: salt, basalt rock, limestone, kaolin

CHIEF CROPS: bananas, corn, beans, sweet potatoes, sugarcane, coffee, peanuts

GOVERNMENT TYPE: republic

CAPITAL: Praia (pop., 107,000)

INDEPENDENCE DATE: July 5, 1975

WEBSITE: virtualcapeverde.net/

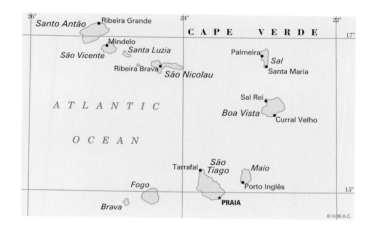

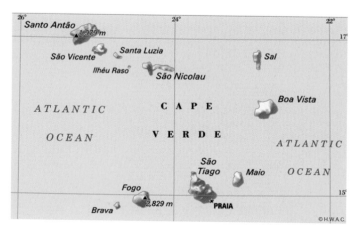

The landlocked Central African Republic is a huge monotonous plateau, bordered by scattered hills in the northeast and southwest. Stretches of grassy savanna and woodlands, in which there is an abundance of wildlife, make it a land of stunning beauty. The Oubangui (Ubangi) and the tributaries of the Chari (Shari) are the major rivers. The climate is tropical, with hot, dry winters and mild to hot wet summers. Isolation in the heart of Africa is the main problem of the nation, a problem compounded by a paucity of resources and a small population. However, cotton production has increased greatly in recent years and provides a major export. Diamonds and timber are major exports. However, cotton, coffee and tobacco also contribute to exports and income. Belgium and other European Union countries are the major recipient of the country's exports.

There are more than 80 ethnic groups in the Central African Republic. The major groups are the Baya, the Banda and the Mandjia. The Sara, Mboum, M'Baka and Yakoma make up a small minority. Half the population is Christian - split equally between Protestant and Roman Catholic. Muslims form a smaller group. Sangho is the national language; French is the official language. Bangui is the capital.

For centuries, the area was a crossroads for numerous migrations by various groups, mainly of Bantu origin. In the nineteenth century, French expeditions penetrated the country, which was named Ubangi-Shari after its two main rivers. Early in the twentieth century the country became one of the territories of French Equatorial Africa. In 1960 the area became a fully independent nation under the name Central African Republic. In 1966 Jean-Bedel Bokassa seized the government, and ten years later proclaimed himself emperor. Bokassa was unseated in 1979, after a regime of cruelty and repression. Civilian rule was established in 1993 and lasted until 2003 when the government was deposed in a military coup which established a transitional government.

> **Did you know?** In the early 1960s the Central African Republic was a center of Chinese influence in Africa.

The government still does not fully control the countryside, where pockets of lawlessness persist.

AREA: 240,535 sq mi (622,984 sq km) rain forest in the southwest.

■ **CLIMATE:** The climate is tropical, with hot, dry winters and mild to hot wet summers.

■ **PEOPLE:** There are more than 80 ethnic groups in the Central African Republic. The major groups are the Baya, the Banda and the Mandjia. The Sara, Mboum, M'Baka and Yakoma make up a small minority.

POPULATION: 4,303,356

LIFE EXPECTANCY AT BIRTH (YEARS): male, 39.7; female, 43.1

LITERACY RATE: 60%

ETHNIC GROUPS: Baya 33%, Banda 27%, Mandjia 13%, Sara 10%, Mboum 7%, M'Baka 4%, Yakoma 4%

PRINCIPAL LANGUAGES: French (official), Sangho (national), tribal languages

CHIEF RELIGIONS: indigenous beliefs 35%, Protestant 25%, Roman Catholic 25%, Muslim 15%

■ **ECONOMY:** Diamonds and timber are major exports. However, cotton, coffee and tobacco also contribute to exports and income.

GOVERNMENT TYPE: in transition

CAPITAL: Bangui (pop., 689,000)

INDEPENDENCE DATE: August 13, 1960

MONETARY UNIT: CFA franc

GDP: $4.2 billion (2004 est.)

PER CAPITA GDP: $1,100

INDUSTRIES: diamond mining, sawmills, breweries, textiles, footwear, assembly of bicycles and motorcycles

MINERALS: diamonds, uranium, gold, oil

CHIEF CROPS: cotton, coffee, tobacco, manioc, yams, millet, corn, bananas

WEBSITE: www.state.gov/r/pa/ei/bgn/4007.htm

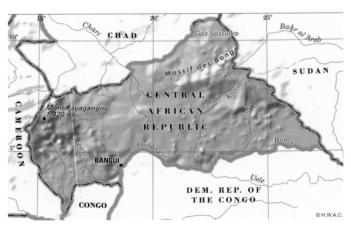

Woman pounding casaava root into fufu.

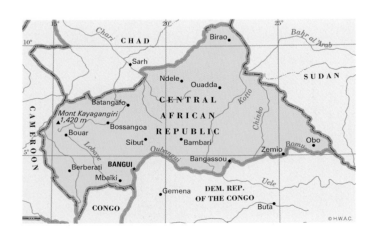

Chad suffers from isolation, internal strife and a loss of arable land and is one of the most underdeveloped countries in the world. Landlocked, the country is shaped like a shallow basin, rimmed by mountain ranges on the north and east. The northern part of the country is desert, while the central plain is hot and dry savanna, with a brief rainy season. The southern lowlands are tropical, with a wooded savanna and seasonal rains. The two chief rivers are the Chari and the Logone. On the western border, Lake Chad is believed to be the remnant of an inland sea. Desertification in the northern part of the savanna country is a problem. With its productive area more than a thousand miles from any seaport, Chad is difficult to reach. There is no railroad, and much of the network of dirt roads and tracks is impassable during the rainy season. Petroleum resources are being developed but cotton, cattle and gum arabic make up the bulk of Chad's non-oil exports. Cotton is the major cash crop, accounting for at least half its exports. Most exports go to the United States and China.

The population is made up of more than 200 distinct groups divided between Sudanic northerners and Nilotic southerners. The official languages are French and Arabic. More than half the population is Muslim; the remainder is Christian or animist. N'Djamena is the capital and largest city.

Outdoor tailor

Chad was the home of a succession of African kingdoms before the French takeover at the end of the nineteenth century. As one of the four territories of French Equatorial Africa, Chad was the first territory to rally to DeGaulle in World War II. In 1960 independence was proclaimed but conflicts soon arose between northern Muslim and southern Christian groups, resulting in years of civil war. In 1980 Libyan troops invaded Chad in support of the northern rebels but were forced out in 1987. In 1994 the International Court of Justice ruled that the Aozou Strip between Chad and Libya belongs to Chad.

Did you know? Now partially desert, Chad was a fertile country in ancient times.

AREA: 495,755 sq mi (1,284,000 sq km)

■ **CLIMATE:** The north is desert, while the central plain is hot and dry with a brief rainy season. The southern lowlands are warm and more humid with seasonal rains.

■ **PEOPLE:** The population is made up of more than 200 distinct groups divided between Sudanic northerners and Nilotic southerners.

POPULATION: 9,944,201

LIFE EXPECTANCY AT BIRTH (YEARS): male, 47.0; female, 50.1

LITERACY RATE: 40%

ETHNIC GROUPS: about 200 groups; largest are Arabs in north and Sara in south

PRINCIPAL LANGUAGES: French, Arabic (both official); Sara; more than 120 different languages and dialects

■ **ECONOMY:** One of the most underdeveloped countries in the world. Petroleum resources are being developed but cotton, cattle and gum arabic make up the bulk of Chad's non-oil exports.

CHIEF RELIGIONS: Muslim 51%, Christian 35%, animist 7%, other 7%

CAPITAL: N'Djamena (pop., 797,000)

INDEPENDENCE DATE: August 11, 1960

GOVERNMENT TYPE: republic

MONETARY UNIT: CFA franc

GDP: $15.7 billion (2004 est.)

PER CAPITA GDP: $1,600

INDUSTRIES: cotton textiles, meatpacking, beer brewing, natron, soap, cigarettes, construction materials

MINERALS: petroleum (unexploited but exploration under way), uranium, natron, kaolin

CHIEF CROPS: cotton, sorghum, millet, peanuts, rice, potatoes, manioc

WEBSITE: www.chadembassy.org/site/index.cfm?lang=1

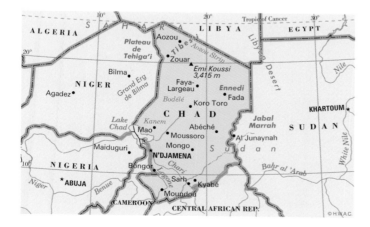

Chile stretches some 2650 miles along the Pacific coast of South America and is at no point wider than 250 miles. Far out in the Pacific are Easter Island (Isla de Pascua or Rapa Nui), Isla Sala y Gómez and the Juan Fernández Islands. At the very southern tip of the country, just north of Cape Horn, Chile occupies the western half of Tierra del Fuego. The towering Andes dominate most of the eastern frontier. The central region where the climate is of the temperate Mediterranean type, is agricultural. The north contains the Atacama Desert, one of the driest areas of the globe, while the forested south is cool and damp.

Chile has immense natural resources and is one of the world's leading copper producers. Copper, iron ore, nitrates, precious metals, and molybdenum are also important. Timber and offshore fish are also important resources. Chile is a major producer of wheat, grapes, apples and other fruits, potatoes and sugar beets. Chilean wines are world renowned. Industrial activity is strong, especially in mineral refining, metal manufacturing, food processing, fish processing, finished textiles, paper and wood products. Exports go to the United States, Japan, China, South Korea and the Netherlands.

Nearly all of the population is of European and European-Indian descent. Roman Catholicism is the religion for 90 percent of the people, and Spanish is the universal language. Santiago, the capital, is the metropolis of the nation. The port city of Valparaíso and Concepción are important centers.

> **Did you know?** Chilean poets Gabriela Mistral and Pablo Neruda won Nobel Prizes.

Before the Spanish conquest in the sixteenth century, the northern portion of the country was under the rule of the Inca Empire, and the south was mainly controlled by the Araucanian Indians, who were to prove fiercely hostile to the Spanish colonists until the end of the nineteenth century. During most of its colonial history, Chile was a captaincy general dependent on the viceroyalty of Peru. Chilean independence was obtained from Spain under the leadership of José de San Martín and Bernardo O'Higgins in 1818. Between 1879 and 1884, Chile defeated Peru and Bolivia in the War of the Pacific, acquiring the mineral-bearing northern desert region. In 1970, Chilean voters elected Socialist Salvador Allende Gossens president, the first Marxist so elected in the Americas. However, Allende was overthrown and then killed in September 1973, in a military coup led by army commander General Augusto Pinochet. Civilian rule was not restored until 1989. The country has advanced economically in recent years. Chile joined the North American Free Trade Agreement (NAFTA) in 1994.

AREA: 292,260 sq mi (756,950 sq km)

■ **CLIMATE:** The northern Atacama Desert is one of the world's driest areas, while the south is cool and damp. The central region is Mediterranean temperate, while the frigid Andes dominate most of the eastern frontier.

Atacama desert

■ **PEOPLE:** Nearly all of the population is of European and European-Indian descent.

POPULATION: 16,134,219

LIFE EXPECTANCY AT BIRTH (YEARS): male, 73.1; female, 79.8

LITERACY RATE: 95.2%

ETHNIC GROUPS: European and mestizo 95%, Amerindian 3%

PRINCIPAL LANGUAGES: Spanish (official), Araucanian

CHIEF RELIGIONS: Roman Catholic 89%, Protestant 11%

■ **ECONOMY:** Chile's immense resources include copper, iron ore, nitrates and precious metals. Timber and fish are also important. A major producer of grapes, apples and other fruits; Chilean wines are world renowned.

MONETARY UNIT: peso

GDP: $169.1 billion (2004 est.)

PER CAPITA GDP: $10,700

INDUSTRIES: mining, foodstuffs, fish processing, iron and steel, wood and wood products, transport equipment, cement, textiles

MINERALS: copper, timber, iron ore, nitrates, precious metals, molybdenum

CHIEF CROPS: wheat, corn, grapes, beans, sugar beets, potatoes, fruit

GOVERNMENT TYPE: republic

CAPITAL: Santiago (pop., 5,478,000)

INDEPENDENCE DATE: September 18, 1810

WEBSITE: www.chileangovernment.cl

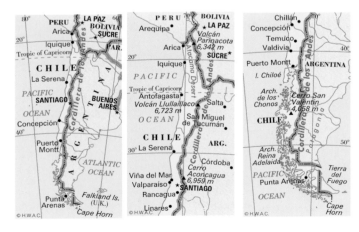

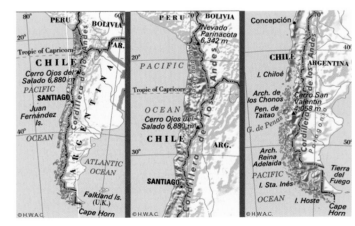

The oldest continuing civilization on earth, China has a recorded history stretching back more than 4,000 years. With its more than one billion inhabitants, China is the most populous nation on the globe. It is also the third-largest country in area. The eastern part of the country consists of fertile plains and deltas, but the western two-thirds consists mostly of mountains, high plateaus (Tibet) and deserts. Offshore are the large islands of Taiwan (administered separately by the Nationalist Government) and Hainan. The country's two great rivers are the Huang (Yellow) and the Chang (Yangtze); also important are the Amur and Xi (Si). China enjoys an extremely diverse climate; tropical in the south to subarctic in the north. The vast land has huge stores of natural resources: coal, iron ore, petroleum, tin and tungsten, among other metals. China has the world's greatest potential for hydroelectric power.

China is among the world's largest producers of rice, wheat, potatoes, corn, peanuts, tea, millet, barley, cotton and oilseeds. Electronics, machinery, apparel, furniture, and optical and medical equipment are the most important exports, primarily to the United States Japan and Western Europe. In recent decades China's industrial production has been surging. Steel, machinery, armaments, textiles and consumer goods lead the list.

Did you know? The giant panda, native to western China, is an endangered species.

Birth control and enforced family size restrictions have curtailed China's formerly rapid population growth. Han Chinese make up 92 percent of the population, but Tibetans, Uygurs and Mongols are other notable ethnic groups. Although the Chinese speak many widely divergent dialects, Mandarin, based on Beijing speech, is the basis of the national language. All dialects are written in a uniform ideographic script. The long-established religions are Confucianism, Buddhism and Daoism (Taoism). The average Chinese practices a mixture of all three faiths. There are small Muslim and Christian communities. While China has many cities with more than one million people, Shanghai and Beijing, the capital, are the greatest centers.

The historical Chinese dynasties date from the beginnings of Chinese civilization in the Yellow River valley before 2000 B.C. Modern Chinese history begins with the overthrow of the last imperial dynasty in 1912 and the establishment of a republic. The following years saw great turmoil, with conflicts between the Chinese government forces, warlords, Communists and, most of all, Japanese invaders from 1931 through 1945. In 1949 the Communists came to power, establishing the People's Republic of China. The Nationalists retreated to the island of Taiwan. In 1950 China overran Tibet. Until the late 1970s, the country experienced a period of radical experiments, including the "Cultural Revolution," which impeded economic growth. After that time China changed to a more flexible economy and opened itself to contacts with the outside world. However, political freedom is still tightly controlled.

Li River and Pinnacles

AREA: 3,705,405 sq mi (9,596,960 sq km)

CLIMATE: The country's extremely diverse climate ranges from tropical in the south to subarctic in the north.

PEOPLE: Han Chinese make up most of the population, but Tibetans, Uygurs and Mongols are other notable ethnic groups.

POPULATION: 1,313,973,713

LIFE EXPECTANCY AT BIRTH (YEARS): male, 70.4; female, 73.7

LITERACY RATE: 81.5%

ETHNIC GROUPS: 56 groups; Han 92%; also Zhuang, Manchu, Hui, Miao, Uygur, Yi, Tujia, Tong, Tibetan, Mongol, et al.

PRINCIPAL LANGUAGES: Mandarin (official), Yue (Cantonese), Wu (Shanghainese), Minbei (Fuzhou), Minnan (Hokkien-Taiwanese), Xiang, Gan, others

CHIEF RELIGIONS: officially atheist; Buddhism, Taoism; some Muslims, Christians

ECONOMY: A world supplier of rice, wheat, potatoes, corn, peanuts, tea, millet and barley, China also has huge stores of coal, iron ore, petroleum, tin, tungsten and hydroelectric power. Electronics, apparel, and machinery are key exports.

MONETARY UNIT: renminbi

GDP: $7,262 billion

PER CAPITA GDP: $5,600

INDUSTRIES: iron and steel, coal, machine building, armaments, textiles and apparel, petroleum, cement, chemical fertilizers, footwear, toys, food processing, automobiles, consumer electronics, telecommunications

MINERALS: coal, iron ore, petroleum, natural gas, mercury, tin, tungsten, antimony, manganese, molybdenum, vanadium, magnetite, aluminum, lead, zinc, uranium

CHIEF CROPS: rice, wheat, potatoes, sorghum, peanuts, tea, millet, barley, cotton, oilseed

GOVERNMENT TYPE: Communist Party-led state

CAPITAL: Beijing (pop., 10,848,000)

INDEPENDENCE DATE: 221 BC

WEBSITE: www.china-embassy.org/eng

In the northwest corner of South America, the Colombia fronts on both the Caribbean Sea and the Pacific Ocean. The three towering parallel ranges of the Andes mountains divide the nation into a flat coastal area, a highland or plateau region, and eastern plains. The climate ranges from tropical along the coast and eastern plains to cooler in the highlands. Colombia's chief river, the Magdalena, traverses almost the length of the country from south to north, as does the parallel Cauca. The eastern plains, known as the Llanos, are drained by tributaries of the Amazon, including the Guaviare, the Caquetá and the Putumayo. The country is rich in the variety of its forest cover, ranging from mangroves along the coast to commercially valuable trees in the highlands. Colombia is blessed with natural resources, including petroleum, natural gas, coal, emeralds, gold, lead, copper and platinum. A major oil find in 1993 in eastern Colombia sparked the rapid development of oil and coal reserves. Coffee is the chief crop but Colombia also produces cut flowers, bananas, rice and corn. The raising of livestock, cattle, pigs and sheep contributes one-third of the agricultural output. Industry is increasing in the production of textiles and garments, chemicals, metal products, cement, cardboard containers, plastic resins and manufactures, beverages, wood products, pharmaceuticals, machinery and electrical equipment. Petroleum, coffee, coal, bananas and cut flowers are exported to the United States, Venezuela and Ecuador.

Did you know?
Colombia is the world's principal source of emeralds.

More than half the population is of mixed Indian and European descent. Other important ethnic groups include people of European origin and of African ancestry. Spanish, the official language, is spoken by all but a few Indian tribes. Roman Catholicism is the religion of 95 percent of the population. The capital, Bogotá, is the largest city. Medellín and Cali both have more than a million inhabitants. Barranquilla on the Caribbean Sea is a major port.

Prominent among pre-Colombian cultures was that of the highland Chibchas. The founding of Bogotá in 1538 by the Spaniards established Colombia as the nucleus of New Granada, a vast territory that included parts of Panama, Venezuela and Ecuador. By defeating Spanish royalist forces in 1819, Simón Bolívar secured the independence of the new republic of Greater Colombia, which included the former territory of New Granada. However, in 1830 Greater Colombia broke up into separate republics. In 1863 the nation took its present name of Colombia. A major problem of recent years is the processing and export of illicit drugs.

Venta de artesnias en raquira

AREA: 439,735 sq mi (1,138,910 sq km)

■ **CLIMATE:** From tropical along the coast and eastern plains to cooler in the highlands.

■ **PEOPLE:** More than half the population is of mixed Indian and European descent. Other important ethnic groups include people of European origin and of African ancestry.

POPULATION: 43,593,035

LIFE EXPECTANCY AT BIRTH (YEARS): male, 67.6; female, 75.4

LITERACY RATE: 91.3%

ETHNIC GROUPS: mestizo 58%, European 20%, Creole 14%, black 4%, black-Amerindian 1%, Amerindian 3%

PRINCIPAL LANGUAGE: Spanish (official)

CHIEF RELIGION: Roman Catholic 90%

■ **ECONOMY:** Natural resources include petroleum, natural gas, coal, gold, emeralds and platinum. Coffee is the chief crop but Colombia also produces cut flowers, bananas, rice and corn. Industries include textiles and garments, chemicals and metal products.

MONETARY UNIT: peso

GDP: $281.1 billion (2004 est.)

PER CAPITA GDP: $6,600

INDUSTRIES: textiles, food processing, oil, clothing and footwear, beverages, chemicals, cement, gold, coal, emeralds

MINERALS: petroleum, natural gas, coal, iron ore, nickel, gold, copper, emeralds

CHIEF CROPS: coffee, cut flowers, bananas, rice, tobacco, corn, sugarcane, cocoa beans, oilseed, vegetables

GOVERNMENT TYPE: republic

CAPITAL: Bogotá (pop., 7,290,000)

INDEPENDENCE DATE: July 20, 1810

WEBSITE: www.colombiaemb.org

The small island group of the Comoros, which gained independence from France in 1975, lies in the Mozambique Channel between Mozambique and Madagascar. Three large islands, Grande Comore (Njazidja), Anjouan (Nzwani) and Mohéli (Mwani), and a number of smaller ones form this nation, which also lays claim to French-administered Mayotte. The tropical climate, with a hot rainy season from November to April, becomes more temperate the rest of the year. With poor transport, a young, rapidly growing population and negligible resources, Comoros is one of the world's poorest countries. Attempts have been made to develop tourism, but agriculture still accounts for most of its economic activity. Vanilla, cloves, perfume essences and copra are its chief exports, mainly to the United States and France. Comoros is the world's leading producer of ylang-ylang (used in perfume essences) and is the second-largest producer of vanilla.

The people are largely descendants of Muslim settlers with strains from Africa and Madagascar. There is a small European minority. The major religion is Islam, but there is a small Catholic minority. While Arabic and French are the official languages, most speak Comoran, a Swahili dialect. Moroni on Grande Comore is the capital and chief town

Did you know? Ylang-ylang, a major export, is a perfume made from a native tree.

Comoros has endured 19 coups or attempted coups since gaining independence from France in 1975. In 1997, the islands of Anjouan and Moheli declared independence from Comoros. In 1999, military chief Col. Azali seized power. He pledged to resolve the secessionist crisis through a confederal arrangement named the 2000 Fomboni Accord. In December 2001, voters approved a new constitution and presidential elections took place in the spring of 2002. Each island in the archipelago elected its own president and a new union president took office in May 2002.

AREA: 838 sq mi (2,170 sq km)

CLIMATE: The tropical climate, with a hot rainy season from November to April, becomes more temperate the rest of the year.

PEOPLE: Most of the people share African-Arab origins. There is a small European minority.

POPULATION: 690,948

LIFE EXPECTANCY AT BIRTH (YEARS): male, 59.3; female, 63.9

LITERACY RATE: 57.3%

ETHNIC GROUPS: Antalote, Cafre, Makoa, Oimatsaha, Sakalava (all are mostly an African-Arab mix)

PRINCIPAL LANGUAGES: Arabic, French (both official); Shikomoro (a blend of Swahili and Arabic)

CHIEF RELIGION: Muslim (official) 98%

ECONOMY: One of the world's poorest countries, agriculture still accounts for most economic activity. Vanilla, cloves, ylang-ylang (used in perfume essences) and copra are its chief exports. Attempts have been made to develop tourism.

MONETARY UNIT: franc

GDP: $441 million (2002 est.)

PER CAPITA GDP: $700

INDUSTRIES: tourism, perfume distillation

CHIEF CROPS: vanilla, cloves, perfume essences, copra, coconuts, bananas, cassava

CAPITAL: Moroni (pop., 53,000)

INDEPENDENCE DATE: July 6, 1975

GOVERNMENT TYPE: in transition

WEBSITE: www.state.gov/r/pa/ei/bgn/5236.htm

Two franc Moheli stamp 1906

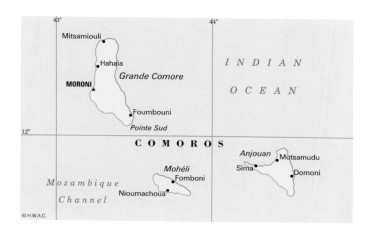

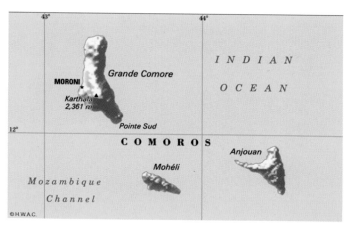

The Democratic Republic of the Congo, slightly more than one-quarter the size of the United States, occupies most of the Congo basin. Its only outlet to the sea is a narrow strip of land on the north bank of the Congo estuary. The huge Congo basin, a low-lying bowl-shaped plateau sloping toward the west, is covered by rainforest. On the south are shrub and savanna lands; high mountains lie to the east. The D.R. Congo's chief rivers are the Congo and its many tributaries, including the Ubangi, Lualaba, Lomami, Kasai and Kwango. The tropical climate is hot and humid in the equatorial river basin, but cooler in the highlands. The D.R. Congo's vast mineral wealth consists of copper, cobalt, uranium ore, diamonds, tin, manganese and gold. Some oil is produced; forestry is important. The main cash crops are coffee, palm oil and rubber. Exports of copper, coffee, diamonds, cobalt and petroleum are shipped to Belgium, Finland, the United States, and China.

The three largest ethnic groups of the indigenous Bantu people are the Mongo, Luba and Kongo. A small Hamitic group of Azande also inhabit the region. Roman Catholics are 50 percent of the population; Protestants (20 percent), Kimbanguists (10 percent) and Muslims (10 percent) make up the remainder. French is the official language; Lingala, Kingwana, Kikongo and Tshiluba are also widely spoken. Kinshasa, formerly Leopoldville, is the capital and largest city.

> **Did you know?** This country, the former Belgian Congo, lies east of the Congo Republic

During the first century B.C., the Bantu people spread into the Congo Basin. The powerful kingdom of the Kongo was an important Bantu state before Portugal reached the mouth of the Congo River in 1483. In 1885 King Leopold II of Belgium set up the Congo Free State and became its absolute monarch. In 1908 the Congo Free State became the Belgian Congo. The colony was granted independence in 1960 as the Democratic Republic of the Congo. Years of civil war, rebellion and secessionist movement kept the new nation in turmoil and crippled economic development. In 1971 the country was renamed the Republic of Zaire. President Mobutu Sese Seko, who has ruled Zaire since 1965 with an iron hand, has been accused of mismanaging the economy and of enriching himself at the people's expense. Refugees flooding into Zaire from neighboring Rwanda in 1994 have put a further strain in the nation's economy. The country was renamed The Democratic Republic of the Congo in 1997 after a political coup.

AREA: 905,567 sq mi (2,345,410 sq km)

■ **CLIMATE:** A hot and humid tropical climate in the equatorial river basin becomes cooler in the highlands.

■ **PEOPLE:** The largest ethnic groups of the indigenous Bantu people are the Mongo, Luba and Kongo.

POPULATION: 62,660,551

Kinshasa

LIFE EXPECTANCY AT BIRTH (YEARS): male, 47.1; female, 51.3
LITERACY RATE: 77.3%
ETHNIC GROUPS: over 200 groups; the four largest, the Mongo, Luba, Kongo (all Bantu), and Mangbetu-Azande (Hamitic), make up 45% of the population
PRINCIPAL LANGUAGES: French (official), Lingala, Kingwana (a Swahili dialect), Kikongo, Tshiluba
CHIEF RELIGIONS: Roman Catholic 50%, Protestant 20%, Kimbanguist 10%, Muslim 10%

■ **ECONOMY:** Vast mineral wealth includes copper, cobalt, diamonds, gold and other minerals. Some oil is produced and forestry is important. Main cash crops are coffee, rubber, palm oil, cotton, cocoa, sugar and tea.

MONETARY UNIT: Congolese franc
GDP: $42.7 billion (2004 est.)
PER CAPITA GDP: $700
INDUSTRIES: mining, mineral processing, consumer products, cement
MINERALS: cobalt, copper, cadmium, petroleum, industrial and gem diamonds, gold, silver, zinc, manganese, tin, germanium, uranium, radium, bauxite, iron ore, coal
CHIEF CROPS: coffee, sugar, palm oil, rubber, tea, quinine, cassava, palm oil, bananas, root crops, corn, fruits
GOVERNMENT TYPE: republic with strong presidential authority (in transition)
CAPITAL: Kinshasa (pop., 5,277,000)
INDEPENDENCE DATE: June 30, 1960
WEBSITE: www.state.gov/r/pa/ei/bgn/2823.htm

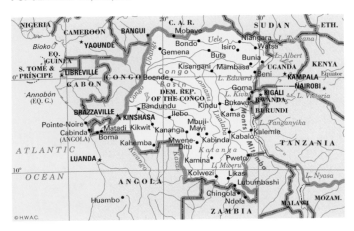

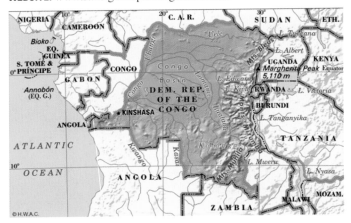

The Republic of the Congo consists of a coastal plain along a short frontage on the Atlantic Ocean, savanna, highlands and a plateau. Roughly one-half the land area is covered by dense equatorial forest, and a quarter is covered by marshes. The main rivers are the Congo, Oubangi and the Sangha. The climate is tropical, with constant high temperatures and humidity. The production of crude oil, centered in offshore wells near Pointe Noire, dominate the economy and exports. Timber and timber products are also an important source of export income. There are reserves of potash, lead, zinc, copper, iron ore and gold. Cash crops include coffee and cocoa. Industries are limited to brewing, sugar and flour milling. Trade is primarily with China, Taiwan, North Korea and the United States.

The largest of more than a dozen indigenous ethnic Bantu groups are the Bacongo, Vili, Bateke, M'Bochi and Sangha. French is the official language, but Lingala and Kikongo are the principal spoken languages. Half the population is Christian, 48 percent is Animist, and 2 percent is Muslim. Brazzaville, the capital and the port of Pointe Noire are the only large cities.

Before the nineteenth century, the territory of the present nation was divided between the two great African kingdoms of Loango and Congo. In the late nineteenth century, Count Pierre Savorgnan de Brazza established French control of the area north of the Congo river. Independence was gained in 1960.

AREA: 132,047 sq mi (342,000 sq km)

CLIMATE: The climate is tropical, with constant high temperatures and humidity.

PEOPLE: The largest of more than a dozen indigenous ethnic Bantu groups are the Bacongo, Vili, Bateke, M'Bochi and Sangha.

POPULATION: 3,702,314

LIFE EXPECTANCY AT BIRTH (YEARS): male, 48.5; female, 50.6

LITERACY RATE: 74.9%

ETHNIC GROUPS: Kongo 48%, Sangha 20%, M'Bochi 12%, Teke 17%

PRINCIPAL LANGUAGES: French (official), Lingala, Monokutuba, Kikongo, many local languages and dialects

CHIEF RELIGIONS: Christian 50%, animist 48%, Muslim 2%

> **Did you know?** This Congo was a colony of France before gaining independence.

Katanga cross - a form of archaic money from the Katanga Province

ECONOMY: The production of crude oil, from offshore wells near Pointe Noire, dominate the economy. Timber and timber products are also an important source of export income. Trade is primarily with China, Taiwan, North Korea and the United States.

MONETARY UNIT: CFA franc

GDP: $2.3 billion (2004 est.)

PER CAPITA GDP: $800

INDUSTRIES: petroleum extraction, cement, lumber, brewing, sugar, palm oil, soap, flour, cigarettes

MINERALS: petroleum, potash, lead, zinc, uranium, copper, phosphates, natural gas

CHIEF CROPS: cassava, sugar, rice, corn, peanuts, vegetables, coffee, cocoa

GOVERNMENT TYPE: republic

CAPITAL: Brazzaville (pop., 1,080,000)

INDEPENDENCE DATE: August 15, 1960

WEBSITE: www.state.gov/r/pa/ei/bgn/2825.htm

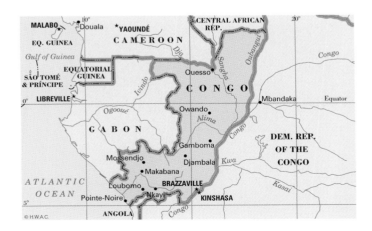

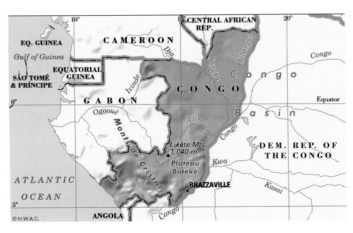

Forests cover two-thirds of the country. Three ranges of volcanic mountains cross the country from north to south. A wide coastal plain borders the Caribbean, and a narrower one edges the Pacific. The climate is tropical, with dry winters and a summer rainy season. Costa Rica's prosperous economy stems from the raising and export of coffee, bananas and sugarcane (which provide more than half the export revenue) and textiles. A strong electronic components and microprocessor industry contribute to the economy. Exports of coffee, bananas, sugar, pineapples, textiles, electronic components and medical equipment go to the United States, Netherlands and Guatemala. Tourism has increased rapidly, attracted by the exotic beauty of the flora and fauna in its forested interior.

The majority of the population is of European descent, chiefly Spanish. There is a large mestizo minority and smaller groups of both African and Chinese origin. Almost all are Roman Catholic in religion. Spanish is the official and predominant language. The descendants of nineteenth-century immigrants in the Limón area speak a Jamaican English dialect. San José, the capital, is the largest city, followed by the port city of Limón.

Did you know? More than 725 species of birds are native to Costa Rica.

Before Costa Rica's colonization in the 1500s by the Spanish, the Guaymi Indians inhabited the country. During the colonial period, it was administered as part of Guatemala. In 1821 Costa Rica became independent from Spain and was annexed by Mexico. Later the Central American countries seceded from Mexico and established the Central American Federation. In 1838 Costa Rica became an independent republic. For more than a hundred years Costa Rica has been considered a model of democratic government and social progress in Central America. Costa Rica (literally "rich coast") enjoys a high standard of living by Latin American standards. There is no regular army, as the constitution forbids armed forces.

AREA: 19,730 sq mi (51,100 sq km)

■ **CLIMATE:** The climate is tropical, though cooler in the highlands, with dry winters and a summer rainy season.

■ **PEOPLE:** The majority of the population is of European and mixed descent, chiefly Spanish. There are small groups of Africans and Chinese.

POPULATION: 4,075,261

ETHNIC GROUPS: European and mestizo 94%, black 3%, Amerindian 1%, Chinese 1%

PRINCIPAL LANGUAGES: Spanish (official), English spoken around Puerto Limon

CHIEF RELIGIONS: Roman Catholic (official) 76%, Protestant 14%

■ **ECONOMY:** A prosperous economy stems from the export (mostly to the U.S.) of coffee, bananas, sugarcane and textiles. Tourism has increased rapidly, attracted by the beauty of the forested interior.

Cataract on the Rio Savegre

MONETARY UNIT: colon

GDP: $38.0 billion (2004 est.)

PER CAPITA GDP: $9,600

INDUSTRIES: microprocessors, food processing, textiles and clothing, construction materials, fertilizer, plastic products

CHIEF CROPS: coffee, pineapples, bananas, sugar, corn, rice, beans, potatoes

LIFE EXPECTANCY AT BIRTH (YEARS): male, 74.1; female, 79.3

LITERACY RATE: 95.5%

CAPITAL: San José (pop., 1,085,000)

GOVERNMENT TYPE: republic

INDEPENDENCE DATE: September 15, 1821

WEBSITE: www.costarica-embassy.org

Côte d'Ivoire (Ivory Coast) takes its name from the trade in ivory begun by the Portuguese late in the sixteenth century. Almost half the country is composed of rain forest; the remainder is grassy and wooded savanna, with mountains in the northeast. The climate is tropical on the coast, changing to semi-arid in the north. One of the world's largest producers of coffee, cocoa and palm oil, the economy is largely agricultural in nature. Industries include the processing of tropical woods, oil refining, textile manufacturing and food processing. Gold and diamond deposits are also being exploited. Exports go primarily to the United States, France and the Netherlands.

The five principal ethnic divisions are the Akan, Krou, Senoufo/Lobi, and the Northern and Southern Mande. The Baoules, in the Akan division, probably comprise the single largest subgroup. The Betes in the Krou division, the Senoufos in the north, and the Malinkes in the northwest and the cities are the next largest groups. French is the official language. Dioula is the most widely spoken of the African languages. Muslims, Christians and animists each form a third of all religious adherents. Abidjan is the country's largest city and its de facto capital. The official capital, Yamoussoukro, was established in 1983.

Abidjan-Plateau

Little is known of the country's past before the first contacts with the Portuguese and French in the sixteenth century. In the late nineteenth century Côte d'Ivoire was organized as a French protectorate. In 1960 independence was achieved and under President Houphouët-Boigny's leadership (1960-1993) with French support, Côte d'Ivoire became the richest and most self-sufficient state in West Africa. However, a minitary coup in December 1999 overthrew the government and has destabilized the country.

Did you know? This nation is the world's leading producer of cocoa beans.

AREA: 124,502 sq mi (322,460 sq km)

■ **CLIMATE:** The climate is tropical on the coast, changing to semi-arid in the north.

■ **PEOPLE:** The five principal ethnic divisions are the Akan, Krou, Senoufo/Lobi, and the Northern and Southern Mande.

POPULATION: 17,654,843

LIFE EXPECTANCY AT BIRTH (YEARS): male, 40.3; female, 44.8

LITERACY RATE: 48.5%

ETHNIC GROUPS: Akan 42%, Voltaiques (Gur) 18%, north Mandes 17%, Krous 11%, south Mandes 10%

PRINCIPAL LANGUAGES: French (official), Dioula, many native dialects

CHIEF RELIGIONS: Muslim 35-40%, Christian 20-30%, indigenous beliefs 25-40%

■ **ECONOMY:** One of the world's largest producers of coffee, cocoa and palm oil, the economy is largely agricultural in nature. Gold and diamond deposits are also being exploited. Exports are primarily to the United States, France and the Netherlands.

MONETARY UNIT: CFA franc

GDP: $24.8 billion (2004 est.)

PER CAPITA GDP: $1,500

INDUSTRIES: foodstuffs, beverages, wood products, oil refining, truck and bus assembly, textiles, fertilizer, electricity

MINERALS: petroleum, natural gas, diamonds, manganese, iron ore, cobalt, bauxite, copper

CHIEF CROPS: coffee, cocoa beans, bananas, palm kernels, corn, rice, manioc, sweet potatoes, sugar, cotton, rubber

GOVERNMENT TYPE: In transition

OFFICIAL CAPITAL: Yamoussoukro (pop., 416,000); seat of government, Abidjan pop., 3,337,000)

INDEPENDENCE DATE: August 7, 1960

WEBSITE: www.state.gov/r/pa/ei/bgn/2846.htm

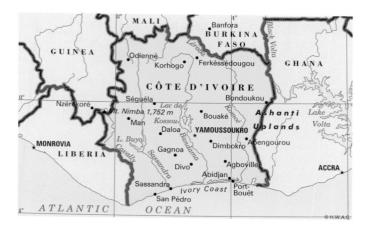

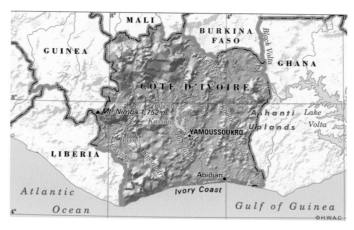

Croatia is geographically diverse, with flat plains along the Hungarian border and mountains and highlands in Dalmatia along the Adriatic coast. Croatia's rivers are the Sava, Drava and Danube. The interior of the country has a continental climate, with hot summers and cold winters, while the coast enjoys mild winters and dry summers. Some coal, petroleum, natural gas, iron ore, bauxite and clays are produced. Wheat, corn, sugar beets, sunflowers, fruit, grapes, livestock, olives and citrus are raised. The fish catch is important. Chemicals, foodstuffs, metal products, machinery, textiles and shipbuilding are leading industries. Machinery, chemicals, food products and fuels are shipped to European Union countries and Slovenia. Privatization of state-run industries is slowly increasing and tourism is on the rise.

Croats make up most of the population, but there is a small Serbian minority. Bosnians, Hungarians and Slovenes are other notable ethnic groups. Croatia is three fourths Roman Catholic. Serbo-Croatian is the dominant language; the Latin alphabet is used. Zagreb is the capital and largest city.

The Croats, a Slavic people, entered the area in the 600s A.D. The Kingdom of Croatia was founded in 925 A.D. In 1102 Hungarian rule was established in Croatia. During the Middle Ages the Venetians controlled the Dalmatian coast. The eastern part of present-day Croatia fell to the Ottoman Turks in 1526. By the 1700s the Hapsburgs had driven out the Turks. Following the defeat of Austria-Hungary in World War I, Croatia became part of the Kingdom of Serbs, Croats and Slovenes, renamed Yugoslavia in 1929. During World War II, a Croatian state controlled by Nazi Germany and Fascist Italy was set up. After the war, Croatia became one of the constituent republics of Yugoslavia. With the breakup of Yugoslavia, Croatia became independent in 1991. Following independence, Serbs gained control of the eastern end of Croatia and of the Serb-inhabited area within Croatia known as Krajina. In 1995 Croatian troops drove Serbian military forces and civilians out of Krajina. Under UN supervision the last Serb-held enclave in eastern Slavonia was returned to Croatia in 1998.

Did you know?
Dubrovnik has a drugstore that first opened in 1317.

AREA: 21,831 sq mi (56,542 sq km)
■ **CLIMATE:** The coast has mild winters and dry summers, while the interior has hot summers and cold winters.
■ **PEOPLE:** Croats make up most of the population, but there is a small Serbian minority. Bosniaks, Hungarians and Slovenes are other notable ethnic groups.

Dubrovnik-Old Harbor at Old City

POPULATION: 4,494,749
LIFE EXPECTANCY AT BIRTH (YEARS): male, 70.2; female, 78.3
LITERACY RATE: 97%
ETHNIC GROUPS: Croat 78%, Serb 12%, Bosniak 1%
PRINCIPAL LANGUAGES Croatian (official), Serbian
CHIEF RELIGIONS: Roman Catholic 88%, Orthodox 5%
■ **ECONOMY:** Machinery, textiles and chemicals, food products and fuels are exported to European Union countries and Slovenia. Privatization of state-run industries is slowly increasing and tourism is on the rise.
MONETARY UNIT: kuna
GDP: $50.3 billion (2004 est.)
PER CAPITA GDP: $11,200
INDUSTRIES: chemicals and plastics, machine tools, fabricated metal, electronics, pig iron and rolled steel products, aluminum, paper, wood products, construction materials, textiles, shipbuilding, tourism
MINERALS: oil, coal, bauxite, iron ore, calcium, natural asphalt, silica, mica, clays, salt
CHIEF CROPS: wheat, corn, sugar beets, sunflower seed, barley, alfalfa, clover, olives, citrus, grapes, soybeans, potatoes
GOVERNMENT TYPE: parliamentary democracy
CAPITAL: Zagreb (pop., 688,000)
INDEPENDENCE DATE: June 25, 1991
WEBSITE: www.vlada.hr/default.asp?ru=2

Teatro Garcia Lorca

Cuba was called in the past the "Pearl of the Antilles." Largest and most westerly island of the West Indies, Cuba lies at the entrance of the Gulf of Mexico and is some 90 miles south of Florida. About three-fifths of the country consists of flat to gently rolling terrain with many wide and fertile valleys and plains. The remainder is mountainous or hilly. Trade winds moderate the tropical climate. The east coast is subject to seasonal hurricanes. Cuba's mineral resources include nickel, cobalt, iron ore, copper, manganese, salt, timber, oil and natural gas. Sugar is the most important crop; tobacco, citrus fruit, coffee and cattle are the leading agricultural products. Cuba's agricultural and mineral exports go mainly to the Netherlands, Canada, Venezuela, Spain and China. Industry is limited to textiles and the processing of minerals and agricultural crops. Most industries are owned and run by the government, though a small private sector is tightly controlled and regulated.

Nearly 90 percent of the population is of European and mixed European and African ancestry. Spanish is the official and universal language. Cubans were predominantly Roman Catholic before Castro. Havana, the capital, has a population of more than two million people; Santiago de Cuba and Camagüey are also important.

Did you know? The United States has leased a naval base at Guantánamo Bay since 1903.

Following the discovery of Cuba by Columbus in 1492, the island remained under Spanish rule until almost the end of the nineteenth century. After a revolt against Spain in 1895 and the brief Spanish American War of 1898, Cuba became an independent republic, though under U.S. protection until 1934. In 1959 the coming to power of Fidel Castro transformed Cuba into a socialist state modeled on the Soviet Union. Private property was nationalized. Worsening relations and the severing of diplomatic ties by the United States culminated in the abortive Bay of Pigs invasion. In 1962 the installation of Soviet missiles in Cuba led to a U.S. naval blockade. The loss of massive amounts of economic aid from the former Soviet Bloc after 1989 and the over thirty-year U.S. ban on trade with Cuba have crippled the economy and precipitated a severe economic depression.

AREA: 42,803 sq mi (110,860 sq km)

CLIMATE: Trade winds moderate the tropical climate.The east coast is subject to seasonal hurricanes.

PEOPLE: Nearly 90 percent of the population is of European and mixed European and African ancestry.

POPULATION: 11,382,820

LIFE EXPECTANCY AT BIRTH (YEARS):MALE, 75.1; female, 79.8

LITERACY RATE: 97%

ETHNIC GROUPS: Creole 51%, white 37%, black 11%, Chinese 1%

PRINCIPAL LANGUAGE: Spanish (official)

CHIEF RELIGIONS: Roman Catholic, Santeria

ECONOMY: Most industries are owned and run by the government, though a small private sector is tightly controlled and regulated. Cuba's agricultural and mineral exports go mainly to the Netherlands, Canada, Venezuela, Spain and China.

MONETARY UNIT: peso

GDP: $33.9 billion (2004 est.)

PER CAPITA GDP: $3,000

INDUSTRIES: sugar, petroleum, tobacco, chemicals, construction, mining, cement, agricultural machinery, biotechnology

CHIEF CROPS: sugar, tobacco, citrus, coffee, rice, potatoes, beans

MINERALS: cobalt, nickel, iron ore, copper, manganese, salt, silica, petroleum

GOVERNMENT TYPE: Communist state

INDEPENDENCE DATE: May 20, 1902

CAPITAL: Havana (pop., 2,189,000)

WEBSITE: www.cubagov.cu/ingles

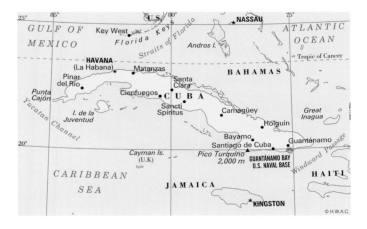

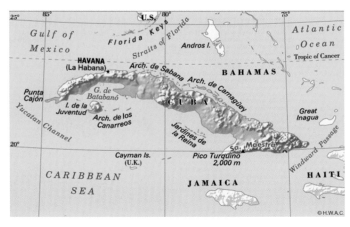

Present-day Cyprus is divided into two separate states. The central and southwestern part of the island is controlled by the Republic of Cyprus, the only internationally recognized government and home of the Greek population. The northeast portion of the island is ruled by the Turkish Republic of Northern Cyprus, which has been recognized only by Turkey.

Mountains in the north and south rim a central plain. The temperate Mediterranean climate features hot dry summers and cool wet winters. The island possesses deposits of copper, pyrites, asbestos, gypsum and marble. Major agricultural and export crops are potatoes, grapes, olives and citrus fruits. Food and beverages, pharmaceuticals, and textile production are the chief industries. Tourism is the most important economic activity. Most economic activity is centered in the Greek-inhabited Republic of Cyprus. Trade is primarily with Greece, Italy, Germany, the United Kingdom and France.

The Greeks in the Greek Republic constitute more than three-quarters of the population of the island. Turks make up less than 20 percent and reside in the Turkish area. The Greek population is of the Greek Orthodox faith, and the Turkish population is of the Muslim faith. In addition to the Greek and Turkish languages, English is widely spoken. Nicosia is the largest city and serves as capital for both sectors, as the border between the two states bisects the city. There are two British armed forces bases on the island.

Did you know? Center of a kingdom in the 7th century BC, Nicosia is one of the world's oldest cities.

The Greeks first settled the island before 1000 B.C. In the sixteenth century, the Ottoman Turks conquered the island. Administration was transferred to Britain in 1878. Independence was officially proclaimed in 1960. However, the Greek community clamored for "enosis," union with Greece. Following independence, years of violence between the Greek and Turkish ethnic communities ended when a Turkish force invaded and occupied 40 percent of the island in 1974. In 1975 the Turkish Cypriots proclaimed their own state in northern Cyprus.

Cyprus' membership to the European Union on May 1, 2004 has been an important milestone in its economic development.

AREA: 3,571 sq mi (9,250 sq km)

■ **CLIMATE:** The country has a temperate Mediterranean climate, with hot, dry summers, and cool, rainy winters.

■ **PEOPLE:** Though historically the two ethnic groups were evenly distributed throughout the island, today Southern Cyprus is predominantly Greek while the north is mostly Turkish.

POPULATION: 784,301

LIFE EXPECTANCY AT BIRTH (YEARS): male, 75.1; female, 79.9

LITERACY RATE: 97%

ETHNIC GROUPS: Greek 85%, Turkish 12%

PRINCIPAL LANGUAGES: Greek, Turkish (both official); English

CHIEF RELIGIONS: Greek Orthodox 78%, Muslim 18%

Paphos

■ **ECONOMY:** Cyprus is known for citrus, grapes, olives, lamb and dairy products. Other exports include copper, pharmaceuticals, cement and clothing. Trade is primarily with Greece, Italy, Germany, the United Kingdom and France.

MONETARY UNIT: pound

GDP: Greek Cypriot area, $15.7 billion (2004 est.); Turkish Cypriot area, $4.5 billion (2004 est.)

PER CAPITA GDP: Greek Cypriot area, $20,300; Turkish Cypriot area, $7,100

INDUSTRIES: food, beverages, textiles, chemicals, metal products, tourism, wood products

MINERALS: copper, pyrites, asbestos, gypsum, salt, marble, clay earth pigment

CHIEF CROPS: potatoes, citrus, vegetables, barley, grapes, olives, vegetables

GOVERNMENT TYPE: republic

CAPITAL: Nicosia (pop., 205,000)

INDEPENDENCE DATE: August 16, 1960

WEBSITE: www.cyprusembassy.net

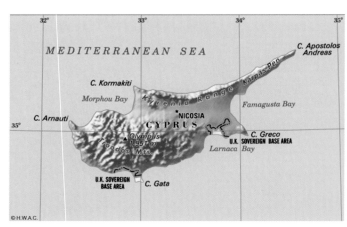

Until January 1, 1993, what is now the Czech Republic consisted of Bohemia and Moravia, the western half of landlocked Czechoslovakia in Central Europe. Czechoslovakia then split into two separate states — the Czech Republic and Slovakia. Bohemia in the west consists of rolling plains, hills, and plateaus surrounded by low mountains. Moravia, in the east, is very hilly. The major river system of the republic is the Vltava (Moldau), which flows into the Labe (Elbe). The temperate climate has cool summers and cold, cloudy and humid winters. Coal, clay and graphite are the chief mineral resources. Diversified crop and livestock production includes grains, potatoes, sugar beets, hops, fruit, hogs, cattle and poultry. The most important manufactures are motor vehicles, machinery, iron, steel and chemicals, which are mainly exported to Slovakia, Poland, France, Austria, Italy and the Netherlands.

Czechs make up more than 90 percent of the population, but there is a small minority of Moravians and Slovaks. Roman Catholics are the largest of the religious groups. Czech is the dominant language. The beautiful capital city of Prague is the largest urban center. Brno and Ostrava also rank high in population.

> **Did you know?**
> The Czech Republic and Slovakia formed a single country from 1918 until 1993.

During the Middle Ages the Czechs established the Kingdom of Bohemia, which was an important participant in medieval European history. During the religious wars of the Reformation, the Czech lands came under the control of the House of Hapsburg. In 1918, following the defeat of Austria-Hungary in World War I, Czechoslovakia was proclaimed an independent republic, incorporating the Czech lands and Slovakia. The Sudeten region was severed from Czechoslovakia as a result of the Munich Pact of 1938, and Nazi Germany occupied Bohemia and Moravia in 1939. After the defeat of Nazi Germany in World War II, Czechoslovakia suffered a Communist coup, which transformed the state into a communist "peoples republic." In late 1989 country-wide demonstrations resulted in the fall of the Communist Party. The Czech and Slovak units agreed to separate peacefully in late 1992. The Czech Republic became a European Union (EU) member on May 1, 2004.

AREA: 30,450 sq mi (78,866 sq km)

CLIMATE: The temperate climate has cool summers and cold, cloudy, humid winters.

Prague

PEOPLE: Czechs make up most of the population, but there is a small minority of Moravians and Slovaks.

POPULATION: 10,235,455

LIFE EXPECTANCY AT BIRTH (YEARS): male, 72.5; female, 79.2

LITERACY RATE: 99.9%

ETHNIC GROUPS: Czech 81%, Moravian 13%, Slovak 3%

PRINCIPAL LANGUAGES: Czech (official), German, Polish, Romani

CHIEF RELIGIONS: atheist 40%, Roman Catholic 39%, Protestant 5%, Orthodox 3%

ECONOMY: The country's most important manufactures include motor vehicles, machinery, iron, steel and chemicals, which are mainly exported to Slovakia, Poland, France and Austria.

MONETARY UNIT: koruna

GDP: $172.2 billion (2004 est.)

PER CAPITA GDP: $16,800

INDUSTRIES: metallurgy, machinery and equipment, motor vehicles, glass, armaments

MINERALS: coal, kaolin, clay, graphite

CHIEF CROPS: wheat, potatoes, sugar beets, hops, fruit

GOVERNMENT TYPE: republic

CAPITAL: Prague (pop., 1,170,000)

INDEPENDENCE DATE: January 1, 1993

WEBSITE: www.czech.cz

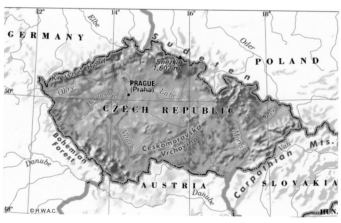

The constitutional monarchy of Denmark sits strategically between the Baltic and the North seas. It borders Germany on the south and lies across the Skagerrak and Kattegat straits from Norway and Sweden. The country consists of the Jutland Peninsula and about 500 islands, the main islands being Sjaelland, Fyn, Falster, Lolland, Langeland and Bornholm. The Faroe Islands and Greenland are self-governing overseas divisions of the Danish realm. The country has a temperate climate, often rainy, humid and cloudy, with windy winters and cool summers. A member of the European Union, Denmark's prosperous economy is based on technologically advanced agriculture, small-scale industry and foreign trade. Its rich agricultural production includes meat, dairy products, grain, potatoes, sugar beets and fish.

Its chief industries are food processing, machinery, textiles, chemicals, shipbuilding, furniture and windmills. Meat, dairy products, chemicals and machinery head its list of exports. Trading partners include Germany, Sweden, U.K., U.S., Norway, Japan and east European countries.

> **Did you know?** The island of Greenland is a self-governing part of Denmark.

The Danes are a Scandinavian people; there is a small community of Greenland Inuit (Eskimos), emigrants and Faroese emigrants from the Danish colonies. The predominant religion is Lutheranism. Danish is the universal language. Copenhagen, the charming capital and the country's largest city, is found on the island of Sjaelland. Tivoli, the city's pleasure garden, is world famous. Other cities are Århus and Ålborg on the Jutland Peninsula, and Odense on the island of Fyn. Denmark's population is highly literate and has produced many prominent writers, including the famed author Hans Christian Andersen. The Little Mermaid, one of his most beloved characters, is memorialized in a statue that sits overlooking the capital's harbor.

Danish Vikings were prominent in Norse raids on Western Europe. During the nineteenth and twentieth centuries, the Danish economy grew and the populace attained high living

standards. However, Denmark suffered military defeat at the hands of the Prussians and Austrians in 1864 and was occupied by Germany during World War II. Denmark has been a member of NATO since its founding in 1949, and is one of the few countries to exceed the United Nations goal of contributing 0.7% of Gross National Product to development assistance. Though a member since 1973, the rest of the EU has agreed to exempt Denmark from certain aspects of the European Union, including a common defense, a common currency, EU citizenship, and certain aspects of legal cooperation.

AREA: 16,639 sq mi (43,094 sq km)

■ **CLIMATE:** The country has a temperate climate, often rainy, humid and cloudy, with windy winters and cool summers.

■ **PEOPLE:** Mostly Scandinavians, with small communities of Greenland Inuit (Eskimos) and Faroese from the Danish colonies.

POPULATION: 5,450,661

LIFE EXPECTANCY AT BIRTH (YEARS): male, 75.2; female, 79.8

LITERACY RATE: 100%

ETHNIC GROUPS: Mainly Danish; German minority in south

PRINCIPAL LANGUAGES: Danish (official), Faroese, Greenlandic (an Inuit dialect), German

Nyhaven

CHIEF RELIGIONS: Evangelical Lutheran (official) 95%, other Christian 3%, Muslim 2%

■ **ECONOMY:** Machinery, meat, fish and dairy products, chemicals, shipbuilding, furniture and windmills head Denmark's list of exports. Trading partners include Germany, Sweden, U.K., U.S., Norway, Japan and east European countries.

MONETARY UNIT: krone

GDP: $174.4 billion (2004 est.)

PER CAPITA GDP: $32,200

INDUSTRIES: food processing, machinery and equipment, textiles and clothing, chemical products, electronics, construction, furniture, shipbuilding

MINERALS: petroleum, natural gas, salt, limestone, stone, gravel and sand

CHIEF CROPS: barley, wheat, potatoes, sugar beets

GOVERNMENT TYPE: constitutional monarchy

CAPITAL: Copenhagen (pop., 1,066,000)

INDEPENDENCE DATE: 10th century

WEBSITE: www.ambwashington.um.dk/en

The Northeast African country of Djibouti takes its name from its capital and chief city, a port at the western end of the Gulf of Aden and the southern entrance of the Red Sea. Djibouti consists of an arid, rocky coastal plain and an inland plateau separated by central mountains. The desert climate is extremely hot and very dry. Almost entirely lacking in resources, Djibouti exists chiefly as a transshipping point to the outer world for a large part of Ethiopia's trade. The port of Djibouti is the terminus for the Ethiopia-Djibouti railroad, built by French interests to connect Addis Ababa with the sea. The economy is based on services connected with the country's strategic location and its status as a free trade zone. Djibouti has one of the most liberal economic regimes in Africa, with almost unrestricted banking and commerce sectors.

The population is nearly two-thirds Somali (chiefly Issas), and about one-third Afar. Islam is the religion for almost the entire population. Somali and Afar are spoken most, although French is the official language.

In 1884 the Protectorate of French Somaliland was established. In 1967 the protectorate was renamed the French Territory of the Afars and Issas in recognition of the two major ethnic groups. In 1977, the territory, last remnant of the vast French African empire, became independent.

Did you know? Djibouti is on a dangerous strait, the Bab al-Mandab ("gate of tears").

AREA: 8,880 sq mi (23,000 sq km)

CLIMATE: The desert climate is extremely hot and very dry.

PEOPLE: The population is nearly two-thirds Somali (chiefly Issas), and about one-third Afar.

POPULATION: 486,530

LIFE EXPECTANCY AT BIRTH (YEARS): male, 41.8; female, 44.4

LITERACY RATE: 46.2%

ETHNIC GROUPS: Somali 60%, Afar 35%

PRINCIPAL LANGUAGES: French, Arabic (both official); Afar, Somali

Farside

CHIEF RELIGIONS: Muslim 94%, Christian 6%

ECONOMY: With few natural resources and little industry, Djibouti exists chiefly as a transshipping point for most of Ethiopia's trade, due to the country's strategic location and its status as a free trade zone.

MONETARY UNIT: Djibouti franc (DJF)

GDP: $619 million (2003 est.)

PER CAPITA GDP: $1,300

INDUSTRIES: construction, agricultural processing

CHIEF CROPS: fruits, vegetables

GOVERNMENT TYPE: republic

CAPITAL: Djibouti (pop., 502,000)

INDEPENDENCE DATE: June 27, 1977

WEBSITE: www.state.gov/r/pa/ei/bgn/5482.htm

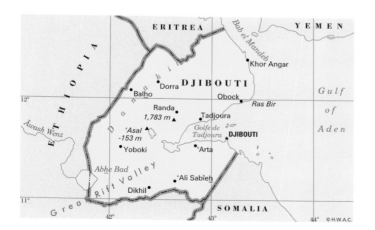

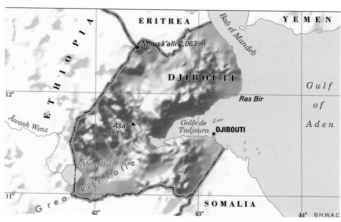

Dominica, northernmost of the Windward Islands, lies between Guadeloupe and Martinique. The wild, natural beauty of the heavily forested and rugged mountains of this island contrasts with the beaches and tourist resorts of other Caribbean islands. A tropical climate, moderated by northeast trade winds, is subject to occasional hurricanes and tropical storms. Efforts are being made to develop a tourist industry. However, the economy is chiefly agricultural, based on the production of bananas, citrus, mangoes, root crops and coconuts. Bananas are the main export, shipped mostly to the U.K. and many Caribbean countries.

While English is the official language, a patois based on French and containing many African elements is widely spoken. The island's population is nearly all of African or mixed African-European origin, but there is a small Carib-Indian community. Roseau is the capital and largest city.

Dominica, named for Sunday, the day of the week on which tradition says Columbus first sighted the island in 1493, was originally occupied by peaceful Arawak Indians. Warlike Caribs conquered the Arawaks in the 1300s. Permanent occupation by Europeans did not occur until the mid-eighteenth century when French settlements were made. In 1783 the British took control, holding the island until independence was granted in 1978.

Did you know?
Dominica was sighted and named by Christopher Columbus in 1493.

Calibishie

CHIEF RELIGIONS: Roman Catholic 77%, Protestant 15%

■ **ECONOMY:** Efforts are being made to develop a tourist industry. However, the economy is chiefly agricultural. Bananas are the main export, shipped mostly to the U.K. and many Caribbean countries.

CAPITAL: Roseau (pop., 27,000)

MONETARY UNIT: East Caribbean dollar

GDP: $384 million (2003 est.)

PER CAPITA GDP: $5,500

INDUSTRIES: soap, coconut oil, tourism, copra, furniture, cement blocks, shoes

CHIEF CROPS: bananas, citrus, mangoes, root crops, coconuts, cocoa

GOVERNMENT TYPE: parliamentary democracy

INDEPENDENCE DATE: November 3, 1978

WEBSITE: www.ndcdominica.dm

AREA: 291 sq mi (754 sq km)

■ **CLIMATE:** Tropical climate moderated by northeast trade winds, with occasional hurricanes and tropical storms.

■ **PEOPLE:** The population is nearly all of African or mixed African-European origin, but there is a small Carib-Indian community.

POPULATION: 68,910

LIFE EXPECTANCY AT BIRTH (YEARS): male, 71.5; female, 77.4

LITERACY RATE: 94%

ETHNIC GROUPS: black, Carib Amerindian

PRINCIPAL LANGUAGES: English (official), French patois

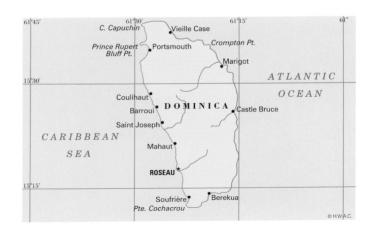

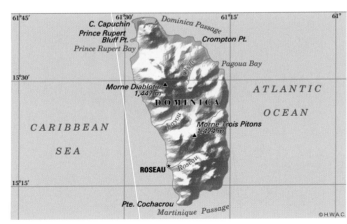

Sharing Hispaniola with Haiti, the Dominican Republic occupies the eastern two-thirds of the island, which lies between the Atlantic Ocean and the Caribbean Sea. The terrain is rugged; four mountain ranges traverse the country from east to west. Fertile valleys lie between the mountains. The tropical climate varies little in temperature, but rainfall varies seasonally. Nickel and gold are mined. Agriculture is a key sector of the economy; sugar is the dominant commodity. Textiles, sugar, coffee, ferronickel and cocoa are exported, chiefly to the United States. Free trade zones have fostered economic growth, especially in the manufacture of wearing apparel. Tourism and supporting services is also a growing industry.

The population is primarily Creole of mixed African and European descent. There is also a significant minority of Europeans and a smaller minority of African origin. Haitians form the largest foreign minority group. Spanish is the official and universal language, and Roman Catholicism is the dominant religion. Santo Domingo is the capital and largest metropolitan center. Founded in 1496, it is the oldest European settlement in the Western Hemisphere. Christopher Columbus is buried in the city's cathedral.

Columbus visited Hispaniola in 1492, setting the stage for the Spanish conquest of the Caribbean. Following shifting ownership by France, Spain and Haiti, the Dominican Republic became independent in 1844. The United States intervened militarily twice in the history of the republic, between 1916 and 1924 and again in 1965.

> **Did you know?** U.S. marines occupied this nation in 1916–24 and intervened in 1965.

AREA: 18,815 sq mi (48,730 sq km)

■ **CLIMATE:** The tropical climate varies little in temperature, but rainfall varies seasonally.

■ **PEOPLE:** The population is primarily Creole of mixed African and European descent. There is also a significant minority of Europeans and a smaller minority of African origin. Haitians form the largest foreign minority group.

POPULATION: 9,183,984

LIFE EXPECTANCY AT BIRTH (YEARS): male, 66.0; female, 69.4

LITERACY RATE: 82.1%

Zona Colonial

ETHNIC GROUPS: Creole 73%, white 16%, black 11%

PRINCIPAL LANGUAGE: Spanish (official)

CHIEF RELIGION: Roman Catholic 95%

■ **ECONOMY:** Services have overtaken agriculture due to an increase in tourism. Free trade zones have fostered economic growth. Textiles, sugar, coffee, ferronickel and cocoa are exported, chiefly to the United States.

MONETARY UNIT: peso

GDP: $55.7 billion (2004 est.)

PER CAPITA GDP: $6,300

INDUSTRIES: tourism, sugar processing, mining, textiles, cement, tobacco

MINERALS: nickel, bauxite, gold, silver

CHIEF CROPS: sugarcane, coffee, cotton, cocoa, tobacco, rice, beans, potatoes, corn, bananas

GOVERNMENT TYPE: republic

CAPITAL: Santo Domingo (pop., 1,865,000)

INDEPENDENCE DATE: February 27, 1844

WEBSITE: www.domrep.org/home.htm

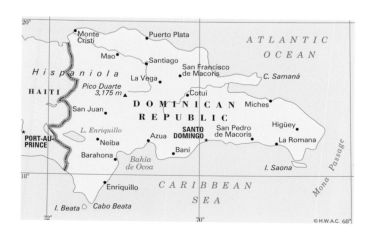

Located in Southeast Asia, northwest of Australia in the Lesser Sunda Islands; "Timor-Leste" includes the eastern half of Timor Island, the Oecussi (Ambeno) region on the northwest portion of Timor Island, and the islands of Pulau Atauro and Pulau Jaco. The climate is tropical, hot and semi-arid with distinct rainy and dry seasons. The terrain is mountainous, while floods, landslides, earthquakes and tsunamis are common. Natural Resources include gold, petroleum, natural gas, manganese and marble. Although the poorest nation in Asia, oil and natural gas offer great hope for the economy. The major cash crops are coffee, rice, corn, cassava, sweet potatoes, soybeans, cabbage, mangoes, bananas and vanilla. Industries include printing, soap manufacturing, handicrafts and woven cloth. Exports include coffee, sandalwood and marble, oil and natural gas. Major trading partners are Indonesia, Australia, the United States, Western Europe and Japan.

The people are of mixed Malay and Pacific Islander descent. There are also small groups of Papuans and Chinese. Most people are Roman Catholic, though there are small groups of Muslims and Protestants. Tetum and Portuguese are the official languages, though Indonesian and English are also spoken. Dili is the capital and chief city.

Did you know? East Timorese voted for independence from Indonesia in 1999.

Portuguese and Dutch traders made the first western contact with Timor in the early 16th century. Sandalwood and spice traders, as well as missionaries, maintained sporadic contact until 1642, when the Portuguese moved into Timor in strength. The Portuguese and the Dutch, based at the western end of the island in Kupang, battled for influence until the present-day borders were agreed to in 1906. Imperial Japan occupied East Timor from 1942-45. Portugal resumed colonial authority over East Timor in 1945 after World War II. Following a military coup in Lisbon in 1974, Portugal began to leave East Timor. Political tensions-exacerbated by Indonesian involvement heated up, and in 1975, the Timorese Democratic Union Party (UDT) launched a coup d'état in Dili.

In the following civil war, the Revolutionary Front for an Independent East Timor (FRETILIN) pushed UDT forces into Indonesian West Timor. Shortly after this, Indonesian forces began incursions into East Timor. In November, FRETILIN declared East Timor an independent state. Indonesia responded by launching a full-scale military invasion in December. The Indonesian occupation of Timor was initially characterized by a program of brutal military repression. Beginning in the late 1980s, however, the Indonesians began to emphasize economic development and job creation while maintaining a strict policy of political repression, although serious human rights violations continued. Estimates of the number of Timorese who lost their lives to violence and hunger during the Indonesian occupation range from 100,000 to 250,000. In August of 1999, Indonesia held a referendum in which the people of East Timor voted overwhelmingly for independence. In September, 1999 the Australian-led peace-keeping troops of the International Force for East Timor were deployed to bring violence to an end. East Timor became a fully independent republic with a parliamentary form of government on May 20, 2002, after approximately two and a half years under the authority of the UN Transitional Administration in East Timor.

Native dress

AREA: 5,740 sq mi (14,880 sq km)

CLIMATE: Tropical, hot and semi-arid with distinct rainy and dry seasons. Floods, landslides earthquakes and tsunamis are common.

PEOPLE: The people are of mixed Malay and Pacific Islander descent. There are also small groups of Papuans and Chinese.

POPULATION: 1,062,777

LIFE EXPECTANCY AT BIRTH (YEARS): male, 63.3; female, 67.9

LITERACY RATE: 48%

ETHNIC GROUPS: Austronesian; Papuan

PRINCIPAL LANGUAGES: Tetum, Portuguese (both official); Indonesian, English, other native languages

CHIEF RELIGIONS: Roman Catholic 90%, Muslim 4%, Protestant 3%

ECONOMY: The poorest nation in Asia, oil and gas offer great hope for the economy. Exports include coffee, sandalwood and marble. Major trading partners are Australia, Europe, Japan and the United States.

MONETARY UNIT: U.S. dollar and Indonesian rupiah

GDP: $370 million (2004 est.)

PER CAPITA GDP: $400

INDUSTRIES: printing, soap manufacturing, handicrafts, woven cloth

MINERALS: gold, petroleum, natural gas, manganese, marble

CHIEF CROPS: coffee, rice, maize, cassava, sweet potatoes, soybeans, cabbage, mangoes, bananas, vanilla

GOVERNMENT TYPE: republic

CAPITAL: Dili (pop., 49,000)

INDEPENDENCE DATE: May 20, 2002

WEBSITE: timor-leste.gov.tl

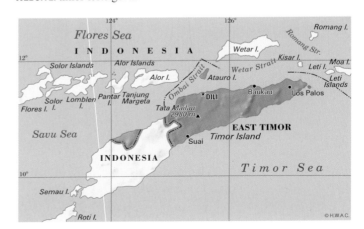

The country takes its name from the Equator, which bisects the country's northern region. The Galápagos Islands, some 600 miles west of the mainland, are part of the national territory. About one-quarter of the country consists of a coastal plain ("Costa"). Another one-quarter forms the Sierra, or highlands, lying between two chains of the Andes. The Oriente, or eastern jungle, covers the remaining half of the country. The climate is tropical along the coast and in the Amazon jungle lowlands. Temperatures are cooler inland at higher elevations. Ecuador has substantial oil deposits. Fish and shrimp are important resources, as is timber, especially balsawood. Bananas are the chief agricultural product, but coffee, cocoa, cut flowers and livestock also rank high. Petroleum is the chief export along with bananas, shrimp, coffee and cut flowers. Exports go mainly to the United States, but also to Panama, Peru and Italy.

Most of the people are mestizos - of mixed Indian and Spanish descent. People of Indian background form one-quarter of the population; smaller European and African components make up the remainder. Spanish is the dominant language. Quechua is the most important of the Indian tongues. Roman Catholicism is the chief religion. The major port is Guayaquil. Quito, the capital, has long been considered one of the most beautiful cities in South America.

The Incas ruled Ecuador until their empire fell to the Spanish conquistadors in 1533. With the end of Spanish rule in 1822, the country was for a time part of Greater Colombia, which embraced Ecuador, Colombia, Panama and Venezuela. In 1942 an agreement was signed between Ecuador and Peru to settle their boundary disputes in the Oriente region. However, since then, further disputes have broken out over the boundary, the latest in 1995 was resolved by a peace agreement with Peru in October of 1998.

Did you know? The Galápagos Islands in the Pacific make up a province of Ecuador.

AREA: 109,483 sq mi (283,560 sq km)

■ **CLIMATE:** The climate is tropical along the coast and in the Amazon jungle lowlands. Temperatures are cooler inland at higher elevations.

■ **PEOPLE:** The indigenous population is primarily mestizo (Spanish-Indian). There is also a significant Indian minority and small groups of Europeans and Africans.

POPULATION: 13,547,510

LIFE EXPECTANCY AT BIRTH (YEARS): male, 73.2; female, 79.0

LITERACY RATE: 90.1%

Cotopaxi

ETHNIC GROUPS: mestizo 65%, Amerindian 25%, black 3%

PRINCIPAL LANGUAGES: Spanish (official), Amerindian languages (especially Quechua)

CHIEF RELIGION: Roman Catholic 95%

■ **ECONOMY:** Petroleum is the chief export along with bananas, shrimp, coffee and cut flowers. Exports go mainly to the United States, but also to Panama, Peru and Italy.

MONETARY UNIT: U.S. dollar

GDP: $49.5 billion (2004 est.)

PER CAPITA GDP: $3,700

INDUSTRIES: petroleum, food processing, textiles, metal work, paper and wood products, chemicals, plastics, fishing, lumber

MINERALS: petroleum

CHIEF CROPS: bananas, coffee, cocoa, rice, potatoes, manioc (tapioca), plantains, sugarcane

CAPITAL: Quito (pop., 1,451,000)

INDEPENDENCE DATE: May 24, 1822

GOVERNMENT TYPE: republic

WEBSITE: www.ecuador.org/main.htm

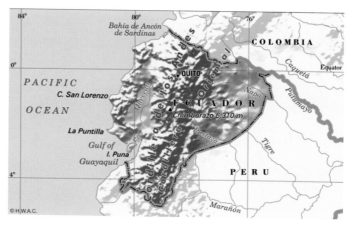

The geography of Egypt is dominated by the fertile Nile Valley and delta, where the great pyramids and the temples of the pharaohs are found. In contrast, the remainder of the country is a vast desert plateau with only a few oases under cultivation. The vital Suez Canal separates the land from the Sinai Peninsula on the east. Hot dry summers and moderate winters characterize the desert climate. Petroleum and natural gas are leading natural resources; there are also considerable deposits of phosphates and iron ore. Cotton is the great agricultural crop and chief export. Other crops are rice, corn and wheat, all grown on irrigated land, as is cotton. Textiles, clothing, food processing and chemicals are the major industries. Besides cotton, petroleum and clothing are the leading exports. Major trading partneres include the EU, U.S., Middle East and Japan. A thriving media and movie industry, and tourism give the economy a major boost.

Egyptians make up most of the population. Ethnic minorities include Bedouin Arab nomads, Berbers and Nubians. Arabic is the official and universal language although English and French are widely understood by the educated classes. About 94 percent of the population is Sunni Muslim. Coptic Christians and others constitute the remainder. Cairo, the capital, and Alexandria are the chief cities.

Nile River, Aswan

The history of Egypt dates back 5,000 years. A succession of dynasties held sway in the great Nile Valley civilization, followed by Persian, Greek, Roman and Byzantine rule. Arab invaders in 639 A.D. introduced Islam. In 1517 Egypt came under the control of the Ottoman Turks. In the late nineteenth century Egypt came under British influence. With the decline of western domination, Egypt became a republic in 1952. In 1956 Egypt nationalized the Suez Canal. Israel, France and Britain attacked Egypt, but were forced to withdraw under pressure from the United States, the Soviet Union and the United Nations. Although Israel and Egypt had fought against each other in four wars between 1948 and 1973, the two nations signed a peace treaty in 1979.

Did you know?
Archaeological records of ancient Egypt date back 6,000 years.

AREA: 386,662 sq mi (1,001,450 sq km)

■ **CLIMATE:** While regular flooding of the Nile Valley made this civilization possible, the country has a desert climate, with hot, dry summers, and moderate winters.

■ **PEOPLE:** A fairly homogenous ethnic group, Egyptians retain strong genetic ties to their ancient forebears. Ethnic minorities include Bedouin Arab nomads and Nubians.

POPULATION: 78,887,007

LIFE EXPECTANCY AT BIRTH (YEARS): male, 68.2; female, 73.3

LITERACY RATE: 51.4%

ETHNIC GROUPS: Egyptian Arab 99%

PRINCIPAL LANGUAGES: Arabic (official), English, French

CHIEF RELIGIONS: Muslim (official; mostly Sunni) 94%, Coptic Christian and other 6%

■ **ECONOMY:** Egypt exports petroleum, natural gas, iron ore and other natural resources. A thriving media and movie industry, and tourism give its economy a major boost.

MONETARY UNIT: pound

GDP: $316.3 billion (2004 est.)

PER CAPITA GDP: $4,200

INDUSTRIES: textiles, food processing, tourism, chemicals, hydrocarbons, construction, cement, metals

MINERALS: petroleum, natural gas, iron ore, phosphates, manganese, limestone, gypsum, talc, asbestos, lead, zinc

CHIEF CROPS: cotton, rice, corn, wheat, beans, fruits, vegetables

GOVERNMENT TYPE: republic

CAPITAL: Cairo (pop., 10,834,000)

INDEPENDENCE DATE: February 28, 1922

WEBSITE: www.sis.gov.eg

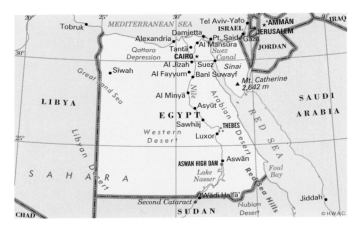

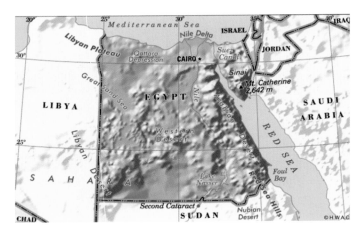

El Salvador is the smallest of the Central American nations. Mountain ranges running east to west divide the country into a narrow Pacific coastal belt on the south; a central region of valleys and plateaus, where most of the population lives; and a mountainous northern region. The climate is tropical, with a summer rainy season and a winter dry season. The climate is temperate inland at higher elevations. Coffee is the most important commercial crop. Textiles and apparel, light manufacturing, medicines, sugar and shrimp are exported, mainly to the United States.

Almost 90 percent of the population is of mixed European and Indian descent. There are also small groups of Europeans and Amerindians. Spanish is the universal language. Most of the population is Roman Catholic, with a sizable Protestant minority. San Salvador is the capital and largest city.

Following the Spanish conquest of the area in the 1520s, El Salvador was administered as part of the captaincy general of Guatemala. After independence from Spain in 1821, El Salvador was annexed to Mexico and later joined the Central American Federation. In 1841 the country declared its independence. During the 1980s civil war between left-wing guerrillas and successive centrist and right-wing governments wracked the country. After much bloodshed, including nearly 60,000 killed, peace returned in 1992.

Did you know? A 1992 treaty ended a civil war that cost an estimated 75,000 lives.

AREA: 8,124 sq mi (21,040 sq km)

CLIMATE: Tropical, with a summer rainy season and a winter dry season. The climate is temperate inland at higher elevations.

PEOPLE: Most people are of mixed European and Indian descent. There are also small groups of Europeans and Amerindians.

POPULATION: 6,822,378

LIFE EXPECTANCY AT BIRTH (YEARS): male, 67.3; female, 74.7

LITERACY RATE: 71.5%

ETHNIC GROUPS: mestizo 90%, white 9%, Amerindian 1%

PRINCIPAL LANGUAGES: Spanish (official), Nahua

CHIEF RELIGIONS: Roman Catholic 83%, many Protestant groups

Church at Suchitoto

ECONOMY: El Salvador is the smallest country in Central America. Coffee is the most important commercial crop. Textiles and apparel, light manufacturing, medicines, sugar and shrimp are exported, mainly to the United States.

MONETARY UNIT: colon

GDP: $32.4 billion (2004 est.)

PER CAPITA GDP: $4,900

INDUSTRIES: food processing, beverages, petroleum, chemicals, fertilizer, textiles, furniture, light metals

MINERALS: petroleum

CHIEF CROPS: coffee, sugar, corn, rice, beans, oilseed, cotton, sorghum

GOVERNMENT TYPE: republic

CAPITAL: San Salvador (pop., 1,424,000)

INDEPENDENCE DATE: September 15, 1821

WEBSITE: www.elsalvador.org/home.nsf/home

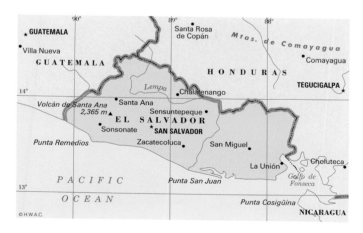

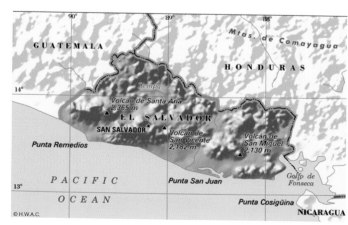

The small Republic of Equatorial Guinea consists of two areas: the mainland, or Río Muni, and the larger island of Bioko (Fernando Po) with the tiny island of Annóbon to the south. In contrast to the islands, which are volcanic, Río Muni contains a coastal plain rising to hills in the interior. The tropical climate is always hot and humid. Bata, on the mainland, is somewhat drier and cooler. Mineral resources are limited, and agriculture is restricted to the raising of cocoa for export and some coffee, cocoa, rice and yams. Timber cutting is also undertaken. The recent discovery of oil has dramatically improved the economy. Exports of petroleum, methanol, timber and cocoa go mainly to the U.S., China and Spain.

The great majority of the population are the Fang of mainland Río Muni. On Bioko the indigenous Bubis are the major ethnic group. Minorities include the Annobonese on Annobon Island, and the Ndowe, Kombe and Bujebas on the coast of Rio Muni. More than 80 percent of the population is Roman Catholic. Spanish is the official language. The capital, Malabo, is located on the island of Bioko, while Bata is the chief town of Río Muni.

Did you know? The capital, Malabo, is located on an island in the Gulf of Guinea.

First visited by the Portuguese in the late 1400s, the area was ceded to Spain in 1778. In 1968 Spain granted independence to Equatorial Guinea.

AREA: 10,831 sq mi (28,051 sq km)

CLIMATE: The tropical climate is always hot and humid. Bata, on the mainland, is somewhat drier and cooler.

PEOPLE: Most of the people are the Fang of Río Muni, while on Bioko the Bubis are the major ethnic group. Minorities include the Annobonese on Annobon and the Ndowe, Kombe and Bujebas on the Rio Muni coast.

POPULATION: 540,109

LIFE EXPECTANCY AT BIRTH (YEARS): male, 53.0; female, 57.4

LITERACY RATE: 78.5%

Malabo waterfront

ECONOMY: The recent discovery of oil has dramatically improved the economy. Exports of petroleum, methanol, timber and cocoa go mainly to the U.S., China and Spain.

MONETARY UNIT: CFA franc

GDP: $1.3 billion (2002 est.)

PER CAPITA GDP: $2,700

INDUSTRIES: petroleum, fishing, sawmilling, natural gas

MINERALS: oil, petroleum, gold, manganese, uranium

CHIEF CROPS: coffee, cocoa, rice, yams, cassava, bananas, palm oil, nuts

ETHNIC GROUPS: Fang 83%, Bubi 10%

PRINCIPAL LANGUAGES: Spanish, French (both official); Fang, Bubi, pidgin English, Portuguese Creole, Ibo

CHIEF RELIGIONS: nominally Christian and predominantly Roman Catholic, traditional practices

GOVERNMENT TYPE: republic

CAPITAL: Malabo (pop., 95,000)

INDEPENDENCE DATE: October 12, 1968

WEBSITE: www.state.gov/r/pa/ei/bgn/7221.htm

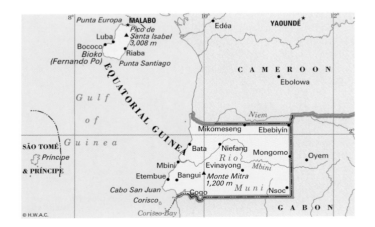

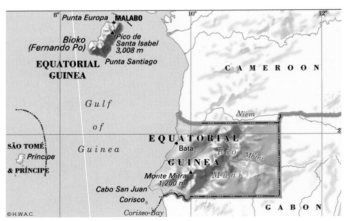

The East African country of Eritrea fronts the Red Sea between Djibouti and Sudan and borders Ethiopia along most of its southern boundary. Highlands are found in the north, and a coastal desert plain lies in the east. Off the coast is the Dahlak Archipelago. The climate varies from hot and arid in the western hills and plains to cooler and wetter in the central highlands. There is a hot, dry desert strip along the Red Sea coast. The chief exploited minerals are gold, copper, iron ore, potash and salt. Millet, sorghum, wheat, barley, flax, cotton, papayas, citrus fruits, bananas, beans and lentils are grown. Trade goods of this very poor country include skins, meat, livestock and gum arabic. Trade is primarily with Saudi Arabia, Yemen, Italy, Djibouti and Sudan.

Half of the population are Tigrays, while another third are Tigre. There are small groups of Saho, Afar, Beja, Bilen and Kunama. Muslim and Christian religions predominate. The languages reflect the ethnic groups. Asmara is the capital. Mits'iwa (Massawa) and Āseb (Assab) are the chief ports.

Did you know? Eritrea was once a colony of Italy.

Originally part of ancient Ethiopia, Eritrea was an Italian colony from 1890 until 1941. After British occupation, Eritrea again became part of Ethiopia in 1952. After years of pro-independence insurgency, Eritrea became independent in 1993.

AREA: 46,842 sq mi (121,320 sq km)

CLIMATE: Hot and arid in the western hills and lowlands, becoming cooler and wetter in the central highlands, with a hot, dry desert strip along the Red Sea.

PEOPLE: Half of the population are Tigrays, while another third are Tigre. There are small groups of Saho, Afar, Beja, Bilen and Kunama.

POPULATION: 4,786,994

LIFE EXPECTANCY AT BIRTH (YEARS): male, 51.3; female, 54.1

LITERACY RATE: 25%

ETHNIC GROUPS: Tigrinya 50%, Tigre and Kunama 40%, Afar 4%, Saho 3%

PRINCIPAL LANGUAGES: Arabic, Tigrinya (both official); Afar, Amharic, Tigre, Kunama, other Cushitic languages

CHIEF RELIGIONS: Muslim, Coptic Christian, Roman Catholic, Protestant

ECONOMY: Trade goods of this very poor country include skins, meat, live-stock and gum arabic. Trade is primarily with Saudi Arabia, Yemen, Italy, Djibouti and Sudan.

MONETARY UNIT: nakfa

GDP: $4.2 billion (2004 est.)

PER CAPITA GDP: $900

INDUSTRIES: food processing, beverages, clothing and textiles

MINERALS: gold, potash, zinc, copper, salt, possibly oil and natural gas

CHIEF CROPS: sorghum, lentils, vegetables, corn, cotton, tobacco, coffee, sisal

GOVERNMENT TYPE: in transition

CAPITAL: Asmara (pop., 556,000)

INDEPENDENCE DATE: May 24, 1993

WEBSITE: www.state.gov/r/pa/ei/bgn/2854.htm

Rashaida family

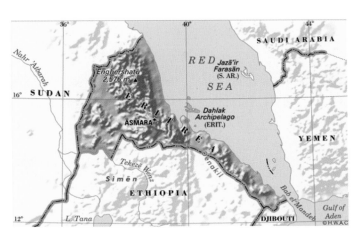

The Republic of Estonia is bordered by Russia in the east along Lake Peipus, and Latvia on the south. The Gulf of Finland lies to the north, the Gulf of Riga to the southwest. Marshy lowlands dominate the country's terrain. Offshore are the large islands of Saaremaa, Hiiumaa and the smaller Muhu. Wet, moderate winters and cool summers typify the maritime climate. The economy benefits from a strong electronics and telecommunications sector. Oil shale, phosphorus, limestone and blue clay are the chief natural resources. Meat, milk, butter, cheese, potatoes, livestock and fish are the chief agricultural products. Leading industries are engineering, electronics, wood and wood products, and textiles. Machinery and equipment, wood and paper, and textiles go mostly to Finland, Sweden, Latvia, Russia and Germany.

Estonians, closely related to the Finns, form more than two thirds of the population. Another quarter are Russians. Ukrainians, Belarusians and Finns make up a small minority. Estonian is the official language.

Most of the people are Lutheran. Tallinn, the capital, is the largest city.

> **Did you know?** Estonia, along with Latvia and Lithuania, split from the Soviet Union in 1991.

The early Estonians were under the rule successively of the Danes, Teutonic Knights, Sweden, and finally, after 1721, Tsarist Russia. In 1918 Estonia became independent, but was annexed to the Soviet Union as a union republic in 1940. On Sept. 6, 1991, Estonia regained its independence. It became a member of the European Union on May 1, 2004.

AREA: 17,462 sq mi (45,226 sq km)

■ **CLIMATE:** Wet, moderate winters and cool summers typify the maritime climate.

■ **PEOPLE:** Estonians, closely related to the Finns, form more than two thirds of the population. Another quarter are Russians. Ukrainians, Belarusians and Finns make up a small minority.

POPULATION: 1,324,333

LIFE EXPECTANCY AT BIRTH (YEARS): male, 65.8; female, 77.3

LITERACY RATE: 100%

ETHNIC GROUPS: Estonian 65%, Russian 28%

PRINCIPAL LANGUAGES: Estonian (official), Russian, Ukrainian, Finnish

Tallinn

CHIEF RELIGIONS: Evangelical Lutheran, Russian Orthodox, Estonian Orthodox

■ **ECONOMY:** The economy benefits from a strong electronics and telecommunications sector. Machinery and equipment, wood and paper, and textiles go mostly to Finland, Sweden, Latvia, Russia and Germany.

MONETARY UNIT: kroon

GDP: $19.2 billion (2004 est.)

PER CAPITA GDP: $14,300

INDUSTRIES: engineering, electronics, wood and wood products, textile, information technology, telecommunications

MINERALS: oil shale, peat, phosphorite, clay, limestone, sand, dolomite, sea mud

CHIEF CROPS: potatoes, vegetables

CAPITAL: Tallinn (pop., 391,000)

INDEPENDENCE DATE: August 20, 1991

GOVERNMENT TYPE: republic

WEBSITE: www.riik.ee/en/

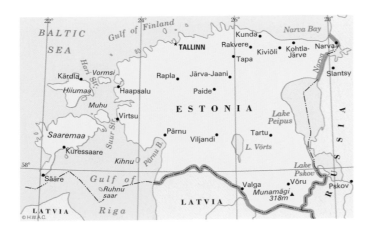

Ethiopia is a large landlocked country in Northeast Africa with a unique people and history. In the center of the country is a high, partly mountainous plateau cut by many rivers and split diagonally by the Great Rift Valley. The land gradually slopes to lowlands in the west and to a plains region in the southeast. The major rivers are the Blue Nile, the Wabe-Shebele-Wenz and the Omo Wenz. Although Ethiopia is quite close to the Equator, there is a wide variation in climate due to the extensive range of topography. Apart from coffee, agriculture consists mostly of subsistence crops - cereals, pulses, sorghum, cane sugar and livestock raising. Industries include textiles, processed foods, construction, cement and hydroelectric power. Coffee, Ethiopia's largest export, generates more than half of its total export earnings. Other exports include qat, gold, leather products, livestock and oilseeds. Main trading partners are Djibouti, Germany, Japan, Saudi Arabia, the United States, United Arab Emirates and Italy. Ethiopia faces difficult economic problems as it is one of the poorest and least developed countries in Africa.

The dominant Amhara of the highlands along with the Tigreans make up 32 percent of the population and are mostly Christian. The Oromo (Galla), of whom some are Christian and some are Muslim, constitute 40 percent of the population. Other groups include the Somali, Sidama, Gurage, Wolaita and Afar. Amhara is the official language. Addis Ababa is the capital and only large city.

Did you know? Ethiopia traces its origins back to the ancient African kingdom of Aksum.

Ethiopia's southeast boundary is in dispute with Somalia.

Isolated from outside influences, Ethiopia developed a culture still suggestive of Biblical times. Among its proudest traditions is that of the descent of Ethiopian emperors from King Solomon and the Queen of Sheba. Christianity was introduced in the fourth century A.D. Emperor Menelik II consolidated the nation during his reign from 1889 to 1913 and defeated an invading Italian army in 1896. The Italians occupied Ethiopia in 1936, but in World War II, British forces drove out the Italians. In 1952 Eritrea was joined to Ethiopia. Army officers brought down the government of Emperor Haile Selassie in 1974. A brutal Marxist regime followed. A revolt for independence raged in Eritrea during this time. Authoritarian government was overthrown in 1991 and was replaced with a more democratic regime. Eritrea broke off from Ethiopia in 1993. The boundaries between the two countries are still in dispute.

AREA: 435,186 sq mi (1,127,127 sq km)

CLIMATE: Though close to the Equator, there is a wide variation in climate due to the extensive range of topography.

Gondar-Facilides Castle

PEOPLE: Three-fourths of the population are Oromo, Amhara, and Tigreans, but there are many other ethnic groups including the Somali, Sidama, Gurage, Wolaita and Afar.

POPULATION: 74,777,981

LIFE EXPECTANCY AT BIRTH (YEARS): male, 40.0; female, 41.8

LITERACY RATE: 35.5%

ETHNIC GROUPS: Oromo 40%, Amhara and Tigre 32%, Sidamo 9%, Shankella 6%, Somali 6%, Afar 4%, Gurage 2%

PRINCIPAL LANGUAGES: Amharic, Tigrinya, Oromigna, Guaragigna, Somali, Arabic, over 200 other languages

CHIEF RELIGIONS: Muslim 45-50%, Ethiopian Orthodox 35-40%, animist 12%

ECONOMY: Coffee is more than half of the total export earnings. Other exports include qat, gold, livestock and leather products. Trading partners include Djibouti, Germany, Japan, Saudi Arabia and the United States.

CAPITAL: Addis Ababa (pop., 2,723,000)

INDEPENDENCE DATE: more than 2,000 years ago (ancient kingdom of Aksum)

GOVERNMENT TYPE: federal republic

MONETARY UNIT: birr

GDP: $54.9 billion (2004 est.)

PER CAPITA GDP: $800

INDUSTRIES: food processing, beverages, textiles, chemicals, metals processing, cement

MINERALS: small reserves of gold, platinum, copper, potash, natural gas

CHIEF CROPS: cereals, pulses, coffee, oilseed, sugarcane, potatoes, qat

WEBSITE: www.ethiopianembassy.org

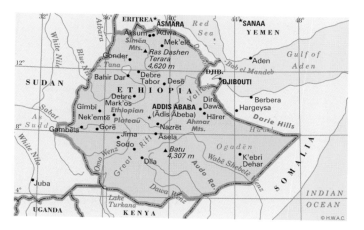

Fiji consists of about 320 Pacific islands, the largest of which is Viti Levu, occupying more than half of Fiji's land area and the seat of the capital and chief city, Suva. Vanua Levu is next in area, while the small island of Rotuma, which lies 240 miles north of Vanua Levu, is third. The larger islands are mountainous and surrounded by coral reefs. The windward sides are covered with tropical forests; the leeward sides contain grassy plains. The tropical marine climate has only slight seasonal temperature variation. Fiji's natural resources consist of timber, fish, gold and copper. Other important industries include sugar and garments. Fiji is a leading voice for the South Pacific in the United Nations. In commerce, Fiji is a transshipment point for trade with the Pacific Islands. The United States, Australia, Western Europe, the Pacific Islands and Japan receive Fiji's exports, which include sugar, garments, gold, timber, fish, mineral water and coconut products. Tourist revenue is increasing. The indigenous Fijians, who constitute more than half of the population, are Melanesians. More than a third of the population is descended from Indian laborers who came to Fiji in the late nineteenth century. There are also small groups of Europeans and Chinese. Half the people are Christian, 38 percent are Hindu, and 8 percent Muslim. English is the official language; Fijian and Hindi are spoken.

Did you know? Only about 100 of Fiji's more than 300 islands and islets are inhabited.

The first European contact with Fiji was by the Dutch navigator Tasman in 1643. In the following century, Captain James Cook reached other islands in the group. Missionaries soon followed and converted native chiefs to Christianity in the early nineteenth century. Britain annexed the islands in 1874. In 1970 Fiji won independence and joined the United Nations.

AREA: 7,054 sq mi (18,270 sq km)

CLIMATE: The tropical marine climate has only slight seasonal temperature variation.

PEOPLE: Fijians (Melanesians) form more than half of the population. Another third are Indo-Fijian. There are also small groups of Europeans and Chinese.

POPULATION: 905,949

LIFE EXPECTANCY AT BIRTH (YEARS): male, 66.7; female, 71.8

LITERACY RATE: 92.5%

Rural Fiji

ETHNIC GROUPS: Fijian 51%, Indian 44%

PRINCIPAL LANGUAGES: English (official), Fijian, Hindustani

CHIEF RELIGIONS: Christian 52%, Hindu 38%, Muslim 8%

ECONOMY: Fiji's exports, which include sugar, garments, gold, timber, fish and mineral water go mainly to the United States, Australia, Western Europe, the Pacific Islands and Japan. Tourist revenue is increasing.

MONETARY UNIT: Fiji dollar

GDP $5.2 billion (2004 est.)

PER CAPITA GDP: $5,900

INDUSTRIES: tourism, sugar, clothing, copra, small cottage industries

MINERALS: gold, copper, offshore oil potential

CHIEF CROPS: sugarcane, coconuts, cassava, rice, sweet potatoes, bananas

GOVERNMENT TYPE: republic

CAPITAL: Suva (pop., 210,000)

INDEPENDENCE DATE: October 19, 1970

WEBSITE: www.fiji.gov.fj

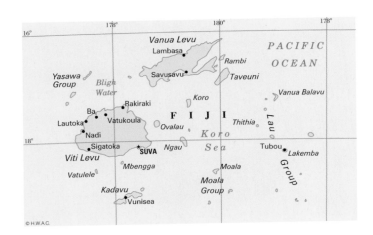

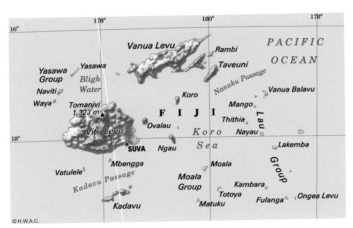

inland, the land of lakes, is fronted by the Gulf of Bothnia on the west and the Gulf of Finland on the south. Sweden, Norway and Russia are its land neighbors. Forests cover 70 percent of its land area. Swamps and the mostly flat plains give way to low mountains in the far north. Offshore between Finland and Sweden is the Ahvenanmaa Archipelago (Åland Islands). The North Atlantic Current, Baltic Sea and the more than 60,000 lakes modify the cold and temperate climate. Mineral resources include zinc, chromium, nickel, copper and iron ore. Vast forests supply a major timber, paper and pulp industry. Agriculturally, livestock and dairy production predominate. The main crops are cereals, sugar beets and potatoes. Fishing is also important.

Besides pulp and paper, shipbuilding, metal products, machinery, furniture, textiles, chemicals, electronics and electrical equipment are important manufactures. The European Union, Russia, United States and China receive most of Finland's exports.

Most of the population is Finnish, but there is a small Swedish-speaking minority along the coast, and a tiny Lapp group in the north. More than 85 percent of the population is Lutheran. Finnish, the official language, is spoken by 93 percent of the population. Swedish, the other official language is spoken by 6 percent. Helsinki is the capital and largest city. The Finns entered what is now Finland by the eighth century A.D.

Did you know? Nearly one-third of Finland lies north of the Arctic Circle.

Beginning in 1200, Sweden gradually conquered Finland. Finland was lost to Russia in 1809, which made it a grand duchy with considerable autonomy. Finnish independence was proclaimed in 1917. In 1939, Soviet troops invaded Finland. Despite strong resistance, Finland was ultimately defeated and forced to cede one-tenth of its territory to the U.S.S.R. In 1941 Finland fought again against the Soviets, but defeat in 1944 forced it to cede additional areas to the U.S.S.R. The last fifty years have seen the growth of a strong Finnish economy. Finland joined the European Union on January 1, 1995.

AREA: 130,130 sq mi (337,030 sq km)

CLIMATE: The North Atlantic Current, Baltic Sea and the more than 60,000 lakes modify the cold and temperate climate.

PEOPLE: Most of the population is Finnish, but there is a small Swedish-speaking minority along the coast, and a tiny Lapp group in the north.

POPULATION: 5,207,000

Savonlinna Heinäkuu

LIFE EXPECTANCY AT BIRTH (YEARS): male, 74.3; female, 81.7

LITERACY RATE: 100%

ETHNIC GROUPS: Finnish 93%, Swedish 6%

PRINCIPAL LANGUAGES: Finnish, Swedish (both official); Russian, Sami

CHIEF RELIGION: Evangelical Lutheran 89%

ECONOMY: Besides pulp and paper, metals, machinery, chemicals and electronics are important exports. Trading partners include the European Union, Russia, United States and China.

MONETARY UNIT: euro

GDP: $136.2 billion (2002 est.)

PER CAPITA GDP: $26,200

INDUSTRIES: metal products, electronics, shipbuilding, pulp and paper, copper refining, foodstuffs, chemicals, textiles, clothing

MINERALS: copper, zinc, iron ore, silver

CHIEF CROPS: barley, wheat, sugar beets, potatoes

GOVERNMENT TYPE: republic

CAPITAL: Helsinki (pop., 936,000)

INDEPENDENCE DATE: December 6, 1917

WEBSITE: www.finland.fi

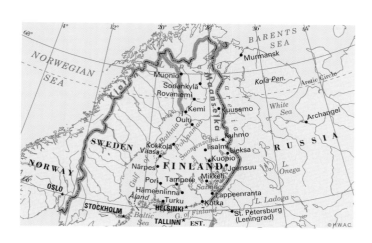

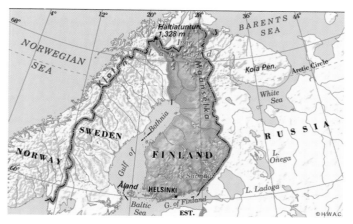

The name La Belle France evokes images of famed cuisine, fine wines and sophistication in a beautiful landscape. The country experiences generally cool winters and mild summers, with mild winters and hot summers along the Mediterranean Sea. Temperatures can be colder inland at higher elevations. Location gave France secure boundaries on four sides - the English Channel on the north, the Atlantic Ocean on the west, the Mediterranean Sea and the Pyrenees in the south and the Alps on the southeast. As a result France has enjoyed relatively stable borders for the last 400 years. In the northwest, Brittany and Normandy are set apart from the rest of France because of their Celtic and Norse beginnings. The Loire valley is noted for its agricultural riches in its vineyards as well as for its magnificent chateaux. In the south Provence is celebrated for its sunny Mediterranean climate along the Riviera and for the vineyards of the Rhône valley. Languedoc's inhabitants speak a dialect almost separate from French, while Auvergne is famous for its location in the heart of the mountainous Massif Central. The Alsace and Lorraine regions have strong Germanic roots. Île de France is home to the center of French unity, the capital and metropolis of France, the city of Paris.

Did you know? Known for its art, culture, and beauty, Paris is called the "City of Light."

Historically, the French are a blend of Latin, Celtic and Germanic ethnic strains. There are also Teutonic, Slavic, Sub-Saharan African, Indochinese, and Basque minorities. North African Muslims form the largest foreign minority group. The unity of the French nation developed early, during the late medieval period of the French monarchy. By the French Revolution in the late eighteenth century, France had become a unique blending of geography, people and government into a single whole. Successive regimes, from Napoleon Bonaparte to Charles de Gaulle, have continued this legacy.

France's natural defensive borders, however, have proved less than effective since Bonaparte's day. Defeated by Prussia in the Franco-Prussian War of 1870, it was forced to cede the provinces of Alsace-Lorraine to a newly-constituted German state, against which it waged war twice in the twentieth century: in World War I, when French territory was the site of many major engagements; and again in World War II, when France was overrun and occupied by Nazi Germany in 1940, with the Allied landing in Normandy in June 1944 and subsequent battles leading to its total liberation.

Today, agricultural riches make France one of the world's leading grain producers and exporters. A long tradition of skilled craftsmanship resulted in world leadership in the arts and in production of luxury goods. France holds a leading position in high-tech fields such as aircraft, space orbiting, pharmaceuticals and electronics. France is one of the founding members of the European Union.

Chateau de Fontainebleau

AREA: 211,210 sq mi (547,030 sq km)

CLIMATE: Mediterranean. Temperatures can be colder inland at higher elevations.

PEOPLE: The French are a blend of Latin, Celtic and Germanic ethnic strains. North African Muslims form the largest foreign minority group.

POPULATION: 60,144,000

LIFE EXPECTANCY AT BIRTH (YEARS): male, 75.6; female, 83.1

LITERACY RATE: 99%

ETHNIC GROUPS: French, with Slavic, North African, Indochinese, Basque minorities

PRINCIPAL LANGUAGES: French (official), Italian, Breton, Alsatian (German), Corsican, Gascon, Portuguese, Provençal, Dutch, Flemish, Catalan, Basque, Romani

CHIEF RELIGIONS: Roman Catholic 83-88%, Muslim 5-10%

ECONOMY: Automobiles, aircraft, pharmaceuticals, electronic components, wine and luxury goods are shipped mostly to the European Union and the United States.

CAPITAL: Paris (pop., 9,658,000)

INDEPENDENCE DATE: 486

GOVERNMENT TYPE: republic

MONETARY UNIT: euro

GDP: $1,540 billion (2002 est.)

PER CAPITA GDP: $25,700

INDUSTRIES: machinery, chemicals, automobiles, metallurgy, aircraft, electronics, textiles, food processing, tourism

CHIEF CROPS: wheat, cereals, sugar beets, potatoes, wine grapes

MINERALS: coal, iron ore, bauxite, zinc, potash

WEBSITE: www.ambafrance–us.org

Gabon is the land where, for fifty-three years, the famous medical missionary, Albert Schweitzer, operated a hospital at Lambaréné. Dense equatorial rain forest covers about 85 percent of the entire country. The coastal plain is deeply indented in the north, while inland there are plateaus and mountains through which the major river, the Ogooué, and its tributaries have carved deep valleys and channels. The tropical climate is always hot and humid with two rainy and two dry seasons. Besides petroleum and natural gas, timber, manganese, uranium, iron ore and gold are important resources. Cocoa, coffee, rubber, sugar, and pineapples are the chief cash crops and forestry is important. Crude oil makes up about three quarters of export income, primarily directed toward the United States, China and France.

The Fang is the largest ethnic group, followed by the Eshira, Bapounou, Nzebi and the Bateke/Obamba. French is the official language. Christians make up more than 60 percent of the population. Libreville is the capital and largest city.

Although Portuguese voyagers visited the coastal area in the late fifteenth century, the country remained largely undisturbed by European influences until the mid-nineteenth century, when the French made treaties with coastal monarchs and penetrated the interior. Independence was gained in 1960. The exploitation of large deposits of manganese and uranium in the 1960s and a major offshore oil field in the 1970s has helped make Gabon one of the more prosperous and stable African countries.

Did you know? Three-quarters of Gabon is covered by a dense rain forest.

AREA: 103,347 sq mi (267,667 sq km)

■ **CLIMATE:** The tropical climate is always hot and humid with two rainy and two dry seasons.

■ **PEOPLE:** The Fang is the largest ethnic group, followed by the Eshira, Bapounou, Nzebi and the Bateke/Obamba.

POPULATION: 1,424,906

LIFE EXPECTANCY AT BIRTH (YEARS): male, 54.9; female, 58.1

LITERACY RATE: 63.2%

ETHNIC GROUPS: Fang, Bapounou, Nzebi, Obamba, European

PRINCIPAL LANGUAGES: French (official), Fang, Myene, Nzebi, Bapounou/Eschira, Bandjabi

CHIEF RELIGION: Christian 55-75%

Libreville-Chancery Building

■ **ECONOMY:** One of the richest countries in Africa, crude oil makes up about three quarters of export income. Exports are primarily directed toward the United States, China and France.

MONETARY UNIT: CFA franc

GDP: $8.0 billion (2004 est.)

PER CAPITA GDP: $5,900

INDUSTRIES: food and beverages, textile, lumber, cement, petroleum extraction and refining, mining, chemicals, ship repair

MINERALS: petroleum, manganese, uranium, gold, iron ore

CHIEF CROPS: cocoa, coffee, sugar, palm oil, rubber

GOVERNMENT TYPE: republic

CAPITAL: Libreville (pop., 611,000)

INDEPENDENCE DATE: August 17, 1960

WEBSITE: www.state.gov/r/pa/ei/bgn/2826.htm

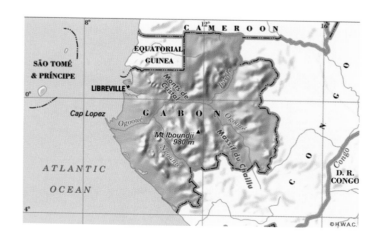

The Gambia in West Africa is a narrow strip seven to twenty miles wide on either side of the Gambia River. The country extends eastward 200 miles from the Atlantic Ocean, and is entirely surrounded by Senegal on the land side. Coastal mangrove swamps graduate to sand hills and plateaus away from the river. The tropical climate is marked by a hot summer rainy season and a cooler dry season in the winter. The economy benefits from a re-export trade built up around its ocean port and low import duties. Peanut products, fish, cotton lint, palm kernels go to India, the European Union and Thailand. Tourism is a growing industry.

The largest ethnic group is the Mandinka, followed by the Fula, Wolof, Jola, Serahule and Serere. Ninety percent of the people are Muslims. English is the official language. Banjul, known as Bathurst in the colonial period, is the capital and largest city.

Reached by Portuguese navigators in the 1400s, the territory became, through purchase in 1588, the first British possession in Africa. In 1965 Gambia became fully independent.

Did you know? This narrow nation lies along both banks of the lower Gambia River.

AREA: 4,363 sq mi (11,300 sq km)

CLIMATE: The tropical climate is marked by a hot summer rainy season and a cooler dry season in the winter.

PEOPLE: The largest ethnic group is the Mandinka, followed by the Fula, Wolof, Jola, Serahule and Serere.

POPULATION: 1,641,564

LIFE EXPECTANCY AT BIRTH (YEARS): male, 52.8; female, 56.9

LITERACY RATE: 47.5%

ETHNIC GROUPS: Mandinka 42%, Fula 18%, Wolof 16%, Jola 10%, Serahuli 9%

PRINCIPAL LANGUAGES: English (official), Mandinka, Wolof, Fula, other native dialects

CHIEF RELIGIONS: Muslim 90%, Christian 9%

ECONOMY: The economy benefits from a re-export trade built up around its ocean port and low import duties. Peanut products, fish, cotton lint, palm kernels go to India, the European Union and Thailand. Tourism is a growing industry.

Banjul Arch

MONETARY UNIT: dalasi

GDP: $2.8 billion (2004 est.)

PER CAPITA GDP: $1,800

INDUSTRIES: processing of peanuts, fish, and hides; tourism; beverages; agricultural machinery assembly; woodworking; metalworking; clothing

CHIEF CROPS: peanuts, millet, sorghum, rice, corn, sesame, cassava, palm kernels

CAPITAL: Banjul (pop., 372,000)

INDEPENDENCE DATE: February 18, 1965

GOVERNMENT TYPE: republic

WEBSITE: www.visitthegambia.gm

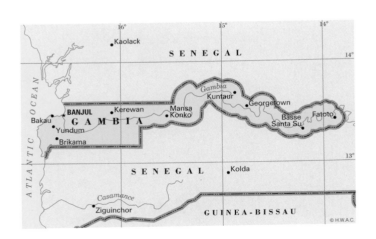

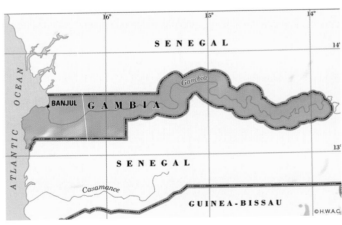

Georgia is mostly mountainous, with the main ridge of the Caucasus (Kavkaz) on the north and the Lesser Kavkaz on the south. Lowlands open to the Black Sea in the west. Good soils occur in the flood plains of the river valleys. The Mediterranean climate is warm and pleasant. The manganese deposits are economically important. Forests, hydropower, coal, iron ore and copper are also significant. Georgia is a major producer of citrus fruits and tea and is also noted for its grapes and excellent wines. The industrial sector produces metals, machinery, aircraft, tower cranes, wood products, chemicals and textiles. Exports, destined for Turkey, Turkmenistan, Russia and Azerbaijan consist of machinery, chemicals, fuel reexports, citrus fruits, tea and wine. The completion in 2005 of the Baku-T'bilisi-Ceyhan oil pipeline and the Baku-T'bilisi-Erzerum gas pipeline for the transport of oil and gas between Europe and Asia has contributed significantly to the economy of the country.

Georgians make up 70 percent of the population. Other important groups include Armenians, Russians and Azerbaijanis. Christians, 83 percent of the population, are followers of the Georgian, Russian and Armenian Orthodox churches; there is a Muslim minority. Georgian is the official language. Tbilisi, the capital, has more than a million inhabitants.

Did you know? Pres. Shevardnadze was the Soviet Union's last foreign minister.

The region was home to the ancient kingdoms of Colchis and Iberia. Christianity entered the area by 400 A.D. The first kingdom of Georgia appeared in 1008. In 1590 the Ottoman Turks conquered Georgia. About two centuries later, in 1801, the area was annexed to Russia. The Soviets made the area the Georgian Soviet Socialist Republic in 1921. In April 1991 Georgia regained its independence. Beset by ethnic and civil strife, Georgia began to stabilize in 1995.

AREA: 26,911 sq mi (69,700 sq km)

■ **CLIMATE:** The Mediterranean climate is mild on the Black Sea coast with cold winters in the mountains.

■ **PEOPLE:** Georgians make up most of the population. Other important groups include Azerbaijanis, Armenians and Russians.

POPULATION: 4,661,473

LIFE EXPECTANCY AT BIRTH (YEARS): male, 72.4; female, 79.4

LITERACY RATE: 99%

Tbilisi-Old Town, Turkish bath houses

ETHNIC GROUPS: Georgian 70%, Armenian 8%, Russian 6%, Azeri 6%

PRINCIPAL LANGUAGES: Georgian (official), Russian, Armenian, Azeri, Abkhaz (official in Abkhazia)

CHIEF RELIGIONS: Georgian Orthodox 65%, Muslim 11%, Russian Orthodox 10%, Armenian Apostolic 8%

■ **ECONOMY:** Exports, destined for Turkey, Turkmenistan, Russia and Azerbaijan consist of machinery, chemicals, citrus fruits, tea and wine. An oil/gas pipeline to Turkey has contributed significantly to the economy.

MONETARY UNIT: lari

GDP: $14.5 billion (2004 est.)

PER CAPITA GDP: $3,100

INDUSTRIES: steel, aircraft, machine tools, electrical appliances, mining, chemicals, wood products, wine

MINERALS: manganese, iron ore, copper, coal, oil

CHIEF CROPS: citrus, grapes, tea, vegetables

GOVERNMENT TYPE: republic

CAPITAL: Tbilisi (pop., 1,064,000)

INDEPENDENCE DATE: April 9, 1991

WEBSITE: www.parliament.ge

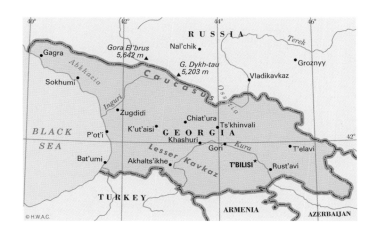

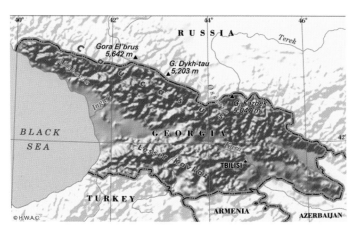

Germany, in the heart of Europe, has been a major participant in European history since medieval times. The country is generally flat in the north and hilly in the central areas, rising to more than 4,000 feet above sea level in the Black Forest and to more than twice that height in the Bavarian Alps. Germany's historic rivers are the Rhine, Danube and Elbe. The climate is temperate and marine-influenced, with cool, cloudy wet winters and summers. Germany is a major producer of hard coal, natural gas, iron, lignite and potash. Agriculture is well diversified in crop and livestock farming. Potatoes, wheat, sugar beets, barley and grapes are important. Germany has an advanced market economy and is a world leader in exports. Highly skilled workers in world-class enterprises manufacture technologically advanced goods. The nation ranks among the largest producers of iron and steel, coal, chemicals, electrical products, ships, vehicles, and electronics in the global economy. Chemicals, motor vehicles, iron and steel products, manufactured goods, textiles and electrical products are shipped mostly to the European Union and the United States. German beer and wine are world famous.

Germans constitute 95 percent of the population. Turks and other eastern and southern European people make up a small but growing group. German is the universal language. Religious adherents are nearly equally divided between Roman Catholics and Protestants; there is a small Muslim minority. Germany's great cities are Berlin, Hamburg, Munich and Cologne. The capital is gradually being shifted from Bonn to Berlin.

> **Did you know?** The environmentalist Green Party helps govern Germany.

For most of Germany's history, political unification proved to be beyond reach. In the eighteenth century, Prussia began to emerge as an important power, and by 1871 the Prussian king was proclaimed emperor of a united Germany. Germany was defeated in World War I, 1914-1918, and the 1930s saw the country's transformation into a brutal police state under the National Socialist Party (Nazis) led by Adolf Hitler. World War II, which resulted in the extermination of 6,000,000 European Jews, ended in total German defeat. Germany was shorn of its eastern territory in East Prussia and Silesia. Millions of lives were lost during the war and in the lost territories after the war. In 1949 Germany was divided into a democratic Federal Republic in the west and a Communist German Democratic Republic in the east. The collapse of Communism throughout Eastern Europe beginning in 1989 resulted in the dissolution of the German Democratic Republic and its absorption into the Federal Republic. The reunited nation has experienced difficulties in modernizing East Germany and integrating

Traditional town plaza

it into the Federal Republic. Germany is one of the founding members of the European Community.

AREA: 137,847 sq mi (357,021 sq km)

CLIMATE: The climate is temperate and marine-influenced, with cool, cloudy wet winters and summers.

PEOPLE: Most of the people are German. Turks and other eastern and southern European people make up a small but growing group.

POPULATION: 82,422,299

LIFE EXPECTANCY AT BIRTH (YEARS): male, 75.5; female, 81.6

LITERACY RATE: 99%

ETHNIC GROUPS: German 92%, Turkish 2%

PRINCIPAL LANGUAGES: German (official), Turkish, Italian, Greek, English, Danish, Dutch, Slavic languages

CHIEF RELIGIONS: Protestant 34%, Roman Catholic 34%, Muslim 4%

ECONOMY: Chemicals, motor vehicles, iron and steel products, textiles and electrical products are shipped mostly to the European Union and the United States. German beer and wine are world famous.

MONETARY UNIT: euro

GDP: $2.174 trillion (2001 est.)

PER CAPITA GDP: $26,200

INDUSTRIES: mining, steel, cement, chemicals, machinery, vehicles, machine tools, electronics, food and beverages, shipbuilding, textiles

MINERALS: iron ore, coal, potash, lignite, uranium, copper, natural gas, salt, nickel

CHIEF CROPS: potatoes, wheat, barley, sugar beets, fruit, cabbages

GOVERNMENT TYPE: republic

CAPITAL: Berlin (pop., 3,327,000)

INDEPENDENCE DATE: January 18, 1871

WEBSITE: www.germany–info.org

Ghana, known as the Gold Coast during the colonial period, is situated on the Gulf of Guinea and is bordered by Côte d'Ivoire on the west, Burkina Faso on the north and Togo on the east. The coastline is a mostly low sandy shore, backed by plains and intersected by rivers, the greatest of which is the Volta. Northward is a belt of tropical rainforest, broken by densely forested hills and rivers. The far north is a region covered by savanna and grassy plains. In the center of the country is Lake Volta, a reservoir formed by the backed-up waters of the Volta River lying behind Akosombo Dam. The tropical climate ranges from warm to hot and humid along the coast to hot and dry in the north. True to its old name, Ghana has significant deposits of gold. Diamonds, manganese and bauxite are also important resources. Cocoa is by far the leading cash crop. Other crops are rice, coffee, cassava and peanuts. There is also a commercial tuna fishing industry. The major industrial activity is the smelting of bauxite into aluminum. Exports, consisting of gold, timber, tuna, bauxite and aluminum, are shipped to Germany, the United States, the United Kingdom and Japan. Tourism has become one of Ghana's largest foreign income earners

Did you know? Ghana's Lake Volta is one of the largest artificially created lakes in the world.

Most of the population is Black African. The major tribes include the Akan (including the Asante), the Moshi-Dagomba, the Ewe, the Ga and the Gurma. Indigenous beliefs have the largest groups of religious followers. Muslims and Christians form lesser groups. English is the official language, but the languages of the various ethnic groups are in common use. Accra is the capital and largest city.

Independent kingdoms comprised Ghana in precolonial times. Following the arrival of the Portuguese in the fifteenth century, the coastal region soon became known as the Gold Coast because of the rich trade in that metal. The gold trade later gave way to the slave trade, which was eventually abolished by the British in the nineteenth century. In 1874 Britain established the colony of the Gold Coast. In 1957 the state of Ghana obtained independence, becoming the first black African colony of a European power to do so.

AREA: 92,456 sq mi (239,460 sq km)

CLIMATE: From warm and dry along the coast to hot and humid in the southwest, the climate becomes hot and dry in the north.

PEOPLE: The principal ethnic groups are the Akan (including the Asante), the Moshi-Dagomba, the Ewe and the Ga.

POPULATION: 22,409,572

LIFE EXPECTANCY AT BIRTH (YEARS): male, 55.4; female, 57.2

LITERACY RATE: 64.5%

Gold mining

ETHNIC GROUPS: Akan 44%, Moshi-Dagomba 16%, Ewe 13%, Ga 8%, Gurma 3%, Yoruba 1%

PRINCIPAL LANGUAGES: English (official); about 75 African languages, including Akan, Moshi-Dagomba, Ewe, and Ga

CHIEF RELIGIONS: Christian 63%, indigenous beliefs 21%, Muslim 16%

ECONOMY: Tourism has become one of Ghana's largest foreign income earners. Exports of gold, cocoa, timber, tuna, bauxite and aluminum, are shipped to the European Union, the United States and Japan.

MONETARY UNIT: cedi

GDP: $48.3 billion (2004 est.)

PER CAPITA GDP: $2,300

INDUSTRIES: mining, lumbering, light manufacturing, aluminum smelting, food processing

MINERALS: gold, diamonds, bauxite, manganese

CHIEF CROPS: cocoa, rice, coffee, cassava, peanuts, corn, shea nuts, bananas

GOVERNMENT TYPE: republic

CAPITAL: Accra (pop., 1,847,000)

INDEPENDENCE DATE: March 6, 1957

WEBSITE: www.ghana.gov.gh

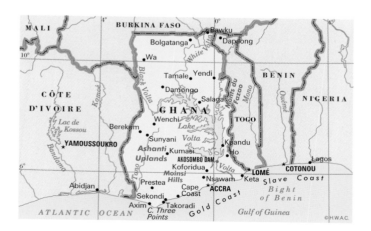

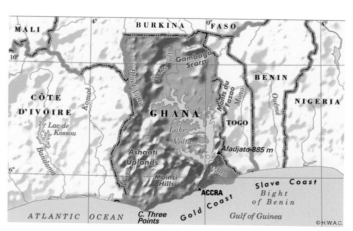

The ancient Greeks are considered to have been the founders of Western civilization and were leaders in art, literature and philosophy. Some of the Hellenic city-states were the world's first democracies. Modern Greece occupies the southern part of the Balkan peninsula and more than 3,000 offshore islands. The large island of Crete is the most prominent. The country is predominantly mountainous, dry and rocky. The coastline is broken up into many peninsulas. Greece has a temperate Mediterranean climate, with mild, wet winters and hot, dry summers. The chief mineral resources are bauxite, lignite, nickel, magnesite, oil and marble. Wheat, corn, sugar beets, olives and olive oil, tomatoes, wine, tobacco, grapes, citrus, livestock and dairy products are the most important agricultural products. Processed foods, textiles, metals, chemicals, petroleum products, and electrical power are the major industries. Food and beverages, manufactured goods, petroleum products, chemicals, textiles, tobacco and olive oil are the chief exports, mainly to the European Union and the United States. Tourism and the Greek merchant marine contribute much to the economy.

Did you know? The Olympics started in Greece; Athens will host the 2004 games.

Greeks constitute 98 percent of the population, and 98 percent are followers of the Greek Orthodox faith. Greek is the universal language. Athens is the capital and greatest city. Thessaloníki is second in size.

Following the golden age of Greece in the fifth century B.C., Greek civilization was spread widely by the conquests of the Macedonian monarch, Alexander the Great. Later, after years of Roman domination, a rebirth of Greek power occurred in the Byzantine Empire of the Middle Ages. This renaissance was eclipsed, however, with the conquest of Greece by the Ottoman Turks in the 1400s. Modern Greece first obtained its freedom in the war of independence against the Turks, 1821-30. The European powers, who had intervened on Greece's behalf, chose a German prince as the nation's first monarch, later to be succeeded by a Danish prince. Greece suffered badly in the Nazi German occupation during World War II and during the civil war between Communist and royalist guerrillas from 1944-1950. The monarchy was overthrown by the military in 1967 and a republic was proclaimed in 1973. Civilian rule returned in 1974.

Greece became a member of the European Union on January 1, 1981.

AREA: 50,940 sq mi (131,940 sq km)

■ **CLIMATE:** Greece has a temperate Mediterranean climate, with mild, wet winters and hot, dry summers.

Santorini

■ **PEOPLE:** Greeks constitute nearly all of the population.

POPULATION: 10,976,000

LIFE EXPECTANCY AT BIRTH (YEARS): male, 76.3; female, 81.7

LITERACY RATE: 97%

ETHNIC GROUPS: Greek 98%

PRINCIPAL LANGUAGES: Greek (official), English, French

CHIEF RELIGIONS: Greek Orthodox (official) 98%, Muslim 1%

■ **ECONOMY:** Food and beverages, petroleum products, chemicals, textiles, tobacco and olive oil are the chief exports, mainly to the European Union and the United States. Tourism and the Greek merchant marine contribute much to the economy.

GOVERNMENT TYPE: parliamentary republic

CAPITAL: Athens (pop., 3,120,000)

INDEPENDENCE DATE: 1829

MONETARY UNIT: euro

GDP: $201.1 billion (2002 est.)

PER CAPITA GDP: $19,000

INDUSTRIES: tourism, food and tobacco processing, textiles, chemicals, metal products, mining, petroleum

MINERALS: bauxite, lignite, magnesite, petroleum, marble

CHIEF CROPS: wheat, corn, barley, sugar beets, olives, tomatoes, tobacco, potatoes

WEBSITE: www.greekembassy.org

The southernmost of the Windward Islands, the island nation of Grenada also includes the island of Carriacou. Volcanic in origin, the islands are chiefly mountainous. The climate is tropical, tempered by northeast trade winds, with infrequent hurricanes. Grenada, known as the "Isle of Spice," is famous for its nutmeg, cocoa and cinnamon. Exports go mainly to the Caribbean, the United States, and the Netherlands. Tourism and offshore banking are leading foreign exchange earners.

The great majority of the people are of African descent, with some South Asians (East Indians) and Europeans. English is the official language, and a French patois is spoken. The leading religious groups are Roman Catholic and Anglican. Saint George's is the capital and largest town.

Invading Caribs expelled the original Arawak inhabitants shortly before the visit of Columbus in 1498. French control of Grenada lasted from 1650 to 1762; two hundred years of British rule followed. Independence was attained in 1974, but the radical New Jewel Movement seized the government in 1979. United States armed forces invaded in 1983 at the request of Grenada's Caribbean neighbors, after a coup by a hard-line faction deposed and executed Prime Minister Maurice Bishop, and the government and its Cuban advisors were removed.

Did you know? Grenada is the smallest independent country in the western hemisphere.

Despite a history of infrequent tropical storms, Hurricane Ivan caused catastrophic damage when it struck the island directly in September, 2004. This category 3 intensity storm was followed in July, 2005 by Hurricane Emily, a category 5 storm which caused even more damage. Reconstruction has proceeded quickly, but much work remains.

AREA: 133 sq mi (344 sq km)

■ **CLIMATE:** The climate is tropical, tempered by northeast trade winds, with infrequent hurricanes.

■ **PEOPLE:** The majority of the people are of African descent with some South Asians (East Indians) and Europeans.

POPULATION: 89,703

LIFE EXPECTANCY AT BIRTH (YEARS): male, 62.7; female, 66.3

LITERACY RATE: 98%

Nutmeg factory

ETHNIC GROUPS: black 82%, Creole 13%

PRINCIPAL LANGUAGES: English (official), French patois

CHIEF RELIGIONS: Roman Catholic 53%, Anglican 14%, other Protestant 33%

■ **ECONOMY:** Known as the "Isle of Spice," Grenada is famous for nutmeg and cocoa. Exports go mainly to the Caribbean, the United States, and the Netherlands. Tourism and offshore banking are leading foreign exchange earners.

MONETARY UNIT: East Caribbean dollar

GDP: $440 million (2002 est.)

PER CAPITA GDP: $5,000

INDUSTRIES: food and beverages, textiles, light assembly operations, tourism, construction

CHIEF CROPS: bananas, cocoa, nutmeg, mace, citrus, avocados, root crops, sugarcane, corn, vegetables

CAPITAL: Saint George's (pop., 33,000)

INDEPENDENCE DATE: February 7, 1974

GOVERNMENT TYPE: parliamentary democracy

WEBSITE: www.grenadagrenadines.com

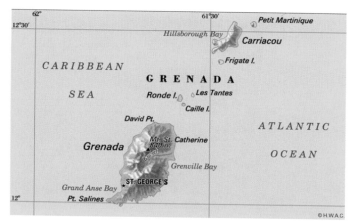

Guatemala is the most populous country in Central America. The central highlands region forms one-fifth of the country's land surface. The Pacific plain is a narrow belt between the mountains and the ocean. While Caribbean lowlands consist of fertile river valleys, the lowland forest of Petén dominates the northern part of the country. The tropical climate is hot and humid in the lowlands, but cooler in the highlands. The chief natural resources are petroleum, nickel, rare woods and fish.

Agriculture dominates the country's economy and exports. The principal crops are sugarcane, coffee, bananas, cardamom, cotton, rice and rubber. Livestock ranching is important. Light manufacturing of clothing and textiles, prepared foods, construction materials, tires and pharmaceuticals form the chief industrial activities. Coffee, bananas, sugar, crude oil, chemical products, clothing, textiles and vegetables are shipped primarily to the United States, Central America and Mexico.

Ethnically the population is divided almost equally between those of Indian ancestry and those of mixed Indian and European ancestry. Spanish, the official language, is spoken by 60 percent of the population. Indian languages, largely Mayan, are spoken by the remaining 40 percent. Roman Catholicism is the dominant religion, although Protestant churches are growing rapidly. The capital, Guatemala, is the largest city.

> **Did you know?**
> Guatemala was the center of the Mayan Empire (3rd-10th cent. AD).

The Mayans flourished in Guatemala before the arrival of the Spanish conquistadors. After gaining its independence from Spain, Guatemala was first annexed to Mexico. It later became part of the United Provinces of Central America. In 1839 Guatemala gained its independence. For more than a century the military governed the country. In the latter part of the twentieth century Guatemala has experienced much political turmoil, with successive governments waging a thirty-six-year-long war against leftist guerrillas. In December 1996 the government signed a peace agreement formally ending the conflict which had left more than 100,000 dead and had created some one million refugees. While conditions have improved, widespread political violence and corruption continue to be a concern.

AREA: 42,043 sq mi (108,890 sq km)

■ **CLIMATE:** The tropical climate is hot and humid in the lowlands, but cooler in the highlands.

Tikal

■ **PEOPLE:** The population is divided between the indigenous Indian people and those of mixed Indian and European ancestry.
POPULATION: 12,293,545
LIFE EXPECTANCY AT BIRTH (YEARS): male, 64.3; female, 66.1
LITERACY RATE: 63.6%
ETHNIC GROUPS: mestizo 55%, Amerindian 43%
PRINCIPAL LANGUAGES: Spanish (official); more than 20 Amerindian languages, including Quiche, Cakchiquel, Kekchi, Mam, Garifuna, and Xinca
CHIEF RELIGIONS: mostly Roman Catholic; some Protestant, indigenous Mayan beliefs
■ **ECONOMY:** Light manufacturing and consumer products form the chief industrial activities. Coffee, bananas, sugar, crude oil, chemical products, clothing, textiles and vegetables are shipped primarily to the United States, Central America and Mexico.
MONETARY UNIT: quetzal
GDP: $59.5 billion (2004 est.)
PER CAPITA GDP: $4,200
INDUSTRIES: sugar, textiles and clothing, furniture, chemicals, petroleum, metals, rubber, tourism
MINERALS: petroleum, nickel
CHIEF CROPS: sugarcane, corn, bananas, coffee, beans, cardamom
GOVERNMENT TYPE: republic
CAPITAL: Guatemala City (pop., 951,000)
INDEPENDENCE DATE: September 15, 1821
WEBSITE: www.guatemala-embassy.org

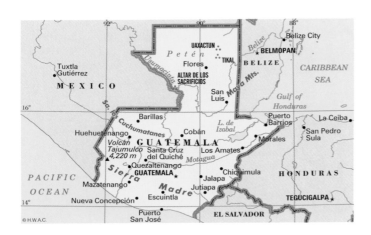

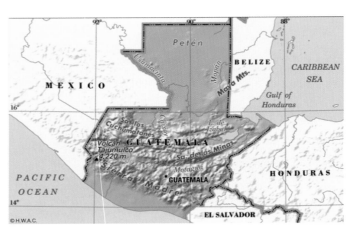

The West African nation of Guinea, one of the world's poorest, consists of a low-lying coastal area, a pastoral plateau, a forest region along the border with Liberia and a dry area in the north. The climate is generally hot and humid. Guinea possesses nearly half of the world's bauxite reserves and is the second largest producer. The production of iron ore and the mining of diamonds are also important. Agriculture is restricted mostly to limited farming of rice, cassava, fonio, millet, corn, coffee, cocoa and pineapples. Alumina and bauxite dominate exports, mainly to the European Union and the United States, along with diamonds, gold and coffee.

The leading ethnic groups are the Peul (Fulani), Malinke and the Soussou. Muslims form the great majority of the population. French is the official language. Each ethnic group has its own language. Conakry is the capital, largest city and chief port.

Between the tenth and fifteenth centuries, Guinea was part of the great African empires of Ghana, Mali and Songhai. From the fifteenth to the nineteenth centuries, Portuguese, Dutch, English and French outposts were established along the cost. A French protectorate was formed in Guinea in 1849. Guinea, the only French West African territory to vote against membership in the French Community, became an independent republic in 1958. The economy has stagnated, as very little foreign investment has been made there.

Did you know? More than one-third of the world's reserves of bauxite are in Guinea.

AREA: 94,926 sq mi (245,857 sq km)

■ **CLIMATE:** The tropical climate is generally hot and humid.

■ **PEOPLE:** The leading ethnic groups are the Peuhl (Fulani), Malinke and the Soussou.

POPULATION: 9,690,222

LIFE EXPECTANCY AT BIRTH (YEARS): male, 48.5; female, 51.0

LITERACY RATE: 35.9%

ETHNIC GROUPS: Peuhl 40%, Malinke 30%, Soussou 20%

PRINCIPAL LANGUAGES: French (official), many African languages

Kissidougou market

CHIEF RELIGIONS: Muslim 85%, Christian 8%, indigenous beliefs 7%

■ **ECONOMY:** Guinea possesses nearly half of the world's bauxite reserves and is the second largest producer. Alumina and bauxite dominate exports, mainly to the European Union and the United States, along with diamonds, gold and coffee.

MONETARY UNIT: franc

GDP: $19.5 billion (2004 est.)

PER CAPITA GDP: $2,100

INDUSTRIES: mining, alumina refining, light manufacturing, agricultural processing

MINERALS: bauxite, iron ore, diamonds, gold, uranium

CHIEF CROPS: rice, coffee, pineapples, palm kernels, cassava, bananas, sweet potatoes

GOVERNMENT TYPE: republic

CAPITAL: Conakry (pop., 1,366,000)

INDEPENDENCE DATE: October 2, 1958

WEBSITE: www.state.gov/r/pa/ei/bgn/2824.htm

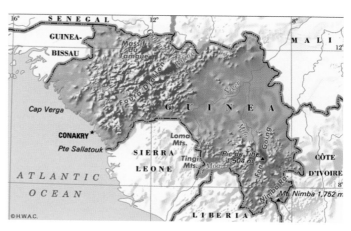

The West African nation of Guinea-Bissau is bordered by Senegal on the north and Guinea on the south. Many islands lying offshore are part of the country. A low coastal plain rises to savanna in the east. The tropical climate is generally hot and humid. Guinea-Bissau is considered one of the poorest countries in the world. Mineral resources consist of little-exploited deposits of bauxite, phosphates and offshore petroleum. Cashews, peanuts, palm kernels and some timber are the chief farm crops, forming nearly 100 percent of exports, which also include fish and shrimp. Guinea-Bissau's exports go primarily to India, the United States and Nigeria.

The largest of the ethnic groups are the Balanta and Fula. There are also smaller groups of Manjaca, Mandinga and Papel. Indigenous beliefs are prevalent, but 30 percent of the population follows Islam. Portuguese is the official language, but Criolo, a creole lingua franca, is spoken throughout Guinea-Bissau. Bissau is the capital.

The Portuguese reached the area in 1446. In 1897 it became a Portuguese colony known as Portuguese Guinea and separated from the Cape Verde islands, to which it had been attached. Years of revolt against the Portuguese began in 1962. In 1974 Guinea-Bissau was the first Portuguese African territory to achieve independence.

Did you know? At carnival time in Guinea-Bissau, people wear masks of sharks, hippos, and bulls.

AREA: 13,946 sq mi (36,120 sq km)

CLIMATE: The tropical climate is generally hot and humid.

PEOPLE: The largest of the ethnic groups are the Balanta and Fula. There are also smaller groups of Manjaca, Mandinga and Papel.

POPULATION: 1,442,029

LIFE EXPECTANCY AT BIRTH (YEARS): male, 45.1; female, 48.9

LITERACY RATE: 34%

ETHNIC GROUPS: Balanta 30%, Fula 20%, Manjaca 14%, Mandinga 13%, Papel 7%

PRINCIPAL LANGUAGES: Portuguese (official), Crioulo, tribal languages

CHIEF RELIGIONS: indigenous beliefs 50%, Muslim 45%, Christian 5%

Bissau seen from Rio Geba

ECONOMY: Cashews, peanuts, palm kernels and some timber are the chief farm crops. Along with fish and shrimp they form nearly all of the country's exports. Guinea-Bissau's exports go primarily to India, the United States and Nigeria.

CAPITAL: Bissau (pop., 336,000)

INDEPENDENCE DATE: September 24, 1973

GOVERNMENT TYPE: republic

MONETARY UNIT: CFA franc

GDP: $1.0 billion (2004 est.)

PER CAPITA GDP: $700

INDUSTRIES: agricultural processing, beer, soft drinks

MINERALS: phosphates, bauxite, petroleum

CHIEF CROPS: rice, corn, beans, cassava, cashew nuts, peanuts, palm kernels, cotton

WEBSITE: www.state.gov/r/pa/ei/bgn/2824.htm

Lying on the northeast coast of South America, the country is divided into a low-lying coastal region, a heavily forested interior and a region of mountains and savanna in the south and west. The Essequibo and the Courantyne are the chief rivers. The tropical climate is moderated by northeast trade winds, with two rainy seasons. Gold, bauxite, diamonds, timber, shrimp and fish are the chief natural resources. Other exports include gold, bauxite, shrimp and timber. Major trading partners include Canada, the United States and the United Kingdom.

Half the population is of East Indian descent, while more than 40 percent are of African and mixed African origin. English is the dominant language. Over half the people are Christian, but a third follow the Hindu religion. Georgetown, the capital, is the only large city.

Originally populated by the Arawak and Carib peoples, Guyana was the subject of contention between the Netherlands and Britain for almost 200 years. Under British rule after 1814, the colony was named British Guiana. In 1966 it became independent and took the name Guyana.

Did you know? Dense forest makes up about 75% of this sparsely populated country.

Conflict between the Hindu majority and the population of African origin has resulted in instability. Guyana became a member of the CARICOM Single Market and Economy in 2006, which should improve economic conditions by increasing markets for its export goods. Venezuela lays claim to all of the area west of the Essequibo River.

AREA: 83,000 sq mi (214,970 sq km)

■ **CLIMATE:** The tropical climate is moderated by northeast trade winds, with two rainy seasons.

■ **PEOPLE:** Half the population is of East Indian descent, while more than 40 percent are of African and mixed African origin.

POPULATION: 767,245

LIFE EXPECTANCY AT BIRTH (YEARS): male, 60.1; female, 64.8

LITERACY RATE: 98.1%

ETHNIC GROUPS: East Indian 50%, black 36%, Amerindian 7%

PRINCIPAL LANGUAGES: English (official), Amerindian dialects, Creole, Hindi, Urdu

CHIEF RELIGIONS: Christian 50%, Hindu 35%, Muslim 10%

■ **ECONOMY:** Sugar and rice are the chief crops and leading agricultural exports. Other exports include gold, bauxite, shrimp and timber. Major trading partners include Canada, the United States and the United Kingdom.

MONETARY UNIT: Guyana dollar

GDP: $2.9 billion (2004 est.)

PER CAPITA GDP: $3,800

INDUSTRIES: sugar, rice milling, timber, textiles, mining

CHIEF CROPS: sugar, rice, wheat, vegetable oils

MINERALS: bauxite, gold, diamonds

CAPITAL: Georgetown (pop., 231,000)

INDEPENDENCE DATE: May 26, 1966

GOVERNMENT TYPE: republic

WEBSITE: www.guyana.org

Guyanese rain forest

Haiti occupies the western third of the island of Hispaniola in the Caribbean Sea. Its only land border is with the Dominican Republic on the east. About two-thirds of the country is mountainous and unsuitable for cultivation. The climate is largely tropical, but is semiarid where the mountains in the east cut off the trade winds. Mineral resources are bauxite, copper, calcium carbonate, gold and marble. One of the poorest countries in North America. Handicrafts, electronics assembly, food processing, beverages, tobacco products and light manufacturing contribute to the economy. Apparel, mangoes, leather and raw hides and seafood are the chief exports, which go mainly to the United States.

Nearly all of Haiti's people are of African or African/European descent. French is the official language, but the vast majority speak Creole. Most of the population is Roman Catholic. Voodoo is widely practiced. Port-au-Prince is the capital and only city of more than one million inhabitants.

Haiti came under French control in the late 1600s. Under the leadership of black leaders such as Toussaint Louverture, Dessalines and Christophe, Haiti gradually threw off French rule between 1793 and 1811. From 1915 to 1934 the United States occupied the country. Then, for over 30 years, the Duvalier family — first François "Papa Doc," as President-for-Life, succeeded after his death in 1971 by Jean-Claude "Baby Doc" — ruled Haiti in dictatorial manner, terrorizing opponents utilizing the dreaded Ton-Ton Macoutes, a combination secret police-death squad organization. "Baby Doc" was ousted in 1989, and in 1990 Father Jean-Bertrand Aristede, a progressive priest, was elected President in a free election. Aristede was deposed by the military in 1991, but returned to power when the U.S. intervened militarily in 1994 to return him to office. His term ended in February, 1996.

Did you know? Haiti is the 2nd-oldest republic, after the United States, in the western hemisphere.

Barred from a new term by the constitution, Aristide agreed to step aside and support a presidential election in December, 1995. Rene Preval, who had been Aristide's Prime Minister in 1991, took 88% of the vote, and was sworn in to a 5-year term in February, 1996. In late 1996 Aristide created a new political party and emerged as the easy victor of controversial elections. He became president again in February, 2001.

This did not, however, put an end to political unrest. In February, 2004 Aristide submitted his resignation as President. Despite significant delays presidential elections took place peacefully in February, 2006.

AREA: 10,714 sq mi (27,750 sq km)

Cap Haitien

CLIMATE: The climate is largely tropical, but is semiarid where the mountains in the east cut off the trade winds.

PEOPLE: Nearly all of Haiti's people are of African or African/European descent.

POPULATION: 8,308,504

LIFE EXPECTANCY AT BIRTH (YEARS): male, 50.5; female, 53.1

LITERACY RATE: 45%

PRINCIPAL LANGUAGES: French, Creole (both official)

ETHNIC GROUPS: black 95%, Creole and other 5%

CHIEF RELIGIONS: Roman Catholic 80%, Protestant 16%; voodoo widely practiced

ECONOMY: One of the poorest countries in North America. Handicrafts, electronics assembly, and light manufacturing contribute to the economy. Apparel, mangoes, leather and raw hides and seafood are chief exports, which go mainly to the United States.

MONETARY UNIT: gourde

GDP: $12.1 billion (2004 est.)

PER CAPITA GDP: $1,500

INDUSTRIES: sugar refining, flour milling, textiles, cement, light assembly industries

MINERALS: bauxite, copper, calcium carbonate, gold, marble

CHIEF CROPS: coffee, mangoes, sugarcane, rice, corn, sorghum

GOVERNMENT TYPE: republic

CAPITAL: Port-au-Prince (pop., 1,961,000)

INDEPENDENCE DATE: January 1, 1804

WEBSITE: www.haiti.org

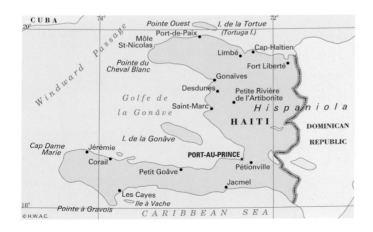

Honduras, located between Guatemala and El Salvador on the west and Nicaragua on the east, fronts on the Caribbean Sea on the north, and has a small Pacific coastline at the Golfo de Fonseca in the south. Except for the Caribbean and Pacific coastal plains, the country is generally mountainous. The climate is subtropical in the lowlands and temperate in the mountains. Gold, silver, lead and zinc are mined. Coffee, bananas, shrimp and lobster, sugar, fruits, basic grains and livestock are the leading agricultural products. Apparel, coffee, shrimp, bananas, palm oil, gold, melons, lobster, lumber and sugar are leading exports, which go mainly to the United States. Honduras has little industry and is one of the poorest countries in the Western Hemisphere.

The population is largely of mixed European and Amerindian derivation. Spanish is the official and predominant language. The people are overwhelmingly Roman Catholic in religion. Tegucigalpa, the capital, and San Pedro Sula are the largest cities.

The Mayan civilization flowered and was centered here before the arrival of Columbus in 1502. Under Spanish rule, Honduras was part of the captaincy general of Guatemala. Spanish rule was overthrown in 1821. In 1838 Honduras became an independent republic, separated from the Central American Federation. In 1969, El Salvador and Honduras fought the brief "Soccer War" over disputed border areas. In 1992, the International Court of Justice awarded most of the disputed territory to Honduras, although delays continue due to technical difficulties. However, Honduras and El Salvador maintain normal diplomatic and trade relations. Honduras also has unresolved maritime border disputes with El Salvador, Nicaragua, Jamaica, and Cuba.

Did you know? About 90% of Hondurans are mestizo (of Spanish and Indian ancestry).

AREA: 43,278 sq mi (112,090 sq km)

◼ CLIMATE: The climate is subtropical in the lowlands and temperate in the mountains.

◼ PEOPLE: The population is mostly of mixed mixed Indian and European descent.

POPULATION: 7,326,496

LIFE EXPECTANCY AT BIRTH (YEARS): male, 65.0; female, 67.4

LITERACY RATE: 74%

Palacio Municipal

ETHNIC GROUPS: mestizo 90%, Amerindian 7%, black 2%, white 1%

PRINCIPAL LANGUAGES: Spanish (official), Garífuna, Amerindian dialects

CHIEF RELIGION: Roman Catholic 97%

◼ ECONOMY: One of the poorest countries in North America. Handicrafts, electronics assembly, and light manufacturing contribute to the economy. Apparel, mangoes, leather and raw hides and seafood are chief exports, which go mainly to the United States.

MONETARY UNIT: lempira

GDP: $18.8 billion (2004 est.)

PER CAPITA GDP: $2,800

INDUSTRIES: sugar, coffee, textiles, clothing, wood products

MINERALS: gold, silver, copper, lead, zinc, iron ore, antimony, coal

CHIEF CROPS: bananas, coffee, citrus

CAPITAL: Tegucigalpa (pop., 1,007,000)

INDEPENDENCE DATE: September 15, 1821

GOVERNMENT TYPE: republic

WEBSITE: www.hondurasemb.org

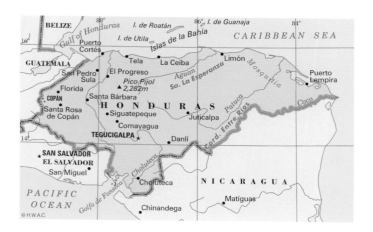

Present-day Hungary includes less than one-third the area that made up the Kingdom of Hungary in the old Austro-Hungarian monarchy before 1918. Most of this landlocked Central European country is a flat plain, except for low mountain ranges in the north and near Lake Balaton. Hungary's great river is the Danube; the Tisza and the Drava are also noteworthy. The climate is temperate with cold, cloudy, humid winters and warm summers. Natural resources include bauxite, coal and natural gas. Hungary's rich farmlands produce diversified crops of wheat, corn, sunflower seeds, wine grapes, potatoes and sugar beets, and there is a well-developed livestock industry. The textile, pharmaceutical, food processing, machinery and motor vehicle industries contribute to a strong economy. Machinery, vehicles, manufactured goods and food products are shipped primarily to countries in the European Union.

Hungarians make up most of the population. There are small Romany, German, and Serb minorities. Large numbers of Hungarians reside outside Hungary's present-day borders in Slovakia, Romania and Serbia. The overwhelmingly dominant language of the people is Hungarian. Sixty-eight percent of the population is Roman Catholic; 25 percent is Protestant. Budapest is the capital and by far the most populous urban center.

Did you know? In 1872 the communities of Buda and Pest united as the city of Budapest.

The Magyars migrated from beyond the Urals near the end of the ninth century A.D., conquering most of present-day Hungary and establishing a dynasty that lasted more than four centuries. The Ottoman Turk conquest of most of Hungary in 1526 resulted in the election of a Hapsburg as ruler of the remainder. By 1686, most of Hungary was liberated from the Turks. Hapsburg rule lasted until 1919, when Hungary was deprived of vast areas that were ceded to Czechoslovakia, Romania and Yugoslavia. Following defeat in World War II, after having sided with Italy and Germany, the country was occupied by Soviet troops. Hungarian Communists seized power by 1949. In 1956 a popular anti-Communist uprising broke out and took over, but was suppressed by Soviet troops. In 1989 the Communists fell from power. Hungary became a member of the European Union on May 1, 2004.

AREA: 35,920 sq mi (93,030 sq km)

■ **CLIMATE:** The climate is temperate with cold, cloudy, humid winters and warm summers.

Budapest-Parliament complex

■ **PEOPLE:** Hungarians make up most of the population. There are small Romany, German, and Serb minorities.

POPULATION: 9,877,000

LIFE EXPECTANCY AT BIRTH (YEARS): male, 67.8; female, 76.8

LITERACY RATE: 99%

ETHNIC GROUPS: Hungarian 90%, Roma 4%, German 3%, Serb 2%

PRINCIPAL LANGUAGES: Hungarian (official), Romani, German, Slavic languages, Romanian

CHIEF RELIGIONS: Roman Catholic 68%, Protestant 25%

■ **ECONOMY:** Hungary's rich farmlands produce a wide range of agricultural products. There is also a well-developed livestock industry. Machinery, vehicles, manufactured goods and food products are shipped primarily to countries in the European Union.

MONETARY UNIT: forint

GDP: $134.7 billion (2002 est.)

PER CAPITA GDP: $13,300

INDUSTRIES: mining, metallurgy, construction materials, processed foods, textiles, pharmaceuticals, motor vehicles

MINERALS: bauxite, coal, natural gas

CHIEF CROPS: wheat, corn, sunflower seed, potatoes, sugar beets

GOVERNMENT TYPE: parliamentary democracy

CAPITAL: Budapest (pop., 1,812,000)

INDEPENDENCE DATE: 1001

WEBSITE: www.eKormanyzat.hu/english

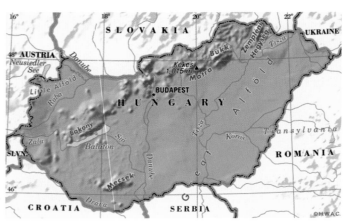

Out in the North Atlantic, closer to Greenland than to Western Europe, lies the rugged, largely desolate island of volcanic origin called Iceland. Its quarter of a million fiercely individualistic inhabitants have a tradition of preserving their heritage. Almost three-quarters of the land consists of glaciers, lakes, a mountainous lava desert and wasteland. The small remainder is used for grazing and cultivation. Most of the inhabitants live on the coast, particularly in the southwest. The temperate climate, moderated by the North Atlantic Current, is marked by mild, windy winters and damp, cool summers. Diatomite is the only significant mineral resource. Geothermal and hydroelectric power are the chief sources of energy. Agriculture is restricted to the growing of potatoes, tomatoes, cucumbers, and turnips and the raising of livestock. Fish processing and aluminum smelting are the most important industries. Ferro-silicon alloy production and information technology also contribute to the economy. Fishing is the most important economic activity, contributing nearly three quarters of the export earnings. Major trading partners include the European Union and the United States. Recent trends in whale watching and ecotourism have expanded tourism. Recent trends in whale watching and ecotourism have expanded tourism.

Did you know? Iceland is home to more than 100 volcanoes and vast lava fields.

The population is a homogeneous mixture of the descendants of Norwegians and Celts, of whom nearly 90 percent are Lutheran. Icelandic is the official and universal language. The capital, Reykjavík, is the only sizable city.

The first permanent settlers arrived from Norway around 870 A.D., bringing with them Irish and Scottish wives and slaves. Originally an independent republic, Iceland came under the rule of the Danish crown in 1381. In 1918 Iceland was declared a sovereign state in union with Denmark. Icelanders voted to terminate that union in 1944 and inaugurated a republic. Iceland has chosen not to join the European Union primarily due to concerns over losing control of fishing resources.

AREA: 39,769 sq mi (103,000 sq km)

■ **CLIMATE:** The temperate climate, moderated by the North Atlantic Current, is mild, with windy winters and damp, cool summers.

■ **PEOPLE:** Most Icelanders are descendants of Norwegian settlers and Celts from the British Isles.

POPULATION: 299,388

LIFE EXPECTANCY AT BIRTH (YEARS): male, 78.2; female, 82.3

Sod-covered rooftops

LITERACY RATE: 99.9%

ETHNIC GROUPS: Icelandic 94%

PRINCIPAL LANGUAGE: Icelandic (official)

CHIEF RELIGION: Evangelical Lutheran 93%

■ **ECONOMY:** Fishing is the most important economic activity, contributing nearly three quarters of the export earnings. Major trading partners include the European Union and the United States. Recent trends in whale watching and ecotourism have expanded tourism.

MONETARY UNIT: krona

GDP: $9.4 billion (2004 est.)

PER CAPITA GDP: $31,900

INDUSTRIES: fish processing, aluminum smelting, ferrosilicon production, geothermal power, tourism

MINERALS: diatomite

CHIEF CROPS: potatoes, turnips

GOVERNMENT TYPE: constitutional republic

CAPITAL: Reykjavík (pop., 184,000)

INDEPENDENCE DATE: June 17, 1944

WEBSITE: www.iceland.is

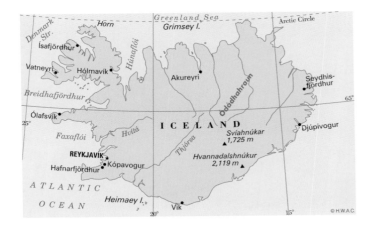

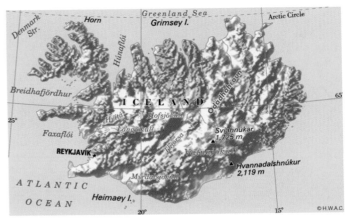

India, occupying most of the Indian subcontinent, is home to more than 800 million people. The country consists of three major topographical areas: the Himalaya mountains, extending along the whole of the northern border; the fertile and heavily population Ganges Plain; and the southern peninsula, including the Deccan Plateau, which is of moderate elevation and is less densely populated. India's great rivers are the Ganges, Brahmaputra, Godavari, Krishna and the Narmada. The climate varies from tropical-monsoon in the south to temperate in the extreme north. India has the fourth-largest coal reserves in the world. Iron ore, manganese, mica, bauxite, titanium ore, chromite, limestone, titanium ore, diamonds, petroleum and natural gas are other important resources. Agriculture dominates the Indian economy. The principal crops are rice, wheat, oilseeds, cotton, jute, tea and sugarcane. India's fish catch ranks among the world's largest. Livestock and poultry are also important. Economic activity is a mixture of traditional village farming, modern agricultural methods, handicrafts and a wide range of modern industries. Textiles, chemicals, food processing, steel, transportarion equipment, fertilizers, cement, mining and petroleum are the most important industrial products. The growing electronic and computer software industry is located in the Bangalore region. Exports of clothing, gems and jewelry, textiles, tea, engineering goods and leather goods flow to the United States, China, the European Union and the United Arab Emirates. Business outsourcing and movie production are growing industries. Tourism is a major contributor to the economy.

> **Did you know?** More than 1,600 languages or dialects are spoken in India.

Two major ethnic strains predominate in India's population; 72 percent are Indo-Aryans who live in the north, and 25 percent are Dravidians who live in the south. An aboriginal population lives in the central part of the country, and some Mongol groups are found in the north. Hindi, spoken by 38 percent of the people, is the official language; English is an associated language. Telugic, Bengali, Marathi, Tamil, Urdu, Gujarati, Kanarese, Punjabi, Oriya and Malayalam are other important languages. The Hindu religion is embraced by 80 percent of the population and Islam by 14 percent. Christians and Sikhs constitute about 2 percent each. Calcutta, Bombay and Delhi, the capital, are the great urban agglomerations. Successive invasions and a long period of subjugation under alien rule have made India what it is today — a land of diverse, often conflicting cultures, religions and peoples. Invading Aryans conquered the flourishing Indus valley civilization about 1500 B.C. Over the next 2000 years a Brahmanic civilization with a caste system developed. European contact with India beginning in 1498 revealed a subcontinent dominated by Mogul rulers who followed Islam. During the 1700s British supremacy was assured with the defeat of French forces. By the beginning of the twentieth century,

Britain ruled the subcontinent, dividing the administration of India into native states and directly ruled British India. In 1947 the subcontinent was partitioned into the independent nations of India and Pakistan. India has come into conflict with Pakistan over nuclear weapons testing, the status of Kashmir, and other territorial problems, as well as with China over the status of India's northern border.

Agra-Taj Mahal

AREA: 1,269,345 sq mi (3,287,590 sq km)

■ **CLIMATE:** The climate varies from tropical-monsoon in the south to temperate in the extreme north.

■ **PEOPLE:** India is nearly three quarters Indo-Aryan, and about one quarter Dravidian. Some Mongol groups are found in the north.

POPULATION: 1,095,351,995

LIFE EXPECTANCY AT BIRTH (YEARS): male, 63.3; female, 64.8

LITERACY RATE: 52%

ETHNIC GROUPS: Indo-Aryan 72%, Dravidian 25%

PRINCIPAL LANGUAGES: Hindi, English, Bengali, Telugu, Marathi, Tamil, Urdu, Gujarati, Malayalam, Kannada, Oriya, Punjabi, Assamese, Kashmiri, Sindhi, and Sanskrit (all official); Hindustani, a mix of Hindi and Urdu spoken in the north, is popular but not official

CHIEF RELIGIONS: Hindu 82%, Muslim 12%, Christian 2%, Sikh 2%

■ **ECONOMY:** Economic activity is a mix of village farming, modern agriculture, handicrafts, outsourcing and industry. Clothing, jewelry, textiles, tea, engineering goods and leather goods go to the United States, China and the European Union.

MONETARY UNIT: rupee

GDP: $3,319 billion (2004 est.)

PER CAPITA GDP: $3,100

INDUSTRIES: textiles, chemicals, food processing, steel, transport equipment, cement, mining, petroleum, machinery, software

MINERALS: coal, iron ore, manganese, mica, bauxite, titanium ore, chromite, natural gas, diamonds, petroleum, limestone

CHIEF CROPS: rice, wheat, oilseed, cotton, jute, tea, sugarcane, potatoes

CAPITAL: New Delhi (pop. of city proper, 300,000)

INDEPENDENCE DATE: August 15, 1947

GOVERNMENT TYPE: federal republic

WEBSITES: indiaimage.nic.in www.indianembassy.org

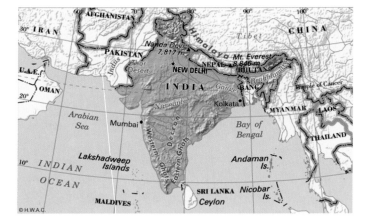

Indonesia, a necklace of 13,662 beautiful tropical islands, lies strung along the Equator. Sumatra, Borneo (the southern half of which is known as Kalimantan), Celebes (Sulawesi), Java, Timor and Halmahera are the largest islands. The western half of New Guinea is the Indonesian province known as Irian Jaya. The large islands have central mountain ranges, which rise from extensive coastal lowlands. Many islands are dotted with volcanoes, both active and dormant, and several earthquakes have devastated many parts of Indonesia. The tropical climate is hot and humid in the lowlands, but more moderate at the higher elevations. Abundant natural resources consist of petroleum and natural gas, bauxite, tin, nickel, copper, gold and coal. Rice, rubber, coffee, palm oil, peanuts, pepper and copra dominate the rich agricultural sector. The leading industries are textiles, garments, footwear, wood and paper products, rubber and chemical fertilizers. The leading exports, petroleum and natural gas, clothing, appliances, plywood, rubber, and various minerals, are directed to Japan, the United States, Singapore and China. Tourism is an important source of revenue.

The principal ethnic groups are the Javanese, Sundanese, Madurese and coastal Malays. Chinese make up the largest foreign minority group. Bahasa Indonesia, a form of Malay, is the official language. Javanese is the most widely spoken local dialect. Muslims make up 80 percent of religious adherents; Christians are 9 percent, Hindus, mainly on Bali, are 2 percent of the people. Jakarta, is the capital and largest city. Surabaya is second-largest.

Did you know?
Indonesia is home to the komodo dragon, largest lizard in the world.

Early in the first millennium A.D., the islands came under the influence of the Indian civilization and of Hinduism and Buddhism. In the 1500s, however, Islam replaced both of these as the dominant religion. In the 1600s, the Dutch emerged as the dominant power in the East Indies, maintaining their rule almost uninterrupted until World War II, when Japan occupied the islands. After the war, independence was obtained despite Dutch resistance. Indonesia gained control of the western half of New Guinea in 1962. In 1965-67, an attempted Communist coup was suppressed with great severity. In 1975 Indonesia invaded Portuguese Timor, followed by an annexation that has not been recognized by the United Nations. In the occupation that followed, an estimated 250,000 Timorese — nearly one-third of the island's population — died of either military-enforced starvation or from direct military repression.

In 1999 a UN supervised referendum resulted in a majority vote for East Timor's independence from Indonesia. In retaliation anti-independence militias, supported by the Indonesian military, began a large-scale campaign of retribution. Most of the country's infrastructure was destroyed. In September, 1999 Australian-led peacekeeping troops brought the violence to an end. East Timor became fully independent in May, 2002, after two and a half years under a UN Transitional Administration.

Bali

AREA: 741,100 sq mi (1,919,440 sq km)

■ **CLIMATE:** The tropical climate is hot and humid in the lowlands, but more moderate at higher elevations.

■ **PEOPLE:** The principal ethnic groups are the Javanese, Sundanese, Madurese and coastal Malays. Chinese form the largest foreign minority group.

POPULATION: 245,452,739

LIFE EXPECTANCY AT BIRTH (YEARS): male, 66.8; female, 71.8

LITERACY RATE: 83.8%

ETHNIC GROUPS: Javanese 45%, Sundanese 14%, Madurese 8%, Malay 8%

PRINCIPAL LANGUAGES: Bahasa Indonesia (official, modified form of Malay), English, Dutch, Javanese, other dialects

CHIEF RELIGIONS: Muslim 88%, Protestant 5%, Roman Catholic 3%, Hindu 2%, Buddhist 1%

■ **ECONOMY:** The leading exports, petroleum and natural gas, clothing, appliances, plywood, rubber, and various minerals, are directed to Japan, the United States, Singapore and China. Tourism is an important source of revenue.

MONETARY UNIT: rupiah

GDP: $827.4 billion (2004 est.)

PER CAPITA GDP: $3,500

INDUSTRIES: petroleum and natural gas, textiles, apparel, footwear, mining, cement, chemical fertilizers, plywood, rubber, food, tourism

MINERALS: petroleum, tin, natural gas, nickel, bauxite, copper, coal, gold, silver

CHIEF CROPS: rice, cassava, peanuts, rubber, cocoa, coffee, palm oil

CAPITAL: Jakarta (pop., 12,296,000)

INDEPENDENCE DATE: August 17, 1945

GOVERNMENT TYPE: republic

WEBSITE: www.embassyofindonesia.org

About two and one-half times larger than Texas, earthquake-prone Iran is a large semiarid plateau with high mountain ranges and much dry desert. The Kārūn and its tributaries form the country's largest river system. Along the Caspian coast the climate is subtropical, while inland it is arid or semiarid. Higher western elevations can see severe weather with heavy snowfall. Iran's oil industry, founded in 1908, is the backbone of the national economy. Other natural resources include iron, coal, chromite, zinc and copper. Modern agriculture and irrigation has opened new markets for Iranian produce. Wheat, rice, sugar beets, tobacco and wool are the leading agricultural and livestock products. Petrochemical and textile manufacturing and food processing are the chief industries. Iran is one of the world's largest oil producers, and also has large reserves of natural gas. Petroleum forms 90 percent of Iran's exports, with carpets a significant part of the remainder. Exports go primarily to Japan and Western Europe.

About half the population is Persian, and a quarter is Azerbaijani; there are many Kurds and Arabs. Ninety-five percent of the population is Shi'a Muslim. Farsi, or Persian, is spoken by 58 percent of the population; Turkic languages are spoken by 26 percent. Tehrān, the capital, is the largest city. Mashhad, Esfahān, Tabrīz and Shīrāz are other major cities.

> **Did you know?** Until the 1930's, Iran was known as Persia.

The Medes and Persians arrived in Iran about 2000 B.C. Beginning in 549 B.C. the Persian Empire ruled much of the Middle East, but was itself conquered by Alexander the Great in 333 B.C. Islam swept the country in the seventh century A.D. Various dynasties were succeeded in 1921 by that of the Pahlavi family. In 1979 the Shah, Mohammad Reza Pahlavi, was overthrown and the monarchy was succeeded by an Islamic republic under the leadership of Ayatollah Ruhollah Khomeini. The seizure of the United States embassy that year resulted in a breakdown in relations between the two countries and a trade embargo. During the 1980s Iran and Iraq waged war along their common border. Iran's relations with many countries has been strained by its attempts to spread its Islamic ideological goals. A report in 2003 provided evidence that Iran, a signatory to the Nuclear Non-Proliferation Treaty, had concealed secret nuclear activities for 18 years. In 2004, Iran agreed to suspend most of its uranium enrichment under a deal with the EU. That promise did not last, however, and since then concerns over Iran's nuclear activities have increased.

Persepolis

AREA: 636,296 sq mi (1,648,000 sq km)

CLIMATE: Conditions range from subtropical on the Caspian coast to arid desert in the eastern and central basins. Higher western elevations can see severe weather with heavy snowfall.

PEOPLE: Most Iranians are of Aryan origin whose ancestors migrated from Central Asia. Iran's nearly 80 diverse ethnic groups include Persians, Kurds, Lurs and Baluchi.

POPULATION: 68,688,433

LIFE EXPECTANCY AT BIRTH (YEARS): male, 68.3; female, 71.1

LITERACY RATE: 72.1%

ETHNIC GROUPS: Persian 51%, Azeri 24%, Gilaki/Mazandarani 8%, Kurd 7%, Arab 3%, Lur 2%, Balochi 2%, Turkmen 2%

PRINCIPAL LANGUAGES: Farsi (Persian; official), Kurdish, Pashto, Luri, Balochi, Gilaki, Mazandarami, Turkic languages (including Azeri and Turkish), Arabic

CHIEF RELIGIONS: Muslim (official; Shi'a 89%, Sunni 10%)

ECONOMY: Iran is one of the world's largest oil producers, and also has large reserves of natural gas. Modern agriculture and irrigation has opened new markets for Iranian produce.

MONETARY UNIT: rial

GDP: $516.7 billion (2004 est.)

PER CAPITA GDP: $7,700

INDUSTRIES: petroleum, petrochemicals, textiles, construction materials, food processing, metal fabricating, armaments

MINERALS: petroleum, natural gas, coal, chromium, copper, iron ore, lead, manganese, zinc, sulfur

CHIEF CROPS: wheat, rice, other grains, sugar beets, fruits, nuts, cotton

CAPITAL: Tehran (pop., 7,190,000)

INDEPENDENCE DATE: April 1, 1979

GOVERNMENT TYPE: Islamic republic

WEBSITES: www.daftar.org/engwww.iran-un.org

Iraq was the site of ancient Sumerian, Babylonian and other civilizations in the valley of its two great rivers, the Tigris and Euphrates. Fertile lowlands along the two rivers interrupt the broad plains that make up most of the country. The plains are rimmed by reedy marshes in the southeast and mountains along the northern and eastern borders. Iraq's climate is mostly of the arid desert type, with mild to cool winters and dry, hot summers. Strong winds cause frequent sandstorms. Northern mountain regions see cold, snowy winters. Petroleum and natural gas are the dominant natural resources. Some phosphates and sulphur are also present and exploited. Iraq is not self-sufficient in food production; wheat, barley, rice and dates are the leading agricultural products. Industry is limited to petrochemicals and food processing. Following the Persian Gulf War of 1990-91, the United Nations embargo on trade with Iraq reduced exports to a minimum. Due to current conflict, the country is in disarray as hostilities hamper efforts to restart the economy.

Arabs make up most of the population; Kurds form a significant minority. Arabic is the official and dominant language. Kurdish is spoken in the northeast. More than 60 percent of the people are Shi`a Muslim, 34 percent are Sunni Muslim, and 3 percent are Christian in religion. Baghdad, the capital, is the largest city. Al Bas¸rah and Mosul are other major cities.

The rule of the ancient civilizations in the Tigris-Euphrates Valley gave way to Persian and Greek domination.

> **Did you know?** Iraq occupies most of historic Mesopotamia.

Islam was introduced in the seventh century A.D. In the 1500s the region fell to Ottoman Turks, under whose rule it remained until World War I. Iraq was made a British mandate under the League of Nations in 1920 and, in 1932, was the first Arab country to become free of Western European control. After 1958 the political environment was strained by numerous coups and by wars with the native Kurds and neighboring Iran. Under the leadership of President Saddam Hussein, Iraq invaded neighboring Kuwait on the Persian Gulf. In 1991 United States and United Nations troops drove the Iraqis out of Kuwait and advanced into Iraq. A cease fire resulted, and trade sanctions were imposed against Iraq. Though Iraq's people are mostly Shi'a Muslims, Hussein's regime favored Sunni Muslims and persecuted the Shi'a and Kurds, causing violent conflict which has erupted since his removal by U.S and coalition forces in 2003. Since then an Iraqui interim government has drafted a permanent constitution and held national elections.

AREA: 168,754 sq mi (437,072 sq km)

Mosque

■ CLIMATE: Iraq has a desert climate with mild winters and hot, cloudless summers. Strong winds cause frequent sandstorms. Northern mountain regions see cold, snowy winters.

■ PEOPLE: Iraq's people are mostly Shi'a Muslims. Hussein's regime favored Sunni Muslims and persecuted the Shi'a and Kurds, causing violent conflict which has erupted since his removal.

POPULATION: 26,783,383

LIFE EXPECTANCY AT BIRTH (YEARS): male, 67.1; female, 69.5

LITERACY RATE: 58%

ETHNIC GROUPS: Arab 75%-80%, Kurdish 15%-20%

PRINCIPAL LANGUAGES: Arabic (official), Kurdish (official in Kurdish regions), Assyrian, Armenian

CHIEF RELIGIONS: Muslim (official; Shi'a 60-65%, Sunni 32-37%)

■ ECONOMY: Iraq's commerce was dominated by the oil sector, but the country is in disarray as hostilities hamper efforts to restart the economy.

CAPITAL: Baghdad (pop., 5,620,000)

INDEPENDENCE DATE: October 3, 1932

GOVERNMENT TYPE: in transition

MONETARY UNIT: dinar

GDP: $54.4 billion (2004 est.)

PER CAPITA GDP: $2,100

INDUSTRIES: petroleum, chemicals, textiles, construction materials, food processing

MINERALS: petroleum, natural gas, phosphates, sulfur

CHIEF CROPS: wheat, barley, rice, vegetables, dates, cotton

WEBSITE: www.state.gov/r/pa/ei/bgn/6804.htm

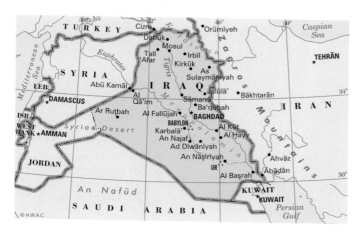

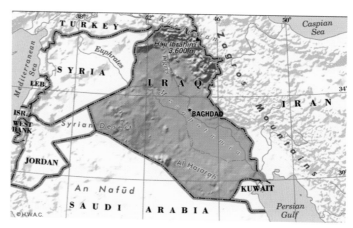

The Republic of Ireland occupies most of the island of that name, except for Northern Ireland, which is part of the United Kingdom. The country is shaped like a basin, with high coasts sloping inland to low-lying plains. The temperate marine climate, moderated by the North Atlantic Current, is overcast about half the time, with mild winters and cool summers. The Shannon, the major river, is also the longest. Peat, natural gas, copper, gypsum, limestone, barite, dolomite, lead and zinc are the chief natural resources. Principal agricultural crops are turnips, barley, potatoes, sugar beets and wheat. Livestock and dairy products are also important. Industry has been growing, with the production of chemicals and pharmaceuticals, textiles, machinery, food processing and brewing as the chief industrial activities. Tourism is a major source of the national income. Exports, consisting of chemicals, data-processing equipment, transport equipment, food and beverages, machinery and live animals, go to the United States and the European Union.

The population is mainly Irish, with an Anglo-Irish minority. English is the language generally used, but Irish Gaelic is spoken, mainly in areas along the western seaboard. Roman Catholics

Did you know? There are no serpents in Ireland, and the only reptile at all is the lizard.

form 93 percent of the population; Anglicans make up 3 percent. Dublin, the capital, is the dominant city. Cork and Limerick are the other major cities.

In the fifth century A.D., Gaelic culture flourished. Irish was one of the first Western European countries to be converted to Christianity. English penetration, beginning in the 1100s, resulted in a centuries-long struggle between the English and the Irish. About one million Irish died of starvation as a result of the 1846-54 potato blight. In the years that followed, more than one and one-half million Irish emigrated, mostly to the United States. The Easter Rebellion against British rule in 1916, though unsuccessful, was the beginning of the final struggle for independence. In 1921 and 1922 the Irish Free State was established, with several counties in Ulster being separated as Northern Ireland. Éire, or Ireland, was proclaimed as the official name of the country in 1937. In 1949 the nation withdrew from the British Commonwealth. Ireland joined the European Union in January, 1973. In 1995, the Irish electorate voted in a referendum to allow divorce in some cases, a move opposed by the powerful Roman Catholic Church hierarchy. A 2004 referendum measure, seeking to bring citizenship laws in line with more restrictive European policies, passed by a wide majority. Persons with non-Irish parents acquire Irish citizenship at birth only if at least one parent has been a resident in Ireland for three years.

Slieve League

AREA: 27,135 sq mi (70,280 sq km)

CLIMATE: The temperate climate, moderated by the North Atlantic Current, is overcast about half the time, with mild winters and cool summers.

PEOPLE: The population is mainly Irish, with an Anglo-Irish minority.

POPULATION: 4,062,235

LIFE EXPECTANCY AT BIRTH (YEARS): male, 74.7; female, 80.2

LITERACY RATE: 98%

ETHNIC GROUPS: Celtic; English minority

PRINCIPAL LANGUAGES: English, Irish Gaelic (both official); Irish Gaelic spoken by small number in western areas

CHIEF RELIGIONS: Roman Catholic 92%, Anglican 3%

ECONOMY: Exports, consisting of chemicals, data-processing equipment, transport equipment, food and beverages, machinery and live animals, go to the United States and the European Union. Tourism is a major source of income.

MONETARY UNIT: euro

GDP: $126.4 billion (2004 est.)

PER CAPITA GDP: $31,900

INDUSTRIES: food products, brewing, textiles, clothing, chemicals, pharmaceuticals, machinery, transport equipment, glass and crystal, software

MINERALS: zinc, lead, natural gas, barite, copper, gypsum, limestone, dolomite, peat, silver

CHIEF CROPS: turnips, barley, potatoes, sugar beets, wheat

CAPITAL: Dublin (pop., 1,015,000)

INDEPENDENCE DATE: December 6, 1921

GOVERNMENT TYPE: parliamentary republic

WEBSITES: www.irlgov.ie/
www.irelandemb.org

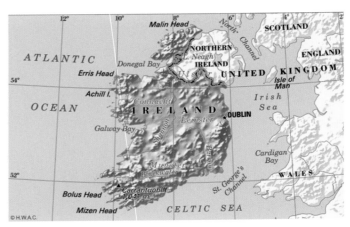

Israel, located at the eastern end of the Mediterranean, is bordered on the north by Lebanon, on the east by Syria and Jordan, and on the south by Egypt. Outside these borders, Israel occupies the West Bank and the Golan Heights. About 50 percent of the country is taken up by the Negev Desert. The remainder consists of a narrow coastal plain in the center, a hilly region to the north, and the Jordan Rift Valley. Israel's climate is hot and dry in southern and eastern desert areas, but the Mediterranean coast is more temperate. The Jordan is the only sizable river. Potash and bromine from the Dead Sea deposits are the chief mineral resources. Israel is largely self-sufficient in food production, except for grains. Citrus and other fruits, vegetables, cotton and livestock are the principal agricultural products. Israel's industries produce textiles and apparel, cut diamonds, processed foods, chemicals, metal products, military equipment, electronic equipment and machinery. Tourism is a major contributor to the economy. Exports include military equipment, cut diamonds, software, semiconductors, chemicals, rubber, plastics, and textiles. Exports go mainly to the United States, as well as to Belgium and Hong Kong.

Though 80% of the population is Jewish, about half of Israeli Jews consider themselves secular in practice. There is also a small Arab minority. Judaism is the faith of 82 percent of the population, Islam is practiced by 14 percent, 2 percent are Christians. Hebrew is the official language, but Arabic is used by the Arab minority. English is widely spoken. Jerusalem is the capital and largest city, followed by Tel Aviv-Yafo and Haifa.

> **Did you know?** The Dead Sea, on Israel's border, is almost 6 times as salty as the ocean.

By about 1000 B.C. a Hebrew kingdom was firmly established at Jerusalem under King David. After the reign of Solomon, the kingdom split into two states, Israel and Judah. The two kingdoms were conquered repeatedly through several centuries, and the Jews were scattered throughout many lands. Following the Muslim conquest of the seventh century A.D., Arab culture became predominant. The nineteenth-century Zionist movement promoted Jewish migration to the land, at that time the Ottoman Turkish province of Palestine. Palestine was occupied during World War I by Britain, which governed it as a League of Nations mandate from 1919 to 1946, and as a United Nations territory from 1946 to 1948. In 1948 Israel was proclaimed a nation and the British withdrew from Palestine. Armies of the surrounding Arab states attacked Israel, but her victory saw Israel in possession of its present-day boundaries. Jordan occupied what is now the West Bank, while Egypt occupied the Gaza Strip. At the end of the Six-Day War in 1967, Israel occupied all of the Sinai Peninsula, the Gaza Strip, all of the West Bank of Jordan and the Golan Heights of Syria. The fourth Arab-Israeli war broke out on Yom Kippur, October 6, 1973. Fighting with

Dome of the Rock

Egypt ceased in January 1974, and in 1979 a peace treaty was signed. By 1982 Israel had completed its evacuation of the Sinai Peninsula. In 1993 Israel signed an agreement with the Palestine Liberation Organization, which recognized Israel's right to exist and established limited Palestinian self-rule in the Gaza Strip and some towns in the West Bank. In 1995, Prime Minister Yitzhak Rabin was assassinated by an Israeli extremist opposed to Rabin's continued withdrawal of Israeli forces from the West Bank. In August, 2005, Israel began its withdrawal from the Gaza Strip, including the dismantling of 17 settlements.

AREA: 8,019 sq mi (20,770 sq km)

■ **CLIMATE:** Israel's climate is hot and dry in southern and eastern desert areas, but the Mediterranean coast is more temperate.

■ **PEOPLE:** Though 80% of the population is Jewish, about half of Israeli Jews consider themselves secular in practice. There is also a small Arab minority.

POPULATION: 6,352,117

LIFE EXPECTANCY AT BIRTH (YEARS): male, 77.1; female, 81.4

LITERACY RATE: 95%

ETHNIC GROUPS: Jewish 80%, Arab and other 20%

PRINCIPAL LANGUAGES: Hebrew, Arabic (both official); English

CHIEF RELIGIONS: Jewish 80%, Muslim (Sunni) 15%, Christian 2%

■ **ECONOMY:** Exports include military equipment, cut diamonds, software, semiconductors, chemicals, rubber, plastics, and textiles. Exports go mainly to the United States, as well as to Belgium and Hong Kong.

CAPITAL: Jerusalem (pop., 686,000)

MONETARY UNIT: new shekel

GDP: $129.0 billion (2004 est.)

PER CAPITA GDP: $20,800

INDUSTRIES: high-tech design and manufactures, wood and paper products, beverages, tobacco, caustic soda, cement, diamond cutting

MINERALS: potash, copper, natural gas, phosphates, magnesium bromide,

CHIEF CROPS: citrus, vegetables, cottonclays, sand

INDEPENDENCE DATE: May 14, 1948

GOVERNMENT TYPE: republic

WEBSITE: www.israelemb.org

The boot-shaped Italian peninsula is bordered by three branches of the Mediterranean: the Tyrrhenian Sea on the west, the Ionian Sea on the south, and the Adriatic Sea on the east. Major offshore islands are Sicily and Sardinia. The country is rugged and mountainous, except for the Po Valley area in the north, the heel of "the boot" in the south, and small coastal areas. The Po is the most important river. Though predominantly Mediterranean, the climate is Alpine in the north, and hot and dry in the south. Though poor in many minerals, Italy's natural resources include coal, natural gas and marble. Principal crops include fruits, vegetables, grapes, potatoes, sugar beets, potatoes, grain and olives. Fishing, beef and dairy products are also important. Tourism is a major contributor to Italy's economic well-being. Since World War II, Italy has developed into a high-ranking industrial nation, producing machinery, steel, chemicals, textiles, motor vehicles, clothing, food and agricultural products which are exported to the European Union and the United States.

Roman Colosseum

The population is primarily Italian, with small groups of Germans, French, Slovenes, Albanians and Greeks. Italian is the official and predominant language. Italy is 98 percent Roman Catholic. Rome, the capital, Milan, Naples, Turin, Genoa and Palermo are the largest cities.

> **Did you know?** There are two independent countries inside Italy: San Marino and Vatican City.

Italy, one of the youngest of Europe's nation-states, is the home of one of its oldest civilizations. About 500 B.C. Rome began its rise to power, supplanting the earlier Etruscan civilization. The Roman Empire fell in the fifth century A.D., and as a result, the Italian peninsula was politically fragmented until modern times. After the great cultural and intellectual flowering of the Renaissance in the late 15th century, the petty states fell increasingly under foreign sway. Between 1860 and 1870, Italy was unified under the leadership of the Kingdom of Sardinia. The country suffered heavy losses in World War I, which was followed by the fascist dictatorship of Benito Mussolini. Mussolini's adherence to Nazi Germany during World War II ultimately resulted in the Allied invasion of Sicily and the mainland, and the toppling of Mussolini's regime. After the war the monarchy was abolished and Italy became a republic. Since that time Italy has enjoyed strong economic growth. Italy is a charter member of the European Community.

AREA: 116,306 sq mi (301,230 sq km)

■ **CLIMATE:** Predominantly Mediterranean, the climate is Alpine in the north, and hot and dry in the south.

■ **PEOPLE:** Primarily Italian, with small groups of Germans, French, Slovenes, Albanians and Greeks.

POPULATION: 58,133,509

LIFE EXPECTANCY AT BIRTH (YEARS): male, 76.6; female, 82.7

LITERACY RATE: 98%

ETHNIC GROUPS: mostly Italian; small minorities of German, Slovene, Albanian

PRINCIPAL LANGUAGES: Italian (official), German, French, Slovenian, Albanian

CHIEF RELIGION: predominantly Roman Catholic

■ **ECONOMY:** Italy produces machinery, steel, chemicals, textiles, motor vehicles, clothing, food and agricultural products which are exported to the European Union and the United States. Tourism is a major contributor to Italy's economic well-being.

MONETARY UNIT: euro

GDP: $1,609 billion (2004 est.)

PER CAPITA GDP: $27,700

INDUSTRIES: tourism, machinery, iron and steel, chemicals, food processing, textiles, motor vehicles, clothing, footwear, ceramics

MINERALS: mercury, potash, marble, sulfur, natural gas, oil, coal

CHIEF CROPS: fruits, vegetables, grapes, potatoes, sugar beets, soybeans, grain, olives

GOVERNMENT TYPE: republic

CAPITAL: Rome (pop., 2,665,000)

INDEPENDENCE DATE: March 17, 1861

WEBSITES: www.italyemb.orgwww.travel.it

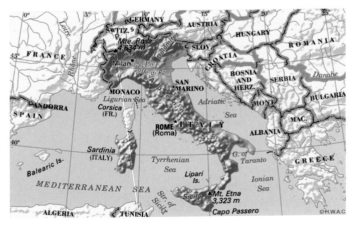

The large island of Jamaica lies in the Caribbean Sea, about 90 miles south of Cuba and 100 miles west of Haiti. Mountains cover most of the island; lowlands stretch across the western end, and a narrow plain covers the south. The tropical climate is hot and humid, but temperate in the interior. Jamaica's major mineral resources are bauxite, gypsum and limestone. Sugar, bananas, coffee, citrus fruits and allspice are important agricultural commodities. The production of rum and textiles, and light manufacturing of metal, chemical and paper products dominate the industrial scene. Tourism is also an important source of income. Exports of alumina, bauxite, sugar, bananas, rum, garments, citrus fruits and coffee go mainly to the United States, European Union and Canada.

The population is largely of African and Afro-European extraction. English is the official and dominant language; a Jamaican Creole is also used. Protestants make up 56 percent of religious adherents, and Roman Catholics form another 5 percent. Others, including Rastafarians and some other spiritual cults, make up 39 percent. Kingston is the capital and largest city.

Jamaica was inhabited by Arawaks when Columbus arrived in 1494. It remained in Spanish hands from early in the 1500s to 1655, when it passed to British control. The island developed a prosperous sugar-producing industry, and a huge population of African slaves was imported to work the island's sugar plantations. With the abolition of slavery in 1833, the plantation economy suffered a severe blow, resulting in long-lasting poverty and social unrest. Britain withdrew in 1962 when Jamaica achieved full independence.

Did you know? Reggae, a mixture of native, rock, and soul music, is from Jamaica.

Ocho Rios

AREA: 4,244 sq mi (10,991 sq km)

■ **CLIMATE:** The tropical climate is hot and humid, but temperate in the interior.

■ **PEOPLE:** The population is largely of African and Afro-European extraction.

POPULATION: 2,758,124

LIFE EXPECTANCY AT BIRTH (YEARS): male, 74.0; female, 78.2

LITERACY RATE: 85%

ETHNIC GROUPS: black 91%, mixed 7%, East Indian and other 2%

PRINCIPAL LANGUAGES: English, patois English

CHIEF RELIGIONS: Protestant 61%, Roman Catholic 4%, spiritual cults and other 35%

■ **ECONOMY:** Exports of alumina, bauxite, sugar, bananas, rum, garments, citrus fruits and coffee go mainly to the United States, European Union and Canada. Tourism is also an important source of income.

MONETARY UNIT: Jamaican dollar

GDP: $11.1 billion (2004 est.)

PER CAPITA GDP: $4,100

INDUSTRIES: tourism, bauxite, textiles, food processing, light manufactures, rum, cement, metal, paper, chemical products

MINERALS: bauxite, gypsum, limestone

CHIEF CROPS: sugarcane, bananas, coffee, citrus, potatoes, vegetables

GOVERNMENT TYPE: parliamentary democracy

CAPITAL: Kingston (pop., 575,000)

INDEPENDENCE DATE: August 6, 1962

WEBSITES: www.cabinet.gov.jm
www.jis.gov.jm

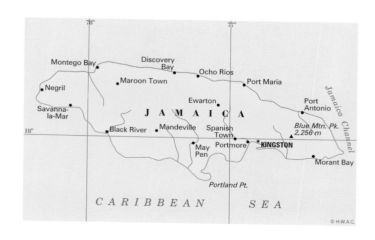

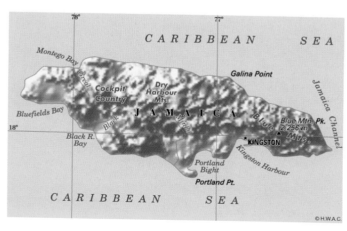

The island country of Japan is an archipelago forming a 2,360-mile-long arc off the east coast of Asia between the Sea of Japan and the Pacific Ocean proper. There are four main islands — Hokkaidō, Honshū, Shikoku and Kyūshū — and more than 3,000 smaller ones. Hills and mountains, many of which are active or dormant volcanoes, cover 72 percent of the country. Because of its unstable geologic position beside the Pacific deeps, numerous earthquakes shake the islands. Japan's climate varies from tropical in the south to cool temperate in the north. Mineral resources are negligible, but some coal and oil is produced. About 50 percent self-sufficient in food production, Japan produces rice, sugar beets, vegetables and fruit, milk, meat and silk. The agricultural economy is highly subsidized and protected. Japan's industrial structure makes it one of the most powerful economies in the world. Motor vehicles and transport equipment, electrical and electronic equipment, chemicals, metals and textiles are the leading products of the industrial sector and the exports that go to Southeast Asia and the United States.

The remarkably homogeneous population is almost entirely Japanese. Koreans make up the largest of the minorities within the country. A small number of native Ainu - aboriginal hunters believed to be of Caucasian origin - live on the northern island of Hokkaidō. Japanese is the official and universal language. Eighty-four percent of the Japanese observe both the Shinto and Buddhist religions; less than 1 percent are Christians. Japan's great cities are the capital, Tōkyō, Yokohama, Ōsaka and Nagoya.

Reliable records of Japanese history date back to 400 A.D. From the sixth to the eighth centuries Japan fell under the strong cultural influence of China, and Buddhism was introduced. In the centuries that followed a feudal system dominated the social structure, and the country existed as a closed society, untouched by other influences. The only contact with the outside world was through Dutch traders in Nagasaki. A United States naval officer, Commodore Perry, forced the opening of Japanese trade to the West in 1854. In the 1860s power became centered in the emperor, whose government proceeded to modernize the country. Japan defeated China in 1895, and in 1905 smashed Russian power in the Far East. In 1931 Japan again began military actions in China. Japanese forces attacked U.S. installations in 1941, and occupied the Philippines, Indochina, Malaya, Singapore and the Dutch East Indies. But Japan was defeated in 1945 with the dropping of atomic bombs on Hiroshima and Nagasaki. Immediately after the war, during the occupation of Japan by the U.S., Japan began the long climb back from destruction and defeat. Since that time Japan has reached the world economic summit through the mastery of high technology, a strong work ethic and government-industrial cooperation.

Did you know? Japan is among the world's largest producers of steel.

Shibuya, Tokyo

AREA: 145,883 sq mi (377,835 sq km)

■ **CLIMATE:** Climate varies from tropical in the south to cool temperate in the north.

■ **PEOPLE:** The remarkably homogeneous population is almost entirely Japanese, with a small native aboriginal Ainu minority living on the northern island of Hokkaido.

POPULATION: 127,463,611

LIFE EXPECTANCY AT BIRTH (YEARS): male, 77.7; female, 84.5

LITERACY RATE: 99%

ETHNIC GROUPS: Japanese 99%; Korean, Chinese, and other 1%

PRINCIPAL LANGUAGES: Japanese (official), Ainu, Korean

CHIEF RELIGIONS: Shinto and Buddhist observed together by 84%

■ **ECONOMY:** Motor vehicles and transport equipment, electrical and electronic equipment, chemicals, metals and textiles are the leading exports, which go to Southeast Asia and the United States.

GOVERNMENT TYPE: parliamentary democracy

CAPITAL: Tokyo (pop., 34,997,000)

INDEPENDENCE DATE: 660 BC

MONETARY UNIT: yen

GDP: $3,745 billion (2004 est.)

PER CAPITA GDP: $29,400

INDUSTRIES: motor vehicles, electronic equipment, machine tools, steel and nonferrous metals, ships, chemicals, textiles, processed foods

CHIEF CROPS: rice, sugar beets, vegetables, fruit

WEBSITES: www.us.emb-japan.go.jp
www.jnto.go.jp

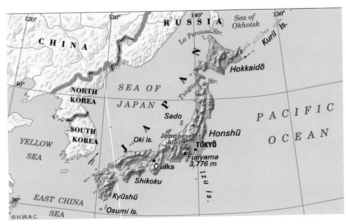

Jordan is a largely uninhabited desert about the size of Portugal. The desert plateau occupies the east, and a highland area borders it on the west. The Jordan River Valley forms the western boundary with Israel and the West Bank. Jordan is largely desert, but it does have a rainy season in the western highlands from November to April. Phosphates and potash are the country's mineral resources. Some wheat, fruits and vegetables are grown on irrigated land. Industry is limited to some textile and fertilizer production. The economy suffers from an unfavorable balance of trade. Phosphate and potash are primary exports. A pipeline from Egypt supplies Jordan's crude oil. Trade agreements allow duty-free textiles and garments into the U.S.

The population is 98 percent Arab, and 92 percent are Sunni Muslim; 8 percent are Christian. Arabic is the official and universal language, but English is widely understood among the upper and middle classes. Ammān, the capital, Irbid and Az Zarqa' are the major cities.

Jordan was the biblical home of the Moabites, the Ammonites, the Edomites and some Hebrew tribes. Islam prevailed in the area in the seventh century A.D. In the 1500s the region became part of the Ottoman Empire. After World War I the area became the Transjordan, a mandate of the League of Nations under Britain. With the end of the mandate in 1949, the Hashemite Dynasty was recognized as ruler of the Transjordan and the country became the Hashemite Kingdom of Jordan. In the following year the West Bank was formally annexed by Jordan. Defeat in the Six-Day War with Israel in 1967 saw the West Bank occupied by Israel. In the 1990s Jordan and Israel signed accords leading to peace.

> **Did you know?**
> Philadelphia was the ancient name for Amman, Jordan's modern capital.

AREA: 145,883 sq mi (377,835 sq km)

■ **CLIMATE:** Climate varies from tropical in the south to cool temperate in the north.

■ **PEOPLE:** The remarkably homogeneous population is almost entirely Japanese, with a small native aboriginal Ainu minority living on the northern island of Hokkaido.

POPULATION: 127,463,611
LIFE EXPECTANCY AT BIRTH (YEARS): male, 77.7; female, 84.5
LITERACY RATE: 99%

Petra

ETHNIC GROUPS: Japanese 99%; Korean, Chinese, and other 1%
PRINCIPAL LANGUAGES: Japanese (official), Ainu, Korean
CHIEF RELIGIONS: Shinto and Buddhist observed together by 84%

■ **ECONOMY:** Motor vehicles and transport equipment, electrical and electronic equipment, chemicals, metals and textiles are the leading exports, which go to Southeast Asia and the United States.
GOVERNMENT TYPE: parliamentary democracy
CAPITAL: Tokyo (pop., 34,997,000)
INDEPENDENCE DATE: 660 BC
MONETARY UNIT: yen
GDP: $3,745 billion (2004 est.)
PER CAPITA GDP: $29,400
INDUSTRIES: motor vehicles, electronic equipment, machine tools, steel and nonferrous metals, ships, chemicals, textiles, processed foods
CHIEF CROPS: rice, sugar beets, vegetables, fruit

WEBSITES: www.us.emb-japan.go.jp
www.jnto.go.jp

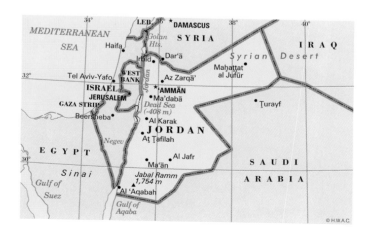

The Central Asian Republic of Kazakhstan was the second-largest constituent republic of the former Soviet Union. Though its borders do not touch the world's oceans, the republic borders the Caspian and Aral seas. Kazakhstan, about the size of Argentina, is essentially a vast flatland extending from the Volga basin on the west to the Altai Mountains in the east. The arid and semiarid continental climate has cold winters and hot summers. The nation possesses vast oil, coal and other mineral resources - iron ore, manganese, chromite, nickel, copper, molybdenum, lead, zinc, uranium and gold. Kazakhstan is a major producer of wheat, barley, cotton and rice. Chief livestock products are dairy goods, leather, meat, and wool. One of the world's top 10 oil-producing nations; oil represents nearly three quarters of overall exports. Steel, nonferrous metals, and machinery are the chief industries. The export of oil, metals, chemicals and machinery go to Russia, China and the European Union.

Kazaks make up more than half of the population, with ethnic Russians comprising another third. Kazak is the official language and is spoken by more than 45 percent of the population. Two-thirds of the population speak Russian, which is used in everyday business. Muslims total 47 percent of religious adherents, and Russian Orthodox form another 44 percent. Almaty, formerly Alma Ata, is the largest city; Qaraghandy (Karaganda) is the second-largest city. Aqmola is the new capital city.

Did you know? The shrinking Aral Sea was once the world's 4th-largest lake.

Kaindy Lake

The Kazaks were originally pastoral nomads in the northern part of Central Asia. A Kazak khanate existed from the late 1400s until the Russian Empire absorbed it during the nineteenth century. During the Soviet period the area became the Kazak Soviet Socialist Republic in 1936. The country became independent in 1991.

AREA: 1,049,155 sq mi (2,717,300 sq km)

■ **CLIMATE:** The arid and semiarid continental climate has cold winters and hot summers.

■ **PEOPLE:** Kazaks make up more than half of the population, with ethnic Russians comprising another third.

POPULATION: 15,233,244

LIFE EXPECTANCY AT BIRTH (YEARS): male, 60.7; female, 71.7

LITERACY RATE: 98.4%

ETHNIC GROUPS: Kazak 53%, Russian 30%, Ukrainian 4%, Uzbek 3%, German 2%, Uighur 1%

PRINCIPAL LANGUAGES: Kazakh, Russian (both official); Ukranian, German, Uzbek

CHIEF RELIGIONS: Muslim 47%, Russian Orthodox 44%

■ **ECONOMY:** Oil represents nearly three quarters of overall exports. Steel, nonferrous metals, and machinery are the chief industries. The export of oil, metals, chemicals and machinery go to Russia, China and the European Union.

MONETARY UNIT: tenge

GDP: $118.4 billion (2004 est.)

PER CAPITA GDP: $7,800

INDUSTRIES: oil, mining, iron and steel, tractors and other agricultural machinery, electric motors, construction materials

MINERALS: petroleum, natural gas, coal, iron ore, manganese, chrome ore, nickel, cobalt, copper, molybdenum, lead, zinc, bauxite, gold, uranium

CHIEF CROPS: spring wheat, cotton

GOVERNMENT TYPE: republic

CAPITAL: Astana (pop., 332,000)

INDEPENDENCE DATE: December 16, 1991

WEBSITE: www.kazakhembus.com

Kenya, the land of the safari, gameparks and alluring green hills, is one of Africa's best-known countries. Tourism has grown spectacularly, becoming the country's largest foreign exchange earner, with annual revenues exceeding those of Kenya's coffee exports. Rugged plateaus and mountains gird the Great Rift Valley in the center and west of the country. To the east are dry bushland and a marshy coastal plain. In the north the land turns to scrub and desert. The country's chief river is the Tana. Kenya's climate varies from tropical along the coast to arid in the interior. Kenya has small reserves of limestone, soda ash, salt, flourspar and gemstones. Coffee, tea, sugarcane, corn, wheat, sisal, are the major crops. Meat and dairy products are also important. Petroleum refining, grain and sugar milling, cement, beer and soft drinks, textiles and light manufacturing dominate the industrial sector. Exports, mainly tea, coffee, and horticultural products, flow primarily to the European Union and neighboring African countries.

African safari route

The Kikuyu make up 22 percent of the population, followed by the Luhya at 14 percent, the Luo (14 percent), the Kalinjin (11 percent), the Kamba (11 percent), the Kisii (6 percent) and the Meru (5 percent). English and Swahili are the official languages, but there are many indigenous tongues. Roman Catholics account for 28 percent of the country's religious adherents; 26 percent are Protestants; 18 percent are followers of indigenous beliefs and 6 percent are Muslim. Nairobi, the capital, is the largest city in population, followed by the port city of Mombasa.

Did you know? Kenya's diverse wildlife is protected in dozens of national parks.

Kenya's coast was familiar to mariners in past eras, including Phoenicians, Egyptians, Greeks, Arabs and Portuguese. Britain gained a foothold in the nineteenth century and in 1895 established a protectorate over the area, then known as British East Africa. With the influx of British and South African settlers, the white population continued to dominate Kenya. In 1952 the Mau Mau Rebellion, led by Kikuyu tribesmen, erupted. Brutal slayings were carried out against the white community, which made equally brutal reprisals against the black community. The bitter conflict lasted until 1959, when Africans were granted more — but still a minority — representation in the colonial Legislative Council. In 1963 Kenya attained independence under the leaderships of Jomo Kenyatta, the Kikuyu leader.

AREA: 224,962 sq mi (582,650 sq km)

CLIMATE: Kenya's climate varies from tropical along the coast to arid in the interior.

PEOPLE: The Kikuyu make up 22 percent of the population, followed by the Luhya and the Luo. Other groups include the Kalinjin, the Kamba, the Kisii and the Meru.

POPULATION: 34,707,817

LIFE EXPECTANCY AT BIRTH (YEARS): male, 44.8; female, 45.1

LITERACY RATE: 78.1%

ETHNIC GROUPS: Kikuyu 22%, Luhya 14%, Luo 13%, Kalenjin 12%, Kamba 11%, Kisii 6%, Meru 6%

PRINCIPAL LANGUAGES: English, Swahili (both official); numerous indigenous languages

CHIEF RELIGIONS: Protestant 45%, Roman Catholic 33%, indigenous beliefs 10%, Muslim 10%

ECONOMY: Exports, mainly tea, coffee, and horticultural products, flow primarily to the European Union and neighboring African countries. The tourism sector is Kenya's largest foreign exchange earner.

MONETARY UNIT: shilling

GDP: $34.7 billion (2004 est.)

PER CAPITA GDP: $1,100

INDUSTRIES: small-scale consumer goods, agricultural processing, oil refining, cement, tourism

MINERALS: gold, limestone, soda ash, salt barites, rubies, fluorspar, garnets

CHIEF CROPS: coffee, tea, corn, wheat, sugarcane, fruit, vegetables

GOVERNMENT TYPE: republic

CAPITAL: Nairobi (pop., 2,575,000)

INDEPENDENCE DATE: December 12, 1963

WEBSITE: www.kenyaembassy.com

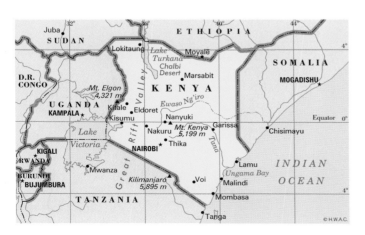

Kiribati, formerly the Gilbert Islands, includes thirty-three Pacific Ocean islands and atolls in the Gilbert, Phoenix and Line groups, plus Banaba (Ocean Island). All but Banaba have coral-ringed lagoons circling the tops of submerged mountains. Moderated by trade winds, the tropical marine climate is hot and humid. Phosphate was produced on Banaba until 1979, but copra is now the main commercial crop and export. Fishing and seaweed also add to the economy. Exports are shipped to Japan, France, Thailand and the United States. Tourism is relatively small, but important to the economy.

The nearly homogeneous Micronesian population speaks Gilbertese, but English is the official language. Roman Catholicism and Protestantism have the most religious adherents. The capital is Bairiki on Tarawa island.

The islands were settled from Samoa in about the thirteenth century. Britain established a protectorate over the Gilberts and the neighboring Ellice Islands (Tuvalu) in 1892. In 1943, Tarawa was the scene of a major battle in the Pacific theater of World War II. Following separation from the Ellice Islands in 1975, the Gilberts became the independent nation of Kiribati in 1979.

Did you know? The nation's 33 islands are scattered over 2 million sq mi (5 million sq km) of ocean.

Caroline Islands - coral beach

AREA: 313 sq mi (811 sq km)

CLIMATE: Moderated by trade winds, the tropical marine climate is hot and humid.

PEOPLE: The population is almost completely Micronesian.

POPULATION: 105,432

LIFE EXPECTANCY AT BIRTH (YEARS): male, 58.3; female, 64.4

LITERACY RATE: NA

ETHNIC GROUPS: Micronesian

PRINCIPAL LANGUAGES: English (official), I-Kiribati

CHIEF RELIGIONS: Roman Catholic 52%, Protestant 40%

ECONOMY: Copra is the main commercial crop and export. Fishing and seaweed also add to the economy. Exports are shipped to Japan, France, Thailand and the United States. Tourism is relatively small, but important to the economy.

MONETARY UNIT: Australian dollar

GDP: $79 million (2001 est.)

PER CAPITA GDP: $800

INDUSTRIES: fishing, handicrafts

CHIEF CROPS: copra, taro, breadfruit, sweet potatoes, vegetables

CAPITAL: South Tarawa (pop., 42,000)

GOVERNMENT TYPE: republic

INDEPENDENCE DATE: July 12, 1979

WEBSITE: www.state.gov/p/eap/ci/kr

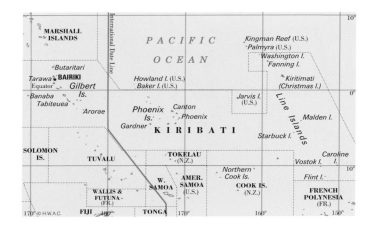

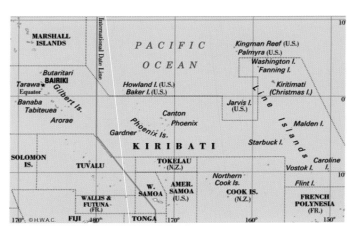

North Korea is one of the world's most isolated nations and is perhaps the most rigidly Communist society remaining on the globe. A land of mountains, North Korea contains thousands of peaks, leaving less than one-fifth of the total area as cultivable. The Yalu is the main river. Rainfall is concentrated in the hot summers of this mostly cold, humid climate. North Korea possesses significant deposits of coal, iron ore, lead, zinc, magnesite, copper, gold and uranium. Rice, corn, grain, soybeans and potatoes are the primary crops. Livestock products include cattle, pigs, pork and eggs. Military products, machine building, chemicals, metallurgy, textiles and food processing are the chief industries. The chief exports are largely mineral ores, non-metal products, machinery and textiles which go to China, South Korea, Thailand, Russia and Japan. It is also believed North Korea earns hundreds of millions of dollars from the unreported sale of missiles, narcotics and counterfeit cigarettes.

The population is Korean, with few minorities. There are small groups of Chinese and Japanese. Korean is the official and universal language. Buddhism and Confucianism were the dominant religions in the past, but under the Communist government religious observance has been discouraged. P'yŏngyang is the capital and largest city. Ch'ŏngjin and Namp'o are other major cities.

Did you know? Settled in 1122 BC, Pyŏngyang is the oldest city on the Korean Peninsula.

As in South Korea, Chinese influence had a major impact well into the nineteenth century. In 1910 all of Korea was annexed by Japan. After World War II, the Soviet Union occupied Korea north of the 38th Parallel, and the communist Democratic People's Republic of North Korea was established in 1948. The North Korean invasion of South Korea in 1950 began the bitter Korean War, in which United States and other United Nations armed forces fought North Korean forces that were supported by the Chinese Communists. Fighting ceased in 1953, leaving Korea divided as before. The nation had existed since then under the strict rule of Kim Il Sung who died in 1994. The current Communist regime under his son, Kim Jong Il, still has no diplomatic relations with the Seoul government, it's neighbor to the south.

North Korea's missile development, as well as its nuclear, chemical and biological weapons programs are a major concern to the international community. North Korea has expelled monitors from the International Atomic Energy Agency and has declared its withdrawl from the International Non-Prolifiration Treaty. In October 2006 it announced it had carried out its first nuclear test, in defiance of international warnings.

Tianchi (Lake of Heaven)

AREA: 46,541 sq mi (120,540 sq km)

■ **CLIMATE:** Rainfall is concentrated in the hot summers of this mostly cold, humid climate.

■ **PEOPLE:** The population is Korean, with few minorities. There are small groups of Chinese and Japanese.

POPULATION: 23,113,019

LIFE EXPECTANCY AT BIRTH (YEARS): male, 68.4; female, 73.9

LITERACY RATE: 99%

ETHNIC GROUP: Korean

PRINCIPAL LANGUAGE: Korean (official)

CHIEF RELIGIONS: activities almost nonexistent; traditionally Buddhist, Confucianist, Chondogyo

■ **ECONOMY:** North Korea has one of the world's most isolated economies. Chief exports are largely mineral ores, non-metal products, military products, machinery and textiles which go to China, South Korea, Thailand, Russia and Japan.

MONETARY UNIT: won

GDP: $40.0 billion (2004 est.)

PER CAPITA GDP: $1,700

INDUSTRIES: military products, machine building, electric power, chemicals, mining, metallurgy, textiles, food processing

MINERALS: coal, lead, tungsten, zinc, graphite, magnesite, iron ore, copper, gold, pyrites, salt, fluorspar

CHIEF CROPS: rice, corn, potatoes, soybeans, pulses

GOVERNMENT TYPE: Communist state

CAPITAL: Pyongyang (pop., 3,228,000)

INDEPENDENCE DATE: September 9, 1948

WEBSITE: www.korea-dpr.com/menu.htm

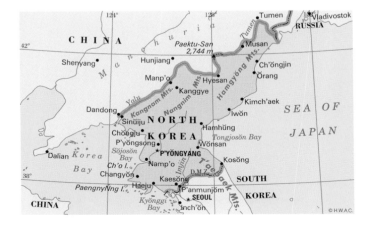

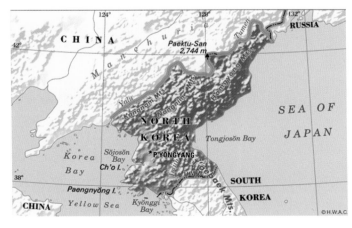

The dynamic growth of South Korean productivity has made this nation a major participant in the world economy. This is surprising, considering the terrible destruction suffered by South Korea during the war of 1950-53. Largely mountainous, the country's arable land is limited to the lowlands and river valleys of the south and southwest where rice, grain and root crops are grown. Rainfall is heavier in the summers of the temperate climate. The Han and the Naktong are the most important rivers. Coal is the chief mineral resource; some tungsten, molybdenum and graphite are produced. Rice, vegetables, fruit, and barley are major crops. Fish, meat and dairy products are also important. The large industrial sector includes electronics and electrical products, telecommunications, motor vehicles, chemicals, steel, and the building of ships. A huge export trade consisting primarily of electronic products (semiconductors, cellular phones and equipment, computers), motor vehicles, steel, ships and petrochemicals go mainly to China, the United States, Japan and Hong Kong.

The Korean population is mostly homogeneous, though there is a small group of Chinese. Korean is the national language; English is widely taught in the schools. Christianity (49 percent) and Buddhism (47 percent) are the dominant religions. The capital, Seoul, is dominant, but Pusan, Taegu and Inch'ŏn are also important cities.

Did you know? The Korean language is written in Han'gul, a language script created in the 1400s.

Chinese culture was highly influential during Korea's history. Japan annexed Korea in 1910. After Japan's defeat in 1945, U. S. forces occupied Korea south of the 38th Parallel. In 1948 the Republic of Korea was established in that area. The invasion by North Korean forces brought on the Korean War of 1950-53. United States and other United Nations forces came to South Korea's defense. A seesaw battle with North Korea and her Chinese allies ended in 1953 with a cease fire, which left Korea divided as before. During the last decades of the twentieth century, South Korea developed a strong export-directed industrial economy.

In 2000 an historic summit between the two Koreas took place hoping to initiate a gradual, long-term unification process. South Korea has sought the elimination of North Korea's nuclear weapons through the Six Party Talks, and has pursued a policy of reconciliation known as the "Peace and Prosperity Policy."

AREA: 38,023 sq mi (98,480 sq km)

CLIMATE: Rainfall is heavier in the summer of the temperate climate.

Seoul-Gyeongbokgung Palace

PEOPLE: The Korean population is mostly homogeneous, though there is a small group of Chinese.

POPULATION: 48,846,823

LIFE EXPECTANCY AT BIRTH (YEARS): male, 72.0; female, 79.5

LITERACY RATE: 98%

ETHNIC GROUP: Korean

PRINCIPAL LANGUAGE: Korean (official)

CHIEF RELIGIONS: Christian 49%, Buddhist 47%, Confucianist 3%

ECONOMY: A huge export trade consisting primarily of semiconductors, cellular phones and equipment, computers, motor vehicles, steel, ships and petrochemicals go mainly to China, the United States and Japan.

MONETARY UNIT: won

GDP: $925.1 billion (2004 est.)

PER CAPITA GDP: $19,200

INDUSTRIES: electronics, automobile production, chemicals, shipbuilding, steel, textiles, clothing, footwear, food processing

MINERALS: coal, tungsten, graphite, molybdenum, lead

CHIEF CROPS: rice, root crops, barley, vegetables, fruit

GOVERNMENT TYPE: republic

CAPITAL: Seoul (pop., 9,714,000)

INDEPENDENCE DATE: August 15, 1948

WEBSITE: www.korea.net

The Persian Gulf state of Kuwait is mainly a flat desert with a few oases. The desert climate has intensely hot summers and short cool winters. Kuwait's petroleum constitutes 10 percent of the world's oil reserves, and her natural gas reserves are also sizable. Agricultural activity is negligible. Industrial activity is related primarily to the exploitation of petroleum. The oil industry, owned by the government, provides most of the country's revenues. Oil exports flow to Japan, South Korea, the United States, Singapore and Taiwan.

Kuwaitis make up nearly half of the population. Foreigners from other Arab countries and from southern Asia make up the remainder. Arabic is the official and universal language, but English is widely spoken. The largely Muslim population is divided between the Shi`a and Sunni sects. The only large urban center is the capital, Al Kuwait.

Before 1897, Kuwait was nominally an Ottoman province. Then British influence became dominant. In 1914 Kuwait was recognized as a fully independent state under British protection. In 1961 Britain recognized Kuwait as a fully independent nation. In 1990 Iraq invaded Kuwait without warning, but was driven out in 1991 by United Nations forces with the United States playing the major role.

AREA: 6,880 sq mi (17,820 sq km)

CLIMATE: This arid country has a dry, desert climate with intensely hot summers and short, cool winters.

PEOPLE: Kuwaitis make up nearly half of the population. Foreigners from other Arab countries and from southern Asia make up the remainder.

POPULATION: 2,418,393

LIFE EXPECTANCY AT BIRTH (YEARS): male, 75.9; female, 77.9

LITERACY RATE: 78.6%

ETHNIC GROUPS: Arab 80%, South Asian 9%, Iranian 4%

Did you know? Kuwait gets its water supply by removing the salt from seawater.

Liberation Tower

PRINCIPAL LANGUAGES: Arabic (official), English

CHIEF RELIGIONS: Muslim 85% (official; Sunni 70%, Shi'a 30%)

ECONOMY: The oil industry, owned by the government, provides most of the country's revenues. Oil exports flow to Japan, South Korea, the United States, Singapore and Taiwan.

MONETARY UNIT: dinar

GDP: $48.0 billion (2004 est.)

PER CAPITA GDP: $21,300

INDUSTRIES: petroleum, petrochemicals, desalination, food processing, construction materials

MINERALS: petroleum, natural gas

GOVERNMENT TYPE: constitutional monarchy

CAPITAL: Kuwait City (pop., 1,222,000)

INDEPENDENCE DATE: June 19, 1961

WEBSITE: www.kuwait-info.org

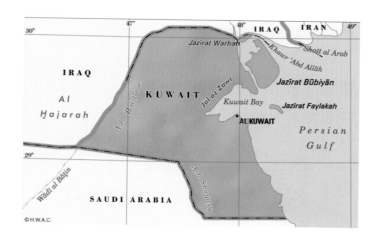

Landlocked Kyrgyzstan borders China along the towering Tian Shan range in the east, Kazakstan on the north, Uzbekistan on the west and Tajikistan to the south. Fertile valleys and basins break up the prevailing mountainous terrain. The cold continental climate ranges from polar in the north to subtropical in the southwest, and becomes moderate in the valleys. The Shū, flowing into Lake Ysyk Kōl, and the Naryn are the chief rivers. Abundant hydropower, significant gold and rare earth metals, locally exploitable coal, oil, and natural gas are important resources, along with deposits of lead, mercury, and antimony. Vast herds of sheep and goats are pastured in the mountain valleys. Crops are chiefly tobacco, cotton, wheat, vegetables and fruits. Industries include small machinery (electric motors, transformers), cotton and wool processing, food processing, construction materials (cement, glass, slate), shoes, furniture and mining. Cotton, wool, meat, tobacco, gold, mercury, uranium, natural gas and hydropower are exported mainly to Switzerland, Kazakhstan, Russia, Afghanistan and China.

Kyrgyz make up two thirds of the population. Russians and Uzbeks make up another quarter. There are small groups of Dungan (ethnic Chinese Muslims), Uighurs, Tatars, and Germans. Kyrgyz is the official language, but Russian is widely used. The population is 70 percent Muslim. Bishkek, formerly Frunze, is the capital and largest city.

The Kyrgyz, coming from the Yenisey valley, drove out the Uighur people from the area of the present republic. Tsarist Russia annexed the area in 1876. In 1936, the area was elevated to the status of a constituent republic of the Soviet Union. Independence was declared in 1991.

Did you know? This Central Asian country is almost entirely mountainous.

AREA: 76,641 sq mi (198,500 sq km)

■ **CLIMATE:** Ranging from polar in the north to subtropical in the southwest; moderate in the valleys.

■ **PEOPLE:** Kyrgyz make up two thirds of the population. Russians and Uzbeks make up another quarter.

POPULATION: 5,213,898

LIFE EXPECTANCY AT BIRTH (YEARS): male, 63.8; female, 72.1

LITERACY RATE: 97%

Burana Tower

ETHNIC GROUPS: Kyrgyz 52%, Russian 18%, Uzbek 13%, Ukrainian 3%, German 2%

PRINCIPAL LANGUAGES: Kyrgyz, Russian (both official); Uzbek

CHIEF RELIGIONS: Muslim 75%, Russian Orthodox 20%

■ **ECONOMY:** Cotton, wool, meat, tobacco, gold, mercury, uranium, natural gas and hydropower are exported mainly to Switzerland, Kazakhstan, Russia, Afghanistan and China.

MONETARY UNIT: som

GDP: $8.5 billion (2004 est.)

PER CAPITA GDP: $1,700

INDUSTRIES: small machinery, textiles, food processing, cement, shoes, sawn logs, refrigerators, furniture, electric motors

MINERALS: gold and rare earth metals, coal, oil, natural gas, nepheline, mercury, bismuth, lead, zinc

CHIEF CROPS: tobacco, cotton, potatoes, vegetables, grapes, fruits and berries

GOVERNMENT TYPE: republic

CAPITAL: Bishkek (pop., 806,000)

INDEPENDENCE DATE: August 31, 1991

WEBSITE: www.kyrgyzstan.org

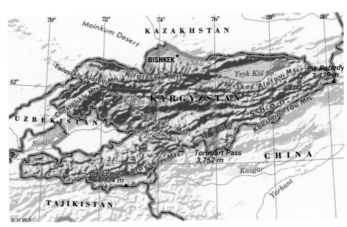

Landlocked Laos consists mostly of rugged jungle-covered mountains, some plains and plateaus and is traversed by the Mekong, the major river. The tropical monsoon climate has rainy summers and dry winters. Subsistence farming consists mainly of the growing of rice and the raising of livestock. Hydroelectric power, timber, gypsum and tin are the major resources. Industry is limited, though garment manufacturing has increased significantly. Garments, gold, copper, electricity, wood and wood products, coffee and tin go mainly to Thailand, Vietnam, France and Germany.

The chief ethnic group is the Lao, comprising half the population. Tai,Tibeto-Burman, Mon-Khmer and Viet-Muong make up the remainder. Lao is the official language, but French and English are spoken. The population is 85 percent Buddhist. Vientiane is the capital and largest city; Louangphrabang and Savannakhet are other important centers.

The Lao people began moving south from China in the thirteenth century, gradually settling in present-day Laos. France established a protectorate in 1893. In 1949 Laos became independent within the French Union. After years of fighting (1953-1975), the communist Pathet Lao assumed control of the government. Since 1986 the government has been decentralizing and encouraging private enterprise. A Bilateral Trade Agreement between the United States and Laos, which took effect in 2005, has resulted in a rise in Lao exports to the United States.

Did you know? In the 1300s, Laos was named the Kingdom of the Million Elephants.

Vientiane-national monument

AREA: 91,429 sq mi (236,800 sq km)

CLIMATE: The tropical monsoon climate has rainy summers and dry winters.

PEOPLE: The chief ethnic group is the Lao, comprising half the population. Tai,Tibeto-Burman, Mon-Khmer and Viet-Muong make up the remainder.

POPULATION: 6,368,481

LIFE EXPECTANCY AT BIRTH (YEARS): male, 52.7; female, 56.8

LITERACY RATE: 57%

ETHNIC GROUPS: Lao Loum 68%, Lao Theung 22%, Lao Soung (includes Hmong and Yao) 9%

PRINCIPAL LANGUAGES: Lao (official), French, English, and various ethnic languages

CHIEF RELIGIONS: Buddhism 60%, animist and other 40%

ECONOMY: Industry is limited, though garment manufacturing has increased significantly. Garments, gold, copper, electricity, wood and wood products, coffee and tin are exported mainly to Thailand, Vietnam, France and Germany.

MONETARY UNIT: kip

GDP: $11.3 billion (2004 est.)

PER CAPITA GDP: $1,900

INDUSTRIES: mining, timber, electric power, agricultural processing, construction, garments, tourism

MINERALS: gypsum, tin, gold, gemstones

CHIEF CROPS: sweet potatoes, vegetables, corn, coffee, sugarcane, tobacco, cotton, tea, peanuts, rice

GOVERNMENT TYPE: Communist

CAPITAL: Vientiane (pop., 716,000)

INDEPENDENCE DATE: July 19, 1949

WEBSITE: www.laoembassy.com/discover/index.htm

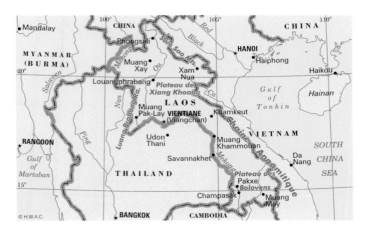

Latvia is situated on the Baltic Sea and the Gulf of Riga, which penetrates deeply into the mainland of the country. Latvia's chief river, the Daugava (Dvina) flows through the country, which is mostly lowland with hills in the west and northeast. Latvia has a wet maritime climate with moderate winters. Peat is the chief natural resource. Limestone, dolomite and timber are also significant. Amber is found along the coast. Agriculture consists principally of cattle and dairy farming. Major crops include cereals, potatoes and timber. Industry is diversified and has been growing since independence; buses, railroad cars, machinery and tools, electronics and textiles are manufactured. Wood products, metals, food products (including alcohol and tobacco), machinery, minerals and textiles go primarily to Lithuania, Estonia, Germany, the United Kingdom, Russia and Sweden.

More than half of the population are Latvians, while nearly a third are Russians. There are also small groups of Belarusians, Ukrainians and Poles. Latvian is the official language; Russian and Lithuanian are also spoken. Lutherans, Roman Catholics and the Russian Orthodox Church form the major religious groups. Riga is the capital and largest city; Daugavpils and Liepāja are other important centers.

Rezekne castle mound

After centuries of rule by the Teutonic Knights, Poland, Sweden and finally Tsarist Russia, Latvia became independent in 1918. In 1940 the U.S.S.R. annexed Latvia. Latvian independence was reestablished in 1991, and the country was admitted to the United Nations. Latvia became a member of the European Union on May 1, 2004.

Did you know? A moat, built in medieval times, surrounds the old section of Riga.

AREA: 24,938 sq mi (64,589 sq km)

CLIMATE: Latvia has a wet maritime climate with moderate winters.

PEOPLE: More than half of the population are Latvians, while nearly a third are Russians. There are also small groups of Belarusians, Ukrainians and Poles.

POPULATION: 2,274,735

LIFE EXPECTANCY AT BIRTH (YEARS): male, 65.9; female, 76.1

LITERACY RATE: 99.8%

ETHNIC GROUPS: Latvian 58%, Russian 30%, Belarusian 4%, Ukrainian 3%, Polish 2%, Lithuanian 1%

PRINCIPAL LANGUAGES: Latvian (official), Russian, Belarusian, Ukrainian, Polish

CHIEF RELIGIONS: Lutheran, Roman Catholic, Russian Orthodox

ECONOMY: Wood products, metals, food products (including alcohol and tobacco), machinery, minerals and textiles go primarily to Lithuania, Estonia, Germany, the United Kingdom, Russia and Sweden.

MONETARY UNIT: lat

GDP: $26.5 billion (2004 est.)

PER CAPITA GDP: $11,500

INDUSTRIES: motor vehicles, railroad cars, synthetic fibers, agricultural machinery, fertilizers, household appliances, pharmaceuticals, processed foods, textiles

MINERALS: peat, limestone, dolomite, amber

CHIEF CROPS: grain, sugar beets, potatoes, vegetables

GOVERNMENT TYPE: republic

CAPITAL: Riga (pop., 733,000)

INDEPENDENCE DATE: August 21, 1991

WEBSITE: www.latvia-usa.org

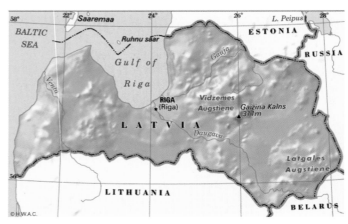

Lebanon is situated on the eastern shore of the Mediterranean and is slightly smaller than Connecticut in area. The Jabal Lubn\Man range stands behind a narrow coastal plain. Farther east is the fertile Al Biqa' (Bekaa Valley). Lebanon's chief river, the Litani, runs down the Al Biqa'. Lebanon has a Mediterranean climate with mild to cool, wet winters, and hot dry summers. The mountains experience heavy winter snows. Citrus and other fruits, vegetables, olives and tobacco are the chief crops. Authentic jewelry, inorganic chemicals, consumer goods, fruit, tobacco, construction minerals, electric power machinery and switchgear, textile fibers and paper go chiefly to Syria, United Arab Emirates, Switzerland, Turkey and Saudi Arabia. Tourism is on the rise.

Arabs constitute 95 percent of the population. There is also a small Armenian minority. Arabic and French are the official languages. The country is 60 percent Islamic and 40 percent Christian in religion. Beirut, the capital, is the largest city; Tripoli is second.

In ancient times Lebanon was the home of sea-trading Phoenicians, and in succeeding centuries was ruled by Assyrians, Persians, Greeks, Romans and Byzantines. Lebanon eventually fell to Islamic invaders, and Islam became the dominant religion. However, many Lebanese remained Christian. Following the collapse of Ottoman rule in 1918, Lebanon, along with Syria, became a French mandate. In 1943 Lebanon gained its independence, and for a time prosperity reigned as Lebanon became a center for commerce and banking in the Middle East.

Did you know? Beirut is found in recorded history as early as the 15th century BC.

In the 1970s, conflicts between Muslims and Christians flared, and activism by Palestinian guerrillas resulted in years of fighting within Lebanon. Intervention by Syrian and Israeli forces occurred at various times, and both occupied parts of the republic. After many years of occupation, Syria withdrew the remainder of its military forces in April, 2005.

In July, 2006, Hezbollah guerillas crossed into Israel, precipitating a war. Israeli ground forces moved against Hezbollah in southern Lebanon. By the wars end in August, an estimated 1200 Lebanese civilians and hundreds of Hezbollah fighters had died. The war temporarily or permanently displaced roughly one-fourth of Lebanon's population. The country, which was already seriously in debt, suffered roughly $5 billion in damages and financial losses.

AREA: 4,015 sq mi (10,400 sq km)

CLIMATE: Lebanon has a Mediterranean climate with mild to cool, wet winters, and hot dry summers. The mountains experience heavy winter snows.

Baalbek-Temple of Baachus

PEOPLE: The people of Lebanon are mostly Arab. There is also a small Armenian minority.

POPULATION: 3,874,050

LIFE EXPECTANCY AT BIRTH (YEARS): male, 69.9; female, 74.9

LITERACY RATE: 86.4%

ETHNIC GROUPS: Arab 95%, Armenian 4%

PRINCIPAL LANGUAGES: Arabic (official), French, English, Armenian

CHIEF RELIGIONS: Muslim 70%, Christian 30%

ECONOMY: Jewelry, chemicals, consumer goods, fruit, tobacco, construction minerals, machinery, textiles and paper go chiefly to Syria, United Arab Emirates, Switzerland, Turkey and Saudi Arabia. Tourism is on the rise.

MONETARY UNIT: pound

GDP: $18.8 billion (2004 est.)

PER CAPITA GDP: $5,000

INDUSTRIES: banking, food processing, jewelry, cement, textiles, mineral and chemical products, wood and furniture products, oil refining, metal fabricating

MINERALS: limestone, iron ore, salt

CHIEF CROPS: citrus, grapes, tomatoes, apples, vegetables, potatoes, olives, tobacco

GOVERNMENT TYPE: republic

CAPITAL: Beirut (pop., 1,792,000)

INDEPENDENCE DATE: November 22, 1943

WEBSITE: www.lebanonembassyus.org

Landlocked Lesotho, surrounded by the Republic of South Africa, consists mostly of highlands, with some plateaus, hills and mountains, and is drained by the Orange River. The climate is temperate, with cool, dry winters and hot, wet summers. Natural resources include agricultural and grazing land, some diamonds, sand, clay and building stones. Subsistence farming crops are chiefly corn, wheat and sorghum. A portion of the adult male workforce is employed in South African mines. There is also a rapidly expanding apparel industry. Exports, mostly clothing, furniture, footwear and wool, go mainly to the United States and nearby African countries.

The population is almost entirely Sotho and is 80 percent Christian. Sesotho and English are the official languages. Maseru is the capital and chief town.

Lesotho became an area of refuge for the Sotho people, driven there by Zulu and Matabele raids and Boer incursions in the early 1800s. The Sotho king sought British protection, and in 1884 Lesotho became the protectorate of Basutoland. The kingdom gained independence in 1966.

AREA: 11,720 sq mi (30,355 sq km)

■ **CLIMATE:** The climate is temperate, with cool, dry winters and hot, wet summers.

■ **PEOPLE:** The population is almost entirely Sotho.

POPULATION: 2,022,331

LIFE EXPECTANCY AT BIRTH (YEARS): Male: 6.8; female, 36.8

LITERACY RATE: 83%

ETHNIC GROUPS: Sotho 99%

PRINCIPAL LANGUAGES: Sesotho, English (both official); Zulu, Xhosa

CHIEF RELIGIONS: Christian 80%, indigenous beliefs 20%

■ **ECONOMY:** A portion of the adult male workforce is employed in South African mines. There is also a rapidly expanding apparel industry. Exports, mostly clothing, furniture, footwear and wool, go mainly to the United States and nearby African countries.

Did you know?
Diamonds are Lesotho's chief export.

Likhoele

MONETARY UNIT: loti
GDP: $5.9 billion (2004 est.)
PER CAPITA GDP: $3,200
INDUSTRIES: food, beverages, textiles, apparel assembly, handicrafts, construction, tourism
MINERALS: diamonds
CHIEF CROPS: corn, wheat, pulses, sorghum, barley
GOVERNMENT TYPE: modified constitutional monarchy
CAPITAL: Maseru (pop., 170,000)
INDEPENDENCE DATE: October 4, 1966
WEBSITE: www.lesotho.gov.ls

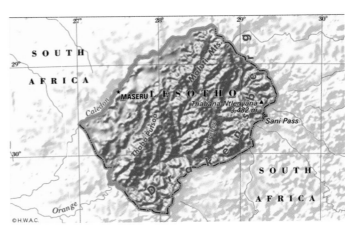

Liberia, Africa's oldest independent republic, is a flat, green country except for some hills in the northeast. The tropical climate has hot, humid summers with frequent heavy showers, and dry winters with hot days to cool nights. Iron ore, diamonds, timber and gold are the chief natural resources, along with unexploited deposits of offshore oil. Coffee, cocoa, rice, cassava, palm oil and sugarcane are the chief crops. Rubber is the chief export, followed by small amounts of cocoa. Major markets include Denmark, Germany, Poland, the United States and Greece.

Indigenous African groups make up 95 percent of the population. Americo-Liberians, the descendants of repatriated slaves, make up another 2.5 percent of the population. There is also a small group of Congo People, descendents of Caribbean immigrants who had been slaves. Traditional African religions are practiced by 70 percent of the population, Islam by 20 percent and Christianity by 10 percent. English is the official language, spoken by 20 percent of the people. The remainder speaks many West African languages. Monrovia is the capital and chief city.

Liberia was once known as the Grain Coast. In ancient times the area was part of the black empires of the sub-Saharan region further north. Early in the nineteenth century the area was colonized by freed black slaves from the United States. The first liberated slaves arrived in 1822, and in 1847 the Republic of Liberia was proclaimed. The nation was ruled by the minority descendants of the American slaves until 1980, when

Did you know? Liberia's pygmy hippopotamus is half the size of the common hippo.

military dictatorships took control. Since then, a 14-year civil war, ending in 2003, has devastated the country, destroying much of Liberia's economy. After two years of a transitional government, peaceful democratic elections took place in 2005.

AREA: 43,000 sq mi (111,370 sq km)

■ **CLIMATE:** The tropical climate has hot, humid summers with frequent heavy showers, and dry winters with hot days to cool nights.

■ **PEOPLE:** Indigenous African groups make up most of the population. A small group of Americo-Liberians, the descendants of repatriated slaves, remain.

POPULATION: 3,042,004

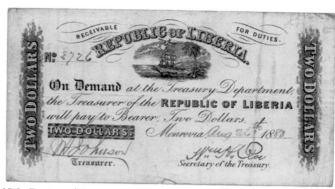

19th Century $2 currency

LIFE EXPECTANCY AT BIRTH (YEARS): male, 46.9; female, 49.0

LITERACY RATE: 38.3%

ETHNIC GROUPS: Kpelle, Bassa, Dey, and other tribes 95%; Americo-Liberians 2.5%, Caribbean 2.5%

PRINCIPAL LANGUAGES: English (official), Mande, West Atlantic, and Kwa languages

CHIEF RELIGIONS: indigenous beliefs 40%, Christian 40%, Muslim 20%

■ **ECONOMY:** Rubber is the chief export, followed by small amounts of cocoa. Major markets include Denmark, Germany, Poland, the United States and Greece. Unexploited offshore oil offers great economic potential.

MONETARY UNIT: Liberian dollar (LRD)

GDP: $2.9 billion (2004 est.)

PER CAPITA GDP: $900

INDUSTRIES: rubber processing, palm oil processing, timber, diamonds

MINERALS: iron ore, diamonds, gold

CHIEF CROPS: rubber, coffee, cocoa, rice, cassava, palm oil, sugarcane, bananas

GOVERNMENT TYPE: in transition

CAPITAL: Monrovia (pop., 572,000)

INDEPENDENCE DATE: July 26, 1847

WEBSITE: www.state.gov/r/pa/ei/bgn/6618.htm

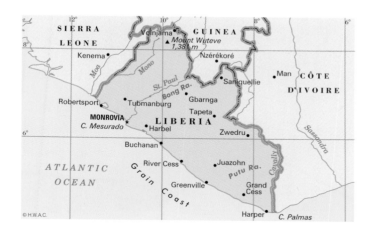

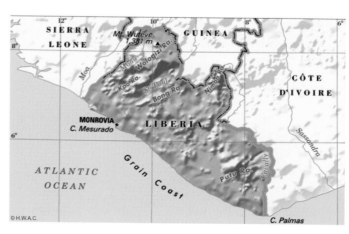

The land that is now Libya was the subject of contention among empires for thousands of years. Though mostly barren, rock-strewn plains and arid deserts, there are elevated regions in the northwest, northeast and extreme south. A strip of Mediterranean climate and vegetation exists along the coast, in contrast to the desert conditions of the vast interior. Some wheat, barley, olives, dates and citrus are grown. Industries include petrochemicals, iron, steel and aluminum, food processing, textiles, handicrafts and cement. Libya is an important producer of petroleum and natural gas, which are the basis of her industrial economy and export trade. Exports, almost entirely petroleum and natural gas, are shipped mainly to the European Union and Turkey.

The population is a mixture of Arabs and Berbers, and is 97 percent Sunni Muslim. Berbers have been largely assimilated into Arabic culture, though scattered Berber communities remain. Arabic is the official and dominant language, but English and Italian are also used. Tripoli is the capital and largest city, followed by Benghāzī. Large numbers of foreigners work in the oil industry.

Libya fell to the Ottoman Turks in 1551 and remained under their domination until Italy took control in 1911. Following Italy's defeat in World War II, Libya was administered by Britain and France. In 1951 the independent Kingdom of Libya was proclaimed. A military junta led by Col. Muammar Qadhafi overthrew the monarchy, and a republic was proclaimed in 1969. Since then Libya has clashed on occasion with Egypt and Chad. In 1986 the United States Air Force bombed Libyan sites on two occasions for firing antiaircraft missiles at American aircraft and for attacks on American servicemen in Europe. The United Nations imposed economic sanctions on Libya in 1992 for her failure to extradite terrorists involved in the 1988 destruction of an American airliner over Scotland. Since the late 1990's, Libya has worked to normalize relations with the West, and has paid some reparations to victims of terrorist activities.

Did you know? Much of Libya lies within the great Sahara Desert.

AREA: 679,362 sq mi (1,759,540 sq km)

CLIMATE: A long, mainly arid, coastal plain has several irrigated areas, with temperatures moderated by the sea. An extreme desert interior lies further south.

PEOPLE: Berbers have been largely assimilated into Arabic culture, though scattered Berber communities remain. Large numbers of foreigners work in the oil industry.

POPULATION: 5,900,754

LIFE EXPECTANCY AT BIRTH (YEARS): male, 74.1; female, 78.6

LITERACY RATE: 76.2%

ETHNIC GROUPS: Arab-Berber 97%

PRINCIPAL LANGUAGES: Arabic (official), Italian, English

CHIEF RELIGION: Muslim (official; mostly Sunni) 97%

ECONOMY: The country's chief exports are oil and natural gas, which go to the European Union and Turkey. Oil gives Libya great wealth, but little of it reaches the people.

MONETARY UNIT: dinar

GDP: $37.5 billion (2004 est.)

PER CAPITA GDP: $6,700

INDUSTRIES: petroleum, food processing, textiles, handicrafts, cement

MINERALS: petroleum, natural gas, gypsum

CHIEF CROPS: wheat, barley, olives, dates, citrus, vegetables, peanuts, soybeans

GOVERNMENT TYPE: Islamic Arabic Socialist "Mass-State"

CAPITAL: Tripoli (pop., 2,006,000)

INDEPENDENCE DATE: December 24, 1951

WEBSITE: www.libya–un.org

Tripoli, Medina

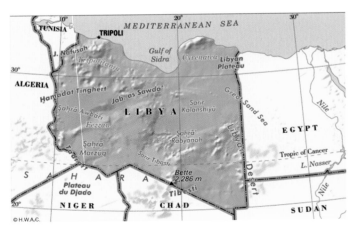

The tiny, landlocked principality of Liechtenstein lies wedged between Austria and Switzerland. One-third of the country is level land bordering the Rhine; an upland occupies the remainder. Liechtenstein's climate is characterized by cold winters and moderately warm summers. Beef and dairy cattle raising is the chief agricultural pursuit. Wheat, barley, corn and potatoes are also grown. Electronics, dental products, metal manufacturing, pharmaceuticals, precision instruments, ceramics and food products are the leading manufactures. Small specialty machinery, dental products, hardware and pottery are chief exports. Trading partners include the European Union, Switzerland, and the United States. Tourism and the sale of postage stamps to collectors also contribute to the economy.

Ethnically, the population is almost entirely Alemannic. There are also small groups of Italians, Swiss, Austrians and Turks. German is the official language. Roman Catholicism is the religion of 87 percent of the population. Vaduz is the capital.

Lithuania consists mostly of fertile lowlands dotted with many small scattered lakes. It has a short coastline on the Baltic Sea, and its chief river is the Nemunas. The wet climate is moderate throughout the year. Natural resources include limestone, clay, sand, gravel, iron ore and granite. Livestock raising and dairy farming are the most important agricultural activities. Grain and potatoes, flax and sugar beets are also grown. Industrial products include machinery, tools, electric motors, television sets, refrigerators and textiles. Exports of mineral products, machinery and appliances, textiles, wood and paper products go mainly to the European Union and Russia.

Did you know? Many international corporations have their headquarters in Liechtenstein.

Lithuanians make up 80 percent of the population; Russians, 9 percent, Poles, 8 percent. The great majority of Lithuanians are Roman Catholic. Lithuanian is the official language. Vilnius, the capital, is the largest city, followed by Kaunas, and the ice-free port of Klaipe'da (Memel).

The ancient realm of Lithuania included large parts of Belarus, Russia and Ukraine in the late Middle Ages. Lithuania merged with Poland in the 1500s and was annexed by Tsarist Russia in 1795. At the end of World War I in 1918, Lithuania became independent. Lithuania was annexed by the Soviet Union in 1940. Independence was regained in 1991. Lithuania became a member of the European Union on May 1, 2004.Following the dissolution of the Germanic Confederation in 1866, Liechtenstein ended its ties to other German states. Since the 1920s, Liechtenstein has formed a customs union with Switzerland.

Balzers

AREA: 62 sq mi (160 sq km)

CLIMATE: The continental climate is marked by cold winters and moderately warm summers.

PEOPLE: Ethnically, the population is almost entirely Alemannic. There are also small groups of Italians, Swiss, Austrians and Turks.

POPULATION: 33,987

LIFE EXPECTANCY AT BIRTH (YEARS): male, 75.8; female, 83.0

LITERACY RATE: 100%

ETHNIC GROUPS: Alemannic 86%; Italian, Turkish, and other 14%

PRINCIPAL LANGUAGES: German (official), Alemannic dialect

CHIEF RELIGIONS: Roman Catholic 80%, Protestant 7%

ECONOMY: Small specialty machinery, dental products, hardware and pottery are chief exports. Trading partners include the European Union, Switzerland, and the United States. Tourism and collectible postage stamps contribute to the economy.

MONETARY UNIT: Swiss franc

GDP: $825 million (1999 est.)

PER CAPITA GDP: $25,000

INDUSTRIES: electronics, metal manufacturing, textiles, ceramics, pharmaceuticals, food products, precision instruments, tourism

CHIEF CROPS: wheat, barley, corn, potatoes

GOVERNMENT TYPE: hereditary constitutional monarchy

CAPITAL: Vaduz (pop., 5,000)

INDEPENDENCE DATE: January 23, 1719

WEBSITE: www.liechtenstein.li/en

Lithuania consists mostly of fertile lowlands dotted with many small scattered lakes. It has a short coastline on the Baltic Sea, and its chief river is the Nemunas. The wet climate is moderate throughout the year. Natural resources include limestone, clay, sand, gravel, iron ore and granite. Livestock raising and dairy farming are the most important agricultural activities. Grain and potatoes, flax and sugar beets are also grown. Industrial products include machinery, tools, electric motors, television sets, refrigerators and textiles. Exports of mineral products, machinery and appliances, textiles, wood and paper products go mainly to the European Union and Russia.

Lithuanians make up 80 percent of the population; Russians, 9 percent, Poles, 8 percent. The great majority of Lithuanians are Roman Catholic. Lithuanian is the official language. Vilnius, the capital, is the largest city, followed by Kaunas, and the ice-free port of Klaipėda (Memel).

The ancient realm of Lithuania included large parts of Belarus, Russia and Ukraine in the late Middle Ages. Lithuania merged with Poland in the 1500s and was annexed by Tsarist Russia in 1795. At the end of World War I in 1918, Lithuania became independent. Lithuania was annexed by the Soviet Union in 1940. Independence was regained in 1991. Lithuania became a member of the European Union on May 1, 2004.

Did you know?
Russians are Lithuania's largest ethnic minority.

AREA: 25,174 sq mi (65,200 sq km)

CLIMATE: The transitional climate is moderate throughout the year with wet summers and winters.

PEOPLE: Lithuanians make up more than 80 percent of the population. Ethnic minorities include Russians and Poles.

POPULATION: 3,585,906

LIFE EXPECTANCY AT BIRTH (YEARS): male, 68.2; female, 79.0

LITERACY RATE: 98%

ETHNIC GROUPS: Lithuanian 81%, Russian 9%, Polish 7%, Belarusian 2%

PRINCIPAL LANGUAGES: Lithuanian (official), Belarusian, Russian, Polish

CHIEF RELIGION: predominantly Roman Catholic

Cottage in Kretinga

ECONOMY: Exports of mineral products, machinery and appliances, textiles, wood and paper products go mainly to the European Union and Russia.

MONETARY UNIT: litas

GDP: $45.2 billion (2004 est.)

PER CAPITA GDP: $12,500

INDUSTRIES: machine tools, electric motors, household appliances, petroleum refining, shipbuilding, furniture making, textiles, food processing, fertilizers, agricultural machinery, optical equipment, electronic components, computers, amber

MINERALS: peat

CHIEF CROPS: grain, potatoes, sugar beets, flax, vegetables

GOVERNMENT TYPE: republic

CAPITAL: Vilnius (pop., 549,000)

INDEPENDENCE DATE: March 11, 1990

WEBSITES: www.president.lt/en www.ltembassyus.org

The trilingual Grand Duchy of Luxembourg lies landlocked between Belgium, Germany and France. The northern part of the country contains the rugged uplands of the Ardennes plateau, while the south consists of undulating terrain drained by the Alzette and Mosel rivers. This modified continental climate has mild winters and cool summers. Iron ore was exploited in the past, but Luxembourg now has little in the way of mineral resources. Grains and wine grapes, along with dairy and livestock raising are the chief agricultural pursuits. Luxembourg's banking and financial services dominate the economy. Steel-making is the major industry, but the production of chemicals, rubber, glass and aluminum are also important. Steel and metal products, chemicals, rubber, machinery and other manufactured equipment are exported to European Union countries.

Luxembourgers are ethnically a Celtic people with a French and German blend. There are also large communities of ethnic Portuguese, Italians, French, Belgians, and Germans. Letzeburgisch, a Germanic dialect, German and French are the official languages. The population is 97 percent Roman Catholic. The capital, Luxembourg, is also the largest city.

Luxembourg was created a Grand Duchy in personal union with the Kingdom of The Netherlands in 1815. In 1839, newly independent Belgium annexed a large part of Luxembourg. The union with the Netherlands was dissolved in 1890.

Did you know?
Luxembourg's capital city is located on the ruins of a Roman settlement.

AREA: 998 sq mi (2,586 sq km)

■ **CLIMATE:** This modified continental climate has mild winters and cool summers.

■ **PEOPLE:** Luxembourgers are ethnically a Celtic people with a French and German blend. There are also large communities of ethnic Portuguese, Italians, French, Belgians, and Germans.

POPULATION: 474,413

LIFE EXPECTANCY AT BIRTH (YEARS): male, 75.3; female, 82.1

Grand Ducal Palace

LITERACY RATE: 100%

ETHNIC GROUPS: Mixture of French and German

PRINCIPAL LANGUAGES: Luxembourgish (national), German, French (official)

CHIEF RELIGION: majority is Roman Catholic; 1979 law forbids collection of such statistics

■ **ECONOMY:** Banking and financial services dominate the economy. Steel and metal products, chemicals, rubber, machinery and other manufactured equipment are exported to European Union countries.

MONETARY UNIT: euro

GDP: $27.3 billion (2004 est.)

PER CAPITA GDP: $58,900

INDUSTRIES: banking, iron and steel, food processing, chemicals, metal products, tires, glass, aluminum

CHIEF CROPS: barley, oats, potatoes, wheat, fruits, wine grapes

GOVERNMENT TYPE: constitutional monarchy

CAPITAL: Luxembourg (pop., 77,000)

INDEPENDENCE DATE: 1839

WEBSITE: www.luxembourg-usa.org

Macedonia, officially referred to by the United States Government as "The Former Yugoslav Republic of Macedonia," is a landlocked Balkan republic situated between Yugoslavia, Bulgaria, Greece and Albania. The mountainous country is punctuated by deep basins and valleys and is drained by the Vardar River. Macedonia's climate has hot, dry summers and autumns and relatively cold winters with heavy snowfall. Iron ore, copper, lead, zinc and chromium are mined. Wine grapes, tobacco, vegetables, milk and eggs are the chief agricultural pursuits. Industries include food processing, beverages, textiles, chemicals and steel. Steel, textile products, chromium, lead, zinc, nickel, tobacco, lamb, and wine flow primarily to Serbia, Germany, Greece and Croatia.

Macedonians make up two thirds of the population. Albanians make up another quarter. There are small groups of Turks, Romas and Serbs. The spoken languages follow the same pattern. Eastern Orthodox religious adherents comprise 67 percent of the population; Muslim adherents, 30 percent. Skopje is the capital and largest city.

Slavs settled the area of the present republic during the sixth century A.D. Macedonia was successively a possession of Greek Byzantium, Bulgaria, Serbia, and finally fell to the Ottoman Turks in the latter half of the 1300s. With the ousting of the Turks in 1912, the region was annexed by Serbia, and after World War I became a part of the successor state of Yugoslavia. In 1991 Macedonia separated from Yugoslavia and attained independence. In 1994 the United States recognized Macedonia's independence, but neighboring Greece disputes the use of the name "Macedonia" for historical and cultural reasons. A small contingent of U.S. troops were flown to Macedonia in 1994 to help forestall another Balkan "powder keg" from detonating. In 1995, Greece ended its embargo against transshipment of Macedonian goods through its territory, which had put a severe strain on Macedonia's economy. The government has reaffirmed its commitment to pursuing membership in NATO and the European Union.

Did you know? Skopje was rebuilt after an earthquake in 1963 destroyed over half the city.

AREA: 9,781 sq mi (25,333 sq km)

■ **CLIMATE:** The country has hot, dry summers and autumns and relatively cold winters with heavy snowfall.

■ **PEOPLE:** Macedonians make up two thirds of the population. Albanians make up another quarter. There are small groups of Turks, Romas and Serbs.

POPULATION: 2,050,554

Ohrid-Saint Panteleimon Monestary

LIFE EXPECTANCY AT BIRTH (YEARS): male, 72.5; female, 77.2

LITERACY RATE: NA

ETHNIC GROUPS: Macedonian 67%, Albanian 23%, Turkish 4%, Roma 2%, Serb 2%

PRINCIPAL LANGUAGES: Macedonian (official), Albanian, Turkish, Romani, Serbo-Croatian

CHIEF RELIGIONS: Macedonian Orthodox 67%, Muslim 30%

■ **ECONOMY:** Steel, textile products, chromium, lead, zinc, nickel, tobacco, lamb, and wine are exported primarily to Serbia, Germany, Greece and Croatia.

MONETARY UNIT: denar

GDP: $14.4 billion (2004 est.)

PER CAPITA GDP: $7,100

INDUSTRIES: mining, textiles, wood products, tobacco, food processing, buses

MINERALS: chromium, lead, zinc, manganese, tungsten, nickel, iron ore, asbestos, sulfur

CHIEF CROPS: rice, tobacco, wheat, corn, millet, cotton, sesame, mulberry leaves, citrus, vegetables

GOVERNMENT TYPE: republic

CAPITAL: Skopje (pop., 447,000)

INDEPENDENCE DATE: September 17, 1991

WEBSITE: www.macedonia.co/uk/mcic

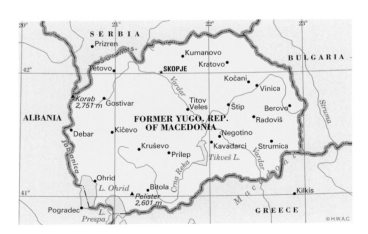

Madagascar, the world's fourth-largest island, is situated in the Indian Ocean, separated from Africa by the Mozambique Channel. A narrow coastal plain rings the high plateau and mountains in the center of the island. Madagascar's wildlife is diverse and unique. The climate is tropical along the coast, temperate inland and arid in the south. Graphite, chromite, coal, bauxite, tar sands and semiprecious stones are mined. Coffee, vanilla, sugarcane, cloves and cocoa are the chief cash crops. Rice and cassava are grown, and cattle-raising is widespread. Industries include food processing, textiles, mining, paper, petroleum refining, glassware, soap, cement, brewing and tanning. Exports of coffee, vanilla and cloves, cotton, chromite and shrimp go to the United States, France and Germany. Apparel exports have become a major source of foreign income.

The population is made up of 18 Malagasy tribes, as well as small groups of Comorans, French, Indians, and Chinese. French and Malagasy are the official languages. Fifty-two percent of the population follow indigenous beliefs; 41 percent are Christian. Antananarivo is the capital and largest city.

The first waves of migration came from present-day Indonesia during the first millennium A.D. Arab seamen reached the island around 900 A.D. France took control of the island in 1896, displacing the native Merina (Hova) Kingdom. Local resistance continued for many years. In 1960 Madagascar became independent. Madagascar was one of the poorest countries in the world, but economic conditions have improved, particularly due to increases in export revenue.

Did you know? The island of Madagascar is the 4th largest in the world.

AREA: 226,657 sq mi (587,040 sq km)

■ **CLIMATE:** The climate is tropical along the coast, temperate inland and arid in the south.

■ **PEOPLE:** The population is made up of 18 Malagasy tribes, as well as small groups of Comorans, French, Indians, and Chinese.

POPULATION: 18,595,469

LIFE EXPECTANCY AT BIRTH (YEARS): male, 54.2; female, 59.0

LITERACY RATE: 80%

ETHNIC GROUPS: Mainly Malagasy (Indonesian-African); also Cotiers, French, Indian, Chinese

Farmland

PRINCIPAL LANGUAGES: Malagasy, French (both official)

CHIEF RELIGIONS: indigenous beliefs 52%, Christian 41%, Muslim 7%

■ **ECONOMY:** Exports of coffee, vanilla and cloves, cotton, chromite and shrimp go to the United States, France and Germany. Apparel exports have become a major source of foreign income.

MONETARY UNIT: ariary

GDP: $14.6 billion (2004 est.)

PER CAPITA GDP: $800

INDUSTRIES: meat processing, soap, breweries, tanneries, sugar, textiles, glassware, cement, automobile assembly, paper, petroleum, tourism

CHIEF CROPS: coffee, vanilla, sugarcane, cloves, cocoa, rice, cassava, beans, bananas, peanuts

MINERALS: graphite, chromite, coal, bauxite, salt, quartz, tar sands, mica, semiprecious stones

GOVERNMENT TYPE: republic

CAPITAL: Antananarivo (pop., 1,678,000)

INDEPENDENCE DATE: June 26, 1960

WEBSITE: www.state.gov/r/pa/ei/bgn/5460.htm

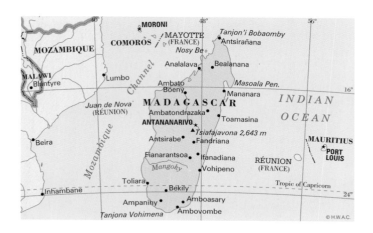

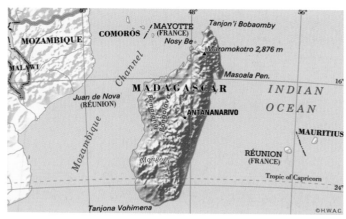

Landlocked Malawi, on the shores of Lake Nyasa (Malawi), is bordered by Tanzania, Mozambique and Zambia. The terrain consists of a narrow, elongated plateau with rolling plains, rounded hills and a few mountains. Malawi's climate is subtropical, with a rainy season from November to May, and a dry season from May to November. Natural resources include limestone, coal and bauxite. There are also unexploited deposits of uranium. Tobacco is the most important crop. Sugarcane, cotton, tea, corn, potatoes, cassava, sorghum and groundnuts are also grown. Tobacco, tea, sugarcane, coffee and peanuts, grown for export, are shipped to the United States, United Kingdom, Germany, South Africa and Egypt.

The Chewa and the Nyanja are the major ethnic groups. Others include the Tumbuka, Yao, Lomwe, Sena and Tonga. English and Chichewa are the official languages. Protestants form 55 percent of the population; Roman Catholics and Muslims each form another 20 percent. Blantyre is the largest city, followed by the capital, Lilongwe.

African kingdoms developed in the area during the 1500s. After Dr. David Livingstone founded missions in Malawi in the mid-nineteenth century, Britain established the Nyasaland Protectorate in 1891. The country gained its independence in 1964 under the name Malawi.

Did you know? Lakes cover nearly one-fourth of Malawi.

Mulanje Mountain

■ **ECONOMY:** Tobacco, tea, sugarcane, coffee and peanuts, grown for export, are shipped to the United States, United Kingdom, Germany, South Africa and Egypt.

MONETARY UNIT: kwacha

GDP: $7.4 billion (2004 est.)

PER CAPITA GDP: $600

INDUSTRIES: tobacco, tea, sugar, sawmill products, cement, consumer goods

MINERALS: limestone, uranium, coal, and bauxite

CHIEF CROPS: tobacco, sugarcane, cotton, tea, corn, potatoes, cassava, sorghum, pulses

GOVERNMENT TYPE: republic

CAPITAL: Lilongwe (pop., 587,000)

INDEPENDENCE DATE: July 6, 1964

WEBSITE: www.malawi.gov.mw

AREA: 45,745 sq mi (118,480 sq km)

■ **CLIMATE:** Malawi's climate is subtropical, with a rainy season from November to May, and a dry season from May to November.

■ **PEOPLE:** The Chewa and the Nyanja are the major ethnic groups. Others include the Tumbuka, Yao, Lomwe, Sena and Tonga.

POPULATION: 13,013,926

LIFE EXPECTANCY AT BIRTH (YEARS): male, 37.1; female, 37.9

LITERACY RATE: 58%

ETHNIC GROUPS: Chewa, Nyanja, Tumbuka, Yao, Lomwe, Sena, Tonga, Ngoni, Ngonde

PRINCIPAL LANGUAGES: Chichewa, English (both official); several African languages

CHIEF RELIGIONS: Protestant 55%, Roman Catholic 20%, Muslim 20%

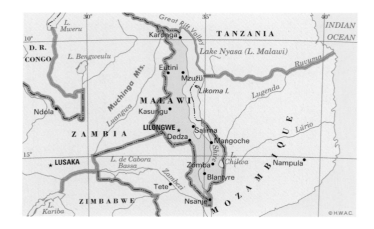

Separated by 400 miles of the South China Sea, the western section of Malaysia occupies the southern part of the Malay Peninsula in the west, and the eastern section includes Sarawak and Sabah on the northern coast of Borneo. The Malay Peninsula consists of a spinal mountain range flanked by coastal plains. In Sabah and Sarawak, coastal plains rise to mountainous interiors. The climate is tropical with annual monsoons. Malaysia possesses major tin deposits. Petroleum and natural gas are found in Sabah and Malaya. Copper, iron ore and bauxite are also important. Plantation rubber, palm oil, rice, coconuts, cocoa, and peppers are important agricultural products; timber logging also contributes to the economy. Electronics, metals, chemicals and textiles are the chief industrial products. Electronic equipment, petroleum and natural gas, palm oil, wood and wood products, rubber and textiles are exported to the United States, Singapore, Japan and China.

Malays make up half of the population while Chinese make up another quarter. There is also a small group of Indians. Islam is the state religion, but the Buddhist, Hindu and Christian communities are significant. Malay is the official language. Chinese dialects, English and Tamil are also spoken. Kuala Lumpur is the capital and largest city.

At the beginning of the thirteenth century, the coasts of Malaya, Sarawak and Sabah were dotted with small ports trading in spices. The lure of the spice trade brought Portuguese, Dutch and British merchant adventurers. By the late nineteenth century, Britain came to dominate the area. Malaya gained independence in 1957, and in 1963 Malaya, Singapore, Sabah and Sarawak joined to form the Federation of Malaysia. In 1965 Singapore seceded from the Federation. Since then, the Malaysian economy has grown remarkably and has produced a moderately high standard of living.

Did you know? The Petronas Towers in the capital are the tallest buildings in the world.

AREA: 127,317 sq mi (329,750 sq km)

■ **CLIMATE:** The climate is tropical with annual monsoons.

■ **PEOPLE:** Malays make up half of the population while Chinese make up another quarter. There is also a small group of Indians.

POPULATION: 23,953,136

LIFE EXPECTANCY AT BIRTH (YEARS): male, 69.3; female, 74.8

LITERACY RATE: 83.5%

ETHNIC GROUPS: Malay and other indigenous 58%, Chinese 24%, Indian 8%

PRINCIPAL LANGUAGES: Malay (official), English, Chinese dialects, Tamil, Telugu, Malayalam, Panjabi, Thai; Iban and Kadazan in the east

CHIEF RELIGIONS: Muslim (official) 60%, Buddhist 19%, Christian 9%, Hindu 6%, Confucianist/Taoist 3%

■ **ECONOMY:** Electronic equipment, petroleum and natural gas, palm oil, wood and wood products, rubber and textiles are exported to the United States, Singapore, Japan and China.

MONETARY UNIT: ringgit

GDP: $229.3 billion (2004 est.)

PER CAPITA GDP: $9,700

INDUSTRIES: rubber/oil-palm goods, light manufacturing, electronics, mining, logging

MINERALS: tin, petroleum, copper, iron ore, natural gas, bauxite

CHIEF CROPS: rubber, palm oil, cocoa, rice, coconuts, pepper

CAPITAL: Kuala Lumpur (pop., 1,352,000)

INDEPENDENCE DATE: August 31, 1957

GOVERNMENT TYPE: federal parliamentary democracy with a constitutional monarch

WEBSITES: www.gov.my www.tourism.gov.my

Kuala Lumpur

Situated in the Indian Ocean about 425 miles from Sri Lanka, the Maldive Islands are flat, with elevations only as high as 10 feet. The tropical climate is hot and humid with annual monsoons. Tourism is the Maldives largest industry. Fishing is the second most important economic activity, and there is limited production of coconuts, corn and sweet potatoes. Fish and fish products are exported to the United States, Thailand, the United Kingdom, Germany, Sri Lanka and Japan.

The people are of mixed Indian, Sinhalese and Arabic descent. Divehi, a dialect of Sinhalese, is the official and universal language, but English is widely spoken. Islam is the state religion. Male is the capital and chief town.

According to legend, it was a Sinhalese prince who was the first sultan, having stayed on to rule after becoming becalmed in the Maldives with his royal bride. In 1887 a sultan placed the islands under British protection. In 1965 the Maldives achieved full independence.

Male

AREA: 116 sq mi (300 sq km)

■ **CLIMATE:** The tropical climate is hot and humid with annual monsoons.

■ **PEOPLE:** The people are of mixed Indian, Sinhalese and Arabic descent.

POPULATION: 359,008

LIFE EXPECTANCY AT BIRTH (YEARS): male, 62.4; female, 65.0

LITERACY RATE: 93.2%

ETHNIC GROUPS: Dravidian, Sinhalese, Arab

PRINCIPAL LANGUAGES: Divehi (Sinhala dialect, Arabic script; official), English

CHIEF RELIGION: Muslim (official; mostly Sunni)

Did you know? None of the Maldives' more than 1,000 islands is larger than 5 sq mi (13 sq km).

■ **ECONOMY:** Tourism is the Maldives largest industry. Fish and fish products are exported to the United States, Thailand, the United Kingdom, Germany, Sri Lanka and Japan.

MONETARY UNIT: rufiyaa

GDP: $1.3 billion (2002 est.)

PER CAPITA GDP: $3,900

INDUSTRIES: fish processing, tourism, shipping, boatbuilding, coconut processing, garments, woven mats, rope, handicrafts, coral and sand mining

CHIEF CROPS: coconuts, corn, sweet potatoes

GOVERNMENT TYPE: republic

CAPITAL: Male (pop., 83,000)

INDEPENDENCE DATE: July 26, 1965

WEBSITE: www.themaldives.com

Tiladummati Atoll
Ceylon
SRI LANKA
North Malosmadulu Atoll
Miladummadulu Atoll
Male Atoll
Ari Atoll
MALE
MALDIVES
Felidu Atoll
Malaku Atoll
INDIAN OCEAN
Kolumadulu Atoll
Haddummati Atoll
One and a Half Degree Channel
Suvadiva Atoll
Addu Atoll Gan
Equator
© H.W.A.C.

Eight Degree Channel
Tiladummati Atoll
Ceylon
SRI LANKA
N. Malosmadulu Atoll
Miladummadulu Atoll
Kardiva Channel
Male Atoll
Ari Atoll
MALE
MALDIVES
Nilandu Atoll
Felidu Atoll
Malaku Atoll
INDIAN OCEAN
Kolumadulu Atoll
Haddummati Atoll
One and a Half Degree Channel
Suvadiva Atoll
Equitorial Channel
Addu Atoll Gan
Equator
© H.W.A.C.

Landlocked Mali, wherein lies Timbuktu, is mainly flat and dry, varying from desolate Sahara in the north to pasture and crop lands in the center, and savannah scrubland in the south. Gold, phosphate, kaolin, salt, and limestone currently mined. Deposits of bauxite, iron ore, manganese, lithium, tin, copper and uranium are unexploited. Millet, rice, corn and peanuts are grown. Cotton and cotton products, gold, livestock and tannery products are exported to China, Pakistan, Thailand and the European Union. Mali remains poor, but economic conditions have improved through economic reform, foreign aid and debt relief. Tourism remains a small, but growing part of Mali's economy.

About half of the population are Mande. There are also significant groups of Peul (Fulani), Voltaic and Songhai. Islam is the religion of 90 percent of the population. French is the official language, but Bambara is spoken by 80 percent of the people. Bamako, the capital, is the only large city.

Modern Mali was a major part of past Sudanic empires - Ghana, Malinké (Mali) and Songhai - that flourished from the eighth through the sixteenth centuries. The golden city of Timbuktu (Tombouctou) was a terminal for trans-Saharan caravan trade during that period. The country came under French control late in the nineteenth century under the name French Sudan. Independence was achieved in 1960, and the country assumed Mali as its name.

Did you know? The ancient empire of Mali extended as far west as the Atlantic Ocean.

AREA: 478,766 sq mi (1,240,000 sq km)

CLIMATE: The varying climate is semitropical in the south, temperate in the center and arid to desolate Sahara in the north.

PEOPLE: About half of the population are Mande. There are also significant groups of Peul (Fulani), Voltaic and Songhai.

POPULATION: 11,716,829

LIFE EXPECTANCY AT BIRTH (YEARS): male, 44.7; female, 45.9

LITERACY RATE: 38%

ETHNIC GROUPS: Mande 50% (Bambara, Malinke, Soninke), Peul 17%, Voltaic 12%, Tuareg and Moor 10%, Songhai 6%

PRINCIPAL LANGUAGES: French (official), Bambara and other African languages

CHIEF RELIGIONS: Muslim 90%, indigenous beliefs 9%

ECONOMY: Cotton and cotton products, gold, livestock and tannery products are exported to China, Pakistan, Thailand and the European Union. Tourism remains a small, but growing part of Mali's economy.

MONETARY UNIT: CFA franc

Mosque

GDP: $11.0 billion (2004 est.)

PER CAPITA GDP: $900

INDUSTRIES: food processing, construction, gold mining

MINERALS: gold, phosphates, kaolin, salt, limestone, uranium

CHIEF CROPS: cotton, millet, rice, corn, vegetables, peanuts

CAPITAL: Bamako (pop., 1,264,000)

GOVERNMENT TYPE: republic

INDEPENDENCE DATE: September 22, 1960

WEBSITE: www.maliembassy.us

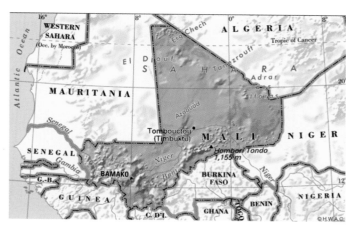

Located in the Mediterranean Sea, about 58 miles south of Sicily and 180 miles from the coast of North Africa, Malta is composed of two main islands, Malta and Gozo. The country consists of a series of low hills with terraced fields on the slopes. The Mediterranean climate has mild, rainy winters and hot, dry summers. Natural resources are limited to limestone and salt. Tourism, ship repair and light manufacturing are the basis of the economy. Exports of machinery and transport equipment, semi-conductors and clothing are directed toward the United States and European Union countries.

The Maltese are chiefly of Phoenician and Carthaginian stock, later mixed with Italians and British. Maltese, a Semitic tongue, and English are the official languages. Roman Catholicism is the religion of 98 percent of the population. Valletta is the capital and chief town.

The strategic importance of Malta has brought it under the control of peoples and empires since the time of the Phoenicians. Greeks, Carthaginians, Romans, Byzantines, Arabs, Normans, the Knights of Malta, the French, and finally the British have ruled the islands. British rule began in 1800. In World War II, Malta, as the "unsinkable aircraft carrier," withstood merciless German and Italian aerial bombardment, earning Britain's George Cross for heroism. Malta became independent in 1964, and joined the European Union on May 1, 2004.

Did you know? Valletta is a 16th-century fortress-city built by the Knights of St. John.

Valletta

AREA: 122 sq mi (316 sq km)

■ **CLIMATE:** The Mediterranean climate has mild, rainy winters and hot, dry summers.

■ **PEOPLE:** The Maltese are chiefly of Phoenician and Carthaginian stock, later mixed with Italians and British.

POPULATION: 400,214

LIFE EXPECTANCY AT BIRTH (YEARS): male, 76.5; female, 81.0

LITERACY RATE: 88.76%

ETHNIC GROUPS: Maltese, other Mediterranean

PRINCIPAL LANGUAGES: Maltese (a Semitic dialect), English (both official)

CHIEF RELIGION: Roman Catholic (official) 91%

GOVERNMENT TYPE: parliamentary democracy

CAPITAL: Valletta (pop., 83,000)

INDEPENDENCE DATE: September 21, 1964

■ **ECONOMY:** Tourism, ship repair and light manufacturing are the basis of the economy. Machinery and transport equipment, semi-conductors and clothing are exported to the United States and European Union countries.

MONETARY UNIT: Maltese lira

GDP: $7.2 billion (2004 est.)

PER CAPITA GDP: $18,200

INDUSTRIES: tourism, electronics, shipbuilding, construction, food and beverages, textiles, footwear, clothing, tobacco

MINERALS: limestone, salt

CHIEF CROPS: potatoes, cauliflower, grapes, wheat, barley, tomatoes, citrus, cut flowers, green peppers

WEBSITE: www.gov.mt/index.asp?l=2

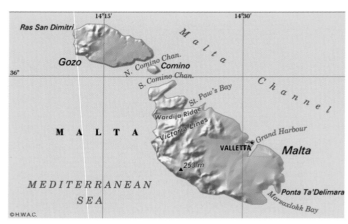

The Marshall Islands form two parallel chains in the North Pacific Ocean about two-thirds of the way between Hawaii and New Guinea. The low coral limestone and sandy islands are , hot and humid and border the typhoon belt. The tropical climate has a wet season from May to November. Coconuts, taro, breadfruit, pigs and chickens are the main agricultural pursuits. Fishing is also important. Copra processing, pearl farming, handicrafts, fish processing, handicrafts and tourism are mainstays of the economy. Copra cake, coconut oil, handicrafts, and fish go to the United States, Japan, Australia, China, Hong Kong, New Zealand and Taiwan.

The Micronesian people are all Christian. English is the official language and is universally spoken, although Malayo-Polynesian languages are also used.

Originally a German protectorate, the islands were placed under a Japanese mandate in 1919. They became part of the United Nations Trust Territory of the Pacific Islands under U.S. control after World War II. The islands of Bikini and Enewetak are former U.S. nuclear test sites. The Republic of the Marshall Islands was proclaimed in 1979. In 1991 the international community recognized the Marshall Islands as independent. Since 1990, the Marshall Islands has offered ship registrations under the Marshall Islands flag. With more than a thousand registered vessels, this has become a growing part of the economy.

Did you know? Bikini Atoll, where the first hydrogen bomb was tested, is located here.

AREA: 70 sq mi (181.3 sq km)

■ **CLIMATE:** These islands are tropical, hot and humid with occasional typhoons, and a wet season from May to November.

■ **PEOPLE:** The native population is almost completely Micronesian. There are small foreign minority groups of Americans, Filipinos, Chinese and Australians.

POPULATION: 60,422

LIFE EXPECTANCY AT BIRTH (YEARS): male, 67.8; female, 71.7

Majuro-Lagoon Shoreline

LITERACY RATE: 93.7%

ETHNIC GROUP: Micronesian

PRINCIPAL LANGUAGES: English, Marshallese (both official); Malay-Polynesian dialects, Japanese

CHIEF RELIGION: mostly Protestant

■ **ECONOMY:** Copra cake, coconut oil, handicrafts, and fish go to the United States, Japan, Australia, China, Hong Kong, New Zealand and Taiwan. Tourism is a growing industry.

MONETARY UNIT: U.S. dollar

GDP: $115 million (2001 est.)

PER CAPITA GDP: $1,600

INDUSTRIES: copra, fish, tourism, craft items from shell, wood, and pearls

MINERALS: deep seabed minerals

CHIEF CROPS: coconuts, tomatoes, melons, taro, breadfruit, fruits

GOVERNMENT TYPE: republic

CAPITAL: Majuro (pop., 25,000)

INDEPENDENCE DATE: October 21, 1986

WEBSITE: www.rmiembassyus.org

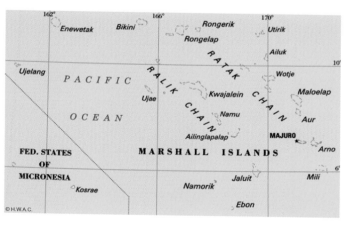

Mauritania is a borderland between Moorish/Arab North Africa and black West Africa. For the most part, the country is flat. The Sahara zone in the north consists of shifting dunes and gravel plains, while the south is more fertile and suitable for cultivation. The desert climate is constantly hot, dry and dusty. Iron ore, gypsum, copper and phosphates are the chief mineral resources. Except in the Senegal river valley, where dates, millet, sorghum and root crops are raised, agriculture is limited to nomadic livestock herding. Offshore fishing also contributes to the economy. Exports, consisting of iron ore and fish products, go to Japan, the European Union, China and Russia. Petroleum reserves are being developed.

Moorish and mixed Moorish-black ethnic groups form 70 percent of the population; another 30 percent are black Africans residing in the Senegal river valley. Hasamiya Arabic is the official language. The population is entirely Muslim. Nouakchott is the capital and chief city.

The original inhabitants, a Sudanic black people, were conquered in the 1000s A.D. by the Berbers, who in turn were conquered by Arabs in the sixteenth century. France established control in 1903. In 1960 Mauritania won full independence. In 1976 Mauritania obtained the southern third of Western Sahara. However, in 1979 Mauritania abandoned the area, and Morocco promptly occupied it.

Did you know? Little plant life and few animals exist in the Sahara in northern Mauritania.

AREA: 397,955 sq mi (1,030,700 sq km)

CLIMATE: The desert climate is constantly hot, dry and dusty.

PEOPLE: Moorish and mixed Moorish-black ethnic groups make up two thirds of the population. Another third are black Africans residing in the Senegal river valley.

POPULATION: 3,177,388

LIFE EXPECTANCY AT BIRTH (YEARS): male, 50,2; female, 54.6

LITERACY RATE: 41.2%

Nouakchott marche

ETHNIC GROUPS: mixed Maur/black 40%, Maur 30%, black 30%

PRINCIPAL LANGUAGES: Hassaniya Arabic, Wolof (both official); Fulani, Pulaar, Soninke (all national); French

CHIEF RELIGION: predominantly Muslim (official)

ECONOMY: Exports, consisting of iron ore and fish products, go to Japan, the European Union, China and Russia. Petroleum reserves are being developed.

MONETARY UNIT: ouguiya

GDP: $5.5 billion (2004 est.)

PER CAPITA GDP: $1,800

INDUSTRIES: fish processing, mining

MINERALS: iron ore, gypsum, copper, phosphate, diamonds, gold, oil

CHIEF CROPS: dates, millet, sorghum, rice, corn, dates

GOVERNMENT TYPE: Islamic republic

CAPITAL: Nouakchott (pop., 600,000)

INDEPENDENCE DATE: November 28, 1960

WEBSITE: www.ambarim-dc.org

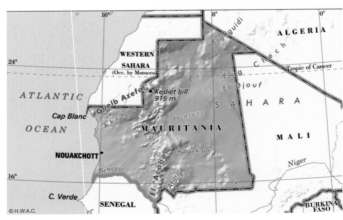

Encircled by coral reefs and the blue-green Indian Ocean, Mauritius is the perfect model of a placid tropical island. The island of Mauritius is volcanic in origin; the mountains which rise from the shore ring a central plateau. Dependencies include Rodrigues and distant smaller islands. Southeast trade winds modify the tropical climate. There is a warm, dry winter and a hot, wet summer. Sugarcane is by far the leading crop. Tea, vegetables, fruits and livestock are also raised. Fishing contributes to the economy. Sugar processing, textiles and clothing, watches, jewelry, cut flowers and optical goods are the chief manufactures. These goods are exported to the European Union and the United States. Tourism is also important.

Indo-Mauritians make up two thirds of the population; Creoles (of African descent) make up another quarter. There are small groups of Sino- and Franco-Mauritians. English is the official language, but many people speak a Creole patois, which is basically French. Fifty-two percent are Hindu, 28 percent are Christian, and 17 percent are Muslim. Port Louis is the capital and largest city.

Did you know? The island of Mauritius is almost entirely surrounded by coral reefs.

Originally settled by the Dutch, the island of Mauritius was occupied by France in the early eighteenth century. In 1814 the island was ceded to Britain. The growth of the sugar industry resulted in the importation of many indentured workers from India. Independence was gained in 1968.

Mauritius has one of the strongest economies in Africa. Economic growth was first driven by sugar, then textiles and tourism. More recently financial services and information technology have emerged as important sectors of the economy

AREA: 788 sq mi (2,040 sq km)

■ **CLIMATE:** Southeast trade winds modify the tropical climate. There is a warm, dry winter and a hot, wet summer.

■ **PEOPLE:** Indo-Mauritians make up two thirds of the population; Creoles (of African descent) make up another quarter. There are small groups of Sino- and Franco-Mauritians.

POPULATION: 1,240,827

LIFE EXPECTANCY AT BIRTH (YEARS): male, 68.1; female, 76.1

Port Louis

LITERACY RATE: 82.9%

ETHNIC GROUPS: Indo-Mauritian 68%, Creole 27%, Sino-Mauritian 3%, Franco-Mauritian 2%

PRINCIPAL LANGUAGES: English (official), Creole, French, Hindi, Urdu, Hakka, Bhojpuri

CHIEF RELIGIONS: Hindu 52%, Christian 28%, Muslim 17%

■ **ECONOMY:** Sugar processing, textiles and clothing, watches, jewelry, cut flowers and optical goods are the chief manufactures. These goods are exported to the European Union and the United States. Financial services are of growing importance.

MONETARY UNIT: Mauritian rupee

GDP: $15.7 billion (2004 est.)

PER CAPITA GDP: $12,800

INDUSTRIES: food processing, textiles, clothing, chemicals, metal products, transport equipment, nonelectrical machinery, tourism

CHIEF CROPS: sugarcane, tea, corn, potatoes, bananas, pulses

GOVERNMENT TYPE: republic

CAPITAL: Port Louis (pop., 143,000)

INDEPENDENCE DATE: March 12, 1968

WEBSITE: www.gov.mu

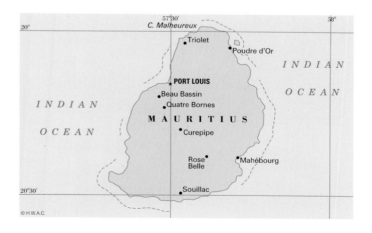

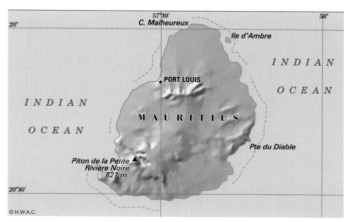

Mexico is the third-largest in area of the Latin-American republics, and is the most populous Spanish-speaking country in the world. The country consists of a large central plateau flanked by the eastern and western coastal ranges of the Sierra Madre. The peninsula of Baja California is the westernmost extremity, while the Yucatan peninsula is at the eastern end of the nation. From a desert plain in the north, the plateau rises to 8,000 feet near Mexico City. Mexico's climate varies from tropical to desert. On the northern border, the Río Bravo del Norte (Rio Grande) is the largest river. Mexico is a leading producer of petroleum and silver. Copper, gold, lead, zinc and natural gas are also exploited. The major cash crops are corn, beans, tobacco, feed grains, fruit, cotton, coffee, sugarcane and tomatoes. Food and beverages, tobacco, chemicals, steel, textiles, clothing and motor vehicles are leading industrial products. Crude oil, oil products, manufactured goods, silver, motor vehicles, coffee and cotton are the chief exports, most of which are shipped to the United States. Tourism is a major economic activity.

The population is nearly two thirds an Indian-Spanish mix and nearly one third Amerindian. The remainder are mostly Caucasian. Spanish is the official and predominant language. Some Indian tongues are spoken. Roman Catholicism is the religion of 89 percent of the population; 6 percent of the population belongs to Protestant sects. Mexico City is the capital and largest city. Guadalajara and Monterrey each have more than one million people.

Did you know? Mexico City is built on the site of the Aztec settlement of Tenochtitlán.

Before the Spanish conquest of Mexico in 1519, Indian civilizations flourished there for centuries. In 1810 Mexico gained its independence from Spain. Between 1836 and 1848, Mexico lost vast areas in the north, including Texas, to the United States. France attempted to establish a puppet empire under Austrian-born Emperor Maximilian, 1864-67. Benito Ju\Aarez led a popular revolt that ended French control. Between 1910 and 1917 Mexico was the scene of a revolt led by Carranza, Villa and Zapata against large estate owners. In 1994 Mexico joined the North American Free Trade Agreement (NAFTA) with the United States and Canada. Financial problems have hindered the economy since then.

AREA: 761,606 sq mi (1,972,550 sq km)

■ **CLIMATE:** Mexico's climate varies from tropical to desert.

Chichen Itza-Piramide de Kukulkan

■ **PEOPLE:** The population is nearly two thirds an Indian-Spanish mix and nearly one third Amerindian. The remainder are mostly Caucasian.

POPULATION: 107,449,525

LIFE EXPECTANCY AT BIRTH (YEARS): MALE, 72.2; female, 77.8

LITERACY RATE: 89.6%

ETHNIC GROUPS: mestizo 60%, Amerindian 30%, white 9%

PRINCIPAL LANGUAGES: Spanish (official), Náhuatl, Maya, Zaptec, OTOMI, Miztec, other indigenous

CHIEF RELIGIONS: Roman Catholic 89%, Protestant 6%

■ **ECONOMY:** Crude oil, oil products, manufactured goods, silver, motor vehicles, coffee and cotton are the chief exports, most of which are shipped to the United States. Tourism is a major economic activity.

CAPITAL: Mexico City (pop., 18,660,000)

INDEPENDENCE DATE: September 16, 1810

GOVERNMENT TYPE: federal republic

MONETARY UNIT: new peso

GDP: $1,006 billion (2004 est.)

PER CAPITA GDP: $9,600

INDUSTRIES: food and beverages, tobacco, chemicals, iron and steel, petroleum, mining, textiles, clothing, motor vehicles, consumer durables, tourism

MINERALS: petroleum, silver, copper, gold, lead, zinc, natural gas

CHIEF CROPS: corn, wheat, soybeans, rice, beans, cotton, coffee, fruit, tomatoes

WEBSITE: www.presidencia.gob.mx/?NLang=en

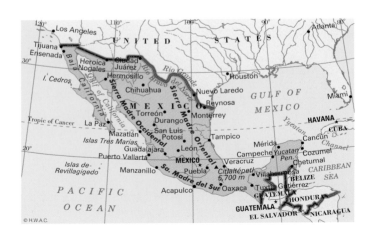

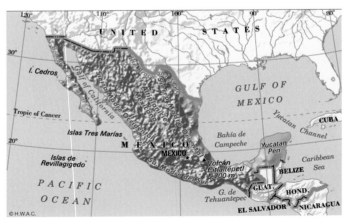

The Federated States of Micronesia, formerly known as the Caroline Islands, lie in the Western Pacific Ocean east of the Philippines and just north of the equator. Varying geologically from high mountainous islands to low coral atolls, Micronesia has a tropical climate with heavy year-round rainfall and occasional typhoons. The leading crops are black pepper, tropical fruits and coconuts. Industries include fish processing, handicrafts, wood and pearls. More than half of the country's work force are government employees. Tourism is developing. Fish, garments, kava and black pepper are the major exports. Trading partners include the United States and Japan.

Nine Micronesian and Polynesian groups comprise the ethnic structure. English is the official and common language; Trukese, Pohnpeian, Yapese and Kosrean are spoken. Almost all of the population is Christian.

Micronesia was probably settled from the East Indies and Melanesia after 1500 B.C. Loosely controlled by Spain after 1686, the islands passed to Germany in 1899. The islands became a mandate of Japan under the League of Nations after World War I. Following Japan's defeat in World War II, in 1947 Micronesia became part of the United Nations Trust Territory of the Pacific Islands governed by the United States. The Federation came into being in 1979 and was accepted as a fully independent member of the United Nations in 1991.

Did you know? The United States is pledged to defend Micronesia, which has no army.

AREA: 271 sq mi (702 sq km)

██ **CLIMATE:** Micronesia has a tropical climate with heavy year-round rainfall and occasional typhoons.

██ **PEOPLE:** Nine Micronesian and Polynesian groups comprise the ethnic structure.

POPULATION: 108,004

LIFE EXPECTANCY AT BIRTH (YEARS): male, 67.7; female, 71.3

LITERACY RATE: 89%

Nukuoro Atoll

ETHNIC GROUPS: 9 distinct Micronesian and Polynesian groups

PRINCIPAL LANGUAGES: English (official), Trukese, Pohnpeian, Yapese, Kosrean, Ulithian, Woleaian, Nukuoro, Kapingamarangi

CHIEF RELIGIONS: Roman Catholic 50%, Protestant 47%

██ **ECONOMY:** More than half of the country's work force are government employees. Fish, garments, kava and black pepper are the major exports. Trading partners include the United States and Japan. Tourism is developing.

MONETARY UNIT: U.S. dollar

GDP: $277 million (2004 est.)

PER CAPITA GDP: $2,000

INDUSTRIES: tourism, construction, fish processing, craft items from shell, wood, and pearls

MINERALS: deep-seabed minerals

CHIEF CROPS: black pepper, tropical fruits and vegetables, coconuts, cassava, sweet potatoes

GOVERNMENT TYPE: republic

CAPITAL: Palikir, on Pohnpei (pop., 7,000)

INDEPENDENCE DATE: November 3, 1986

WEBSITE: www.fsmgov.org

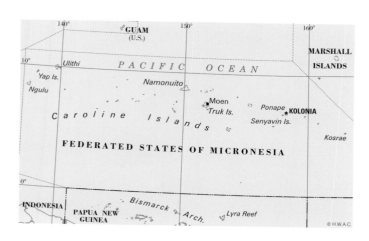

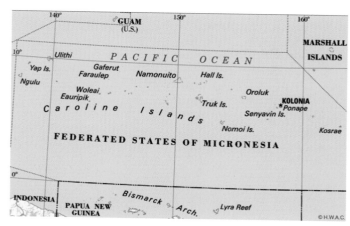

Moldova, landlocked between Romania and Ukraine, forms a large part of the Bessarabian area bordered by the Dnestr and Prut rivers. A strip of Moldova extends eastward across the Dnestr river. The rolling steppe has a climate of moderate winters and warm summers. The country is one of the poorest in Europe. Mining of lignite, phosphates, gypsum and limestone contribute to the economy. Vegetables, fruits, wine grapes, grain, sugar beets, sunflower seeds, meat, milk and eggs are the chief agricultural products. Processed foods, wine, metal processing, machinery production, textiles and shoes are the main industries. Foodstuffs, wine, textiles, footwear and machinery go to Russia, Italy, Romania, Germany, Ukraine and Belarus.

Moldovan-Romanians make up more than three fourths of the population. There are small minorities of Ukrainians, Russians, Turkic Gagauz, Bulgarians and Romanians. Moldovan, virtually the same as Romanian, is the official language. More than 98 percent are adherents of the Eastern Orthodox churches. Chişinău (Kishinev) is the capital and largest city.

Long contested between the Ottoman Turks and Tsarist Russia, the area west of the Dnestr came under Romanian rule in 1918. Bessarabia was then ceded to the U.S.S.R. in 1940. A major part of Bessarabia, plus the Moldovan autonomous area across the Dnestr, was then established as a constituent republic of the Soviet Union. In 1991 Moldova became independent. Separatist groups have been active in the strip east of the Dnestr.

Did you know?
Moldova was at times part of Romania and the Soviet Union.

Moldavian orthodox church

AREA: 13,067 sq mi (33,843 sq km)

■ **CLIMATE:** The country has moderate winters and warm summers.

■ **PEOPLE:** Moldovan-Romanians make up more than three fourths of the population. There are small minorities of Ukrainians, Russians, Turkic Gagauz, Bulgarians and Romanians.

POPULATION: 4,466,706

LIFE EXPECTANCY AT BIRTH (YEARS): male, 60.9; female, 69.4

LITERACY RATE: 96%

ETHNIC GROUPS: Moldovan/Romanian 65%, Ukrainian 14%, Russian 13%

PRINCIPAL LANGUAGES: Moldovan (official), Russian, Gagauz (a Turkish dialect)

CHIEF RELIGION: Eastern Orthodox 99%

■ **ECONOMY:** One of the poorest countries in Europe. Foodstuffs, wine, textiles, footwear and machinery are exported to Russia, Italy, Romania, Germany, Ukraine and Belarus.

MONETARY UNIT: leu

GDP: $8.6 billion (2004 est.)

PER CAPITA GDP: $1,800

INDUSTRIES: food processing, agricultural machinery, foundry equipment, household appliances, hosiery, sugar, vegetable oil, shoes, textiles

MINERALS: lignite, phosphorites, gypsum, limestone

CHIEF CROPS: vegetables, fruits, wine, grain, sugar beets, sunflower seed, tobacco

GOVERNMENT TYPE: republic

CAPITAL: Chisinau (pop., 662,000)

INDEPENDENCE DATE: August 27, 1991

WEBSITE: www.turism.md/eng

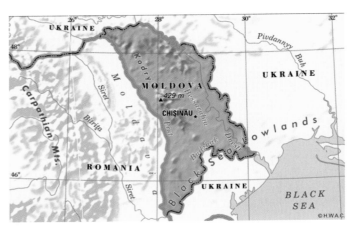

Minuscule Monaco, a coastal enclave on the Mediterranean surrounded by France, is the second-smallest independent state in the world. Crammed into its small area are pleasant Riviera weather, scenery to match, and the Monte-Carlo casino, a gambling paradise. The principality consists of three main areas: La Condamine, Monte-Carlo and Monaco, the capital district. Tourism dominates the economy, but the country has successfully diversified into services and small, high-value-added industries. The principality has full customs integration with France and uses the French franc as currency.

Monegasques form 16 percent of the population. French make up nearly half of the population, while Italians comprise another 16 percent. French is the official language. Roman Catholicism is the religion of 95 percent of the population.

Monaco was occupied by the Phoenicians from the 10th to the 5th century B.C. and then by the Greeks. During the early Christian era it was dominated by Rome until occupied by the barbarians and Saracens. In 1191 A.D., the Genoese took possession of Monaco; the Grimaldi family took control of the principality in 1297 A.D. Monaco became a French protectorate in 1861. In July 1918, a treaty was signed providing for limited French protection over Monaco. In 1993, Monaco became an official member of the United Nations.

Did you know? This rich but tiny country is the most densely populated in the world.

Harbor View

AREA: 0.75 sq mi (1.95 sq km)

■ **CLIMATE:** Mediterranean Riviera weather, with mild, wet winters and hot, dry summers.

■ **PEOPLE:** Monegasques form 16 percent of the population. French make up nearly half of the population, while Italians comprise another 16 percent.

POPULATION: 32,543

LIFE EXPECTANCY AT BIRTH (YEARS): male, 75.5; female, 83.5

LITERACY RATE: 99%

ETHNIC GROUPS: French 47%, Monegasque 16%, Italian 16%

PRINCIPAL LANGUAGES: French (official), English, Italian, Monegasque

CHIEF RELIGION: Roman Catholic (official) 90%

■ **ECONOMY:** Tourism dominates the economy, but the country has successfully diversified into services and small, high-value-added industries.

GOVERNMENT TYPE: constitutional monarchy

CAPITAL: Monaco (pop., 32,000)

INDEPENDENCE DATE: 1419

MONETARY UNIT: euro

GDP: $870 million (2000 est.)

PER CAPITA GDP: $27,000

INDUSTRIES: tourism, construction, small-scale industrial and consumer products

WEBSITE: www.monaco-consulate.com

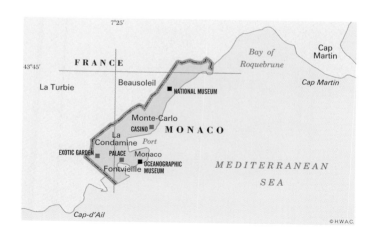

One of the most thinly populated countries in the world, Mongolia is three times as large as France, but most of its territory is desert and semiarid rangeland. Wedged between China and Russia, Mongolia has long been a cause of friction between the two superstates. The country is essentially a huge steppe plateau bordered on the south by the Gobi Desert. Large daily and seasonal temperature variations and little precipitation characterize the continental climate. Mongolia's natural resources include coal, copper, molybdenum, phosphates, tin, nickel, zinc, fluorspar, gold, and petroleum. Livestock is an important part of the economy. Some grain is grown. Industries include mining (primarily copper and gold), building materials, animal product processing, natural fiber manufacturing, food and beverages. Exports of copper, livestock, apparel, wool, cashmere and hides flow mainly to China, the United States and the United Kingdom. Because of Mongolia's remoteness and natural beauty, the tourism sector has recently shown signs of rapid growth.

Naadam festival

Mongols (predominantly Khalkha) make up most of the population and are predominantly Tibetan Buddhists. There are also small groups of Turkic (mostly Kazakh) and Tungusic. Khalkha Mongol is most prevalent language. Ulaanbaatar (Ulan Bator) is the capital and chief city.

Did you know? Rugged Mongolia is the world's most sparsely populated country.

The Mongols were united in the 1200s under the leadership of Genghis Khan, who established a far-flung Eurasian empire. In 1691 the northern Mongols accepted Chinese authority and remained under their rule until the twentieth century. Communist rule was inaugurated with the proclamation of the Mongolian People's Republic in 1924. Parties opposing the Communists were legalized in 1990.

AREA: 604,250 sq mi (1,565,000 sq km)

■ **CLIMATE:** Large daily and seasonal temperature variations and little precipitation characterize the continental climate.

■ **PEOPLE:** Mongols (predominantly Khalkha) make up most of the population. There are also small groups of Turkic (mostly Kazakh) and Tungusic.

POPULATION: 2,832,224

LIFE EXPECTANCY AT BIRTH (YEARS): male, 62.0; female, 66.5

LITERACY RATE: 97.8%

ETHNIC GROUPS: Mongol 85%, Turkic 7%, Tungusic 5%

PRINCIPAL LANGUAGES: Khalkha Mongol, Turkic, Russian

CHIEF RELIGION: Tibetan Buddhist Lamaism 96%

■ **ECONOMY:** Exports of copper, livestock, apparel, wool, cashmere and hides flow mainly to China, the United States and the United Kingdom. The tourism sector has recently shown signs of rapid growth.

CAPITAL: Ulaanbaatar (pop., 812,000)

INDEPENDENCE DATE: July 11, 1921

GOVERNMENT TYPE: republic

MONETARY UNIT: tugrik

GDP: $5.3 billion (2004 est.)

PER CAPITA GDP: $1,900

INDUSTRIES: construction materials, mining, food and beverages, processing of animal products

MINERALS: oil, coal, copper, molybdenum, tungsten, phosphates, tin, nickel, zinc, wolfram, fluorspar, gold, silver, iron, phosphate

CHIEF CROPS: wheat, barley, potatoes, forage crops

WEBSITE: www.mongolianembassy.us

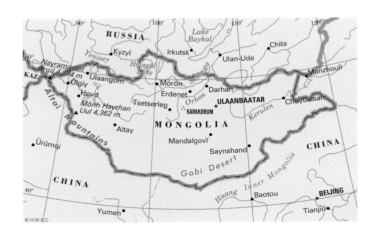

Montenegro was originally part of the former Socialist Federal Republic of Yugoslavia. The terrain is varied. The southwestern Adriatic coast has a high shoreline with a few nearby islands. Beyond the central plains, mountainous regions with thick forests are found in the north and east. The major rivers are the Morac̆a, Tara, and the Lim. The climate is generally Mediterranean, with hot, dry summers and relatively cold winters and heavy snow in the mountains. Natural resources include bauxite and hydroelectric power. Cereals, tobacco, potatoes, citrus fruits, olives and grapes are grown. Sheep are also raised. Aluminum and steelmaking, agricultural processing and consumer goods are the leading industries. Switzerland, Italy, Bosnia and Herzegovenia, and Serbia are the country's traditional trading partners, with most of Montenegro's aluminum output going to Switzerland. Tourism and tourism investments, particularly along the Adriatic coast, are expanding rapidly.

Montenegrins make up nearly half of the population while Serbians comprise another third. There are small groups of Bosniaks, Albanians and Muslims. The population is three quarters Orthodox Christian, 18 percent Muslim and 4 percent Roman Catholic. Serbo-Croatian is the dominant language; Albanian is spoken by 5 percent of the people. The Cyrillic alphabet is used. Podgorica is the capital and chief city.

> **Did you know?** Recently created Montenegro was once a part of Serbia.

The South Slavs entered the region in the 600s A.D. By the 1300s Serbia controlled a large empire on the Balkan Peninsula. In 1389 an Ottoman Turkish victory at Kosovo placed Serbia under Ottoman rule. Montenegro became a refuge for Serbs after the defeat at Kosovo. In 1799 the Turks recognized Montenegro's independence. The Serbian struggle for independence during the nineteenth century resulted in total freedom from Turkish rule in 1878. At the end of World War I in 1918, a united Kingdom of Serbs, Croats and Slovenes was proclaimed, later renamed Yugoslavia in 1929. In 1945, after World War II, a Communist republic was established, consisting of the six federal republics of Serbia, Montenegro, Macedonia, Croatia, Bosnia and Herzegovina and Slovenia. In 1991 federal Yugoslavia broke up. Serbia then sent arms to Serb rebels in Croatia and Bosnia. As a result, the United Nations imposed economic sanctions on Serbia and Montenegro in 1992; the sanctions were not lifted until 1996. In February, 2003, the Yugoslav parliament ratified the Constitutional Charter, establishing a new state union and changing the name of the country from Yugoslavia to Serbia and Montenegro. In May, 2006, the Republic of Montenegro dissolved its political union with Serbia and declared independence on June 3. The country became a member of the United Nations on June 28, 2006.

Kotor

AREA: 5,333 sq mi (13,812 sq km)

■ **CLIMATE:** Generally Mediterranean, with hot, dry summers, cold winters and heavy snow in the mountains.

■ **PEOPLE:** Montenegrins make up nearly half of the population while Serbians comprise another third. There are small groups of Bosnians, Albanians and Muslims.

POPULATION: 620,150

LIFE EXPECTANCY AT BIRTH (YEARS): male, 71; female, 76

LITERACY RATE: 93%

ETHNIC GROUPS: Montenegrins 43%, Serbs 32%, Bosniaks 8%, Albanians 5%

PRINCIPAL LANGUAGES: Serbian of the Ijekavian dialect (official), Albanian

CHIEF RELIGIONS: Orthodox 74%, Muslim 18%, Roman Catholic 2%

■ **ECONOMY:** Exports, consisting of iron ore and fish products, go to Japan, the European Union, China and Russia. Petroleum reserves are being developed.

GOVERNMENT TYPE: republic

CAPITAL: Podgorica (pop., 179,500)

INDEPENDENCE DATE: June 3, 2006

MONETARY UNIT: euro

GDP: $1.91 billion (2005 est.)

PER CAPITA GDP: $3,100

INDUSTRIES: Mining, manufacturing, chemicals, clothing, textiles, forestry

MINERALS: coal, bauxite, aluminum

CHIEF CROPS: olives, wine, potatoes, corn, citrus fruits, vegetables

WEBSITE: www.gom.cg.yu/eng.com

Geographically, Morocco is the westernmost Arab country, the only one to border the Atlantic coast of North Africa. The center is occupied by the dry, rocky Atlas Mountains, which slope downward to narrow fertile coastal plains along the Mediterranean and the Atlantic. In the south is the Sahara. Morocco's climate is Mediterranean, becoming more extreme in the interior. Morocco possesses the world's largest phosphate reserves; iron ore, manganese, lead, zinc, and copper are exploited. Wheat and barley, wine grapes, citrus fruits, vegetables, olives and livestock are chief agricultural commodities. Fishing is also important. Phosphate mining, the manufacture of leather goods and textiles, food processing, construction and public works are the leading industries. Marrakech is a major tourist center. Clothing, fish, chemicals, transistors, phosphates, fruits and vegetables are exported primarily to the European Union as well as to India and the United States.

The Arab-Berber ethnic group accounts for 99 percent of the population. Islam is the religion of 99 percent of the people. French is much used in business, although Arabic is the official language. Casablanca is Morocco's metropolis. Rabat is the capital; Fès and Marrakesh are other large cities.

Conquered by the Arabs in 683 A.D., Morocco became an independent kingdom in 788. The Almoravid Dynasty ruled an area stretching from Senegal to northern Spain from 1090 to 1140. In 1912 Morocco became a protectorate, with most of the country administered by France. Spain controlled the northern zone along the Mediterranean, and a southern zone was administered as part of Spanish Sahara. Tangier was declared an international zone. In 1956 Morocco was reunited under the Sultanate. In 1976 Morocco and Mauritania divided the disputed Western Sahara, but in 1979 Mauritania withdrew from its territory, which was then occupied by Morocco. Relations between Morocco and Algeria remain strained.

> **Did you know?** Morocco has the broadest plains and highest mountains in North Africa.

Casbah, Ait Ben Haddou

LIFE EXPECTANCY AT BIRTH (YEARS): male, 68.1; female, 72.7

LITERACY RATE: 43.7%

ETHNIC GROUPS: Arab-Berber 99%

PRINCIPAL LANGUAGES: Arabic (official), Berber dialects, French, Spanish, English

CHIEF RELIGION: Muslim (official) 99%

■ **ECONOMY:** Clothing, fish, chemicals, transistors, phosphates, fruits and vegetables are exported primarily to the European Union as well as to India and the United States. Tourism is an important source of revenue.

CAPITAL: Rabat (pop., 1,759,000)

INDEPENDENCE DATE: March 2, 1956

GOVERNMENT TYPE: constitutional monarchy

MONETARY UNIT: dirham

GDP: $134.6 billion (2004 est.)

PER CAPITA GDP: $4,200

INDUSTRIES: mining, food processing, leather goods, textiles, construction, tourism

MINERALS: phosphates, iron ore, manganese, lead, zinc

CHIEF CROPS: barley, wheat, citrus, wine, vegetables, olives

WEBSITE: www.mincom.gov.ma/

AREA: 172,414 sq mi (446,550 sq km)l

■ **CLIMATE:** A Mediterranean climate along the coast gives way to a harsh desert interior.

■ **PEOPLE:** Most Moroccans are Sunni Muslims of Arab, Berber or mixed Arab-Berber heritage. Arabs invaded in the 7th and the 11th centuries, establishing their culture in the process.

POPULATION: 33,241,259

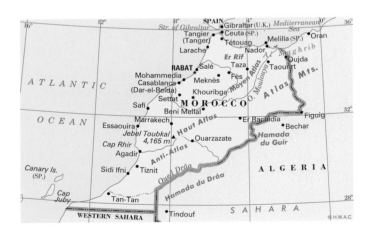

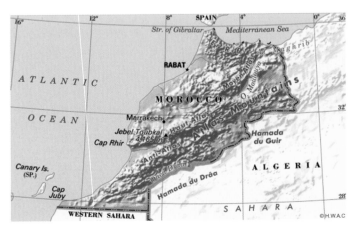

On the east coast of Africa, Mozambique extends more than 1500 miles along the Mozambique Channel, an arm of the Indian Ocean. Lowlands along the coast rise to an 8000-foot plateau, with mountains to the north. Tropical to sub-tropical; the northern coastal plain is hot and humid, while it is cooler to the south and inland. The Ruvuma, Lúrio, Zambezi, Save and Limpopo are the chief rivers. Coal, natural gas, titanium, tantalite and graphite are mined. Cash crops include cotton, cashew nuts, sugarcane, tea, cassava, corn, coconuts, sisal, citrus and tropical fruits, potatoes and sunflowers. Beef and poultry are also raised. Shrimp are gathered off the coast. Industries include food, beverages, chemicals, aluminum, natural gas, textiles, cement, glass and tobacco. Exports of aluminum, cashews, prawns, cotton, sugar, citrus, timber, bulk electricity, natural gas go to Belgium, the Netherlands, South Africa and Zimbabwe. Mozambique's national output of goods declined during the 1980s because of internal disorders, but has improved in recent years.

The people are nearly all of Bantu stock, including Makua, Tsonga, Makonde and Sena. There are also small European, Euro-African and Indian minorities. Portuguese is the official language, but many indigenous languages are spoken. Sixty percent of the population follow indigenous beliefs; 30 percent are Christian, and 10 percent are Muslim. Maputo is the capital and largest city.

Bantu peoples entered Mozambique from Central Africa after 1000 A.D. Arab traders touched on the coast before the arrival of the Portuguese under Vasco da Gama in 1498. The Portuguese developed trading posts and a thriving slave trade in the following centuries. After eleven years of guerrilla warfare, Mozambique was granted independence in 1975. However, civil war between the leftist FRELIMO (Mozambique Liberation Front) and the South Africa-backed RENAMO (Mozambique National Resistance) raged throughout the country until 1992. The country's first multi-party elections took place in October 1994, with FRELIMO presidential candidate winning a plurality of the popular vote. By mid-1995 more than 1.7 million Mozambican refugees had returned.

Did you know?
Mozambique has 10 major ethnic groups, and none forms a majority.

AREA: 309,496 sq mi (801,590 sq km)

CLIMATE: Tropical to sub-tropical; the northern coastal plain is hot and humid, while it is cooler to the south and inland.

Nampula

PEOPLE: The people are nearly all of Bantu stock, including Makua, Tsonga, Makonde and Sena. There are also small European, Euro-African and Indian minorities.

POPULATION: 19,686,505

LIFE EXPECTANCY AT BIRTH (YEARS): male, 37.8; female, 36.3

LITERACY RATE: 42.3%

ETHNIC GROUPS: Shangaan, Chokwe, Manyika, Sena, Makua

PRINCIPAL LANGUAGES: Portuguese (official) and dialects, English

CHIEF RELIGIONS: indigenous beliefs 50%, Christian 30%, Muslim 20%

ECONOMY: Exports of aluminum, cashews, prawns, cotton, sugar, citrus, timber, bulk electricity, natural gas go to Belgium, the Netherlands, South Africa and Zimbabwe.

CAPITAL: Maputo (pop., 1,221,000)

INDEPENDENCE DATE: June 25, 1975

GOVERNMENT TYPE: republic

MONETARY UNIT: metical

GDP: $23.4 billion (2004 est.)

PER CAPITA GDP: $1,200

INDUSTRIES: food, beverages, chemicals, petroleum products, textiles, cement, glass, asbestos, tobacco

MINERALS: coal, titanium, natural gas, tantalum, graphite

CHIEF CROPS: cotton, cashew nuts, sugarcane, tea, cassava, corn, coconuts, sisal, citrus and tropical fruits

WEBSITE: www.embamoc-usa.org

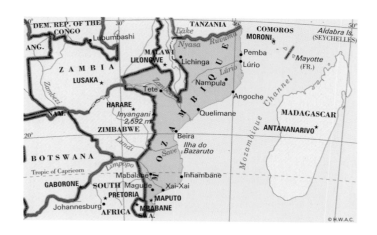

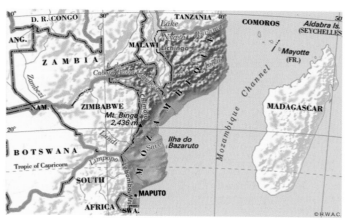

Bagan

The Union of Myanmar, more familiarly known as Burma, is rimmed on the north, east and west by mountain ranges forming a giant horseshoe. Within this mountain barrier is a great central basin, home to most of the country's population. The Irrawaddy, Salween and Sittang rivers flow south through the country and empty into the Andaman Sea. The monsoon climate is cloudy, rainy and hot in the summer and mild, with little rainfall in the winter. The country is rich in petroleum and natural gas as well as tin, copper, antimony, zinc and tungsten. Lead, coal, limestone and precious stones, of which Burmese rubies are notable, are also present. Self-sufficient in food, Myanmar produces paddy rice, pulses, beans, oil seed, groundnuts and sugarcane. The world's largest stand of hardwood trees is found here. Teak is the chief wood harvested. Industrial activity, largely government-controlled, includes agricultural processing, knit and woven apparel, wood and wood products, copper, tin, tungsten, iron, construction materials, pharmaceuticals, fertilizers and natural gas. Fish and fish products also contribute to the economy. Export revenues come from natural gas, teak and forest products, agricultural products, garments and marine products. Exports go to Thailand, India, China and Japan. Myanmar is one of the world's largest producers of illicit opium. Although Myanmar remains a poor Asian country, its rich resources furnish the potential for substantial long-term growth. Tourist potential is great but remains undeveloped.

Did you know?
Myanmar is widely known as the Land of Golden Pagodas.

More than two thirds of the population is Burman. Almost 10 percent is of Shan extraction, while those of Karen descent comprise about 7 percent and the Rakhine make up another 4 percent. There are small groups of Chinese, Mon and Indians. Almost 90 percent of the population follows the Buddhist religion. Burmese is the official and predominant language, but minority groups speak their own languages. Rangoon (Yangon) is the capital and largest city. Fabled Mandalay, famous for its many pagodas and center of Buddhism, is the second-largest city. A new administrative capital, begun in 2005, is under construction and development at Nay Pyi Taw.

Mongol peoples from Tibet moved into present-day Burma before the ninth century, settling along the Irrawaddy river. Burma was annexed piecemeal by Britain in the nineteenth century. It obtained dominion-like status in 1937. The Japanese occupation of Burma during World War II saw Burmese nationalists first fight the British and then the Japanese, whom they found were worse oppressors. Since 1948, when Burma became independent, the government has waged war with Karen and Shan insurgents, who want independence.

In 1988, a new ruling junta deposed the Burmese Socialist Party, suspended the constitution, and established the State Law and Order Restoration Council. They ruled by martial law until elections were held in May, 1990. The National League for Democracy party won an overwhelming victory. However, the junta refused to honor the results, and instead imprisoned many political activists. The ruling junta changed the country's name to "Myanmar," but the democratic opposition does not recognize the name change and maintains use of the name "Burma."

AREA: 261,970 sq mi (678,500 sq km)

■ **CLIMATE:** The monsoon climate is cloudy, rainy and hot in the summer and mild, with little rainfall in the winter.

■ **PEOPLE:** More than two thirds of the population is Burman. Almost 10 percent is of Shan extraction. There are small groups of Karen, Rakhine, Chinese and Mon.

POPULATION: 47,382,633

LIFE EXPECTANCY AT BIRTH (YEARS): male, 54.2; female, 57.9

LITERACY RATE: 83.1%

ETHNIC GROUPS: Burman 68%, Shan 9%, Karen 7%, Rakhine 4%, Chinese 3%, Indian 2%, Mon 2%

PRINCIPAL LANGUAGES: Burmese (official); many ethnic minority languages

CHIEF RELIGIONS: Buddhist 89%, Christian 4%, Muslim 4%, animist 1%

■ **ECONOMY:** Export revenues come from natural gas, teak and forest products, agricultural products, garments and marine products. Exports go to Thailand, India, China and Japan. Tourist potential is great but remains undeveloped.

GOVERNMENT TYPE: military

CAPITAL: Yangon (Rangoon) (pop., 3,874,000)

INDEPENDENCE DATE: January 4, 1948

MONETARY UNIT: kyat

GDP: $74.3 billion (2004 est.)

PER CAPITA GDP: $1,700

INDUSTRIES: agricultural processing, knit and woven apparel, wood and wood products, mining, construction materials, pharmaceuticals, fertilizer

MINERALS: petroleum, tin, antimony, zinc, copper, tungsten, lead, coal, marble, limestone, precious stones, natural gas

CHIEF CROPS: rice, pulses, beans, sesame, groundnuts, sugarcane

WEBSITE: www.state.gov/r/pa/ei/bgn/35910.htm

Famous for its national parks and wildlife, Namibia lies on the coast of southwestern Africa. The country is mostly a high plateau. On the coast, the Namib desert stretches for 1000 miles, and the Kalahari Desert of sand and limestone lies to the east. The Caprivi Strip, 20 to 50 miles wide and some 300 miles long, extends inland and eastward from the northeast corner of the country. Namibia's climate is hot and dry; rainfall is sparse and erratic. Diamonds and uranium are the chief mineral resources. Copper, gold, lead, zinc, tin, and salt are mined. Millet, sorghum, peanuts and grapes are grown. Livestock-raising is the major source of cash income, but fishing also contributes to the economy. The leading exports are diamonds, copper, gold, zinc, lead, uranium, beef, cattle, fish and karakul pelts, which go mainly to South Africa and the United States. Tourism is a rapidly growing sector of the Namibian economy.

About half of the population is Ovambo. Other ethnic groups include the Kavango, Herero, Damara, Nama, Caprivian, San (Bushmen), Baster and Tswana. Roughly 6 percent of the population is white, mostly of South African and German descent. English is the official language, but the majority speak indigenous languages, Afrikaans and German. Christianity is the dominant religion. Windhoek is the capital and chief city.

The original inhabitants, the Bushmen, were largely displaced by incoming Bantu peoples before the nineteenth century. Germany established a protectorate in Namibia in the 1890s, following the prior British annexation of the Walvis Bay area. After World War I, the League of Nations made South-West Africa, as it was then known, a mandate to be administered by South Africa. Following World War II, South Africa refused to place South-West Africa under the United Nations trusteeship system. Namibia achieved independence in 1990, ending many years of contention between South Africa and the U.N. South Africa turned over Walvis Bay to Namibia in 1994.

Did you know? Namibia is the world's 2nd-most thinly populated country.

AREA: 318,696 sq mi (825,418 sq km)

■ **CLIMATE:** The semidesert climate is hot and dry. Rainfall is sparse and erratic.

■ **PEOPLE:** About half of the population is Ovambo. Other ethnic groups include the Kavango, Herero, Damara, Nama, Caprivian, San (Bushmen), Baster and Tswana.

POPULATION: 2,044,147

Sand dunes

LIFE EXPECTANCY AT BIRTH (YEARS): male, 42.4; female, 38.6

LITERACY RATE: 38%

ETHNIC GROUPS: Ovambo 50%, Kavangos 9%, Herero 7%, Damara 7%, white 6%, mixed 7%

PRINCIPAL LANGUAGES: English (official), Afrikaans, German, Oshivambo, Herero, Nama

CHIEF RELIGIONS: Lutheran 50%, other Christian 30%, indigenous beliefs 10-20%

■ **ECONOMY:** The leading exports are diamonds, copper, gold, zinc, lead, uranium, beef, cattle, fish and karakul pelts, which go mainly to South Africa and the United States. Tourism is a rapidly growing sector of the economy.

GOVERNMENT TYPE: republic

CAPITAL: Windhoek (pop., 237,000)

INDEPENDENCE DATE: March 21, 1990

MONETARY UNIT: Namibia Dollar (NAD)

GDP: $14.8 billion (2004 est.)

PER CAPITA GDP: $7,300

INDUSTRIES: meatpacking, fish processing, dairy products, mining

MINERALS: diamonds, copper, uranium, gold, lead, tin, lithium, cadmium, zinc, salt, vanadium, natural gas

CHIEF CROPS: millet, sorghum, peanuts

WEBSITE: www.namibianembassyusa.org

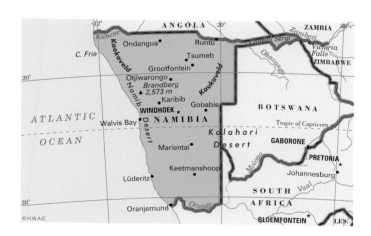

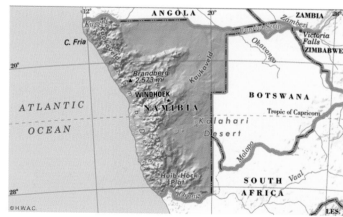

The barren central plateau of the tiny Pacific island of Nauru consists of large phosphate deposits, the result of centuries of bird droppings. The island is tropical with a monsoon season from November to February and unreliable rainfall. Phosphate, much prized as fertilizer, is the island's main natural resource and its only export. Export partners include South Africa, Germany, India and Japan. This unique export helped give the people of Nauru one of the highest per capita incomes in the world. However, phosphate reserves have been significantly depleted in recent years. Some environmentalists say the island is so ecologically devastated now that the inhabitants may soon have to be relocated elsewhere. Agriculture is limited to coconuts and coconut products.

Nauruans comprise most of the population. Other Pacific islanders, Chinese and Europeans make up the remainder. Nauruan is the official language; English is used for most government and commercial purposes. Two-thirds of the population is Protestant, and one-third is Roman Catholic in religion.

Germany annexed the island in 1888. After World War I, Nauru was administered as a League of Nations mandate under Australia, Britain, and New Zealand. Following Japanese occupation in World War II, the island was placed under United Nations trusteeship, with Australia acting as administrator on behalf of the three mandate nations. Nauru declared independence in 1968, becoming the world's smallest independent republic. The country joined the United Nations in 1999.

Denigomodu and Nibok

> **Did you know?**
> Phosphate reserves, from bird droppings, are nearly used up.

AREA: 8 sq mi (21 sq km)

■ **CLIMATE:** Tropical with a monsoon season (November to February); unreliable rainfall.

■ **PEOPLE:** Nauruans comprise most of the population. Other Pacific islanders, Chinese and Europeans make up the remainder.

POPULATION: 13,287

LIFE EXPECTANCY AT BIRTH (YEARS): male, 58.8; female, 66.1

LITERACY RATE: NA

ETHNIC GROUPS: Nauruan 58%, other Pacific Islander 26%, Chinese 8%, European 8%

PRINCIPAL LANGUAGES: Nauruan (official), English

CHIEF RELIGIONS: Protestant 66%, Roman Catholic 33%

■ **ECONOMY:** Phosphates are the main natural resource and only export. Export partners include South Africa, Germany, India and Japan. However, phosphate reserves have been significantly depleted in recent years.

GOVERNMENT TYPE: republic

CAPITAL: offices in Yaren District

INDEPENDENCE DATE: January 31, 1968

MONETARY UNIT: Australian dollar

GDP: $60 million (2001 est.)

PER CAPITA GDP: $5,000

Industries: mining, offshore banking, coconut products

MINERALS: phosphates

CHIEF CROPS: rice, corn, wheat, sugarcane, root crops

WEBSITE: www.un.int/nauru

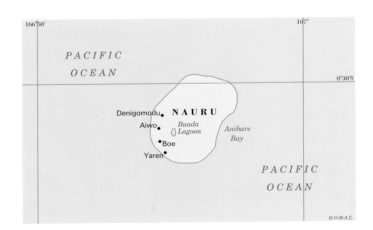

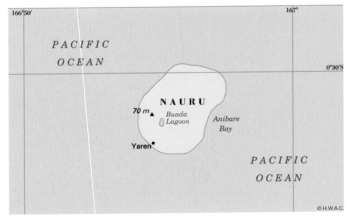

Nepal is a land of green valleys and the towering Himalayan mountains, including Mount Everest, the world's highest peak. The climate varies from cool summers and severe winters in the north to subtropical summers and mild winters in the south. There is a monsoon season from June through September. There are small deposits of quartz, lignite, limestone, magnesite, zinc, copper, iron, mica, lead, and cobalt. Rice, wheat, maize, sugarcane, oilseed, jute, millet and potatoes are the chief subsistence crops. Jute milling, textile production,cigarettes, cement, and brick are the chief industries. Political instability has negatively affected tourism. Exports of carpets, clothing, leather and jute goods go mainly to India, the United States and Germany.

The Nepalese are descendants of migrations from India and Tibet. Ethnic groups include the Chhettri, Brahman, Magar, Tharu, Tamang and Newar. Nepali is the official language, but twenty other languages are spoken. Hinduism is embraced by 90 percent of the population. Nepal is the only official Hindu state in the world. Kāthmāndu is the capital and chief city.

The modern kingdom of Nepal was established in 1768 by the ruler of Gurkha, a small principality west of Kāthmāndu. In 1990 the king proclaimed a constitution establishing a democratic system of government. In 1994, the ruling Nepali Congress Party lost a vote of no confidence in parliament. The resulting elections saw the Communist Party win the most seats in the legislature, with their parliamentary leader becoming the first democratically-elected Communist prime minister on the continent.

> **Did you know?** A mysterious creature called the yeti is said to roam Nepal's mountain peaks.

In June, 2001, the Crown Prince Dipendra reportedly killed his father, the King and most of the ruling family, before killing himself. Two days later, the late King's surviving brother Gyanendra was proclaimed King.

Annapurna

AREA: 54,363 sq mi (140,800 sq km)

■ **CLIMATE:** Tropical with a monsoon season (November to February); unreliable rainfall.

■ **PEOPLE:** Nauruans comprise most of the population. Other Pacific islanders, Chinese and Europeans make up the remainder.

POPULATION: 28,287,147

LIFE EXPECTANCY AT BIRTH (YEARS): male, 59.7; female, 59.1

LITERACY RATE: 27.5%

ETHNIC GROUPS: Newar, Indian, Gurung, Magar, Tamang, Rai, Limbu, Sherpa, Tharu

PRINCIPAL LANGUAGES: Nepali (official); about 30 dialects and 12 other languages

CHIEF RELIGIONS: Hindu (official) 86%, Buddhist 8%, Muslim 4%

■ **ECONOMY:** Phosphates are the main natural resource and only export. Export partners include South Africa, Germany, India and Japan. However, phosphate reserves have been significantly depleted in recent years.

MONETARY UNIT: rupee

GDP: $39.5 billion (2004 est.)

PER CAPITA GDP: $1,500

INDUSTRIES: tourism, carpet, textile, rice, jute, sugar, oilseed mills, cigarette, cement and brick production

MINERALS: quartz, lignite, copper, cobalt, iron ore

CHIEF CROPS: rice, corn, wheat, sugarcane, root crops

GOVERNMENT TYPE: constitutional monarchy

CAPITAL: Kathmandu (pop., 741,000)

INDEPENDENCE DATE: 1768

WEBSITE: www.nepalembassyusa.org

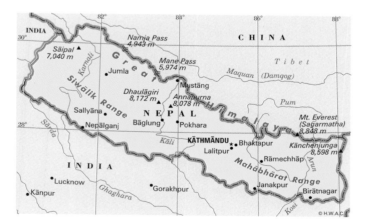

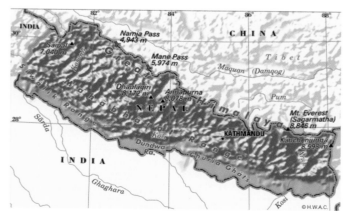

The Netherlands, as the name suggests, lies partly below sea level. Except for some hills in the southeast, the country is low and flat. More than one-fifth of the land has been reclaimed from the sea and is protected by dikes. In 1932 a barrier dam closed the North Sea mouth of the Zuider Zee, creating a vast freshwater lake, the IJsselmeer. The Dutch have carved habitable tracts from the waters, increasing the Netherlands' arable land by a tenth. Following a destructive storm in 1953, dams were built to keep the sea out of the southern estuaries. The Rhine and the Maas are the country's chief rivers. The temperate maritime climate has cool summers and moderate winters. Oil and natural gas are key resources. Peat, limestone, salt, sand and gravel also contribute to the economy. Livestock, dairy and poultry are important agricultural products. Flower bulbs, cut flowers, vegetables and fruits, sugar beets, potatoes, wheat and barley are also raised. The service industry, including hotels, restaurants, transport, communications, banking and business services generate three quarters of the country's income. Agro-industries, metal and engineering products, electrical equipment, chemicals, natural gas, petroleum and microelectronics are the leading industrial activities. Exports, headed by machinery and equipment, mineral fuels, chemicals, processed foods and agricultural products go mainly to the European Union.

Did you know? Much of the nation is below sea level and protected by dikes.

The people are mostly Dutch. There are small minorities of Moroccans, Turks and Surinamese. Roman Catholics make up 34 percent of the population; Protestants form 25 percent; 36 percent are unaffiliated. Dutch is the official and predominant language. Frisian is spoken in the north. The largest city is Amsterdam, co-capital with The Hague. The great port of Rotterdam is the second-largest city.

Celtic and Germanic tribes settled the area. The West Franks gradually conquered the region in the third century A.D. In the sixteenth century, the area passed to Charles V of the House of Hapsburg and then to his son, Philip II of Spain. Between 1568 and 1581, the Dutch waged war against Spain and gained their independence. During the seventeenth and eighteenth centuries, the Dutch built a vast overseas empire, and the Netherlands became one of the world's leading maritime and commercial powers. From 1815 to 1830 the kingdom of the Netherlands included Belgium, which seceded to form a separate nation. During World War II German forces overran the Netherlands and subjected the country to ruthless occupation. After World War II, the country gradually shed most of its large colonial-era empire— from Indonesia in the east to Suriname in the west. However, the "ABC Islands" in the Caribbean — Aruba, Bonaire and Curaçao — remain under Dutch authority. The Netherlands is one of the founding members of the European Community.

Amsterdam Canals

AREA: 16,033 sq mi (41,526 sq km)

CLIMATE: The temperate maritime climate has cool summers and moderate winters.

PEOPLE: The people are mostly Dutch. There are small minorities of Moroccans, Turks and Surinamese.

POPULATION: 16,491,461

LIFE EXPECTANCY AT BIRTH (YEARS): male, 76.2; female, 81.3

LITERACY RATE: 99%

ETHNIC GROUP: Dutch 83%

PRINCIPAL LANGUAGES: Dutch (official), Frisian, Flemish

CHIEF RELIGIONS: Roman Catholic 31%, Protestant 21%, Muslim 4%

ECONOMY: Exports, headed by machinery and equipment, mineral fuels, chemicals, processed foods and agricultural products go mainly to the European Union.

MONETARY UNIT: euro

GDP: $481.1 billion (2004 est.)

PER CAPITA GDP: $29,500

INDUSTRIES: agroindustries, metal and engineering products, electrical machinery and equipment, chemicals, petroleum, construction, microelectronics, fishing

MINERALS: natural gas, petroleum

CHIEF CROPS: grains, potatoes, sugar beets, fruits, vegetables

GOVERNMENT TYPE: parliamentary democracy under a constitutional monarch

CAPITALS: Amsterdam (pop., 1,145,000); seat of government, The Hague (pop., 705,000)

INDEPENDENCE DATE: 1579

WEBSITE: www.netherlands-embassy.org/homepage.asp

New Zealand consists of two principal islands in the South Pacific, North Island and South Island, separated by Cook Strait. North Island contains 72 percent of the country's population. Rolling hills and fertile coastal plains ascend to volcanic mountain peaks in that island's center. Bordered by a coastal plain on the east, the Southern Alps extend the entire length of South Island. New Zealand's climate is temperate to subtropical, with sharp regional contrasts. Natural gas, ironsand, coal and gold and are produced. Wool, meat and dairy products come from livestock-raising, the chief agricultural activity. Wheat, fruits and vegetables are also grown. The fish catch is important, as is forestry. Food processing; petroleum, coal and chemical products; textiles, wood and paper products; metal products and machinery are the chief industries. Exports, chiefly dairy products, meat, forest/wood/paper products, machinery and equipment, fruit and fish go to Australia, the United States, Japan and China.

Europeans comprise three quarters of the population; Maoris, a Polynesian people, form another ten percent. There are small minorities of Asians and Pacific Islanders. English is the official and dominant language. Some Maoris speak their native tongue. Protestants make up 52 percent of the population; Roman Catholics are another 15 percent. Auckland, Christchurch and Wellington, the capital, are the chief cities.

The Maoris reached the islands in the fourteenth century A.D. The Dutch explorer Tasman sighted the islands in 1642, and British explorer James Cook visited in 1769. During the nineteenth century large-scale British immigration began, producing conflicts with the native Maori people. New Zealand won Dominion status in 1907.

Did you know? Some 1,500 of the nation's plants grow nowhere else in the world.

AREA: 103,738 sq mi (268,680 sq km)

CLIMATE: New Zealand's climate is temperate to subtropical, with sharp regional contrasts.

PEOPLE: Europeans comprise three fourths of the population; Maoris, a Polynesian people, form another ten percent. There are small minorities of Asians and Pacific Islanders.

POPULATION: 4,076,140

LIFE EXPECTANCY AT BIRTH (YEARS): male, 75.5; female, 81.6

LITERACY RATE: 99%

ETHNIC GROUPS: New Zealand European 75%, Maori 10%, other European 5%, Pacific Islander 4%

Mount Cook (Aoraki)

PRINCIPAL LANGUAGES: English, Maori (both official)

CHIEF RELIGIONS: Protestant 52%, Roman Catholic 15%

ECONOMY: Exports, chiefly dairy products, meat, forest/wood/paper products, machinery and equipment, fruit and fish go to Australia, the United States, Japan and China. Tourism is a major economic activity.

MONETARY UNIT: New Zealand dollar

GDP: $92.5 billion (2004 est.)

PER CAPITA GDP: $23,200

INDUSTRIES: food processing, wood and paper products, textiles, machinery, transport equipment, banking and insurance, tourism, mining

MINERALS: natural gas, iron ore, sand, coal, gold, limestone

CHIEF CROPS: wheat, barley, potatoes, pulses, fruits, vegetables

GOVERNMENT TYPE: parliamentary democracy

CAPITAL: Wellington (pop., 343,000)

INDEPENDENCE DATE: September 26, 1907

WEBSITES: www.govt.nzwww.nzembassy.com/home.cfm?c=31

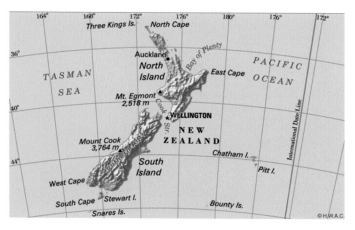

Nicaragua, the largest of the Central American republics, faces the Caribbean Sea on the east and the Pacific Ocean on the west. Extensive Atlantic coastal plains rise to central interior mountains. Volcanoes interrupt the narrow Pacific coastal plain. Nicaragua's climate is tropical in the lowlands and cooler in the highlands. Hurricanes are common. Nicaragua is one of the Western Hemisphere's poorest countries. Gold, silver and copper are chief mineral resources. Tungsten, lead and zinc are also mined. The chief crops are coffee, bananas, sugarcane, cotton, rice, beans and corn. Livestock-raising and dairy are also important. Industries include processed food, textiles, petroleum, chemicals, metal products and beverages. Foodstuffs, coffee, sugar, chemicals, gold and bananas are exported, mainly to Central America, the United States and the European Union.

Ethnically, more than two thirds of the population is mestizo (Spanish-Indian). There are significant minorities of white, black and native Indian. Roman Catholicism is the religion of 95 percent of the population. Spanish is the official and dominant language; various Indian tongues are spoken along the Caribbean coast. Managua is the capital and largest city.

Various Indian tribes inhabited Nicaragua before the arrival of the Spanish in 1552. During the Spanish colonial period, Nicaragua was part of the captaincy general of Guatemala. Nicaragua gained independence in 1821, and with other Central American republics was annexed to Mexico.

Did you know? The eastern shore is called Costa de Mosquitos (Mosquito Coast).

Later, Nicaragua became part of the Central American Federation. In 1838 Nicaragua became a separate republic. From 1912 to 1934, the United States military forces intervened intermittently in Nicaragua. Anastasio Somoza and his family dominated the country from 1934 to 1979, when Sandinista rebels came to power. The anti-Sandinista Contra movement attempted unsuccessfully to overthrow the regime during the 1980s. However, in 1990 free elections resulted in the defeat of the Sandinista candidate for president.

Nicaragua began free market reforms in 1991, and the economy began expanding in 1994. Rapid expansion of the tourist industry has made it one of the nation's largest sources of foreign exchange. The Central American Free Trade Agreement (CAFTA) came into force between the United States and Nicaragua on April 1, 2006.

AREA: 49,998 sq mi (129,494 sq km)

CLIMATE: The climate is tropical in the lowlands and cooler in the highlands. Hurricanes are common.

Playa Marsella

PEOPLE: Ethnically, more than two thirds of the population is mestizo (Spanish-Indian), 17 percent is white, 9 percent is black, and 5 percent native Indian.

POPULATION: 5,570,129

LIFE EXPECTANCY AT BIRTH (YEARS): male, 68.0; female, 72.2

LITERACY RATE: 68.2%

ETHNIC GROUPS: mestizo 69%, white 17%, black 9%, Amerindian 5%

PRINCIPAL LANGUAGES: Spanish (official), indigenous languages, English on Atlantic coast

CHIEF RELIGION: Roman Catholic 85%

ECONOMY: Foodstuffs, coffee, sugar, chemicals, gold and bananas are exported, mainly to Central America, the United States and the European Union. Tourism is expanding.

MONETARY UNIT: gold cordoba

GDP: $12.3 billion (2004 est.)

PER CAPITA GDP: $2,300

INDUSTRIES: food processing, chemicals, machinery and metal products, textiles, clothing, petroleum refining and distribution, beverages, footwear, wood

CHIEF CROPS: coffee, bananas, sugarcane, cotton, rice, corn, tobacco, sesame, soya, beans

MINERALS: gold, silver, copper, tungsten, lead, zinc

GOVERNMENT TYPE: republic

CAPITAL: Managua (pop., 1,098,000)

INDEPENDENCE DATE: September 15, 1821

WEBSITE: www.consuladodenicaragua.com

Bleak mountains punctuate the rocky desert that covers the northern four-fifths of Niger. The productive southern area, watered in part by the Niger River, is semiarid savanna, subject to droughts and floods. Niger has large uranium ore deposits. Coal, tin, iron ore, gold and phosphates are also mined. Cowpeas, cotton, peanuts, millet, sorghum and rice are the cash crops; livestock-raising also contributes to the economy. Industries include textiles, cement, soap, and beverages. Niger is one of the poorest countries in the world. Uranium, livestock, cowpeas, and onions are exported to France, Nigeria and the United States.

More than half of Niger's people are Hausa; the Djerma form another quarter. Fulani and Tuareg are significant minorities. The country is 80 percent Muslim. French is the official language, but most of the people speak Hausa. Niamey is the capital and only large city.

During the pre-European period, Niger was a battleground for the Ghana, Mali, Songhai and Bornu empires, and also for Arabs, Berbers and Tuaregs, among others. France occupied the country in the late nineteenth century. Niger gained its independence in 1960.

Niamey Mosque

AREA: 489,191 sq mi (1,267,000 sq km)

■ **CLIMATE:** The mainly desert climate is hot, dry, and dusty. The south is semiarid savanna, subject to droughts and floods.

■ **PEOPLE:** More than half of Niger's people are Hausa; the Djerma form another quarter. Fulani and Tuareg are significant minorities.

POPULATION: 12,525,094

LIFE EXPECTANCY AT BIRTH (YEARS): male, 42.4; female, 42.0

LITERACY RATE: 15.3%

ETHNIC GROUPS: Hausa 56%, Djerma 22%, Fula 9%, Tuareg 8%, Beri Beri (Kanouri) 4%

PRINCIPAL LANGUAGES: French (official); Hausa, Djerma, Fulani (all national)

CHIEF RELIGION: Muslim 80%

■ **ECONOMY:** Niger is one of the poorest countries in the world. Uranium, livestock, cowpeas, and onions are exported to France, Nigeria and the United States.

Did you know? Niger was part of noted ancient and medieval African empires.

MONETARY UNIT: CFA franc

GDP: $9.7 billion (2004 est.)

PER CAPITA GDP: $900

INDUSTRIES: mining, cement, brick, textiles, food processing, chemicals

MINERALS: uranium, coal, iron ore, tin, phosphates, gold, petroleum

CHIEF CROPS: cowpeas, cotton, peanuts, millet, sorghum, cassava, rice

GOVERNMENT TYPE: republic

CAPITAL: Niamey (pop., 890,000)

INDEPENDENCE DATE: August 3, 1960

WEBSITE: www.nigerembassyusa.org

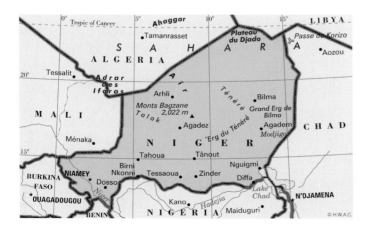

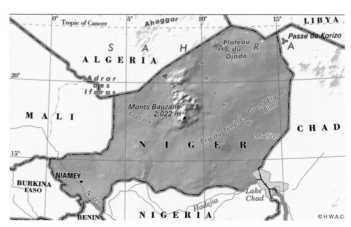

Nigeria is the most populous country in Africa. In the southern lowlands, branches of the Niger delta intersect mangrove swamps. Inland the swamps merge into central hills and plateaus. In the north, the savanna borders the southern part of the Sahara. The climate is equatorial in the south, tropical in the center and arid in the north. Nigeria is a major producer of oil and natural gas. There are also significant deposits of iron ore, coal, limestone, lead and zinc. Cash crops are cocoa, peanuts, palm oil, corn, rice, sorghum, millet, cassava, yams and rubber. Livestock, fishing and forestry resources are important. Textiles, cement, food products, footwear, chemicals and metal products are major industries. Exports are 95 percent oil; cocoa and rubber are also traded. Nigeria's exports go mostly to the United States, Brazil and Spain.

The nation has great ethnic diversity. There are more than 250 ethnic groups in the country. The largest are the Hausa and Fulani in the north, the Yoruba in the southwest and the Ibos (Igbos) in the southeast. English is the official language, but Hausa, Yoruba, Ibo and Fulani are widely spoken. The nation is 50 percent Muslim and 40 percent Christian. Lagos is the largest city, followed by Ibadan and Ogbomosho. The new city of Abuja became the capital in 1991.

Nigeria's earliest known culture, the Nok, held sway from about 700 to 200 B.C. During the Middle Ages, great empires and cultures flourished in both the northern and southern parts of the country. By 1400 A.D. Islam was firmly established in the north. Between the fifteenth and nineteenth centuries Portugal and Britain engaged in commerce and slave trading in Nigeria. Between 1861 and 1914, Britain gradually established administrative control over the country. Nigeria became independent in 1960 as a federal state. From 1967 to 1970 the federal government suppressed the secessionist republic of Biafra in the southeast. Though the discovery and development of oil in the Niger delta in 1956 have resulted in major growth.

> **Did you know?** Nigeria is the biggest oil-producing country in Africa.

In 1993 results of a presidential election, deemed to be Nigeria's fairest, indicated that wealthy Yoruba businessman M.K.O. Abiola had won a decisive victory. However, President Babangida, annulled the election, throwing Nigeria into turmoil. Although some progress has been made, the resulting political instability and inflation continue to hurt economic conditions.

AREA: 356,669 sq mi (923,768 sq km)

■ **CLIMATE:** The climate is equatorial in the south, tropical in the center and arid in the north.

Abuja-Parliament House

■ **PEOPLE:** There are more than 250 ethnic groups in the country. The largest are the Hausa and Fulani in the north, the Yoruba in the southwest and the Ibos (Igbos) in the southeast.

POPULATION: 131,859,731

LIFE EXPECTANCY AT BIRTH (YEARS): male, 50.9; female, 51.1

LITERACY RATE: 57.1%

ETHNIC GROUPS: more than 250; Hausa and Fulani 29%, Yoruba 21%, Igbo (Ibo) 18%, Ijaw 10%

PRINCIPAL LANGUAGES: English (official), Hausa, Yoruba, Igbo (Ibo), Fulani

CHIEF RELIGIONS: Muslim 50%, Christian 40%, indigenous beliefs 10%

■ **ECONOMY:** Nigeria is a major producer of oil and natural gas. Exports are 95 percent oil; cocoa and rubber are also traded. Nigeria's exports go mostly to the United States, Brazil and Spain.

GOVERNMENT TYPE: republic

CAPITAL: Abuja (pop., 452,000)

INDEPENDENCE DATE: October 1, 1960

MONETARY UNIT: naira

GDP: $125.7 billion (2004 est.)

PER CAPITA GDP: $1,000

INDUSTRIES: petroleum extraction, mining, agricultural processing, cotton, rubber, wood, hides and skins, textiles, cement and other construction materials, footwear, chemicals, fertilizer, printing, ceramics, steel

MINERALS: natural gas, petroleum, tin, columbite, iron ore, coal, limestone, lead, zinc

CHIEF CROPS: cocoa, peanuts, palm oil, corn, rice, sorghum, millet, cassava, yams

WEBSITE: www.nigeriaembassyusa.org

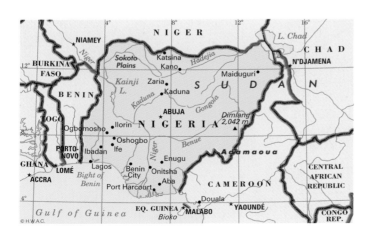

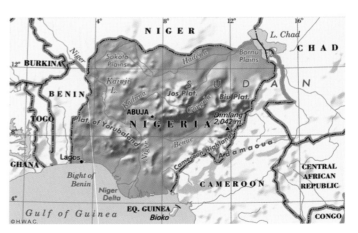

Lying atop Western Europe with nearly half its 1,100-mile length north of the Arctic Circle, Norway is the most sparsely populated country on the continent. Many fjords deeply indent the coast. From the coast the land rises to high plateaus and mountain ranges that are cut by fertile valleys and rapid rivers. Many lakes dot the landscape. Modified by the North Atlantic Current, the climate is temperate along the coast and colder in the interior. The offshore North Sea oil deposits have made Norway, along with Britain, Europe's major petroleum producer. Iron ore, titanium, copper, lead and zinc are important mineral resources. Fishing and forestry are major contributors to the Norwegian economy. Hydro power is a major source of energy. Livestock and dairy are the chief agricultural activities. Barley, oats, wheat, potatoes, fruits and vegetables are also grown. Shipbuilding and the manufacture of machinery, metals, pulp and paper and chemicals are major industrial activities. Petroleum and petroleum products are the major exports.

Norway is one of the world's largest oil exporters, and provides much of western Europe's crude oil and gas. Other exports include machinery and equipment, metals, fish products, chemicals and ships, which go primarily to the European Union. The Norwegian merchant marine is among the world's largest.

The people of Norway are almost entirely Norwegian, although 20,000 Sami (Lapps) live in the north. Norwegian is the official and only language. Evangelical Lutherans comprise 88 percent of the population. Oslo is the capital and largest city, followed by Bergen and Trondheim.

Did you know? Norway has many fjords, steep-sided narrow inlets, in its coastline.

The Norse Viking raids and conquests — from the eighth to the eleventh century — played an important part in European history. During the following centuries, Norway was united with Denmark and Sweden at different times. From 1814 to 1905 the nation existed in a personal union with Sweden under the Swedish monarch. In 1905 Norway became an independent kingdom. From 1940 to 1945 Norway was occupied by Nazi Germany. In 1968 huge oil deposits were discovered in the Norwegian sector of the North Sea. Norway voted against joining the European Union in a 1994 referendum.

AREA: 125,182 sq mi (324,220 sq km)

CLIMATE: Modified by the North Atlantic Current, the climate is temperate along the coast and colder in the interior.

PEOPLE: The people of Norway are almost entirely Norwegian, although 20,000 Sami (Lapps) live in the north.

Grieg Concert Hall

POPULATION: 4,610,820
LIFE EXPECTANCY AT BIRTH (YEARS): male, 76.6; female, 82.2
LITERACY RATE: 100%
ETHNIC GROUPS: Norwegian, Sami
PRINCIPAL LANGUAGES: Norwegian (official), Sami, Finnish
CHIEF RELIGION: Evangelical Lutheran (official) 86%
ECONOMY: Petroleum and petroleum products are the major exports. Others include machinery and equipment, metals, fish products, chemicals and ships, which go primarily to the European Union.
MONETARY UNIT: krone
GDP: $183.0 billion (2004 est.)
PER CAPITA GDP: $40,000
INDUSTRIES: petroleum and gas, food processing, shipbuilding, pulp and paper products, metals, chemicals, timber, mining, textiles, fishing
MINERALS: petroleum, copper, natural gas, pyrites, nickel, iron ore, zinc, lead
CHIEF CROPS: barley, wheat, potatoes
GOVERNMENT TYPE: hereditary constitutional monarchy
CAPITAL: Oslo (pop., 795,000)
INDEPENDENCE DATE: June 7, 1905
WEBSITE: www.norway.no

The coastline of Oman extends about 1,000 miles along the Gulf of Oman and the Arabian Sea. The fertile coastal plain gives way to a range of barren hills and a desert plateau. There is no defined boundary with Saudi Arabia and the United Arab Emirates. Oman has a hot, dry desert interior, but is humid along the coast, allowing for some agriculture. Summer monsoons sometimes occur in the far south. Petroleum is the dominant natural resource, but copper, marble, limestone, gypsum and chromium are also mined. Dates, fruits and vegetables are grown. Fish and livestock are important commodities. Oil is the chief export, shipped mainly to East Asia.

While the population is mostly Arab, there is a large Baluchi minority of Iranian origin. Many foreign workers live here, most from India, Pakistan and Iran. Arabic is the official language. The population is almost entirely Muslim. Muscat is the capital and chief town of the sultanate.

Oman was converted to Islam in the seventh century. Portugal and Ottoman Turkey ruled the region from 1508 to 1749, when the present dynasty assumed power. The area was known as "Muscat and Oman" until 1970, when the name was shortened to Oman. Oman settled its border disputes with the new Republic of Yemen in October, 1992.

Did you know? The average annual rainfall in Oman is less than 4 in (100 mm).

AREA: 82,031 sq mi (212,460 sq km)

CLIMATE: Oman has a hot, dry desert interior, but is humid along the coast, allowing for some agriculture. Summer monsoons sometimes occur in the far south.

PEOPLE: Most Omanis are of Arabic descent, but there is a large Baluchi minority of Iranian origin. Many foreign workers live here, most from India, Pakistan and Iran.

POPULATION: 3,102,229

LIFE EXPECTANCY AT BIRTH (YEARS): male, 70.7; female, 75.2

LITERACY RATE: approaching 80%

ETHNIC GROUPS: Arab, Baluchi, South Asian, African

Monument

PRINCIPAL LANGUAGES: Arabic (official) English, Baluchi, Urdu, Indian Dialects

CHIEF RELIGION: Muslim 75% (official; mostly Ibadhi)

ECONOMY: Oil provides most of Oman's revenue, but agriculture employs more people. Fertile coastal areas produce dates, grains, limes, bananas, vegetables and livestock.

MONETARY UNIT: rial Omani

GDP: $38.1 billion (2004 est.)

PER CAPITA GDP: $13,100

INDUSTRIES: oil and gas, construction, cement, copper

MINERALS: petroleum, copper, asbestos, marble, limestone, chromium, gypsum, natural gas

CHIEF CROPS: dates, limes, bananas, alfalfa, vegetables

GOVERNMENT TYPE: absolute monarchy

CAPITAL: Muscat (pop., 638,000)

INDEPENDENCE DATE: 1650

WEBSITE: www.state.gov/r/pa/ei/bgn/35834.htm

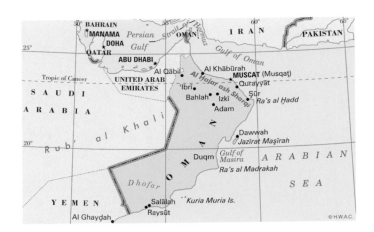

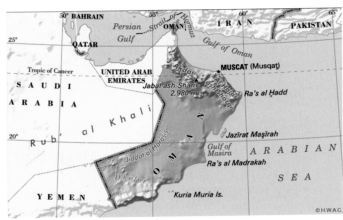

Pakistan extends about 1,000 miles (1610 kilometers) from the Arabian Sea to the mountain wall of the Hindu Kush and the towering peaks of the Karakoram. A barren plain stretches along the foothills of the mountains; in the center is the fertile Indus river plain. The climate is of the hot desert type in most of the country, temperate in the northwest and arctic in the north. Mineral resources include extensive natural gas reserves, limited petroleum, poor-quality coal, iron ore, copper and salt. Pakistan possesses the world's largest contiguous irrigation system, producing cotton, wheat, rice, sugarcane, fruits and vegetables. Beef, mutton, milk and eggs are alos important. Textiles & apparel, food processing, pharmaceuticals, construction materials, shrimp, fertilizer, and paper products are the major industries. Cotton, textiles and clothing are the chief exports, destined for the United States, United Arab Emirates, United Kingdom, China and Germany.

The population is made up chiefly of Punjabi, Sindhi, Pushtan (Pathan) and Baloch (Baluchi) peoples. Islam is the religion of most of the people. Urdu and English are the official languages; Punjabi is spoken by 64 percent of the population. Karachi is the largest city, followed by Lahore and Rawalpindi. Islāmabād is the capital.

In about 2000 B.C. the Indus valley was the home of an ancient civilization, centered on Harappa and Mohenjo-Daro, which was overrun by Aryan invaders about 1500 B.C. Later conquerors were Persians, Greeks under Alexander the Great, Parthians and Kushans. Between the eighth and eleventh centuries invaders from Arabia and Moghuls from the northwest conquered the Indus valley, converting millions of its inhabitants to Islam. Britain conquered the area of present-day Pakistan in the nineteenth century. The departure of the British in 1947 resulted in the creation of a Muslim national homeland split into two widely separated parts. In the west is located what is now present-day Pakistan. The second and more populous part, which is now Bangladesh, was carved from the old colonial state of Bengal. In 1971 an uprising by separatists in the eastern portion resulted in the dispatch of the Pakistani national army to crush the separatists. Finally, in December 1971 Indian forces invaded the eastern area, crushing Pakistani armed forces, resulting in the independence of Bangladesh. Pakistan and India have clashed over the possession of Kashmir twice, in 1947 and 1965.

Did you know? K2, the world's 2nd-highest peak (28,250 ft [8,611 m]), is in the Hindu Kush in Pakistan.

In response to India's nuclear weapons testing, Pakistan conducted its own tests in 1998 increasing tensions in the region. The dispute over Kashmir is ongoing, but recently tensions have been decreasing, including the opening of the border between the two countries.

Chaukundi Tombs

AREA: 310,403 sq mi (803,940 sq km)

■ **CLIMATE:** Most of the country is hot desert. The climate is more temperate in the northwest and arctic in the north.

■ **PEOPLE:** Invaded through the centuries by many cultures, Pakistan's ethnic and religious history is quite diverse. Punjabis are in the majority, followed by the Sindhis, Pashtuns and the Baluchi.

POPULATION: 165,803,560

LIFE EXPECTANCY AT BIRTH (YEARS): male, 61.7; female, 63.6

LITERACY RATE: 42.7%

ETHNIC GROUPS: Punjabi, Sindhi, Pashtun, Balochi

PRINCIPAL LANGUAGES: English, Urdu (both official); Punjabi, Sindhi, Siraiki, Pashtu, Balochi, Hindko, Brahui, Burushaski

CHIEF RELIGIONS: Muslim 97% (official; Sunni 77%, Shi'a 20%)

■ **ECONOMY:** Traditionally agricultural, Pakistan's cultivated land is extensively irrigated. Cotton, wheat and rice are among the most important crops. Tourism is also increasing.

MONETARY UNIT: rupee

GDP: $347.3 billion (2004 est.)

PER CAPITA GDP: $2,200

INDUSTRIES: textiles, food processing, beverages, construction materials, clothing, paper products

MINERALS: natural gas, limited petroleum, poor quality coal, iron ore, copper, salt, limestone

CHIEF CROPS: cotton, wheat, rice, sugarcane, fruits, vegetables

CAPITAL: Islamabad (pop., 698,000)

INDEPENDENCE DATE: August 14, 1947

GOVERNMENT TYPE: republic with strong military influence

WEBSITE: www.pakistan.gov.pk

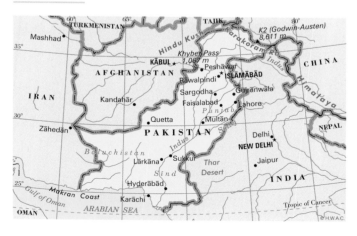

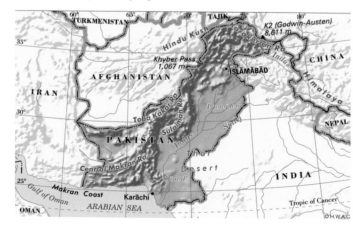

The Republic of Palau, situated 530 miles (853 kilometers) southeast of the Philippines in the North Pacific, is made up of 200 islands, varying from the high, mountainous main island of Babelthuap to low coral islands fringed by barrier reefs. The hot and humid tropical climate has a wet season from May to November. Subsistence farming, some tourism and fishing are the main economic activities. Export products of fish, garments and handicrafts go mainly to the United States, Japan, Taiwan and Singapore.

Palauans are a mixture of Polynesian, Malayan and Melanesian stocks. There are small Filipino and Chinese minorities. English, Palauan and other island languages are official. Various Christian sects and the indigenous Modekngei religion are the chief faiths. The capital, originally located in Koror, on the island of Koror, was moved to the newly built town of Melekeok in 2007.

The islands were under Spanish administration after 1886. In 1899 they were sold to Germany, but in 1921 they became part of the Japanese mandate area. Severe fighting between United States and Japanese troops took place here in 1944. Palau was made part of the United Nations Trust Territory of the Pacific Islands under U.S. administration in 1947. The islands became an autonomous republic in 1981, but did not gain full independence until 1994.

Did you know? Nevada has over 100 times more people than Palau.

Rock Islands

AREA: 177 sq mi (458 sq km)

■ **CLIMATE:** The hot and humid tropical climate has a wet season from May to November.

■ **PEOPLE:** Palauans are a mixture of Polynesian, Malayan and Melanesian stocks. There are small Filipino and Chinese minorities.

POPULATION: 20,303

LIFE EXPECTANCY AT BIRTH (YEARS): male, 66.7; female, 73.2

LITERACY RATE: 92%

ETHNIC GROUPS: Palauan (Micronesian/Malayan/Melanesian mix) 70%, Asian 28%, white 2%

PRINCIPAL LANGUAGES: English (official); Palauan, Sonsorolese, Tobi, Angaur, Japanese (all official in certain states)

CHIEF RELIGIONS: Roman Catholic 49%, Modekngei 30%

■ **ECONOMY:** Subsistence farming, tourism and fishing are the main economic activities. Export products of fish, garments and handicrafts go mainly to the United States, Japan, Taiwan and Singapore.

CAPITAL: Koror (pop., 14,000)

INDEPENDENCE DATE: October 1, 1994

GOVERNMENT TYPE: republic

MONETARY UNIT: U.S. dollar

GDP: $174 million (2001 est.)

PER CAPITA GDP: $9,000

INDUSTRIES: tourism, craft items, construction, garment making

MINERALS: gold, deep-seabed minerals

CHIEF CROPS: coconuts, copra, cassava, sweet potatoes

WEBSITE: www.visit-palau.com

Panama, a narrow serpentine and largely mountainous isthmus connecting North and South America, is bisected by the 51-mile-long (82 kilometer) Panama Canal. Lowlands lie along both coastlines. Rainforests cover the Caribbean side and the eastern part of Panama almost entirely. The tropical maritime climate is hot, humid and cloudy with a long rainy season from May to January. Mahogany forests, copper and shrimp are the country's chief natural resources. Coffee, bananas, vegetables, corn, rice and sugar are the leading crops. Livestock are also raised. Industries include food and drink processing, chemicals, paper products, refined sugar, clothing, furniture and construction. Exports, mainly bananas, shrimp, sugar, coffee and clothing, go to the United States and the European Union. Tourism, particularly Panama Canal cruises, is increasing.

Mestizos of mixed Indian and European ancestry form more than two thirds of the population. There are smaller groups of Amerindian-mixed (West Indian), Caucasian and Amerindian. Roman Catholicism is the religion of 85 percent of the people. Spanish is the official language. Panamá is the capital and chief city. Colón and David are other important cities.

Did you know?
Christopher Columbus visited Panama in 1502.

Following the famous crossing of the isthmus by Balboa in 1513, the area passed into Spanish hands. In 1821 Panama, as part of Colombia, broke away from Spain. From 1881 through 1889 a French company headed by Ferdinand de Lesseps tried unsuccessfully to cut a canal across the isthmus. In 1903 the United States supported a Panamanian revolt against Colombia. The new republic granted control over the Canal Zone to the U.S. In 1914 the Panama Canal was opened after ten years of work.

In 1977, more than sixty years later, the U.S. began the transfer of the Canal Zone to Panama. Economic and military assistance to Panama was frozen in 1987 in response to the political crisis in Panama and an attack on the U.S. Embassy. After nearly two years of political instability, U.S. troops invaded Panama in December 1989. In January 1990, General Manuel Noriega, the Panamanian leader, was arrested and sent to the United States, where he was convicted and imprisoned on charges of drug trafficking. In December of 1999 the United States formally handed over complete control of the Panama Canal to Panama.

AREA: 30,193 sq mi (78,200 sq km)

CLIMATE: The tropical maritime climate is hot, humid and cloudy with a long rainy season from May to January.

Panamá pelicans

PEOPLE: More than two thirds of the population is mestizo (Spanish-Indian). There are smaller groups of Amerindian-mixed (West Indian), Caucasian and Amerindian.

POPULATION: 3,191,319

LIFE EXPECTANCY AT BIRTH (YEARS): male, 69.8; female, 74.6

LITERACY RATE: 90.8%

ETHNIC GROUPS: mestizo 70%, Amerindian-West Indian 14%, white 10%, Amerindian 6%

PRINCIPAL LANGUAGES: Spanish (official), English

CHIEF RELIGIONS: Roman Catholic 85%, Protestant 15%

ECONOMY: Exports, mainly bananas, shrimp, sugar, coffee and clothing, go to the United States and the European Union. Tourism, particularly Panama Canal cruises, is increasing.

MONETARY UNIT: balboa

GDP: $20.6 billion (2004 est.)

PER CAPITA GDP: $6,900

INDUSTRIES: construction, petroleum refining, brewing, cement, sugar milling

MINERALS: copper

CHIEF CROPS: bananas, rice, corn, coffee, sugarcane, vegetables

GOVERNMENT TYPE: republic

CAPITAL: Panamá (pop., 930,000)

INDEPENDENCE DATE: November 3, 1903

WEBSITE: www.visitpanama.com

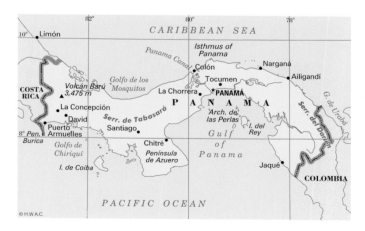

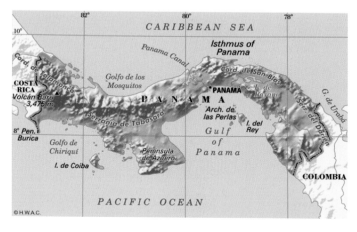

apua New Guinea occupies half the island of New Guinea and includes the offshore Bismarck Archipelago plus other islands. A high mountain ridge bisects the New Guinea portion and includes broad upland valleys and plains. Vast swamps take up much of the coast. The climate is tropical, with slight seasonal temperature variations. There is a northwest monsoon from December through March and a southeast monsoon from May through October. Papua New Guinea produces much copper and gold as well as oil and natural gas. Coffee, cocoa, copra, sugar, palm oil, tea and rubber are the chief cash crops. Forestry is important, as is fishing for tuna and lobsters. Copra crushing, palm oil processing, plywood and wood chip production, gold, silver, and copper mining, construction and crude oil production are major industries. Oil, gold, copper, gold, timber, palm oil, coffee and shellfish are the chief exports destined for Australia, Japan, Germany and China.

The indigenous population of Papua New Guinea is one of the most heterogeneous in the world. Papua New Guinea has several thousand separate communities, most with only a few hundred people. The population is made up of two major groups - Papuans in the interior and on the south coast, and Melanesians on the north coast and on the islands. Seven hundred and fifteen indigenous languages are spoken; pidgin English is widely used. Protestantism is the religion of 45 percent of the population, while Roman Catholicism is followed by 22 percent. Port Moresby is the capital and chief city.

> **Did you know?** More than 700 languages are spoken by hundreds of isolated tribes.

Humans arrived in New Guinea perhaps as early as 50,000 B.C. Germany took control of the northern coast and islands in the late nineteenth century. Britain established a protectorate over the southern area, Papua, in 1884. The British turned Papua over to Australia in 1906. Following Australian seizure during World War I, the German area, the Territory of New Guinea, was placed under a League of Nations mandate administered by Australia. The area was the scene of fierce fighting between invading Japanese forces and Allied troops during World War II. Papua and New Guinea were united administratively in 1949. In 1975 the country was granted independence.

AREA: 178,703 sq mi (462,840 sq km)

■ **CLIMATE:** The climate is tropical, with slight seasonal temperature variations. There are two monsoon seasons.

■ **PEOPLE:** The indigenous population is made up of two major groups - Papuans in the interior and on the south coast, and Melanesians on the north coast and on the islands.

New Guinea sculpture

POPULATION: 5,670,544

LIFE EXPECTANCY AT BIRTH (YEARS): male, 62.4; female, 66.8

LITERACY RATE: 64.5%

ETHNIC GROUPS: Melanesian, Papuan, Negrito, Micronesian, Polynesian

PRINCIPAL LANGUAGES: English (official), pidgin English, Motu; 715 indigenous languages

CHIEF RELIGIONS: indigenous beliefs 34%, Roman Catholic 22%, Protestant 44%

■ **ECONOMY:** Oil, gold, copper, gold, timber, palm oil, coffee and shellfish are the chief exports destined for Australia, Japan, Germany and China.

GOVERNMENT TYPE: parliamentary democracy

CAPITAL: Port Moresby (pop., 275,000)

INDEPENDENCE DATE: September 16, 1975

MONETARY UNIT: kina

GDP: $12.0 billion (2004 est.)

PER CAPITA GDP: $2,200

INDUSTRIES: copra and palm oil processing, wood products, mining, construction, tourism

MINERALS: gold, copper, silver, natural gas, oil

CHIEF CROPS: coffee, cocoa, coconuts, palm kernels, tea, rubber, sweet potatoes, fruit, vegetables

WEBSITE: www.pngtourism.org.pg

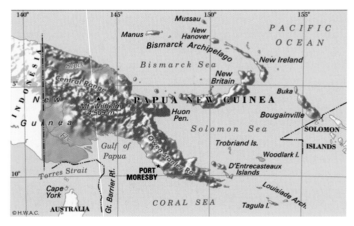

Landlocked Paraguay is divided into two regions by the Paraguay River. The eastern part consists of rolling terrain with tropical forests and fertile grasslands. To the west is the Chaco, a low plain covered with marshes and dense scrub forests. Paraguay's climate varies from temperate east of the Paraguay River to semiarid in the far west. Hydroelectric power is an important source of energy. Timber is the major natural resource. Cotton, sugarcane and soybeans are the chief cash crops; livestock-raising is also important. Manufacturing includes sugar, cement, textiles, beverages and wood products. Cotton, soybeans, vegetable oil, timber, meat and meat products and hydroelectric power are exported mostly to neighboring countries.

Paraguay's people are 95 percent mestizos (Spanish and Indian). Roman Catholicism is the religion of 95 percent of the population. A sizable Mennonite community lives in the Chaco. Spanish is the official language. Guarani is the dominant language. Asunción is the capital and chief city.

Spain took control of the area in 1538. From 1605 through 1767, Jesuits established missions and worked among the Guarani Indians. In 1811 Paraguay became independent. Between 1865 and 1870 Paraguay was disastrously defeated in a war against Argentina, Brazil and Uruguay, losing much territory and more than half its population. The Chaco War of 1932-35 with Bolivia brought Paraguay victory but resulted in economic distress. In 1993, Paraguay was returned to civilian rule after the toppling of military dictator General Alfredo Stroessner, who had ruled uninterrupted from 1954 to 1989.

> **Did you know?**
> Paraguay named a department in honor of U.S. Pres. Rutherford Hayes.

AREA: 157,047 sq mi (406,750 sq km)

■ **CLIMATE:** The climate varies from temperate east of the Paraguay River to semiarid in the far west.

■ **PEOPLE:** Paraguay's people are 95 percent mestizos (Spanish and Indian).

POPULATION: 6,506,464

LIFE EXPECTANCY AT BIRTH (YEARS): male, 72.1; female, 77.3

Iguacu Falls

LITERACY RATE: 92.1%

ETHNIC GROUPS: mestizo 95%

PRINCIPAL LANGUAGES: Spanish, Guaraní (both official)

CHIEF RELIGION: Roman Catholic 90%

■ **ECONOMY:** Paraguay has a predominantly agricultural economy. Cotton, soybeans, vegetable oil, timber, meat and meat products and hydroelectric power are exported mostly to neighboring countries.

GOVERNMENT TYPE: republic

CAPITAL: Asunción (pop., 1,639,000)

INDEPENDENCE DATE: May 14, 1811

MONETARY UNIT: guarani

GDP: $29.9 billion (2004 est.)

PER CAPITA GDP: $4,800

INDUSTRIES: sugar, cement, textiles, beverages, wood products

CHIEF CROPS: cotton, sugarcane, soybeans, corn, wheat, tobacco, cassava, fruits, vegetables

MINERALS: iron ore, manganese, limestone

WEBSITE: www.paraguay.com

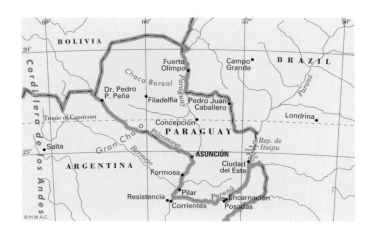

Peru, home of the great pre-Colombian Inca civilization, is situated on the west coast of South America just south of the Equator. The country is divided into a narrow coastal desert; the high sierra, the zone of the great Andean cordilleras; and the eastern lowlands (La Montaña), with uncharted hills, forests and tropical jungles. The climate varies from tropical in the east to dry desert in the west. The Ucayali and the Marañón, both tributaries of the Amazon, are the chief rivers. Peru is an important producer of silver, copper, gold, iron, lead and zinc; petroleum, natural gas and coal are also exploited. The chief commercial crops are coffee, cotton and sugarcane, but rice, corn, plantains, potatoes, livestock and poultry are also raised. Anchovy fishing is the most important fishing activity, although the vagaries of offshore currents cause fluctuations in the catch. Services make up more than half of the domestic economy. Food and beverages, textiles and apparel, metals, minerals, petroleum and fish processing are the leading industries. Mineral exports consistently account for the most significant part of Peru's export revenue. Copper, gold, zinc, petroleum, fishmeal, textiles, apparel and coffee are exported to the United States, China, Chile and Canada. Tourism has grown substantially in recent years.

Amerindians account for nearly half of the population; mestizos (Spanish-Indian) make up another third. There are also small groups of Europeans, Africans, Japanese and Chinese. Spanish and Quechua are the official languages. Roman Catholicism is the chief religion. Lima is the capital and chief city.

Did you know? The Inca empire had its base in Peru's mountains.

Preceding the great Inca civilization, other advanced cultures once existed in Peru, including the Chavin, Tiahuanaco, Mochica and Chimu. In 1532 the Inca Empire fell to the Spanish conquistador, Francisco Pizarro. Peru was the center of the Spanish Viceroyalty of New Castilia, with its capital at Lima. Peru gained independence from Spain with the victories of the revolutionary armies led by San Martín and Bolívar. Territory in the south was lost in the unsuccessful 1879-84 War of the Pacific with Chile. For many years during the twentieth century, Peru has been in dispute with Ecuador over their common boundary.

AREA: 496,226 sq mi (1,285,220 sq km)

CLIMATE: The climate varies from tropical in the east to dry desert in the west; temperate to frigid in the Andes.

PEOPLE: Amerindians account for nearly half of the population; mestizos (Spanish-Indian) make up another third. There are also small groups of Europeans, Africans, Japanese and Chinese.

Machu Picchu

POPULATION: 28,302,603

LIFE EXPECTANCY AT BIRTH (YEARS): male, 67.5; female, 71.0

LITERACY RATE: 88.3%

ETHNIC GROUPS: Amerindian 45%, mestizo 37%, white 15%

PRINCIPAL LANGUAGES: Spanish, Quechua (both official); Aymara

CHIEF RELIGION: Roman Catholic (official) 90%

ECONOMY: Copper, gold, zinc, petroleum, fishmeal, textiles, apparel and coffee are exported to the United States, China, Chile and Canada. Tourism has grown substantially in recent years.

MONETARY UNIT: new sol

GDP: $155.3 billion (2004 est.)

PER CAPITA GDP: $5,600

INDUSTRIES: mining, petroleum, fishing, textiles, clothing, food processing, cement, auto assembly, steel, shipbuilding, metal fabrication

MINERALS: copper, silver, gold, petroleum, iron ore, coal, phosphate, potash

CHIEF CROPS: coffee, cotton, sugarcane, rice, wheat, potatoes, corn, plantains, coca

GOVERNMENT TYPE: republic

CAPITAL: Lima (pop., 7,899,000)

INDEPENDENCE DATE: July 28, 1821

WEBSITE: www.peru.info/perueng.asp

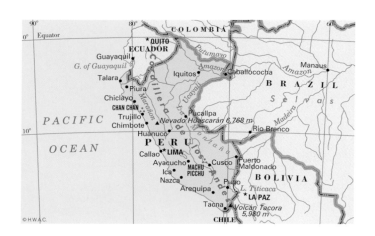

The Philippine archipelago of 7,007 islands stretches about 1,100 miles (1770 kilometers) along the south east rim of Asia. Most of the larger islands — Luzon, Mindanao, Samar, Negros, Palawan, Panay and Mindoro — are mountainous, with volcanoes, extensive coastal plains, wide valleys and hot springs. The tropical marine climate has a northeast monsoon season from November to April, and a southwest monsoon season from May to October. The islands have large deposits of cobalt, nickel, silver, gold and copper. Fisheries and forest resources are also notable. Major crops include sugarcane, coconuts, rice, corn, bananas, pineapples and mangoes. livestock and poultry are also raised. Clothing, textile and pharmaceutical manufacturing and electronic assembly are the main industries. Exports, largely electronics, textiles, coconut products, copper, fish, bananas and sugar go predominantly to the United States and Japan.

The dominant Filipino ethnic stock is Malay, which includes Tagalog, Cebuano and Ilocano. There is also a significant Chinese minority. Filipino (based on Tagalog) and English are the official languages. Eighty-three percent of the population is Roman Catholic; 9 percent are Protestant, and 5 percent are Muslim. Manila is the capital and largest city, followed by Quezon City and Davao.

Did you know? Japan occupied the Philippines in World War II.

Before the coming of Europeans, the Philippine archipelago was an area of trade and settlement for Southeast Asian people of Malay stock. By 1571 Spain had assumed control, and for the next 300 years ruled the islands as a colony. In 1898, following the Spanish-American War, control of the Philippines was ceded to the United States. However, pro-independence guerrilla warfare raged against the Americans until 1905. In 1941 Japan attacked the islands and occupied them until 1945. In 1946 the independent Republic of the Philippines was proclaimed. Widespread unrest and violence led by Communist Huk guerrillas were not put down until 1954. A long-standing Muslim Moro revolt has seethed on the southern island of Mindanao. After sixteen years of authoritarian rule (1969-1986), President Ferdinand Marcos was overthrown by the military in a coup that followed on the heels of a popular mobilization demanding that 1985 presidential candidate Corazon Aquino — widow of slain Marcos opponent, Benigno Aquino, who lost to Marcos in what most observers called a "stolen" election — replace Marcos as President. The military then installed Aquino as President; she held office until 1989, in an administration that was itself the target of several failed army-led coups. She was succeeded in 1989 by Fidel V. Ramos, a former military man, who was re-elected in 1992 and 1995. In

October 1995 he signed an agreement bringing the military insurgency to an end. Joseph Estrada, democratically elected president in 1998, was succeeded by his vice president Gloria Arroyo in 2001 after widespread demonstrations that followed the breakdown of Estrada's impeachment trial on corruption charges.

Manila

AREA: 115,831 sq mi (300,000 sq km)

CLIMATE: The tropical marine climate has a northeast monsoon season from November to April, and a southwest monsoon season from May to October. Typhoons are common.

PEOPLE: The dominant Filipino ethnic stock is Malay, which includes Tagalog, Cebuano and Ilocano. There is also a significant Chinese minority.

POPULATION: 89,468,677

LIFE EXPECTANCY AT BIRTH (YEARS): male, 66.7; female, 72.6

LITERACY RATE: 94.6%

ETHNIC GROUPS: Christian Malay 91.5%, Muslim Malay 4%, Chinese 1.5%

PRINCIPAL LANGUAGES: Filipino, English (both official); many dialects

CHIEF RELIGIONS: Roman Catholic 83%, Protestant 9%, Muslim 5%

ECONOMY: Exports, largely electronics, textiles, coconut products, copper, fish, bananas and sugar go predominantly to the United States and Japan.

GOVERNMENT TYPE: republic

CAPITAL: Manila (pop., 10,352,000)

INDEPENDENCE DATE: July 4, 1946

MONETARY UNIT: peso

GDP: $430.6 billion (2004 est.)

PER CAPITA GDP: $5,000

INDUSTRIES: textiles, pharmaceuticals, chemicals, wood products, food processing, electronics assembly

MINERALS: petroleum, nickel, cobalt, silver, gold, salt, copper

CHIEF CROPS: rice, coconuts, corn, sugarcane, bananas, pineapples, mangoes

WEBSITES: www.philippineembassy-usa.org www.gov.ph

Poland's position in the center of Europe has made it the scene of centuries-long conflicts. Except for mountains on its southern border, the country consists mainly of lowlands. The Vistula (Wisła), Oder (Odra), Bug and Warta are the main rivers. Poland's temperate continental climate is characterized by cold, cloudy, moderately severe winters and mild summers with frequent showers and thundershowers. Coal, sulfur, copper, natural gas, silver and lead are the chief mineral resources. The leading crops are grains, potatoes and oilseed. Poland is a major producer of livestock, poultry and dairy products. Major industries include machine building, iron and steel, glass, mining, shipbuilding, textiles and apparel, chemicals, food processing and beverages. Exports of machinery, cars, ships, metals and apparel are sent primarily to the European Union.

Poles make up most of the population. There are small groups of Germans, Ukrainians and Belorussians. Roman Catholicism is the religion of 95 percent of the people. Polish is the national language. Warsaw is the capital and largest city, followed by Łódź and Kraków (Cracow).

Did you know? More than 9,300 lakes dot the Polish countryside.

Wrocław

The Slavic tribes of the region were united and converted to Christianity in the tenth century A.D. During the Middle Ages, Poland united with Lithuania as a great European power. Between 1772 and 1795 Poland was divided between Prussia, Austria and Russia. In 1918 an independent Polish republic was proclaimed. Nazi Germany and the Soviet Union invaded Poland and partitioned the country in 1939. All Poland came under Nazi rule in 1941, resulting in the extermination of six million Poles, half of them Jews. Soviet troops expelled the Germans in 1944-45, and a Communist regime came to dominate the country in 1947. Postwar Poland was forced to cede the prewar eastern area to the U.S.S.R. As compensation, Poland received a portion of Germany up to the Oder and Neisse rivers. The German population was expelled, and Poles were settled in their place. Outbursts against Communist rule occurred in 1956, 1970, 1976 and through the 1980s. From 1989 through 1991 the Communists lost power and were supplanted by a pro-Solidarity Movement government. However, by 1995 the Solidarity leaders' economic reforms displeased many Poles, who that year voted a former Communist into office as President. Poland joined the European Union on May 1, 2004. In the year after it joined the EU, Poland experienced an overall growth in exports of thirty percent.

AREA: 120,728 sq mi (312,685 sq km)

■ **CLIMATE:** The temperate continental climate is characterized by cold, cloudy, moderately severe winters and mild summers with frequent showers and thundershowers.

■ **PEOPLE:** Poles make up most of the population. There are small groups of Germans, Ukrainians and Belorussians.

POPULATION: 38,536,869

LIFE EXPECTANCY AT BIRTH (YEARS): male, 70.0; female, 78.5

LITERACY RATE: 99%

ETHNIC GROUPS: Polish 98%, German 1%

PRINCIPAL LANGUAGES: Polish (official), Ukrainian, German

CHIEF RELIGION: Roman Catholic 95%

■ **ECONOMY:** Exports of machinery, cars, ships, metals and apparel are sent primarily to the European Union. In the year after joining the EU, Poland's overall growth in exports increased thirty percent.

CAPITAL: Warsaw (pop., 2,200,000)

INDEPENDENCE DATE: November 11, 1918

GOVERNMENT TYPE: republic

MONETARY UNIT: zloty

GDP: $463.0 billion (2004 est.)

PER CAPITA GDP: $12,000

INDUSTRIES: machine building, iron and steel, mining, chemicals, shipbuilding, food processing, glass, beverages, textiles

CHIEF CROPS: potatoes, fruits, vegetables, wheat

MINERALS: coal, sulfur, copper, natural gas, silver, lead, salt

WEBSITES: www.polandembassy.org   www.poland.pl

Portugal, occupying the western portion of the Iberian peninsula, is divided by the Tagus river into two distinct regions; the north, being mountainous, and the south, consisting of rolling plains. The Douro is Portugal's other major river. Outside the mainland, the Atlantic islands of the Azores and Madeira are integral parts of Portugal. The maritime temperate climate is cool and rainy in the north, warmer and drier in the south. Portugal has deposits of tungsten, iron, copper, tin, zinc, and uranium ore. Cork forests and sardine fisheries are other important resources. Grain, potatoes, olives and grapes, along with livestock and poultry are the chief agricultural products. Textiles, clothing and footwear, wood and cork, pulp and paper, chemicals, canned fish and wine are the leading industrial products. Tourism contributes heavily to the economy. Clothing and footwear, motor vehicle parts, canned fish, wine, cork, metals, electronics and electrical equipment are the chief exports, going mainly to the European Union.

The people are largely of homogeneous Mediterranean stock. There are small groups of black Africans and Eastern Europeans. Portuguese is the official and universal language. The population is 97 percent Roman Catholic. Lisbon is the capital and largest city. Porto is second in size.

Following rule by the Romans, Visigoths, and Moors, Portugal was established as an independent state in 1140 A.D. Portuguese discoveries sponsored by Prince Henry the Navigator in the 1400s sparked the growth of a huge overseas empire, including Brazil, large parts of Africa and strategic outposts from Arabia through the coast of India and the East Indies to the Far East. By the twentieth century, Portugal's overseas possessions were largely reduced to Angola and Mozambique in Africa. Both became independent in 1975. Internally, the monarchy was deposed in 1910 and replaced by a republic. After forty-two years of dictatorial rule, a bloodless coup established a democratic regime in 1974. Portugal became a member of the European Union on January 1, 1986.

Did you know? Portugal is one of the world's largest producers of cork.

AREA: 35,672 sq mi (92,391 sq km)

CLIMATE: The maritime temperate climate is cool and rainy in the north, warmer and drier in the south.

Castle of Leira

PEOPLE: The people are largely of homogeneous Mediterranean stock. There are small groups of black Africans and Eastern Europeans.

POPULATION: 10,605,870

LIFE EXPECTANCY AT BIRTH (YEARS): male, 74.1; female, 80.9

LITERACY RATE: 87.4%

ETHNIC GROUPS: mainly Portuguese

PRINCIPAL LANGUAGE: Portuguese (official)

CHIEF RELIGION: Roman Catholic 94%

ECONOMY: Clothing and footwear, motor vehicle parts, canned fish, wine, cork, metals and electronics are the chief exports, going mainly to the European Union. Tourism contributes heavily to the economy.

MONETARY UNIT: euro

GDP: $188.7 billion (2004 est.)

PER CAPITA GDP: $17,900

INDUSTRIES: textiles, footwear, pulp and paper, cork, metalworking, oil refining, chemicals, fish canning, wine, tourism

MINERALS: tungsten, iron ore, uranium ore, marble

CHIEF CROPS: grain, potatoes, olives, grapes

GOVERNMENT TYPE: republic

CAPITAL: Lisbon (pop., 1,962,000)

INDEPENDENCE DATE: 1143

WEBSITE: www.presidenciarepublica.pt/en/main.html

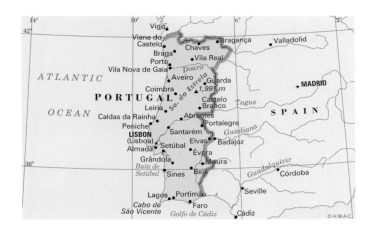

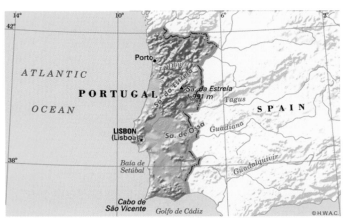

Qatar forms a 100-mile-long (161 kilometer) desert peninsula, stretching north from Arabia into the Persian Gulf. The land is a low, hot dry plain of nearly flat limestone overlain by sand and gravel, with mild pleasant winters and very hot, humid summers. Oil and natural gas are Qatar's great natural resources. Commercial fishing is increasing in importance. Some food is raised on irrigated land. Steel and petrochemicals are produced. Exports, largely petroleum products, flow to Japan, South Korea, Singapore and India. Oil has given Qatar a per capita Gross Domestic Product comparable to those of the leading industrial countries, which allows for free health care and education for all of its citizens.

Arabs make up 40 percent of the population; Pakistanis are 18 percent; Indians, 18 percent; Iranians, 10 percent. The population is 95 percent Muslim descended from tribes which came to Qatar in the 18th century. Many foreigners emigrated, mostly from Asian nations, to work in the oil industry. Arabic is the official language; English is commonly used as a second language. Doha is the capital and chief city.

Qatar was originally under Persian rule. From 1871 through 1913, it was occupied by Ottoman Turks. In 1916 Qatar came under British protection and in 1971 declared its independence. In 1995 Shaikh Khalifa Bin Hamad al-Thani was overthrown as Amir by his son, Crown Prince and Defense Minister Shaikh Hamad Bin Khalifa, in a bloodless coup June 27. The former head of state had previously deposed his cousin as Amir in 1972, soon after independence. He appointed his son as Crown Prince and Defense Minister in 1977, and ever since the younger Khalifa had effectively ruled the country, until recently, when his father tried to reassert his influence. The coup was unanimously supported by the royal family, the governing Cabinet, the Consultative Council, and the military. In 2001, Qatar resolved its longstanding border dispute over the Hawar Islands with Bahrain, and over its southern border with Saudi Arabia.

Did you know? Qatar is a flat desert region, where plant life of any kind is scarce.

AREA: 4,416 sq mi (11,437 sq km)

■ **CLIMATE:** Much of Qatar is a low, barren desert plain with mild pleasant winters and very hot, humid summers.

Doha Palace

■ **PEOPLE:** Arabs make up 40 percent of the population. Signficant groups of Pakistanis and Indians are followed by smaller groups of Iranians and others.

POPULATION: 885,359

LIFE EXPECTANCY AT BIRTH (YEARS): male, 70.9; female, 76.0

LITERACY RATE: 79%

ETHNIC GROUPS: Arab 40%, Pakistani 18%, Indian 18%, Iranian 10%

PRINCIPAL LANGUAGES: Arabic (official), English

CHIEF RELIGION: Muslim (official) 95%

■ **ECONOMY:** Oil and natural gas provide most of Qatar's export revenue, which allows for free health care and education for all citizens. Major trading partners include Japan, South Korea, Singapore and India.

MONETARY UNIT: riyal

GDP: $19.5 billion (2004 est.)

PER CAPITA GDP: $23,200

INDUSTRIES: oil production and refining, fertilizers, petrochemicals, steel reinforcing bars, cement

MINERALS: petroleum, natural gas

CHIEF CROPS: fruits, vegetables

GOVERNMENT TYPE: traditional monarchy

CAPITAL: Doha (pop., 286,000)

INDEPENDENCE DATE: September 3, 1971

WEBSITE: english.mofa.gov.qa

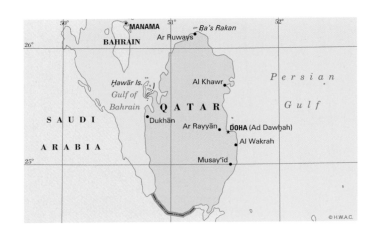

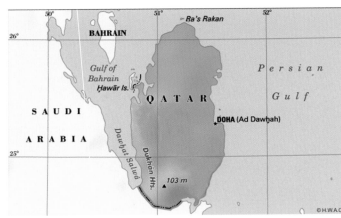

The Carpathian mountains and the Transylvanian Alps form a semicircle through the center of Romania, separating the Moldavian plains in the east, and the Wallachian plain in the south from the Transylvanian plateau in the northwest. The temperate climate has cold, cloudy winters with frequent snow and fog and sunny summers with occasional showers and thunderstorms. The chief natural resources are reserves of petroleum (now declining), natural gas, coal, iron ore and salt. Romania is a major producer of wheat and corn; sugar beets, sunflower seeds, potatoes and livestock are also raised. Forestry is also important. Machine building, mining, construction materials, metal production, chemicals, oil refining, food processing, textiles and clothing are the chief industries. Textiles, chemicals, light manufactures, wood products, fuels, processed metals, machinery and equipment are exported mostly to the European Union and Turkey.

Romanians make up 89 percent of the population; Hungarians are 9 percent. Seventy percent of the population is Romanian Orthodox. Romanian, a Romance tongue, is the official language; Hungarian and German are also spoken. Bucharest is the capital and largest city.

Ancient Dacia, comprising most of present-day Romania, was part of the Roman Empire until the third century A.D. Goths, Huns, Avars, Slavs and Mongols later overran the region. In the thirteenth century, the principalities of Wallachia and Moldavia were established, but by the 1500s both had come under the rule of the Ottoman Turks. In the early nineteenth century, although technically remaining part of the Ottoman Empire, both actually became Russian protectorates. Independence was attained in 1878. After World War I, Romania gained Bessarabia from Russia, Bukovina from Austria and Transylvania from Hungary. In 1940, the Soviet Union annexed Bessarabia and Bukovina. A Communist government was set up after World War II. In late 1989 the Communist government was overthrown, and long-time Communist party boss Nicolas Ceaucescu was executed. Romania became a member of the European Union on January 1, 2007.

> **Did you know?** The real Dracula, Prince Vlad, lived in Romania in the 1400s.

AREA: 91,699 sq mi (237,500 sq km)

■ CLIMATE: The temperate climate has cold, cloudy winters with frequent snow and fog and sunny summers with occasional showers and thunderstorms.

■ PEOPLE: Romanians make up most of the population. There are small groups of Hungarians and Romas.

Sighisoara-Clock Tower

POPULATION: 22,303,552

LIFE EXPECTANCY AT BIRTH (YEARS): male, 67.6; female, 74.8

LITERACY RATE: 97%

ETHNIC GROUPS: Romanian 90%, Hungarian, Roma, and others 10%

PRINCIPAL LANGUAGES: Romanian (official), Hungarian, German, Romani

CHIEF RELIGIONS: Romanian Orthodox 70%, Roman Catholic 6%, Protestant 6%

■ ECONOMY: Textiles, chemicals, light manufactures, wood products, fuels, processed metals, machinery and equipment are exported mostly to the European Union and Turkey.

MONETARY UNIT: lei

GDP: $171.5 billion (2004 est.)

PER CAPITA GDP: $7,700

INDUSTRIES: textiles, footwear, light machinery, auto assembly, mining, timber, construction materials, metallurgy, chemicals, food processing, petroleum refining

MINERALS: petroleum, natural gas, coal, iron ore, salt

CHIEF CROPS: wheat, corn, sugar beets, sunflower seed, potatoes, grapes

GOVERNMENT TYPE: republic

CAPITAL: Bucharest (pop., 1,853,000)

INDEPENDENCE DATE: May 9, 1877

WEBSITES: www.roembus.org
www.gov.ro/engleza/index.html

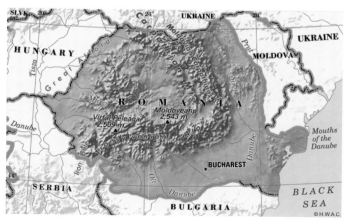

Although not the superpower that the former Soviet Union was, the Russian Federation is still the world's largest country in area. It extends almost 6,000 miles (9,660 kilometers) from east to west and is mostly a broad plain, with low hills west of the Ural mountains, great coniferous forests and tundra in Siberia, and uplands and mountains along its southern border. The chief rivers are the Ob', Yenisey, Lena and Volga. European Russia has a northern continental climate; subarctic conditions exist in Siberia; a frigid tundra climate is found in the far north, while semiarid conditions prevail in the south. Russia possesses a wide base of natural resources including major deposits of oil, natural gas, coal, timber and many strategic minerals. Vast acres produce grain, sugar beets, sunflower seeds, meat, milk, vegetables and fruit. Russian industry turns out road and rail vehicles, aircraft and spacecraft, ships, steel, machinery, electronic equipment and consumer goods. Exports of petroleum, natural gas, wood products, metals and machinery flow to the European Union, United States, Ukraine and China.

Russians make up more than three fourths of the population. There are small groups of Tatars and Ukrainians. Russian is the official and dominant language. The Russian Orthodox Church is the largest religious group. Moscow is the capital and largest city, followed by St. Petersburg, formerly Leningrad.

About the fifth century A.D. Slavs began to people the Russian steppes. Between 862 and 879 Rurik, a Scandinavian chieftain, established the first city state at Novgorod. His successor enlarged the territory and made Kiev his capital. In 1237 Mongol (Tatar) hordes overran Russia, initiating two centuries of the "Tatar Yoke." Following the decline of the Mongols, the Russian state under the tsars grew in all directions from its beginning in the principality of Moscow. Starting in 1581, Russia expanded into Siberia and reached the Pacific in the 1600s. Russia continued to expand to the west during the 1700s, and during the nineteenth century annexed vast areas in the Caucasus and Central Asia. Military setbacks during World War I led to the overthrow of the tsar. The succeeding provisional government was ousted in turn by the Bolsheviks, led by Lenin, who ended the war by surrendering much territory. In 1922 four Communist-ruled states formed the Union of Soviet Socialist Republics. After the death of Lenin in 1924, the U.S.S.R. spent long years under the ruthless dictatorship of Josef Stalin. The country suffered greatly in the war with German invaders, 1941-45. With victory, the U.S.S.R. regained most of the land lost in 1917 and dominated Eastern Europe. Starting in 1989, unrest in Eastern European satellites, economic problems and ethnic separatism within the U.S.S.R. led to the breakup of the Soviet Union

Did you know? Lake Baykal, the world's deepest freshwater lake, is in Siberia.

late in 1991. The fifteen constituent republics became independent states. Russia, the largest of the states, was established as the Russian Federation. However, ethnic separatist movements still trouble the Federation.

In 2005 Russia and China ratified the treaty dividing the islands in the Amur, Ussuri and Argun rivers. This represented the closing chapter of their centuries-long border dispute.

Moscow-St. Basil's Cathedral

AREA: 6,592,769 sq mi (17,075,200 sq km)

 **CLIMATE:** European Russia has a northern continental climate; subarctic conditions exist in Siberia; a frigid tundra climate is found in the far north, while semiarid conditions prevail in the south.

■ **PEOPLE:** Russians make up more than three fourths of the population. There are small groups of Tatars and Ukrainians.

POPULATION: 142,893,540

LIFE EXPECTANCY AT BIRTH (YEARS): male, 59.9; female, 73.3

LITERACY RATE: 98%

ETHNIC GROUPS: Russian 82%, Tatar 4%, Ukrainian 3%, Chuvash 1%, Bashkir 1%, Belarusian 1%, Moldavian 1%

PRINCIPAL LANGUAGES: Russian (official), many others

CHIEF RELIGIONS: Russian Orthodox, Muslim

■ **ECONOMY:** Petroleum, natural gas, wood products and machinery go to the European Union, United States, Ukraine and China.

MONETARY UNIT: ruble

GDP: $1,408 billion (2004 est.)

PER CAPITA GDP: $9,800

INDUSTRIES: mining, extractive industries, machineery, shipbuilding, vehicles, commercial equipment, construction equipment, instruments, consumer durables, textiles, foodstuffs, handicrafts

CHIEF CROPS: grain, sugar beets, sunflower seed, vegetables, fruits

MINERALS: large variety, including oil, natural gas, coal, diamonds, strategic minerals

GOVERNMENT TYPE: federal republic

CAPITAL: Moscow (pop., 10,469,000)

INDEPENDENCE DATE: August 24, 1991

WEBSITE: www.russianembassy.org

Landlocked Rwanda is surrounded by the Democratic Republic of the Congo, Uganda, Tanzania and Burundi. Known as the "Land of a Thousand Hills," the country consists largely of grassy uplands and hills that roll down southeastward from the volcanoes in the northwest. The climate is temperate, with two rainy seasons. In the mountains it is mild, with a possibility of frost and snow. Gold, tin and tungsten are mined. Coffee, tea, bananas, beans, sorghum and potatoes are grown along with chrysanthemums used in pyrethrum based insecticides. Livestock-raising is important. Cement, agricultural products, beverages, soap, furniture, shoes, plastic goods, textiles, cigarettes and and pyrethrum are the chief industries. Tea, coffee, hides, iron and tin ore, and pyrethrum are exported to Indonesia, China, and Germany.

Ethnically, 90 percent of the population is Hutu, 9 percent Tutsi and 1 percent Twa (Pygmy). Kinyarwanda and French are the official languages; Sixty-five percent of the population is Roman Catholic. Kigali is the capital and chief city.

By the fifteenth century the original Bantu Hutus and the Pygmies were conquered by the invading Tutsi, a tall, cattle-keeping people, who imposed a feudal overlordship on the indigenous population. In 1885 Germany took over the region. Along with Burundi, Rwanda was made a League of Nations mandate administered by Belgium after World War I. In 1959 a bloody Hutu revolt overthrew the Tutsi monarchy. In 1962 Rwanda became independent. Massive civil war in 1994 resulted in the deaths of over 500,000 people, primarily Tutsis, and the exit of more than a million people into neighboring countries.

Did you know? The source of the Nile River has been located in Rwanda.

In 2003, Rwanda adopted a new constitution that led to Paul Kagame being elected the country's first post civil war president in August. Rwanda then held its first-ever legislative elections in October.

AREA: 10,169 sq mi (26,338 sq km)

CLIMATE: The climate is temperate, with two rainy seasons. In the mountains it is mild, with a possibility of frost and snow.

PEOPLE: Ethnically, most of the population is Hutu. There is a significant Tutsi minority and a small Twa (pygmy) population.

POPULATION: 8,648,248

Kigali

LIFE EXPECTANCY AT BIRTH (YEARS): male, 38.4; female, 40.0

LITERACY RATE: 48%

ETHNIC GROUPS: Hutu 84%, Tutsi 15%, Twa (Pygmy) 1%

PRINCIPAL LANGUAGES: Kinyarwanda, French, English (all official); Swahili

CHIEF RELIGIONS: Roman Catholic 57%, Protestant 26%, Adventist 11%, Muslim 5%

ECONOMY: Tea, coffee, hides, iron and tin ore, and pyrethrum are exported to Indonesia, China, and Germany.

MONETARY UNIT: franc

GDP: $10.4 billion (2004 est.)

PER CAPITA GDP: $1,300

INDUSTRIES: cement, agricultural products, small-scale beverages, soap, furniture, shoes, plastic goods, textiles, cigarettes

MINERALS: gold, tin ore, tungsten ore, methane

CHIEF CROPS: coffee, tea, pyrethrum, bananas, beans, sorghum, potatoes

GOVERNMENT TYPE: republic

CAPITAL: Kigali (pop., 656,000)

INDEPENDENCE DATE: July 1, 1962

WEBSITE: www.gov.rw

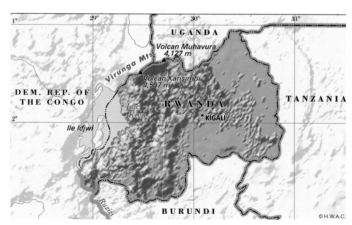

Saint Kitts and Nevis, in the eastern Caribbean Sea, are located about one-third of the way between Puerto Rico and Trinidad and Tobago. The islands are volcanic in origin and have mountainous interiors. The tropical, humid climate is tempered by constant sea breezes and little temperature change. There is a rainy season from May to November with occasional hurricanes. Sugarcane is raised, along with subsistence crops of rice, yams and bananas. Financial and business services, tourism, light manufacturing, sugar processing, cotton, salt, copra, clothing, footwear, beverages, and tobacco contribute to the economy. Exports of machinery, food, electronics, sugar, clothing, beverages, and tobacco go mainly to the United States, Portugal, the United Kingdom and Canada. Tourism is now the chief source of the islands foreign exchange.

The people are mostly of black African descent. There are small minorities of British, Portuguese and Lebanese. Protestantism is the religion of 76 percent of the population; Roman Catholicism is the religion of 11 percent. English is the language of the islands. Basseterre, the capital, is the chief town.

The British colonized Saint Kitts (formerly Saint Christopher) in 1625, and Nevis in 1628. The island of Anguilla to the north was associated with Saint Kitts and Nevis after 1825, but in 1980 separated from them. Saint Kitts and Nevis became independent from Britain in 1983.

Did you know? In 1493, Columbus named Saint Kitts for his patron, Saint Christopher.

In 1998, a vote in Nevis to separate from St. Kitts failed to secure the required two-thirds majority. However Nevis continues in its efforts to try and separate from St. Kitts.

AREA: 101 sq mi (261 sq km)

■ **CLIMATE:** The tropical, humid climate is tempered by constant sea breezes and little temperature change. Rainy season May to November with occasional hurricanes.

■ **PEOPLE:** The people are mostly of black African descent. There are small minorities of British, Portuguese and Lebanese.

POPULATION: 39,000

View of Caribbean

LIFE EXPECTANCY AT BIRTH (YEARS): male, 68.8; female, 74.6

LITERACY RATE: 97%

ETHNIC GROUP: black, British, Portuguese, Lebanese

PRINCIPAL LANGUAGE: English (official)

CHIEF RELIGIONS: Anglican, other Protestant, Roman Catholic

■ **ECONOMY:** Exports of machinery, food, electronics, sugar, clothing, beverages, and tobacco go mainly to the United States, Portugal, the United Kingdom and Canada. Tourism is an important source of revenue.

MONETARY UNIT: East Caribbean dollar

GDP: $339 million (2002 est.)

PER CAPITA GDP: $8,200

INDUSTRIES: sugar processing, tourism, cotton, salt, copra, clothing, footwear, beverages

CHIEF CROPS: sugarcane, rice, yams, vegetables, bananas

GOVERNMENT TYPE: constitutional monarchy

CAPITAL: Basseterre (pop., 12,000)

INDEPENDENCE DATE: September 19, 1983

WEBSITE: www.stkittsnevis.net

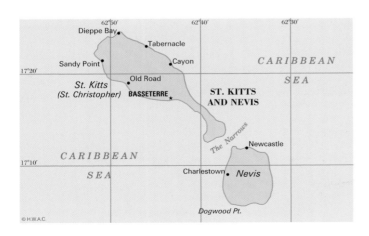

Of volcanic origin, the Caribbean island of Saint Lucia is mountainous, with broad fertile valleys. The breathtaking beauty of its forested mountains and sandy beaches beckons tourists. Northeast trade winds moderate its humid tropical climate. There is a rainy season May to August with occasional hurricanes. Bananas, cocoa, coconut and citrus fruits are the chief commercial crops. The manufacture of clothing and the assembly of electronic components are the main industries. Tourism is the driving force of the economy. Bananas and clothing are the main exports along with cocoa, vegetables, fruits and other agricultural products. Exports go mainly to the United Kingdom and the United States.

Most of the population is of African ancestry. There are small groups of East Indians, Europeans and people of mixed descent. Ninety percent of the population is Roman Catholic. English is the official language; a French patois is widely spoken. Castries is the capital and chief town.

The warlike Caribs were the last of successive waves of Amerindian migrations that had begun in the 1300s. Britain and France struggled for possession of the island after 1605. Britain took full control of Saint Lucia in 1814. A plantation economy based on imported black African slaves flourished until slavery was abolished in 1834. Saint Lucia obtained independence from Britain in 1979.

Did you know?
Bananas are the principal export of this island country.

AREA: 238 sq mi (616 sq km)

■ **CLIMATE:** Northeast trade winds moderate this humid tropical climate.There is a rainy season May to August with occasional hurricanes.

■ **PEOPLE:** Most of the population is of African ancestry. There are small groups of East Indians, Europeans and people of mixed descent.

POPULATION: 168,458

LIFE EXPECTANCY AT BIRTH (YEARS): male, 69.5; female, 76.9

LITERACY RATE: 67%

ETHNIC GROUPS: black 90%, mixed 6%, East Indian 3%, white 1%

Marigot Bay

PRINCIPAL LANGUAGES: English (official), French patois

CHIEF RELIGIONS: Roman Catholic 90%, Protestant 10%

■ **ECONOMY:** Tourism is the driving force of the economy. Bananas and clothing are the main exports along with cocoa, fruits and vegetables. Exports go mainly to the United Kingdom and the United States.

GOVERNMENT TYPE: parliamentary democracy

CAPITAL: Castries (pop., 14,000)

INDEPENDENCE DATE: February 22, 1979

MONETARY UNIT: East Caribbean dollar

GDP: $866 million (2002 est.)

PER CAPITA GDP: $5,400

INDUSTRIES: clothing, assembly of electronic components, beverages, corrugated cardboard boxes, tourism

MINERALS: pumice

CHIEF CROPS: bananas, coconuts, vegetables, citrus, root crops, cocoa

WEBSITE: www.stlucia.gov.lc

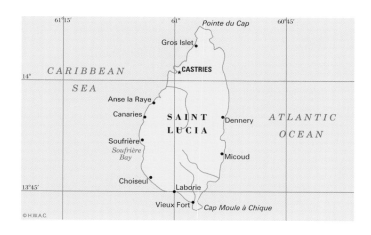

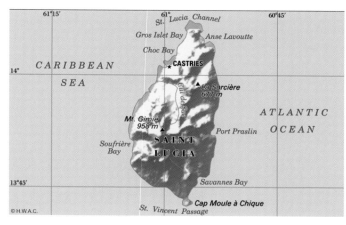

Saint Vincent and the Grenadines are situated in the eastern Caribbean Sea. The island of Saint Vincent is volcanic in origin, with a mountain ridge running its length and rising to Soufrière volcano. The tropical climate has little seasonal temperature variation, a rainy season from May to September and occasional hurricanes. Bananas, coconuts, sweet potatoes and spices are the chief crops. Tourism is an important part of the economy. Offshore banking is growing. Food processing, cement, furniture, clothing and starch are leading industrial products. Bananas, taro and arrowroot starch are the chief exports, going primarily to Caribbean nations and the United Kingdom.

The people are primarily of African descent. There are small groups of mixed peoples, West Indians and Carib Indians. English is the chief language, though some French patois is spoken. Religious groups include Anglicans, Methodists and Roman Catholics. Kingstown is the capital and chief town.

Did you know?
Soufrière, an active volcano in the north, last erupted in 1979.

The earliest known inhabitants were the Arawaks, who were supplanted by the warlike Caribs. Ownership of Saint Vincent and the Grenadines was disputed between the French and British until 1783, when they were formally ceded to Britain. Independence was obtained in 1979.

AREA: 131 sq mi (339 sq km)

■ **CLIMATE:** The tropical climate has little seasonal temperature variation, a rainy season from May to September and occasional hurricanes.

■ **PEOPLE:** Most of the population is of African ancestry. There are small groups of East Indians, Europeans and people of mixed descent.

POPULATION: 117,848

LIFE EXPECTANCY AT BIRTH (YEARS): male, 71.3; female, 74.9

LITERACY RATE: 96%

Bequia-Port Elizabeth

ETHNIC GROUPS: black 66%, mixed 19%, East Indian 6%, Carib Amerindian 2%

PRINCIPAL LANGUAGES: English (official), French patois

CHIEF RELIGIONS: Anglican 47%, Methodist 28%, Roman Catholic 13%

■ **ECONOMY:** Tourism is the driving force of the economy. Bananas and clothing are the main exports along with cocoa, fruits and vegetables. Exports go mainly to the United Kingdom and the United States.

MONETARY UNIT: East Caribbean dollar

GDP: $342 million (2002 est.)

PER CAPITA GDP: $2,900

INDUSTRIES: food processing, cement, furniture, clothing

CHIEF CROPS: bananas, coconuts, sweet potatoes, spices

GOVERNMENT TYPE: constitutional monarchy

CAPITAL: Kingstown (pop., 29,000)

INDEPENDENCE DATE: October 27, 1979

WEBSITE: www.embsvg.com

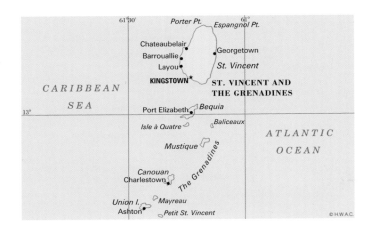

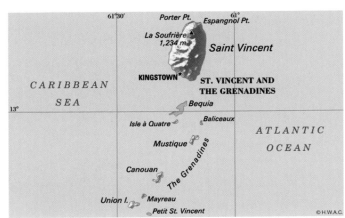

Samoa (formerly Western Samoa), in the South Pacific, lies halfway between Hawaii and New Zealand. Narrow coastal plains, with rugged mountains in the interior, form the two main islands, Savai'i and Upolu. The tropical climate has a rainy season from October to April and a dry season from May to October. Coconuts, bananas, taro, yams and various fruits are the chief agricultural products. Tourism is of growing importance. Fishing is also important. Family remittances from overseas contribute to the economy. The chief exports, coconut oil and cream, cocoa and automotive components are shipped to New Zealand, Australia and American Samoa.

Samoans, who are of Polynesian stock, make up most of the population. The rest are of mixed Euro-Polynesian heritage. The population is almost entirely Christian. Samoan and English are the official languages. Apia is the capital and chief town.

Archaeological evidence suggests that Samoa may have been settled as far back as 1000 B.C. Throughout the nineteenth century the islands were pawns in a struggle for control by the United States, Germany and Britain. In 1899 Eastern Samoa was assigned to the United States, and Western Samoa went to Germany. Following occupation by New Zealand in World War I, the League of Nations assigned Western Samoa as a mandate to New Zealand. In 1946, Western Samoa became a United Nations Trusteeship under New Zealand supervision. In 1962 Western Samoa became independent as a constitutional monarchy, and the name was changed to Samoa in 1997.

Did you know? Native tradition holds that the Polynesian race originated in Samoa.

AREA: 1,137 sq mi (2,944 sq km)

■ **CLIMATE:** The tropical climate has a rainy season from October to April and a dry season from May to October.

■ **PEOPLE:** Samoans, who are of Polynesian stock, make up most of the population. The rest are of mixed Euro-Polynesian heritage.

POPULATION: 176,908

Apia Courthouse

LIFE EXPECTANCY AT BIRTH (YEARS): male, 67.6; female, 73.3

LITERACY RATE: 80%

ETHNIC GROUPS: Samoan 92.5%, Euronesians 7%

PRINCIPAL LANGUAGES: Samoan, English (both official)

CHIEF RELIGION: Christian 99.7%

■ **ECONOMY:** The service sector makes up more than half of the GDP. Tourism is growing. Family remittances from overseas contribute to the economy. Coconut products, cocoa and automotive parts are shipped to New Zealand, Australia and American Samoa.

MONETARY UNIT: tala

GDP: $1.0 billion (2002 est.)

PER CAPITA GDP: $5,600

INDUSTRIES: food processing, building materials, auto parts

CHIEF CROPS: coconuts, bananas, taro, yams

CAPITAL: Apia (pop., 40,000)

GOVERNMENT TYPE: constitutional monarchy

INDEPENDENCE DATE: January 1, 1962

WEBSITE: www.govt.ws

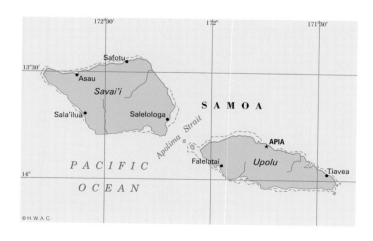

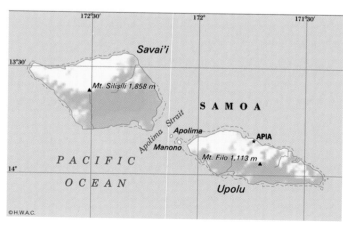

San Marino is the world's oldest republic. Surrounded by Italy, landlocked San Marino lies in the rugged foothills of the Apennines. The Mediterranean climate has mild to cool winters and warm, sunny summers. Building stone is quarried. Wheat, cheese, olive oil, grapes and wine, cattle, pigs and horses are the main agricultural products. Tourism contributes half of the GDP. The banking industry is also important. Textiles, electronics, ceramics and leather manufacturing are the chief industries. Exports of building stone, wine and ceramics go to Italy, with which San Marino enjoys a customs union.

The Sammarinese are of Italian origin; Italian is the official and universal language. Roman Catholicism is the country's religion. San Marino is the capital and chief town.

According to tradition, Marinus, a Christian stonecutter who was later canonized, was the founder of the country in 301 A.D. San Marino is the last of the Italian peninsula's once-numerous city-states.

Guaita fortress overlooking city

AREA: 24 sq mi (61 sq km)

■ **CLIMATE:** The Mediterranean climate has mild to cool winters and warm, sunny summers.

■ **PEOPLE:** The Sammarinese are of Italian origin.

POPULATION: 29,251

LIFE EXPECTANCY AT BIRTH (YEARS): male, 78.0; female, 85.3

LITERACY RATE: 96%

ETHNIC GROUPS: Sammarinese, Italian

PRINCIPAL LANGUAGE: Italian (official)

CHIEF RELIGION: predominantly Roman Catholic

■ **ECONOMY:** Tourism contributes half of the GDP. The banking industry is also important. Exports of building stone, wine and ceramics go

Did you know? San Marino is the 5th-smallest country in the world and claims to be Europe's oldest country, founded in 301 AD.

to Italy, with which San Marino enjoys a customs union.

MONETARY UNIT: euro

GDP: $940 million (2001 est.)

PER CAPITA GDP: $34,600

INDUSTRIES: tourism, banking, textiles, electronics, ceramics, cement, wine

MINERALS: building stone

CHIEF CROPS: wheat, grapes, corn, olives

GOVERNMENT TYPE: republic

CAPITAL: San Marino (pop., 5,000)

INDEPENDENCE DATE: September 3, 301

WEBSITE: www.visitsanmarino.com/defaulte.asp

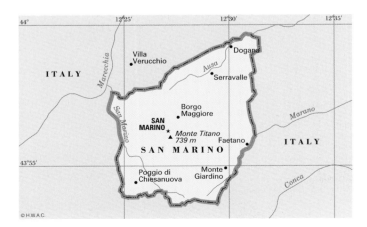

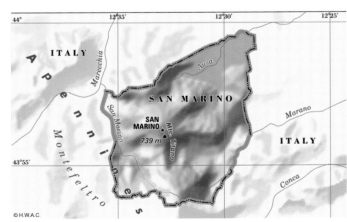

The two islands of São Tomé and Príncipe are in the Gulf of Guinea, just north of the Equator about 125 miles (200 kilometers) off the western coast of Africa. Edged with flat coastal plains, the islands have hilly, wooded interiors. The tropical climate is hot and humid with a wet season from October to May. Cocoa is the dominant crop; coconuts, coffee, copra, bananas and palm kernels are also harvested. Fishing adds to the economy. Industries include light construction, textiles, soap, beer, fish and shrimp processing. Petroleum reserves are being developed. Exports of cocoa, copra, coffee and palm oil go to the European Union and China.

The population is mostly African, with some Portuguese admixture. Portuguese is the official language; a local creole is also spoken. Roman Catholicism is the predominant religion. The town of São Tomé is the capital.

Did you know?
Portugal ruled these islands for nearly 300 years.

Portuguese explorers first found the islands in 1471, and Portuguese later established plantations there, using African slaves. Independence was obtained in 1975. Sao Tome became one of the first African countries to embrace democratic reform in 1990.

São Tomé at the Equator

AREA: 386 sq mi (1,001 sq km)

■ CLIMATE: The climate is tropical with a wet season from October to May.

■ PEOPLE: The population is mostly African, with some mixed Portuguese-Africans.

POPULATION: 193,413

LIFE EXPECTANCY AT BIRTH (YEARS): male, 65.1; female, 68.2

LITERACY RATE: 79.3%

ETHNIC GROUPS: mestizo, black, Portuguese

PRINCIPAL LANGUAGES: Portuguese (official), Creole, Fang

CHIEF RELIGIONS: predominantly Roman Catholic

■ ECONOMY: Exports of cocoa, copra, coffee and palm oil go to the European Union and China. Recently discovered petroleum reserves are being developed.

MONETARY UNIT: dobra

GDP: $214 million (2003 est.)

PER CAPITA GDP: $1,200

INDUSTRIES: light construction, textiles, soap, beer, fish processing, timber

CHIEF CROPS: cocoa, coconuts, palm kernels, copra, cinnamon, pepper, coffee, bananas, papayas, beans

CAPITAL: São Tomé (pop., 54,000)

INDEPENDENCE DATE: July 12, 1975

GOVERNMENT TYPE: republic

WEBSITE: www.saotome.org

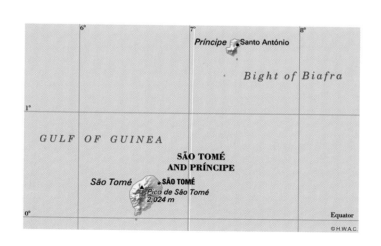

The world's millions of adherents of Islam regard Saudi Arabia with a special reverence because it contains Mecca, holiest of holy cities. This Arabian peninsula country has the largest reserves of petroleum in the world and is the largest exporter of that vital energy source. Saudi Arabia is nine-tenths covered by a barren plateau, including the Rub` al Khali and the An Nafūd desert regions. The desert climate is harsh and dry, with great extremes of temperature. Besides great reserves of oil and natural gas, there are deposits of gold, iron ore and copper. On irrigated lands subsidized by the government, wheat, barley, vegetables, dates and other fruits and livestock are produced. Oil refining and petrochemicals dominate industrial production. Saudi Arabia is the world's largest exporter of petroleum, with about one quarter of the world's petroleum reserves. Petroleum and petroleum products make up 90 percent of exports, which go to the United States, Japan, South Korea, China and the European Union. Pilgrims to Mecca provide substantial income.

The population is 90 percent Arab and 100 percent Muslim. It includes more than six million expatriates from several Southeast Asian countries. Because of the oil industry, most Saudis live in densely packed cities. Arabic is the official and popular language. Riyadh is the capital and largest city, followed by Jiddah and Mecca.

Did you know? Mecca, the birthplace of Muhammad, is the holiest city of Islam.

Arabia has been inhabited by nomadic Semitic tribes for thousands of years. Followers of Mohammed, who was born in Mecca in the sixth century A.D., conquered most of the area between Persia in the east and Spain in the west. Emerging from exile, Ibn Saud founded the Kingdom of Saudi Arabia by conquest between 1902 and 1932. In 1936 oil was discovered near the Persian Gulf, inaugurating the climb to economic power. During the Persian Gulf War of 1990-91, Saudi Arabia served as the base from which United Nations forces regained Kuwait from Iraq.

AREA: 756,985 sq mi (1,960,582 sq km)

■ **CLIMATE:** A hot and dry climate with great extremes of temperature. Nearly half the country is uninhabited desert.

■ **PEOPLE:** The population is nearly all Arab and includes more than six million expatriates from several Southeast Asian countries.

POPULATION: 27,019,731

LIFE EXPECTANCY AT BIRTH (YEARS): male, 73.3; female, 77.3

LITERACY RATE: 78%

ETHNIC GROUPS: Arab 90%, Afro-Asian 10%

Diriyah

PRINCIPAL LANGUAGE: Arabic (official)

CHIEF RELIGION: Muslim (official)

■ **ECONOMY:** Petroleum and petroleum products make up 90 percent of exports, which go to the United States, Japan, South Korea, China and the European Union. Pilgrims to Mecca provide substantial income.

MONETARY UNIT: riyal

GDP: $310.2 billion (2004 est.)

PER CAPITA GDP: $12,000

INDUSTRIES: oil production and refining, basic petrochemicals, cement, construction, fertilizer, plastics

MINERALS: petroleum, natural gas, iron ore, gold, copper

CHIEF CROPS: wheat, barley, tomatoes, melons, dates, citrus

GOVERNMENT TYPE: constitutional monarchy with strong Islamic influence

CAPITAL: Riyadh (pop., 5,126,000)

INDEPENDENCE DATE: September 23, 1932

WEBSITE: www.saudiembassy.net

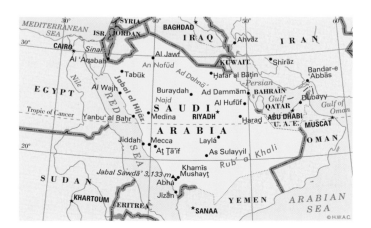

Senegal occupies a transitional zone in West Africa between the Sahara and the equatorial jungle. In the north is a semi-desert region; open savanna is in the center and in the south; the climate is hot and humid. The Senegal is the chief river. Phosphates are the chief mineral resource. Fishing helps to support the economy. Peanuts and cotton are the major cash crops. Petroleum refining and the processing of fish and agricultural products are the chief industries. Exports of fish, cotton, peanuts, phosphates and petroleum products go mainly to India, the European Union and several West African countries.

Wolof, Fulani and Serer are the main ethnic divisions. The country is 92 percent Muslim. French is the official language, but the people speak various African languages. Dakar is the capital and chief city.

Senegal was dominated by the Muslim Tukulers until 1893, when the French conquered the area. Dakar was the capital of vast French West Africa until Senegal became independent in 1960. The country now has one of the most stable governments in Africa.

Street scene

AREA: 75,749 sq mi (196,190 sq km)

CLIMATE: Semi-desert in the north with open savanna in the center and a hot and humid climate in the south.

PEOPLE: Wolof, Fulani (Peulh) and Serer are the main ethnic divisions. There are small groups of Jola, Mandinka and others.

Did you know? Senegal is among the world's largest producers of peanuts.

POPULATION: 11,987,121

LIFE EXPECTANCY AT BIRTH (YEARS): male, 54.9; female, 58.2

LITERACY RATE: 39.1%

ETHNIC GROUPS: Wolof 43%, Pular 24%, Serer 15%, Jola 4%, Mandinka 3%, Soninke 1%

PRINCIPAL LANGUAGES: French (official), Wolof, Pulaar, Jola, Mandinka

CHIEF RELIGIONS: Muslim 94%, Christian 5%

ECONOMY: Exports of fish, cotton, peanuts, phosphates and petroleum products go mainly to India, the European Union and several West African countries.

MONETARY UNIT: CFA franc

GDP: $18.4 billion (2004 est.)

PER CAPITA GDP: $1,700

INDUSTRIES: agricultural and fish processing, mining, fertilizer production, petroleum refining, construction materials

MINERALS: phosphates, iron ore

CHIEF CROPS: peanuts, millet, corn, sorghum, rice, cotton, tomatoes, green vegetables

GOVERNMENT TYPE: republic

CAPITAL: DAKAR (pop., 2,167,000)

INDEPENDENCE DATE: April 4, 1960

WEBSITE: www.state.gov/r/pa/ei/bgn/2862.htm

Serbia, along with Montenegro, are all that remain of the former Socialist Federal Republic of Yugoslavia. The terrain is varied. The landlocked country borders the forested hills of Montenegro on the southwest. In the north are rich fertile plains; in the east and southeast, more rugged terrain prevails. The major rivers are the Danube, Morava, Drina and Sava. The north has a continental climate, with cold winters, hot, humid summers and well-distributed rainfall. The central portion is continental and Mediterranean. The south has hot, dry summers and autumns, and relatively cold winters with heavy snowfall inland. Coal, petroleum, natural gas, antimony, copper, lead, zinc, gold and silver are mined. Cereals and vegetables are grown. Livestock and dairy products add to the economy. Sugar, agricultural machinery, electrical and communication equipment, paper and pulp, lead and transportation equipment are leading industries. Exports of manufactured goods, food and live animals, machinery and transport equipment go to Italy, Germany and Bosnia and Herzegovina.

Serbs make up a large majority of the population. There are small minorities of Hungarians, Bosnians, Albanians and Montenegrins. The population is 85 percent Orthodox Christian, 5 percent Roman Catholic and 3 percent Muslim.

Did you know? In 2003, Yugoslavia turned into a union of its last 2 republics, Serbia and Montenegro.

Serbo-Croatian is the dominant language; Hungarian is spoken by 4 percent of the people. The Cyrillic alphabet is used. Belgrade is the capital and chief city.

The South Slavs entered what is now Serbia in the 600s A.D. By the 1300s Serbia controlled a large empire on the Balkan Peninsula. In 1389 an Ottoman Turkish victory at Kosovo placed Serbia under Ottoman rule. Montenegro became a refuge for Serbs after the defeat at Kosovo. In 1799 the Turks recognized Montenegro's independence. The Serbian struggle for independence during the nineteenth century resulted in total freedom from Turkish rule in 1878. At the end of World War I in 1918, a united Kingdom of Serbs, Croats and Slovenes was proclaimed, later renamed Yugoslavia in 1929. In 1945, after World War II, a Communist republic was established, consisting of the six federal republics of Serbia, Montenegro, Macedonia, Croatia, Bosnia and Herzegovina and Slovenia. In 1991 federal Yugoslavia broke up. Serbia then sent arms to Serb rebels in Croatia and Bosnia. As a result, the United Nations imposed economic sanctions on Serbia and Montenegro in 1992; the sanctions were not lifted until 1996. In February, 2003, the Yugoslav parliament ratified the Constitutional Charter, establishing a new state union and changing the name of the country from Yugoslavia to Serbia and Montenegro.

In May, 2006, the Republic of Montenegro dissolved its political union with Serbia and declared independence on June 3. The parliament of Serbia then stated that the Republic of Serbia was the

Zrenjanin City Hall

continuity of the state union. It changed the name of the country from Serbia and Montenegro to the Republic of Serbia, retaining membership in all international organizations and bodies.

AREA: 34,185 sq mi (88,538 sq km)

■ **CLIMATE:** The north is continental, with cold winters and hot, humid summers. The center is continental and Mediterranean. The south has hot, dry summers and autumns, and relatively cold snowy winters.

■ **PEOPLE:** Serbs make up a large majority of the population. There are small minorities of Hungarians, Bosnians, Albanians and Montenegrins.

POPULATION: 10,212,395

LIFE EXPECTANCY AT BIRTH (YEARS): male, 71.9; female, 77.1

LITERACY RATE: 93%

ETHNIC GROUPS: Serbian 63%, Albanian 14%

PRINCIPAL LANGUAGES: Serbian 63%, Albanian 17%, Hungarian 3%

CHIEF RELIGIONS: Orthodox 65%, Muslim 19%, Roman Catholic 4%

■ **ECONOMY:** Exports of manufactured goods, food and live animals, machinery and transport equipment go to Italy, Germany and Bosnia and Herzegovina.

GOVERNMENT TYPE: federal republic

CAPITAL: Belgrade (pop., 1,118,000)

INDEPENDENCE DATE: February 4, 2003

MONETARY UNIT: new dinar

GDP: $26.3 billion (2004 est.)

PER CAPITA GDP: $2,400

INDUSTRIES: machine building, metallurgy, mining, consumer goods, electronics, petroleum products, chemicals, pharmaceuticals

MINERALS: oil, gas, coal, antimony, copper, lead, zinc, nickel, gold, pyrite, chrome

CHIEF CROPS: cereals, fruits, vegetables, tobacco

WEBSITE: www.gov.yu

The Seychelles, a ninety-island archipelago in the Indian Ocean, are a beautiful tropical paradise, largely isolated from the rest of the world. Mahe, the mountainous main island, takes up just over half the total area of the country. The other islands are flat, elevated coral reefs. The climate of the Seychelles is equable and healthful, although quite humid. Coconuts, cinnamon, vanilla, sweet potatoes, tapioca and bananas are the chief cash crops. Tuna fishing is important. Tourism dominates the economy. Exports of fish, copra and cinnamon bark flow mainly to the European Union and Japan.

Did you know? French planters and their slaves first settled in the Seychelles in 1768.

Ethnically, the Seychellois are a mixture of Asians, Africans and Europeans. English and French are the official languages, but the people primarily speak Creole. Victoria is the capital and chief town.

The Seychelles were unclaimed and uninhabited until 1742, when the French governor of Mauritius sent an expedition to the islands. In 1814 the Seychelles passed to the British; they became a crown colony in 1903, and in 1976 became independent.

AREA: 176 sq mi (455 sq km)

■ **CLIMATE:** The tropical marine climate has a monsoon season from March to September.

■ **PEOPLE:** Seychellois are Creole, a mixture of Asian, African and European.

POPULATION: 81,541

LIFE EXPECTANCY AT BIRTH (YEARS): male, 66.1; female, 77.1

LITERACY RATE: 58%

ETHNIC GROUPS: mainly Seychellois (mix of French, African, and Asian)

PRINCIPAL LANGUAGES: English, French, Creole (all official)

CHIEF RELIGIONS: Roman Catholic 87%, Anglican 7%

■ **ECONOMY:** Tourism dominates the economy. Exports of fish, copra and cinnamon bark are mainly sent to the European Union and Japan.

Victoria

MONETARY UNIT: rupee

GDP: $626 million (2002 est.)

PER CAPITA GDP: $7,800

INDUSTRIES: fishing, tourism, coconut and vanilla processing, rope, boat building, printing, furniture, beverages

CHIEF CROPS: coconuts, cinnamon, vanilla, sweet potatoes, cassava, bananas

GOVERNMENT TYPE: republic

CAPITAL: Victoria (pop., 25,000)

INDEPENDENCE DATE: June 29, 1976

WEBSITE: www.seychelles.com

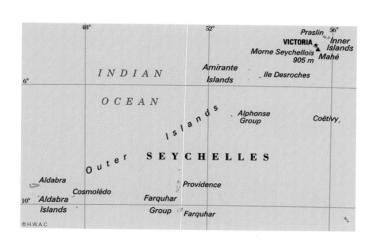

The West African country of Sierra Leone consists of a coastal plain of mangrove swamp that gradually gives way to wooded hills. An upland plateau occupies the interior, and there are mountains near the eastern border. The tropical climate is hot and humid with a rainy season from May to December. Diamonds, bauxite and titanium ore are the chief minerals, followed by gold, iron ore and chromite. Coffee, cocoa, rice, palm kernels, peanuts and vegetables are the chief crops. Mining, forestry, fishing, beverages and cigarettes are chief industries. Exports of titanium ore, diamonds, bauxite, coffee, cocoa and fish go to Belgium, Germany, the United States and India.

The Temne and the Mende are the chief ethnic groups. Less than 2 percent are Creoles, descendants of freed slaves, mostly from the Americas. The population is 60 percent Muslim. English is the official language, but the people speak various African vernaculars. Freetown is the capital and chief city.

Originally divided into many kingdoms, the area was reached in 1460 by the Portuguese, who named it Sierra Leone, meaning "lion mountain." In 1787 a group of abolitionists founded Freetown to resettle freed slaves from Britain and from captured slave ships. The settlement became a crown colony in 1808; in 1896 the interior was made a British protectorate. Sierra Leone became independent in 1961. In recent years civil war hindered economic development, but recent political stability has led to an improving economic environment.

Did you know? Freetown was founded in 1787 as a haven for freed slaves.

AREA: 27,699 sq mi (71,740 sq km)

CLIMATE: The tropical climate is hot and humid with a rainy season from May to December.

PEOPLE: The Temne and Mende are the chief ethnic groups. Less than 2 percent are Creoles, descendants of freed slaves, mostly from the Americas.

POPULATION: 6,005,250

LIFE EXPECTANCY AT BIRTH (YEARS): male, 40.2; female, 45.2

LITERACY RATE: 31.4%

Rural life

ETHNIC GROUPS: Temne 30%, Mende 30%, other tribes 30%; Creole 10%

PRINCIPAL LANGUAGES: English (official), Mende in the south, Temne in the north, Krio (English Creole)

CHIEF RELIGIONS: Muslim 60%, indigenous beliefs 30%, Christian 10%

ECONOMY: Exports of titanium ore, diamonds, bauxite, coffee, cocoa and fish go to Belgium, Germany, the United States and India.

MONETARY UNIT: leone

GDP: $3.1 billion (2003 est.)

PER CAPITA GDP: $500

INDUSTRIES: mining, small-scale manufacturing, petroleum refining

MINERALS: diamonds, titanium ore, bauxite, iron ore, gold, chromite

CHIEF CROPS: rice, coffee, cocoa, palm kernels, palm oil, peanuts

GOVERNMENT TYPE: republic

CAPITAL: Freetown (pop., 921,000)

INDEPENDENCE DATE: April 27, 1961

WEBSITE: www.embassyofsierraleone.org

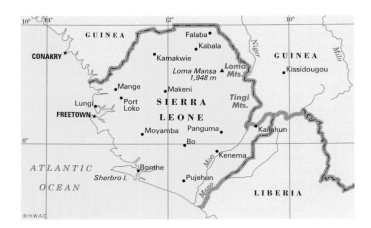

The island of Singapore lies south of the Malay peninsula, separated by the Selat Johor. Except for a central plateau, most of the low-lying island consists of swamp and jungle. The tropical climate is hot, humid and rainy with two distinct monsoon seasons. Singapore has an open entrepreneurial economy with a strong manufacturing sector and excellent international trading links. Major agricultural products include poultry, orchids, vegetables, fruits and ornamental fish. Banking and shipping are very important. The major industries are petroleum refining, chemicals and pharmaceuticals, biotechnology, rubber products and electronics, ship and oil rig repair, food and beverages, printing and publishing. Exports are dominated by petroleum and rubber products, computer and electronic equipment, chemicals and transport equipment, which go to China, Malaysia, the United States and the European Union.

Did you know?
Singapore has one of the highest standards of living in Asia.

Chinese make up three fourths of the population; Malays and Indians are other major groups. Chinese, Malay, Tamil and English are the official languages. Buddhism, Christianity, Islam and Hinduism are the chief religions.

In 1819, Sir Stamford Raffles of the British East India Company founded a trading post on the island. Singapore became part of the British Straits Settlement in 1826, and in 1946 became a separate British crown colony. Singapore joined Malaya, Sarawak and Sabah in 1963 to form the independent Federation of Malaysia. In 1965 Singapore withdrew from the Federation and became a separate independent state.

AREA: 267 sq mi (693 sq km)

■ **CLIMATE:** The tropical climate is hot, humid and rainy with two distinct monsoon seasons.

■ **PEOPLE:** Chinese make up three fourths of the population; Malays and Indians are other major groups.

POPULATION: 4,492,150

LIFE EXPECTANCY AT BIRTH (YEARS): male, 79.0; female, 84.3

LITERACY RATE: 93.5%

ETHNIC GROUPS: Chinese 77%, Malay 14%, Indian 8%

PRINCIPAL LANGUAGES: Chinese, Malay, Tamil, English (all official)

CHIEF RELIGIONS: Buddhist, Muslim, Christian, Taoist, Hindu

■ **ECONOMY:** Exports are dominated by petroleum and rubber products, computer and electronic equipment, chemicals and transport equipment, which go to China, Malaysia, the United States and the European Union.

Downtown

GOVERNMENT TYPE: republic

CAPITAL: Singapore (pop., 4,253,000)

INDEPENDENCE DATE: August 9, 1965

MONETARY UNIT: Singapore dollar

GDP: $120.9 billion (2004 est.)

PER CAPITA GDP: $27,800

INDUSTRIES: electronics, chemicals, financial services, oil-drilling equipment, petroleum refining, rubber products, processed food and beverages, ship repair, entrepot trade, biotechnology

CHIEF CROPS: rubber, copra, fruit, orchids, vegetables

WEBSITE: www.gov.sg

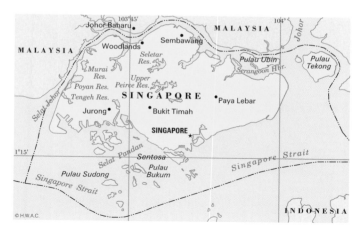

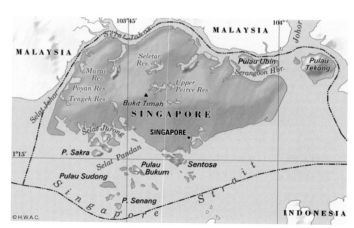

Landlocked Slovakia in Central Europe has rugged mountains in the center and northern part, and has lowlands in the south; the temperate climate has cool summers and cold, cloudy winters. The chief rivers are the Danube, Vah and Hron. Slovakia has significant deposits of coal and small amounts of iron ore, copper and manganese. Crops and livestock include grains, potatoes, sugar beets, hops, fruit, hogs, cattle and poultry. Forestry is important. Chemicals, metals, transport vehicles, machinery, paper, printing and food processing are the leading industrial products. Vehicles and other machinery, iron and steel, chemicals, fuels, plastics and agricultural products are exported mostly to the European Union.

Slovaks make up the majority of the population. There are small groups of Hungarians, Romas, Czechs, Ruthenians and Ukranians. Slovak is the official language. Sixty percent are Roman Catholic. Bratislava is the capital and chief city, followed by Kosˇice.

The Slavic-speaking Slovaks were absorbed by the Kingdom of Hungary in 1000 A.D. Slovakia remained under Hungarian and Austrian control until 1918. After World War I it became part of the new Czechoslovak state. In 1939 Slovakia, with German encouragement, seceded from Czechoslovakia. After World War II, the Slovak area rejoined the reconstituted Czechoslovak state. From 1948 until 1989, when the Communist Party collapsed, Czechoslovakia was a Communist-controlled state. Slovakia separated peacefully from the Czech Republic on January 1, 1993. Slovakia officially became a member of NATO in March, 2004 and joined the European Union in May, 2004.

Did you know?
Bratislava served as the capital of Hungary from 1541 to 1784.

AREA: 18,859 sq mi (48,845 sq km)

■ **CLIMATE:** The temperate climate has cool summers and cold, cloudy winters.

■ **PEOPLE:** Slovaks make up the majority of the population. There are small groups of Hungarians, Romas, Czechs, Ruthenians and Ukranians.

POPULATION: 5,439,448

LIFE EXPECTANCY AT BIRTH (YEARS): male, 70.2; female, 78.4

LITERACY RATE: NA

Oravsky Podámok-Orava Castle

ETHNIC GROUPS: Slovak 86%, Hungarian 11%, Roma 2%

PRINCIPAL LANGUAGES: Slovak (official), Hungarian

CHIEF RELIGIONS: Roman Catholic 60%, Protestant 8%, Orthodox 4%

■ **ECONOMY:** Vehicles and other machinery, iron and steel, chemicals, fuels, plastics and agricultural products are exported mostly to the European Union.

GOVERNMENT TYPE: republic

CAPITAL: Bratislava (pop., 425,000)

INDEPENDENCE DATE: January 1, 1993

MONETARY UNIT: koruna

GDP: $78.9 billion (2004 est.)

PER CAPITA GDP: $14,500

INDUSTRIES: metal and metal products, food and beverages, electricity, chemicals and manmade fibers, machinery, paper and printing, earthenware and ceramics, transport vehicles, textiles, electrical and optical apparatus, rubber products

MINERALS: coal, iron ore, copper, manganese, salt

CHIEF CROPS: grains, potatoes, sugar beets, hops, fruit

WEBSITES: www.slovakembassy-us.org
www.government.gov.sk/english/

Slovenia is bordered by Italy, Austria, Hungary and Croatia, with a small coastal strip on the Gulf of Trieste. Slovenia is a land of mountains interspersed with valleys. The eastward-flowing rivers, including the Sava and the Drava, traverse the valleys. The interior climate has hot summers and cold winters. Lignite coal and mercury are produced. Timber is also important. Livestock-raising dominates agriculture along with poultry and milk. Crops include wine grapes, potatoes, hops, wheat and corn. Metal products, electronics, chemicals, wood products, vehicles and textiles are the leading industries. Machinery, transportation equipment, electrical and optical equipment, chemicals, basic metals and fabricated products are shipped to the European Union.

Slovenes make most of the population. There are also small groups of Croats, Serbs and Bosniaks. The majority of the people are Roman Catholic. Slovenian is spoken by most of the population. Ljubljana is the capital and chief city; Maribor is second in size.

Slovenes spread into the area in the seventh century A.D. However, the Slovenes fell under German control in the late 700s. With the collapse of Austria-Hungary in 1918, Slovenia became part of Yugoslavia. In 1991, Slovenia broke away from Yugoslavia and became independent. It joined the European Union in May, 2004.

Predjama Castle

Did you know?
Slovenia is the most prosperous of the former Yugoslav republics.

AREA: 7,827 sq mi (20,273 sq km)

CLIMATE: The interior climate has hot summers and cold winters.

PEOPLE: Slovenes make most of the population. There are also small groups of Croats, Serbs and Bosniaks.

POPULATION: 2,011,070

LIFE EXPECTANCY AT BIRTH (YEARS): male, 72.2; female, 79.9

LITERACY RATE: 99%

ETHNIC GROUPS: Slovene 88%, Croat 3%, Serb 2%, Bosniak 1%

PRINCIPAL LANGUAGES: Slovenian (official), Serbo-Croatian

CHIEF RELIGION: Roman Catholic 71%

ECONOMY: Machinery, transportation equipment, electrical and optical equipment, chemicals, basic metals and fabricated products are shipped to the European Union.

MONETARY UNIT: euro

GDP: $39.4 billion (2004 est.)

PER CAPITA GDP: $19,600

INDUSTRIES: metallurgy and metal products, electronics, trucks, electric power equipment, wood products, textiles, chemicals, machine tools

MINERALS: coal, lead, zinc, mercury, uranium, silver

CHIEF CROPS: potatoes, hops, wheat, sugar beets, corn, grapes

GOVERNMENT TYPE: republic

CAPITAL: Ljubljana (pop., 256,000)

INDEPENDENCE DATE: June 25, 1991

WEBSITE: www.sigov.si

The Solomon Islands lie just east of Papua New Guinea in the South Pacific Ocean. The larger islands have a mountainous spine that on one side drops steeply to sea level, and on the other drops through a series of foothills to the coast. Humid weather varies from warm to hot. Reserves of gold, bauxite and phosphates are the chief resources. Fishing and forestry also contribute to the economy. Cocoa, coconuts, palm oil and kernels, and rice are produced. Chief industries include fish processing, lumber, boats, rattan and wood furniture, and mining. Tourism, particularly diving, is an important service industry. Exports of timber, fish, copra, cocoa and palm oil go to China, South Korea, Thailand, Japan and the Philippines.

Melanesians form 93 percent of the population. Religious groups include Anglicans (34 percent), Roman Catholics (19 percent) and Baptists (17 percent). English is the official language; Melanesian pidgin is the common language in much of the country. Honiara, on Guadalcanal, is the capital and chief town.

Ancestors of the present Melanesian inhabitants entered the area from the Malay archipelago sometime after 1000 B.C. In the late nineteenth century, Britain established a protectorate over the Solomons. During World War II, Japan invaded the Solomons, but an American counteroffensive, beginning at Guadalcanal, drove the invaders from the islands. Independence from Britain came in 1978. The Asian economic crisis and ethnic violence in 2000 led to government insolvency by 2002. Exports of palm oil and gold ceased while exports of timber fell. With the help of an Australian-led multinational force, political and economic stability are now beginning to recover.

Did you know? The islands' mountains are of volcanic origin and heavily wooded.

AREA: 10,985 sq mi (28,450 sq km)

■ **CLIMATE:** The tropical monsoon climate varies from warm to hot.

■ **PEOPLE:** Melanesians form most of the population. There are small Polynesian and Micronesian minorities.

POPULATION: 552,438

LIFE EXPECTANCY AT BIRTH (YEARS): male, 69.9; female, 75.0

LITERACY RATE: NA

Malaita

ETHNIC GROUPS: Melanesian 93%, Polynesian 4%, Micronesian, European, and others 3%

PRINCIPAL LANGUAGES: English (official), Melanesian pidgin, and 120 indigenous languages

CHIEF RELIGIONS: Anglican 45%, Roman Catholic 18%, other Christian 35%

■ **ECONOMY:** Tourism, particularly diving, is an important service industry. Exports of timber, fish, copra, cocoa and palm oil go to China, South Korea, Thailand, Japan and the Philippines.

GOVERNMENT TYPE: in transition

CAPITAL: Honiara (pop., 56,000)

INDEPENDENCE DATE: July 7, 1978

MONETARY UNIT: Solomon Islands dollar (SBD)

GDP: $800 million (2002 est.)

PER CAPITA GDP: $1,700

INDUSTRIES: fish, mining, timber

CHIEF CROPS: cocoa, beans, coconuts, palm kernels, rice, potatoes, vegetables, fruit

MINERALS: gold, bauxite, phosphates, lead, zinc, nickel

WEBSITE: www.commerce.gov.sb

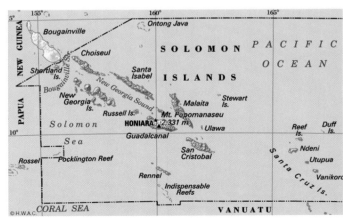

ocated in eastern Africa and bordering the Indian Ocean, much of Somalia is arid or semiarid with two distinct monsoon seasons. The northern region is mountainous; the southern part is mostly desert, but with a large fertile area. Two large rivers flowing from Ethiopia, the Webe Shabeele and Webi Jubba cross the fertile area. Uranium ore, iron, tin, gypsum and salt deposits have been found. Livestock raising is important. Bananas, sorghum, corn and sugarcane are raised. Some fishing is carried on. Despite the lack of a functioning central government, Industries include telecommunications, livestock, fishing, textiles, transportation and limited financial services. Exports, consisting of livestock, hides, fish, charcoal, bananas and scrap metal are shipped to the United Arab Emirates, Yemen and Oman.

Somalis make up most of the population. There is a small mostly Bantu and Arab minority. Almost all of the people are Sunni Muslim. Somali is the official language. Mogadishu is the capital and chief city.

Somalia is reputedly the source of the biblical frankincense and myrrh. In the nineteenth century Britain occupied the northwest portion, and Italy, the east and southeast. Following its defeat in World War II, Italy renounced colonial rights to its portion of Somalia and was given a trusteeship to prepare the former possession for independence. In 1960 British and Italian Somaliland were united as the independent Somali Republic, which was renamed Somalia in 1969. Border clashes between Somalia and neighboring Ethiopia occurred sporadically in the 1970s. Civil war broke out between rival factions in 1991, resulting in high casualties, famine and the complete collapse of the central government. In 1992 the United Nations, with the aid of the United States, undertook the delivery of food to end the famine. Because of ongoing civil clashes, the U.S. and U.N. forces withdrew by 1995.

Did you know?
Frankincense and myrrh are the major forestry products of Somalia.

In the 21st century Somalia gained greater international attention as a possible entry point for international terrorism. The Inter-governmental Authority on Development (IGAD) formed a transitional government, including a Transitional Parliament, a Transitional Federal Government and a transitional President, Prime Minister and cabinet.

AREA: 246,201 sq mi (637,657 sq km)

■ **CLIMATE:** Mostly desert, much of Somalia is hot and humid between two distinct monsoon seasons.

■ **PEOPLE:** Somalis make up most of the population. There is a small mostly Bantu and Arab minority.

Mosque

POPULATION: 8,863,338

LIFE EXPECTANCY AT BIRTH (YEARS): male, 46.0; female, 49.5

LITERACY RATE: 37.8%

ETHNIC GROUPS: Somali 85%, Bantu and other 15%

PRINCIPAL LANGUAGES: Somali, Arabic (both official); Italian, English

CHIEF RELIGION: Sunni Muslim (official)

■ **ECONOMY:** Exports, consisting of livestock, hides, fish, charcoal, bananas and scrap metal are shipped to the United Arab Emirates, Yemen and Oman.

MONETARY UNIT: shilling

GDP: $4.6 billion (2004 est.)

PER CAPITA GDP: $600

INDUSTRIES: sugar refining, textiles, wireless communication

MINERALS: uranium and largely unexploited reserves of iron ore, tin, gypsum, bauxite, copper, salt, natural gas, likely oil reserves

CHIEF CROPS: bananas, sorghum, corn, coconuts, rice, sugarcane, mangoes, sesame seeds, beans

GOVERNMENT TYPE: in transition

CAPITAL: Mogadishu (pop., 1,175,000)

INDEPENDENCE DATE: July 1, 1960

WEBSITE: www.state.gov/r/pa/ei/bgn/2863.htm

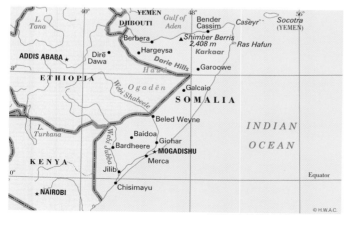

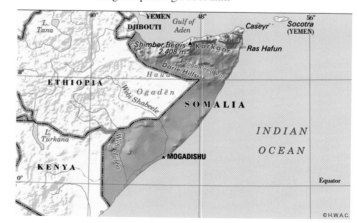

The Republic of South Africa, lying at the extreme southern tip of the continent, consists of a narrow coastal belt of lowlands extending into a great interior plateau. Major rivers include the Orange, Vaal and Limpopo. The mostly semiarid climate is subtropical along the coast. South Africa has large amounts of gold, coal, platinum, diamonds, copper, iron ore, manganese, uranium ore, chromium, nickel, lead, antimony and natural gas. The diversified agricultural sector produces cattle, sheep, corn, wheat, sugarcane, wine grapes, fruits and vegetables. Industries include automobile assembly, metal-working, machinery, iron and steel, chemicals and textiles. Fisheries are important. South Africa's huge export trade of gold, other minerals and metals, foodstuffs, chemicals, motor vehicles and parts is shipped to the European Union, the United States, East Asia and Sub-Saharan Africa.

Black Africans make up three fourths of the population. Other groups include whites, "coloureds" (mixed Bushmen, Hottentot, Malay and white) and Indians. South Africans speak eleven official languages, including Afrikaans, English, Zulu, Xhosa, Sotho and Tswana. Christians include most whites and "coloureds" and about 60 percent of blacks, Hindus include 60 percent of Indians, and Muslims are 2 percent. Pretoria is the administrative capital; Cape Town is the legislative capital, and Bloemfontein is the judicial capital. Cape Town and Johannesburg are the largest cities.

Before the seventeenth century, incoming Bantu peoples were pushing the original Bushmen and Hottentot inhabitants into remote areas. The first Dutch settlers established the Cape Colony in 1652. In 1814 Britain gained possession of the colony from the Netherlands. As a result, the Boers (descendants of Dutch settlers) migrated northeast in the Great Trek. During the Boer War (1899-1902), Britain clashed with the Boer republics of the Transvaal and the Orange Free State. Following the Boer defeat, British sovereignty over present-day South Africa was acknowledged. The Union of South Africa, comprising the Cape, Natal, Transvaal and the Orange Free State was formed in 1910. In 1948 apartheid (i.e., separation of the races with whites in political control) was established as official state policy. South Africa became a republic in 1951 and withdrew from the Commonwealth. Between 1976 and 1981 so-called independence was granted to four black homelands, which went unrecognized internationally and were later abolished. After long years of black struggle and under the pressure of international sanctions, the new constitution of 1994 provided suffrage for all races.

Did you know? South Africa mines more gold than any other country in the world.

Cape Town Waterfront

AREA: 471,010 sq mi (1,219,912 sq km)

CLIMATE: The mostly semiarid climate is subtropical along the coast.

PEOPLE: Black Africans make up three fourths of the population. Other groups include whites, "coloureds" (mixed Bushmen, Hottentot, Malay and white) and Indians.

POPULATION: 44,187,637

LIFE EXPECTANCY AT BIRTH (YEARS): male, 44.0; female, 44.0

LITERACY RATE: 85%

ETHNIC GROUPS: black 75%, white 14%, mixed 8%, Indian 3%

PRINCIPAL LANGUAGES: Afrikaans, English, Ndebele, Pedi, Sotho, Swazi, Tsonga, Tswana, Venda, Xhosa, Zulu (all official)

CHIEF RELIGIONS: Christian 68%, indigenous beliefs and animist 29%

ECONOMY: South Africa's huge export trade of gold, other minerals and metals, foodstuffs, chemicals, motor vehicles and parts is shipped to the European Union, the United States, East Asia and Sub-Saharan Africa.

MONETARY UNIT: rand

GDP: $491.4 billion (2004 est.)

PER CAPITA GDP: $11,100

INDUSTRIES: mining, automobile assembly, metalworking, machinery, textile, iron and steel, chemicals, fertilizer, foodstuffs

MINERALS: gold, chromium, antimony, coal, iron ore, manganese, nickel, phosphates, tin, uranium, gem diamonds, platinum, copper, vanadium, salt, natural gas

CHIEF CROPS: corn, wheat, sugarcane, fruits, vegetables

GOVERNMENT TYPE: republic

CAPITALS: Pretoria (administrative) (pop., 1,209,000), Cape Town (legislative) (pop., 2,967,000), Bloemfontein (judicial) (pop., 381,000)

INDEPENDENCE DATE: May 31, 1910

WEBSITE: www.gov.za

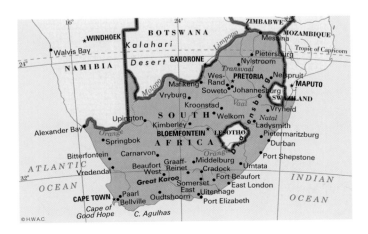

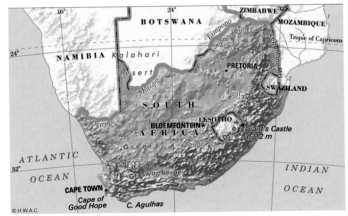

Spain, occupying most of the Iberian peninsula, has played an important part in world history. Most of the country is a high plateau divided by mountains and broad depressions. The landmass rises sharply from the sea, leaving a narrow coastal plain except in the Andalusian lowlands in the south. Also included as integral parts of Spain are the Balearic Islands, the Canary Islands, Ceuta and Melilla. Spain's chief rivers are the Ebro, Duero, Tagus (Tajo) and Guadiana. The temperate climate has hot summers and cold winters in the interior; the coast is more moderate. Coal, iron, uranium, lead, zinc, copper, pyrites, fluorspar, gypsum, mercury, tungsten, kaolin, potash and hydroelectric power are produced. Grain, vegetables, olives, wine grapes, sugar beets, sunflower seed and citrus fruits are produced, along with livestock products. Fishing is important. Spain's leading industries include the manufacture of textiles, apparel, footwear, processed foods and beverages, steel, chemicals, automobiles and shipbuilding. Tourism is very important. The chief exports include motor vehicles and machinery, manufactured goods and foodstuffs which are shipped mostly to other European Union countries.

Did you know?
Bullfighting is the national sport of Spain.

Separate ethnic and linguistic groups are represented by the Castilians of central Spain, the Basques in the north, Catalans in the northeast, Galicians in the northwest, Valencians in the east and the Andalusians in the south. The country is 99 percent Roman Catholic. Madrid is the capital and largest city, followed by Barcelona, center of Catalonia, and by Valencia and Seville.

About 1000 B.C. Celtic tribes from the north invaded the Iberian peninsula. Later Phoenicians and Greeks established colonies along the coast. Carthaginian control was followed by Roman rule established between 205 and 178 B.C. Early in the fifth century A.D. Spain was overrun by the Germanic Visigoths, who were themselves conquered by the Islamic Moors in the early 700s. For the next 800 years a Muslim culture flourished throughout Iberia while the Christian kingdoms fought their way back to control of the peninsula. In 1479 Aragon and Castile were united, establishing the boundaries of modern Spain. The momentous year 1492 saw the final expulsion of the Moors from Spain. That same year the departure of Columbus on his voyages of discovery led to the founding of the vast Spanish world empire. However, after the defeat of the Spanish Armada by England in 1588, Spanish power and the empire began a slow decline. In 1931 a republic replaced the monarchy, but it was in turn replaced by a single-party state under Francisco Franco after the Spanish Civil War, 1936-39. On the death of Franco in 1975, Juan Carlos, grandson of the last king, Alfonso XIII, became King of Spain. The last twenty years have seen the growth of the Spanish economy.

Castillo De Colomares

Basque separatist campaigns for autonomy have continued in the northwestern part of the country, including terrorist violence and political assassinations. In recent years a transnational terrorist threat from jihadist terrorists with possible ties to al Qaeda has become a growing concern. Spain became a member of the European Union on January 1, 1986.

AREA: 194,897 sq mi (504,782 sq km)

■ **CLIMATE:** The temperate climate has hot summers and cold winters in the interior. The coast is more moderate.

■ **PEOPLE:** Separate ethnic and linguistic groups are represented by the Castilians of central Spain, the Basques in the north, Catalans in the northeast, Galicians in the northwest, Valencians in the east and the Andalusians in the south.

POPULATION: 40,341,462

LIFE EXPECTANCY AT BIRTH (YEARS): male, 76.0; female, 82.9

LITERACY RATE: 97%

ETHNIC GROUPS: Castilian, Catalan, Basque, Galician

PRINCIPAL LANGUAGES: Castilian Spanish (official), Catalan, Galician, Basque

CHIEF RELIGION: Roman Catholic 94%

■ **ECONOMY:** Chief exports include motor vehicles and machinery, manufactured goods and foodstuffs which are shipped mostly to other European Union countries. Tourism is very important.

MONETARY UNIT: euro

GDP: $937.6 billion (2004 est.)

PER CAPITA GDP: $23,300

INDUSTRIES: textiles and apparel, food and beverages, metals and metal manufactures, chemicals, shipbuilding, automobiles, machine tools, tourism

MINERALS: coal, iron ore, uranium, mercury, pyrites, fluorspar, gypsum, zinc, lead, tungsten, copper, kaolin, potash

CHIEF CROPS: grain, vegetables, olives, wine grapes, sugar beets, citrus

GOVERNMENT TYPE: constitutional monarchy

CAPITAL: Madrid (pop., 5,103,000)

INDEPENDENCE DATE: 1492

WEBSITE: www.embaspain.ca

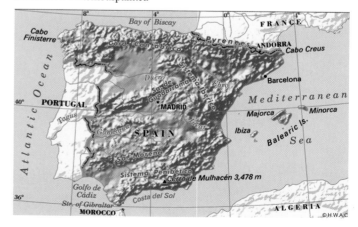

Sri Lanka, formerly known as Ceylon, is a large island lying directly southeast of India across the Palk Strait in the Indian Ocean. A low-lying plain takes up the northern half of the island and continues around the southern coast. The south-central part is mountainous. The tropical climate has a northeast monsoon from December to March and a southwest monsoon from June to October. Limestone, graphite, mineral sands, gems, and phosphates are the chief natural resources. Leading cash crops include rice, tea, rubber, coconut, and spices. Livestock-raising is important. Rubber processing, apparel manufacture, food processing, petroleum refining, textiles, telecommunications, insurance and banking are the main industries. Exports of textiles and apparel, tea, jewelry and gems, refined petroleum, coconut and rubber products go to the United States, the United Kingdom and India. The economy is still recovering from the 2004 tsunami which killed more than 30,000 Sri Lankans and left thousands of others homeless.

Did you know? The Temple of the Tooth in Kandy is said to contain one of the Buddha's teeth.

Sinhalese make up three fourths of the population. Tamils and Moors are the other major groups. Religious adherents include Buddhists (69 percent), Hindus (15 percent), Christians (8 percent) and Muslim (8 percent). Sinhala is the official and national language; Tamil is also a national language. Colombo is the capital and largest city. Sri Jayewardenepura-Kotte is the administrative capital and the site of Parliament.

The Sinhalese came to the island in the sixth century B.C. and were converted to Buddhism in the third century B.C. Tamils entered the northern part of the island from southern India. The Portuguese occupied the coastal areas in the sixteenth century A.D. The Dutch took over Portuguese possessions in the seventeenth century. In 1795 the area fell to Britain. Sri Lanka became independent in 1948, and in 1972 became a republic. Beginning in 1983, the island suffered from clashes between Tamil rebels and government forces. The government declared a unilateral ceasefire in 2002. Despite continued outbreaks of violence, both sides still claim to adhere to the ceasefire.

AREA: 25,332 sq mi (65,610 sq km)

CLIMATE: The tropical climate has a northeast monsoon from December to March and a southwest monsoon from June to October.

PEOPLE: Sinhalese make up three fourths of the population. Tamils and Moors are the other major groups.

POPULATION: 20,222,240

Sigiriya

LIFE EXPECTANCY AT BIRTH (YEARS): male, 70.3; female, 75.6

LITERACY RATE: 90.2%

ETHNIC GROUPS: Sinhalese 74%, Tamil 18%, Moor 7%

PRINCIPAL LANGUAGES: Sinhala, Tamil (both official); English

CHIEF RELIGIONS: Buddhist 70%, Hindu 15%, Christian 8%, Muslim 7%

ECONOMY: Exports of textiles and apparel, tea, jewelry and gems, refined petroleum, coconut and rubber products go to the United States, the United Kingdom and India.

CAPITALS: Colombo (commercial) (pop., 648,000), Sri Jayawardenepura Kotte (administrative) (pop., 117,000)

INDEPENDENCE DATE: February 4, 1948

GOVERNMENT TYPE: republic

MONETARY UNIT: rupee

GDP: $80.6 billion (2004 est.)

PER CAPITA GDP: $4,000

INDUSTRIES: rubber processing, agricultural commodities, clothing, cement, petroleum refining, textiles, tobacco

MINERALS: limestone, graphite, mineral sands, gems, phosphates, clay

CHIEF CROPS: rice, sugarcane, grains, pulses, oilseed, spices, tea, rubber, coconuts

WEBSITE: www.slembassyusa.org

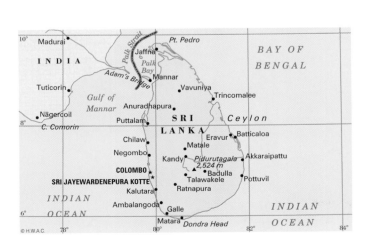

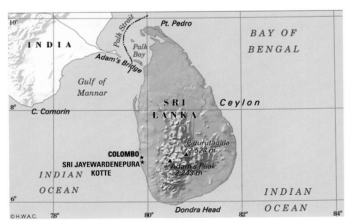

Sudan, in Northeast Africa, is the largest country in area on the continent. It is an immense plateau covered by three distinct natural regions, ranging from the Libyan and Saharan deserts in the north, to grassy plains in the center, to a great swamp and tropical savanna in the south. The chief river is the Nile, formed by the joining of the Blue and White Nile rivers at Khartoum. The northern climate is dry Sahara desert, while the southern climate is humid and tropical. The rainy season varies by region. The country has modest reserves of oil, gold, iron ore, copper, chromite and other industrial metals. Long-staple cotton is the major cash crop. Peanuts, sorghum, millet, wheat, sesame seeds, gum arabic and sugarcane are also grown. Livestock-raising is important. Exports of crude oil and petroleum products, cotton, sesame seeds, sorghum, peanuts, gum arabic, sugar, meat, hides and live animals flow to Egypt, Persian Gulf states, Saudi Arabia and China.

Black Africans make up about half of the population while Arabs make up more than a third. There is also a small number of Beja. The country is 70 percent Sunni Muslim, 5 percent Christian. Twenty-five percent of the people follow indigenous beliefs. Arabic is the official language and the native tongue of a large part of the population; many other languages are spoken. Khartoum is the capital and largest city.

Did you know? Sudan is the largest African country in total area.

Nubia, the northern half of Sudan, played an active part in Egyptian history long before the Christian era. In the fifteenth century A.D. conquering Arabs converted the area to Islam. By 1821, all of Sudan was unified by Egypt. From 1881 to 1885 the Sudanese were led by the Mahdi, a Muslim religious leader, in a successful revolt against Egyptian rule. An Anglo-Egyptian army in 1898-99 defeated the Mahdi's followers and established an Anglo-Egyptian condominium over the area. In 1956 the Sudan was proclaimed an independent republic. Famine and civil strife in the south - where the non-Muslim black population has fought for autonomy from the Arab-dominated north for many years - have crippled the economy. A final Naivasha peace treaty in 2005 has granted southern rebels autonomy for six years, after which a referendum for independence is scheduled.

A separate civil conflict broke out in the western region of Darfur in 2003 has resulted in more than 200,000 deaths and two million displaced people.

AREA: 967,498 sq mi (2,505,810 sq km)

CLIMATE: The northern climate is dry Sahara desert, while the southern climate is humid and tropical. The rainy season varies by region.

PEOPLE: Black Africans make up about half of the population while Arabs make up more than a third. There are also a small number of Beja.

POPULATION: 41,236,378

LIFE EXPECTANCY AT BIRTH (YEARS): male, 57.0; female, 59.4

LITERACY RATE: 46.1%

ETHNIC GROUPS: black 52%, Arab 39%, Beja 6%

PRINCIPAL LANGUAGES: Arabic (official), Nubian, Ta Bedawie; Nilotic, Sudanic dialects; English

CHIEF RELIGIONS: Sunni Muslim 70%, indigenous beliefs 25%, Christian 5%

Khartoum view with traffic

ECONOMY: Crude oil and petroleum products, cotton, sesame seeds, sorghum, peanuts, gum arabic, sugar, meat, hides and live animals go to Egypt, Persian Gulf states, Saudi Arabia and China.

MONETARY UNIT: dinar (SDD)

GDP: $76.2 billion (2004 est.)

PER CAPITA GDP: $1,900

INDUSTRIES: oil, cotton ginning, textiles, cement, edible oils, sugar, soap distilling, shoes, petroleum refining, pharmaceuticals, armaments, automobile/light truck assembly

MINERALS: petroleum, iron ore, copper, zinc, chromium ore, tungsten, mica, silver, gold

CHIEF CROPS: cotton, groundnuts, sorghum, millet, wheat, sugarcane, gum arabic, cassava, mangos, papaya, bananas, sweet potatoes, sesame

GOVERNMENT TYPE: republic with strong military influence

CAPITAL: Khartoum (pop., 4,286,000)

INDEPENDENCE DATE: January 1, 1956

WEBSITE: www.sudanembassy.org

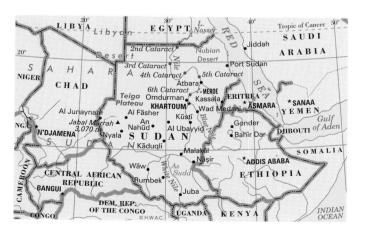

On the east coast of South America and bordering the Atlantic Ocean, Suriname consists of a coastal belt, a central zone of forests and savannas and a southern hill zone. The tropical climate is moderated by trade winds. Suriname is a major source of bauxite as well as lesser amounts of gold, oil, iron ore and other minerals. Forestry and fishing are important economic activities. Rice is the most important agricultural product, followed by bananas, timber, and citrus fruits. Industries include alumina production, oil, gold, fish, shrimp and lumber. Exports of alumina, aluminum, crude oil, gold, lumber, fish and shrimp, rice and bananas go primarily to Norway, the United States, Canada, Belgium and France.

A third of the population is East Indian (Hindustani). There are significant groups of Creoles, Javanese, Bushmen, and people of mixed descent. There are also small groups of Amerindians and Chinese. Religious adherents are 27 percent Hindu, 20 percent Muslim, 25 percent Protestant and 23 percent Roman Catholic. Dutch is the official language; Hindi and Javanese are also spoken. Sranan Tongo is a Creole speech serving as a common language. Paramaribo is the capital and chief city.

The British established their first settlements in 1651. In 1667 Britain traded Suriname to the Netherlands in exchange for Nieuw Amsterdam (New York). With the abolition of slavery in 1863, East Indian and Javanese contract laborers were brought in. Suriname gained independence in 1975.

Paramaribo-Dutch Colonial style houses

AREA: 63,039 sq mi (163,270 sq km)

■ **CLIMATE:** The tropical climate is moderated by trade winds.

Did you know? Most of Suriname's people are of East Indian origin.

■ **PEOPLE:** A third of the population is East Indian (Hindustani). There are significant groups of Creoles, Javanese, Bushmen, and people of mixed descent. There are also small groups of Amerindians and Chinese.

POPULATION: 439,117

LIFE EXPECTANCY AT BIRTH (YEARS): male, 66.8; female, 71.6

LITERACY RATE: 93%

ETHNIC GROUPS: East Indians 37%, Creole 31%, Javanese 15%, Maroons 10%, Amerindian 2%, Chinese 2%, white 1%

PRINCIPAL LANGUAGES: Dutch (official), English, Sranang Tongo (an English Creole), Hindustani, Javanese

CHIEF RELIGIONS: Hindu 27%, Protestant 25%, Roman Catholic 23%, Muslim 20%

■ **ECONOMY:** Exports of alumina, aluminum, crude oil, gold, lumber, fish and shrimp, rice and bananas go primarily to Norway, the United States, Canada, Belgium and France.

GOVERNMENT TYPE: republic

CAPITAL: Paramaribo (pop., 253,000)

INDEPENDENCE DATE: November 25, 1975

MONETARY UNIT: guilder

GDP: $1.9 billion (2004 est.)

PER CAPITA GDP: $4,300

INDUSTRIES: mining, alumina production, oil, lumbering, food processing, fishing

MINERALS: kaolin, bauxite, gold, nickel, copper, platinum, iron ore

CHIEF CROPS: paddy rice, bananas, palm kernels, coconuts, plantains, peanuts

WEBSITE: www.surinameembassy.org

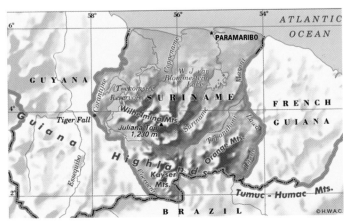

Landlocked Swaziland in southern Africa is almost entirely surrounded by South Africa, except for a stretch of border with Mozambique on the east. The terrain consists mostly of mountains and hills, with some moderately sloping plains. The climate varies from tropical to near temperate. Coal and asbestos are the chief mineral resources, followed by diamonds, quarry stone and talc. Timber is a major natural resource. Sugarcane, corn and citrus fruits are the chief cash crops, along with pineapples, tobacco, rice and peanuts. Livestock-raising is also important. Industries include mining, sugar refining, light manufacturing, wood pulp, textiles, processed foods and consumer goods. Exports of soft-drink concentrate, sugar, fruit, wood pulp and cotton yarn go to South Africa and the European Union.

Did you know? Foreign people and companies own much of the country's land.

The African population is predominantly Swazi with a Zulu minority. The official languages are English and si-Swati. Sixty percent of the population is Christian. Mbabane is the capital and chief town.

Swazis settled in present-day Swaziland in 1820, after being driven out of South Africa by the Zulus. The area later came under British protection. Swaziland became independent in 1968.

AREA: 6,704 sq mi (17,363 sq km)

■ **CLIMATE:** The climate varies from tropical to near temperate.

■ **PEOPLE:** The African population is predominantly Swazi with a Zulu minority.

POPULATION: 1,136,334

LIFE EXPECTANCY AT BIRTH (YEARS): male, 39.1; female, 35.9

LITERACY RATE: 78.3%

ETHNIC GROUPS: African 97%, European 3%

PRINCIPAL LANGUAGES: English, siSwati (both official)

CHIEF RELIGIONS: Christian 60%, Muslim 10%, indigenous and other 30%

■ **ECONOMY:** Exports of soft-drink concentrate, sugar, fruit, wood pulp and cotton yarn go to South Africa and the European Union.

Traditional Swazi ceremonial dance

MONETARY UNIT: lilangeni

GDP: $6.0 billion (2004 est.)

PER CAPITA GDP: $5,100

INDUSTRIES: mining, wood pulp, sugar, soft drink concentrates, textile and apparel

MINERALS: asbestos, coal, clay, cassiterite, gold, diamonds, quarry stone, talc

CHIEF CROPS: sugarcane, cotton, corn, tobacco, rice, citrus, pineapples, sorghum, peanuts

GOVERNMENT TYPE: constitutional monarchy

CAPITALS: Mbabane (pop., 70,000)
Lobamba (legislative)

INDEPENDENCE DATE: September 6, 1968

WEBSITE: www.gov.sz

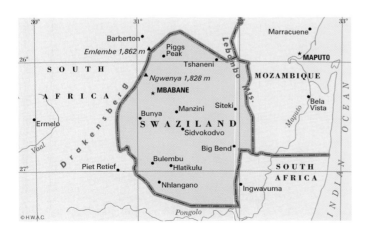

In northern Europe, Sweden occupies the eastern part of the Scandinavian Peninsula. Its seacoast borders primarily on the Gulf of Bothnia and the Baltic Sea. The land is gently rolling in the south and mountainous in the north. About half the country is wooded, and lakes cover some 9 percent of the area. In most of the country the climate is temperate, with cold, cloudy winters and cool, partly cloudy summers; in the north it is subarctic. Sweden is a major producer of iron ore; copper, lead, zinc, gold, silver and tungsten are also mined. Timber is a significant natural resource, and hydroelectric power is an important source of energy. In the agricultural sector, livestock raising predominates; dairy farming is the most important agricultural activity. Barley, wheat and sugar beets are the chief cash crops. Swedish industry is world-renowned for high-quality steel, precision equipment (bearings, radio and telephone parts, armaments), motor vehicles, aircraft, processed foods, wood pulp and paper products. These are shipped primarily to the European Union and the United States. Aided by a long period of neutrality during the two world wars, Sweden has achieved an enviable standard of living under a mixed system of high-tech capitalism and extensive welfare benefits. Privately owned firms account for about 90 percent of industrial output, led by the engineering sector.

The population is mostly Swedish, with small Finnish and Sami (Lapp) minorities. Foreign-born or first-generation immigrants comprise 12 percent of the population. Swedish is the nearly universal language. Ninety-four percent of the population is Evangelical Lutheran. Stockholm is the capital and largest city, followed by Göteborg and Malmö.

> **Did you know?** An ice sheet covered Sweden until about 8,000 years ago.

By the sixth century A.D., Swedes had come to dominate central Sweden, conquering their southern neighbors, the Getes. The Kingdom of Sweden was established in 1000 A.D., and in the 1600s Sweden became a great European power, embracing Finland, Estonia, northern Latvia and the Baltic coast of Germany. In 1709 military decline set in, following a disastrous invasion of Russia. Finland was ceded to Russia in 1809, but Norway came under the Swedish crown in 1814, a union that lasted until 1905. In the closing decades of the twentieth century, inflation, growing unemployment and a loss of competitiveness in international markets have forced cuts in welfare benefits and the curbing of the budget deficit. Sweden became a member of the European Union on January 1, 1995.

AREA: 173,732 sq mi (449,964 sq km)

■ **CLIMATE:** In most of the country the climate is temperate, with cold, cloudy winters and cool, partly cloudy summers; in the north it is subarctic.

Stockholm

■ **PEOPLE:** The population is mostly Swedish, with small Finnish and Sami (Lapp) minorities.

POPULATION: 9,016,596

LIFE EXPECTANCY AT BIRTH (YEARS): male, 78.1; female, 82.6

LITERACY RATE: 99%

ETHNIC GROUPS: Swedish 89%, Finnish 2%; Sami and others 9%

PRINCIPAL LANGUAGES: Swedish (official), Sami, Finnish

CHIEF RELIGION: Lutheran 87%

■ **ECONOMY:** High-quality steel, precision equipment (bearings, radio and telephone parts, armaments), motor vehicles, aircraft, processed foods, wood pulp and paper products are shipped primarily to the European Union and the United States.

MONETARY UNIT: krona

GDP: $255.4 billion (2004 est.)

PER CAPITA GDP: $28,400

INDUSTRIES: iron and steel, precision equipment, pulp and paper products, processed foods, motor vehicles

MINERALS: zinc, iron ore, lead, copper, silver, uranium

CHIEF CROPS: barley, wheat, sugar beets

GOVERNMENT TYPE: constitutional monarchy

CAPITAL: Stockholm (pop., 1,697,000)

INDEPENDENCE DATE: June 6, 1523

WEBSITE: www.sweden.se

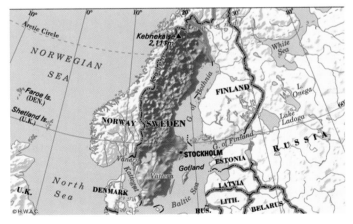

Switzerland is landlocked between Germany, Austria, Liechtenstein, Italy and France. About 60 percent of the country is covered by the Alpine mountain chain running through the south. In the west, the Jura mountains make up 10 percent of the land; the rest is a plateau, with rolling hills and large lakes between the two mountain systems. Switzerland's chief rivers are the Rhine, Rhône, Aare and Inn. The climate is temperate, but varies with altitude and season. The country is rich in forests and water power. Cereals, potatoes, fruit and wine grapes are grown, but livestock and dairy farming predominate. Tourism is vital to the economy, and international banking is very important. The manufacture of machinery, chemicals, pharmaceuticals, watches and clocks, textiles and precision instruments are the chief industries. These products are exported to the European Union and the United States.

Ethnic divisions and language groups are made up of the following: German 74 percent, French 20 percent, Italian 4 percent, Romansch 1 percent. Roman Catholicism is the religion of 48 percent of the people, and Protestantism is 44 percent. Zürich is the largest city, followed by Basel, Geneva and Bern, the capital.

In 1291 the forest cantons of Schwyz, Uri and Unterwalden formed a defensive league against the Hapsburgs. Other cantons joined the league through time, and in 1648 it was recognized as independent. In 1815, the Congress of Vienna guaranteed perpetual neutrality for Switzerland.

Did you know?
Switzerland has not fought in a foreign war since 1515.

In 1960 Switzerland helped form the European Free Trade Area, which did not strive for political union. It became a member of the United Nations in 2002, though it remains outside the European Union.

AREA: 15,942 sq mi (41,290 sq km)

CLIMATE: The climate is temperate, but varies with altitude and season.

PEOPLE: Germans make up about two thirds of the population. Other major groups include French and Italian.

POPULATION: 7,523,934

LIFE EXPECTANCY AT BIRTH (YEARS): male, 77.5; female, 83.3

LITERACY RATE: 99%

ETHNIC GROUPS: German 65%, French 18%, Italian 10%, Romansch 1%

PRINCIPAL LANGUAGES: German, French, Italian (all official); Romansch (semi-official)

CHIEF RELIGIONS: Roman Catholic 46%, Protestant 40%

Rural homes

ECONOMY: Tourism is vital to the economy, and international banking is very important. Machinery, chemicals, pharmaceuticals, watches and clocks, textiles and precision instruments are exported to the European Union and the United States.

MONETARY UNIT: franc

GDP: $251.9 billion (2004 est.)

PER CAPITA GDP: $33,800

INDUSTRIES: machinery, chemicals, watches, textiles, precision instruments

MINERALS: salt

CHIEF CROPS: grains, fruits, vegetables

GOVERNMENT TYPE: federal republic

CAPITAL: Bern (pop., 320,000)

INDEPENDENCE DATE: August 1, 1291

WEBSITE: www.swissemb.org

Ancient Syria is located in southwest Asia and fronts on the Mediterranean Sea. The country consists of a narrow coastal plain, east of which is a highland region continued to the south by the Lebanon and Anti-Lebanon mountains. Fertile plains form the central region, with the Syrian Desert to the southeast. North of the desert region lies the fertile Euphrates river valley. The Orontes is another important river. Syria's climate is mostly of the desert type, with hot, dry sunny summers and mild, rainy winters along the coast. Crude oil and natural gas are major resources. Phosphates, asphalt, rock salt, marble, gypsum, iron ore, chrome and manganese ores are also mined. Cotton, wheat, barley, sugar beets, lentils, olives, fruits and vegetables are major cash crops. Livestock raising is important. Industries include mining, manufacturing, food processing and petroleum. In fact petroleum products account for much of Syria's export earnings. These, along with textiles, cotton, phosphates, fruits and vegetables are sent to Italy, France, Turkey and other Arab countries.

Arabs make up most of the population. Kurds live in the northeast, with Kurdish communities in major cities as well. There is also a small Jewish population. The population is 74 percent Sunni Muslim; Alawite, Druze and other Muslim sects, 16 percent; Christians, 10 percent. Arabic is the official language; Kurdish is spoken by that minority. Damascus is the capital and largest city. Aleppo is second in population.

Did you know? Syria was once part of the empire of Alexander the Great.

Ancient Syria was the home of the Amorites, Aramaeans, Phoenicians and Hebrews. A succession of invaders made Syria a part of the Assyrian, Babylonian, Egyptian, Hittite and Persian empires. Following the rule of Alexander the Great's successors, Syria fell under Roman rule and then became part of the Byzantine Empire. In the seventh century A.D., the country was conquered by the Arabs, and it became the center of a vast Islamic domain. In the twelfth century Syria was the scene of a long struggle between the Christian Crusaders and the Muslim faithful under Saladin. From 1516 to 1918 the Ottoman Turks held sway in Syria. In 1920 Syria was made a French mandate, and in 1946 achieved complete independence. Since independence, Syria has been in conflict with Israel a number of times. It has also occupied parts of Lebanon, but withdrew its troops there in 2005.

AREA: 71,498 sq mi (185,180 sq km)

■ **CLIMATE:** The climate is mostly desert, with hot, dry, sunny summers and mild, rainy winters along the coast.

Church of Aleppo

■ **PEOPLE:** Arabs make up most of the population. Kurds live in the northeast, with Kurdish communities in major cities as well. There is also a small Jewish population.

POPULATION: 18,881,361

LIFE EXPECTANCY AT BIRTH (YEARS): male, 68.5; female, 71.0

LITERACY RATE: 70.8%

ETHNIC GROUPS: Arab 90%, Kurds, Armenians, and other 10%

PRINCIPAL LANGUAGES: Arabic (official), Kurdish, Armenian

CHIEF RELIGIONS: Sunni Muslim 74%, other Muslims 16%, Christian 10%

■ **ECONOMY:** Petroleum products, textiles, cotton, phosphates, fruits and vegetables are sent to Italy, France, Turkey and other Arab countries.

MONETARY UNIT: pound

GDP: $60.4 billion (2004 est.)

PER CAPITA GDP: $3,400

INDUSTRIES: petroleum, textiles, food processing, beverages, tobacco

MINERALS: petroleum, phosphates, chrome and manganese ores, asphalt, iron ore, rock salt, marble, gypsum

CHIEF CROPS: wheat, barley, cotton, lentils, chickpeas, olives, sugar beets

GOVERNMENT TYPE: republic (under military regime)

CAPITAL: Damascus (pop., 2,228,000)

INDEPENDENCE DATE: April 17, 1946

WEBSITE: www.syrianembassy.us

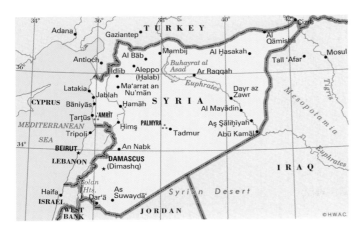

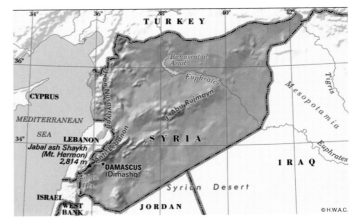

The island of Taiwan is situated off the southeastern coast of mainland China between Taiwan Strait and the Pacific Ocean. The eastern two-thirds of the island are mostly rugged mountains; the west is flat to gently rolling plains. The tropical marine climate has a rainy season from June to August and persistent cloudiness all year. Taiwan has small deposits of coal, natural gas, limestone, marble and asbestos. Rice, vegetables, tea and fruit are the primary agricultural commodities. Livestock include pigs, cattle and poultry. The fisheries are important. Taiwan has a dynamic economy and ranks high among major trading countries. Leading industries are electronics and computer products, chemicals and petrochemicals, textiles, iron and steel, machinery, transport equipment and plastics. Exports of electronics, optical & precision instruments, communications products, textiles, iron and steel, plastic and rubber products go to the United States, China and Japan.

Taiwanese Chinese make up most of the population while mainland Chinese are a significant minority. Mandarin Chinese is the official language; local dialects are spoken. A mixture of Buddhist, Confucian and Taoist teachings is the faith of 93 percent of the people; 5 percent are Christian. Taipei, the capital, is the largest city; Kaohsiung is second.

When the Portuguese visited the island in 1590, they named it Formosa, meaning "beautiful." Chinese emigration to Taiwan began in the 1600s, gradually displacing the original inhabitants, who were of Malay ancestry. At the end of the Sino-Japanese war of 1894-95, the island was ceded to Japan. Taiwan remained in Japanese hands until the end of World War II, when it was restored to China. The Nationalist Kuomingtang government and remnants of the army fled to Taiwan in 1949, when the Communists gained control of the Chinese mainland.

Did you know?
Mainland China claims Taiwan as one of its provinces.

Despite differences between Taiwan and the Peoples Republic of China, contact between the two sides of the Taiwan Strait has grown significantly over the past decade. Taiwan has continued to relax restrictions on unofficial contacts with China. Cross-Strait trade has grown rapidly over the past 10 years. China is Taiwan's largest trading partner, and Taiwan is China's fifth largest. Taipei and Beijing have been cautiously feeling each other out on a series of smaller, intermediary steps, including cross-Strait cargo and passenger charter flights, sale of Taiwan agricultural products in China, and China tourists visiting Taiwan.

AREA: 13,892 sq mi (35,980 sq km)

■ **CLIMATE:** The tropical marine climate has a rainy season from June to August and persistent cloudiness all year.

Taipei

■ **PEOPLE:** Taiwanese Chinese make up most of the population while mainland Chinese are a significant minority.

POPULATION: 23,036,087

LIFE EXPECTANCY AT BIRTH (YEARS): male, 74.3; female, 80.1

LITERACY RATE: 86%

ETHNIC GROUPS: Taiwanese 84%, mainland Chinese 14%, aborigine 2%

PRINCIPAL LANGUAGES: Mandarin Chinese (official), Taiwanese (Min), Hakka dialects

CHIEF RELIGIONS: Buddhist, Confucian, and Taoist 93%; Christian 5%

■ **ECONOMY:** Exports of electronics, optical & precision instruments, communications products, textiles, iron and steel, plastic and rubber products go to the United States, China and Japan.

GOVERNMENT TYPE: democracy

CAPITAL: Taipei (pop., 2,624,000)

INDEPENDENCE DATE: 1949

MONETARY UNIT: Taiwan dollar (TWD)

GDP: $576.2 billion (2004 est.)

PER CAPITA GDP: $25,300

INDUSTRIES: electronics, petroleum refining, chemicals, textiles, iron and steel, machinery, cement, food processing

MINERALS: coal, natural gas, limestone, marble, asbestos

CHIEF CROPS: rice, corn, vegetables, fruit, tea

WEBSITE: www.gio.gov.tw

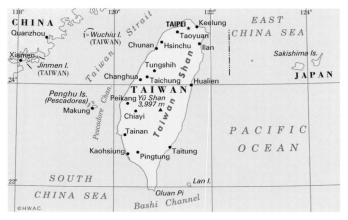

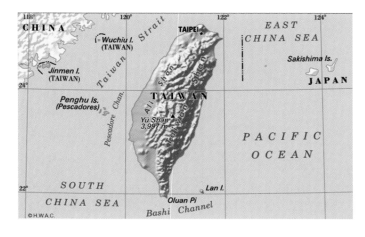

The smallest of the former Soviet republics in Central Asia, landlocked Tajikistan, with its towering peaks of the Pamir and the Alay range, is the site of the highest elevations of the former U.S.S.R. Lowlands are found in the fertile Fergana Valley in the north and also in the southwest. The Syrdar'ya and the Pyandzh are the chief rivers. Tajikistan's climate is hot in summer with mild winters, but is much colder in the Pamir Mountains. Coal, uranium, gold, mercury, lead, some petroleum, zinc, mercury, and antimony are mined. Hydroelectric power is well developed. Cotton is an important crop; fruits, vegetables, grain and livestock are also raised.

Mining, aluminum processing, chemicals and fertilizers, vegetable oil, textiles, machine tools, refrigerators and freezers are major industries. Exports of aluminum, electricity, cotton, fruit vegetable oil and textiles go to the Netherlands, Turkey, Latvia, Russia and Uzbekistan.

Two thirds of the population is Tajik and one fourth are Uzbek. There are small Russian and Kyrgyz minorities. Eighty percent of the people are Sunni Muslims. Tajik is the official language, although Russian is widely used in government and business. Dushanbe is the capital and largest city.

> **Did you know?** The Nurek Dam in Tajikistan is the highest in the world (984 ft [300 m]).

The Tajiks are an Iranian people who brought high agricultural and craft skills to Central Asia. Beginning in the 400s A.D., successive waves of Huns, Chinese, Turkic peoples, Arabs - who introduced Islam in the 700s - and Mongols dominated the region. Tsarist Russia conquered the area in the 1860s and 1870s. In 1929 the Communist-led Tajik Soviet Socialist Republic was established. Tajikistan declared its independence in 1991, but constant political turmoil and fighting have prevailed since then.

AREA: 55,251 sq mi (143,100 sq km)

■ **CLIMATE:** Tajikistan's climate is hot in summer with mild winters, but is much colder in the Pamir Mountains.

■ **PEOPLE:** Two thirds of the population is Tajik and one fourth are Uzbek. There are small Russian and Kyrgyz minorities.

POPULATION: 7,320,815

LIFE EXPECTANCY AT BIRTH (YEARS): male, 61.5; female, 67.6

LITERACY RATE: 98%

Pamir Mountains

ETHNIC GROUPS: Tajik 65%, Uzbek 25%

PRINCIPAL LANGUAGES: Tajik (official), Russian

CHIEF RELIGION: Muslim (Sunni 85%, Shi'a 5%)

■ **ECONOMY:** Exports of aluminum, electricity, cotton, fruit vegetable oil and textiles go to the Netherlands, Turkey, Latvia, Russia and Uzbekistan.

MONETARY UNIT: somoni

GDP: $8.0 billion (2004 est.)

PER CAPITA GDP: $1,100

INDUSTRIES: aluminum, zinc, lead, chemicals and fertilizers, cement, vegetable oil, metal-cutting machine tools, refrigerators and freezers

MINERALS: petroleum, uranium, mercury, brown coal, lead, zinc, antimony, tungsten, silver, gold

CHIEF CROPS: cotton, grain, fruits, grapes, vegetables

GOVERNMENT TYPE: republic

CAPITAL: Dushanbe (pop., 554,000)

INDEPENDENCE DATE: September 9, 1991

WEBSITE: tajikistan.tajnet.com/english/index.html

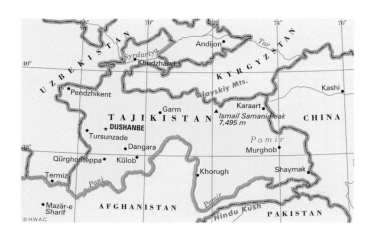

Tanzania, in eastern Africa, a union of Tanganyika and Zanzibar, was the home of some of the oldest forms of human society. A low-lying coastal area on the mainland portion gives way in the west-central region to a high plateau and scattered mountainous zones. Zanzibar, the "Isle of Cloves," is low-lying and formed of coral limestone. The chief rivers are the Rufiji and Ruvuma. Tanzania's climate varies from tropical along the coast to temperate in the highlands. Diamonds and gold are important to the economy. Other major mineral resources include iron ore, coal, nickel, and natural gas. Forest products are important. Hydroelectric power is being developed. Coffee, sisal, tea, cotton, pyrethrum, cashew nuts, tobacco and cloves and are the chief cash crops. Livestock contribute to the economy. Major industries include textiles, mining, the processing of agricultural products and the manufacture of light consumer goods. Exports include coffee, cotton, cashew nuts, cloves, diamonds and other gemstones, gold, manufactured goods and pyrethrum, which are sent to India, the European Union, Japan and China. Tourism is being developed.

Almost all of the people are native African, who belong to more than 120 ethnic groups made up mostly of Bantu stock. On the mainland, 45 percent of the population is Christian, 35 percent is Muslim; Zanzibar is 99 percent Muslim. The official languages are English and Swahili, which is used for communication between ethnic groups. Dar es Salaam is the capital and largest city. Dodoma, in the center of Tanzania, has been designated the new capital and seat of Parliament.

Did you know?
Kilimanjaro, the highest mountain in Africa (19,340 ft [5,895 m]) is in northeast Tanzania.

Archaeological discoveries in the Olduvai Gorge indicate that primitive hominids - the ancestors of modern humans - inhabited Tanzania more than a million years ago. In the tenth century A.D., Arab traders established posts along the east African coast and Zanzibar. In 1505, the posts passed to Portuguese control, but in 1653, Omani Arabs took over the trading posts. Zanzibar itself became ruler of the trading sites in 1856. A British protectorate was established in Zanzibar in 1890. In the following year, the Protectorate of German East Africa was established. As a result of the German defeat in World War I, German East Africa was mandated to Britain in 1920, and the territory's name was changed to Tanganyika. Tanganyika became a trust territory in 1946 and won independence in 1961. In 1963 Zanzibar became independent and in 1964 joined with Tanganyika to form the United Republic of Tanzania. In January 2005, Tanzania became a non-permanent member of the UN Security Council.

Serengeti Nat'l Park-Masai giraffe calf

AREA: 364,900 sq mi (945,087 sq km)

CLIMATE: The climate varies from tropical along the coast to temperate in the highlands.

PEOPLE: Almost all of the people are native African, who belong to more than 120 ethnic groups made up mostly of Bantu stock.

POPULATION: 37,445,392

LIFE EXPECTANCY AT BIRTH (YEARS): male, 43.2; female, 45.6

LITERACY RATE: 67.8%

ETHNIC GROUPS: mainland: Bantu 95%; Zanzibar: Arab, African, mixed

PRINCIPAL LANGUAGES: Swahili, English (both official); Arabic, many local languages

CHIEF RELIGIONS: Christian 30%, Muslim 35%, indigenous beliefs 35%; Zanzibar is 99% Muslim

ECONOMY: Exports include coffee, cotton, cashew nuts, cloves, diamonds and other gemstones, gold, manufactured goods and pyrethrum, which are sent to India, the European Union, Japan and China. Tourism is being developed.

MONETARY UNIT: shilling

GDP: $23.7 billion (2004 est.)

PER CAPITA GDP: $700

INDUSTRIES: agricultural processing, mining, oil refining, shoes, cement, textiles, wood products, fertilizer, salt

MINERALS: tin, phosphates, iron ore, coal, diamonds, gemstones, gold, natural gas, nickel

CHIEF CROPS: coffee, sisal, tea, cotton, pyrethrum, cashew nuts, tobacco, cloves, corn, wheat, cassava, bananas, fruits, vegetables

GOVERNMENT TYPE: republic

CAPITAL: Dodoma (pop., 155,000)

INDEPENDENCE DATE: April 26, 1964

WEBSITE: www.tanzania.go.tz

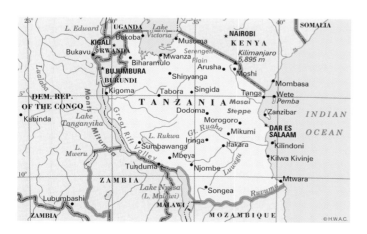

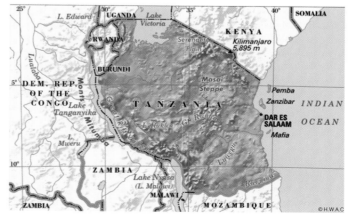

Thailand is favored with superb rice-growing land, vast stands of teak and a guaranteed rainfall that insures agricultural abundance. The core of the country is a central plain, with flat alluvial land watered by a network of canals and irrigation projects. In the north are parallel mountain ranges and fertile valleys running from north to south. To the east is the relatively barren Kho Sawai plateau. North-south mountain ranges dominate peninsular Thailand. The chief rivers are the Mekong and the Chao Phraya and its tributaries. In the summer the southwest monsoon is rainy and warm; in the winter, the northeast monsoon is dry and cool. The country possesses considerable mineral resources, including tin, tungsten, tantalum, lead, lignite, gypsum and natural gas. Thailand is a leading producer of rice and cassava (tapioca). Other crops include rubber, corn, sugarcane, coconuts and soybeans. Teak forests and shrimp fisheries contribute to the economy. Tourism is a vital source of income. The booming industrial sector produces textiles, garments, beverages, integrated circuits, jewelry, plastics, electronics, auto assembly, electrical appliances and food products. Exports include textiles and footwear, fishery products, computers and parts, electronics, electrical appliances, jewelry, rice, tapioca products, integrated circuits, rubber and automobiles are shipped to the United States, the European Union, Japan, China, Singapore and Malaysia. In late December 2004 a major tsunami took 8500 lives and caused massive destruction in the southern provinces. The economy declined severely due to the tsunami catastrophe, drought and violence in the three southernmost provinces, and the sudden drop in tourist arrivals.

The population is three fourths Thai, with a significant Chinese minority. Buddhism is the religion of 95 percent of the population. Thai is the official language and is spoken by most of the people. Bangkok is the capital and largest city. Since 1992, Thailand has been a functioning democracy with constitutional changes of government.

Did you know? Thailand, once called Siam, is where the Siamese cat comes from.

The Thai people moved south from China in the eleventh century A.D. The Thai kingdom was traditionally founded in 1238. Trade was established with Europe and the United States in the eighteenth and nineteenth centuries. A constitutional monarchy replaced the absolute rule of the Thai kings in 1932, but ever since 1958, when a military junta seized control of the government, successive military coups have occurred, limiting chances of democratic reforms. European powers never colonized Thailand, formerly referred to as Siam. Japan briefly occupied the country during World War II. American B-52 bombers were stationed there during the Vietnam conflict. Another legacy of that war was the thousands of refugees - Cambodians fleeing the Khmer Rouge regime in their country and Vietnamese "boat people" - who remained in refugee camps in northeastern Thailand for much of the latter part of the 20th century.

Phang Nga Bay

AREA: 198,456 sq mi (514,000 sq km)

CLIMATE: In the summer the southwest monsoon is rainy and warm; in the winter, the northeast monsoon is dry and cool.

PEOPLE: The population is three fourths Thai, with a significant Chinese minority.

POPULATION: 64,631,595

LIFE EXPECTANCY AT BIRTH (YEARS): male, 69.2; female, 73.7

LITERACY RATE: 93.8%

ETHNIC GROUPS: Thai 75%, Chinese 14%

PRINCIPAL LANGUAGES: Thai, Chinese, Malay, Khmer

CHIEF RELIGIONS: Buddhism (official) 95%, Muslim 4%

ECONOMY: Exports include textiles and footwear, fishery products, computers and parts, electronics, electrical appliances, jewelry, rice, tapioca products, integrated circuits, rubber and automobiles are shipped to the United States, the European Union, Japan, China, Singapore and Malaysia.

MONETARY UNIT: baht

GDP: $524.8 billion (2004 est.)

PER CAPITA GDP: $8,100

INDUSTRIES: tourism, textiles and garments, agricultural processing, beverages, tobacco, cement, light manufacturing, electric appliances and components, computers and parts, integrated circuits, furniture, plastics

MINERALS: tin, rubber, natural gas, tungsten, tantalum, lead, gypsum, lignite, fluorite

CHIEF CROPS: rice, cassava, rubber, corn, sugarcane, coconuts, soybeans

GOVERNMENT TYPE: constitutional monarchy

CAPITAL: Bangkok (pop., 6,486,000)

INDEPENDENCE DATE: 1238

WEBSITE: www.thaiembdc.org

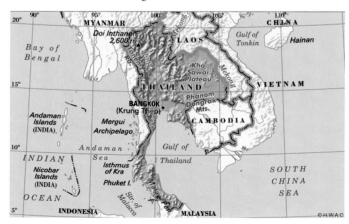

The West African nation of Togo extends inland, finger-like, from its short coastline on the Bight of Benin. Gently rolling savanna in the north is separated from southern plains by central hills. The tropical climate is hot and humid in the south and semiarid in the north. Mineral resources include phosphates, limestone and marble. Togo's economy is heavily dependent on subsistence agriculture, although cash crops of cotton, cocoa, coffee, yams, cassava, corn, millet, sorghum, rice and beans are produced. Livestock and fish contribute to the economy. Chief industries are mining, manufacturing and agricultural processing. Exports, chiefly phosphates, cotton, cocoa and coffee go mainly to West African countries, China and India.

The people are native Africans belonging to more than 35 ethnic groups. The dominant tribes are the Ewe, Mina and Kabye. French is the official language; Ewa, Mina and Kabye are the chief African languages. Indigenous beliefs are followed by 70 percent of the population. Lomé is the capital and chief city.

The Ewes moved into the region from the north between the twelfth and fourteenth centuries A.D. In the late 1400s the Portuguese visited the coast, and the area became a center of the slave trade in the following centuries. Starting in 1884, Germany gradually annexed the region. A French mandate was established in the east following World War I, and a British mandate was formed in the west of Togo. In 1946 the mandates were changed to United Nations Trusteeships. In 1956 British Togoland voted to join the Gold Coast (Ghana) and in 1960 French Togoland became the independent Republic of Togo.

Did you know? Togo is a leading world producer of phosphates.

AREA: 21,925 sq mi (56,785 sq km)

CLIMATE: The tropical climate is hot and humid in the south and semi-arid in the north.

PEOPLE: The people are native Africans belonging to more than 35 ethnic groups. The dominant tribes are the Ewe, Mina and Kabye.

POPULATION: 5,548,702

LIFE EXPECTANCY AT BIRTH (YEARS): male, 51.5; female, 55.5

LITERACY RATE: 51.7%

ETHNIC GROUPS: 37 African tribes; largest are Ewe, Mina, and Kabre

PRINCIPAL LANGUAGES: French (official), Ewe, Mina in the south; Kabye, Dagomba in the north

CHIEF RELIGIONS: indigenous beliefs 51%, Christian 29%, Muslim 20%

ECONOMY: Exports, chiefly phosphates, cotton, cocoa and coffee go mainly to West African countries, China and India.

Cocoa pods

MONETARY UNIT: CFA franc

GDP: $7.6 billion (2001 est.)

PER CAPITA GDP: $1,500

INDUSTRIES: mining, agricultural processing, cement, handicrafts, textiles, beverages

MINERALS: phosphates, limestone, marble

CHIEF CROPS: coffee, cocoa, cotton, yams, cassava, corn, beans, rice, millet, sorghum

GOVERNMENT TYPE: republic

CAPITAL: Lomé (pop., 732,000)

INDEPENDENCE DATE: April 27, 1960

WEBSITE: www.republicoftogo.com/english/index.htm

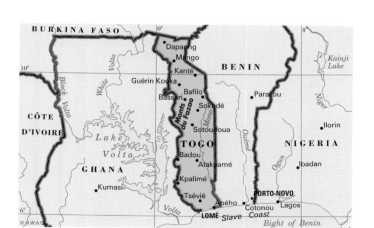

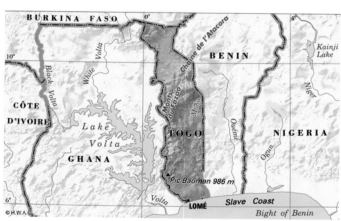

The Kingdom of Tonga consists of an archipelago of 150 islands two-thirds of the way from Hawaii to New Zealand. The eastern chain is low-lying coralline; the western chain is volcanic. Tonga's climate is tropical, modified by tradewinds. Fisheries and tourism are vital to the economy. Family remittances from overseas are important. Coconuts, squash, copra, bananas, vanilla beans and root crops are grown and exported, largely to Japan, New Zealand, the United States, China, Australia and Fiji.

The Tongan people are nearly all Polynesian. Tongan and English are the languages of the country. Free Wesleyans and Latter-day Saints (Mormons) are the two dominant religious groups. Nuku'alofa on Tongatupu is the capital and chief town.

The Dutch visited the islands in 1613. In the nineteenth century the Tongan king made treaties with France, Germany, the United States and Britain, all of which recognized his sovereignty. In 1900 Tonga became a British protectorate, and in 1970 gained its independence.

Royal Palace

AREA: 289 sq mi (748 sq km)

◼ **CLIMATE:** Tonga's climate is tropical, modified by tradewinds.

◼ **PEOPLE:** The Tongan people are nearly all Polynesian.

POPULATION: 114,689

LIFE EXPECTANCY AT BIRTH (YEARS): male, 66.7; female, 71.8

LITERACY RATE: 98.5%

ETHNIC GROUPS: Polynesian

PRINCIPAL LANGUAGES: Tongan, English (both official)

CHIEF RELIGIONS: Wesleyan 41%, Roman Catholic 16%, Mormon 14%

◼ **ECONOMY:** Coconuts, squash, copra, bananas, vanilla beans and root crops are grown and exported, largely to Japan, New Zealand, the United States, China, Australia and Fiji.

> **Did you know?**
> Earthquakes in Tonga cause small islands to suddenly rise or sink.

MONETARY UNIT: pa'anga

GDP: $244 million (2002 est.)

PER CAPITA GDP: $2,300

CAPITAL: Nuku'alofa (pop., 35,000)

INDEPENDENCE DATE: June 4, 1970

GOVERNMENT TYPE: constitutional monarchy

INDUSTRIES: tourism, fishing

CHIEF CROPS: squash, coconuts, copra, bananas, vanilla beans, cocoa, coffee, ginger, black pepper

WEBSITE: www.pmo.gov.to

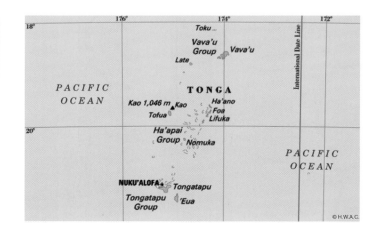

Trinidad and Tobago are the most southerly islands of the Lesser Antilles and sit directly off the coast of northeast Venezuela. Low mountain ranges cross Trinidad from east to west, with flat and well-watered land lying between the north and central ranges. A ridge of volcanic origin runs down the center of Tobago. The tropical climate is marked by a rainy season from June to December. Petroleum, natural gas and asphalt are the chief natural resources. The country's petroleum-based economy affords a high per capita income. Fishing is a key industry. Cocoa, rice, citrus, coffee, sugar, vegetables and poultry are produced. Tourism is of growing importance. Oil refining, chemical manufacturing, printing and food processing are the chief industries. Petroleum and natural gas, chemicals, sugar, cocoa, coffee and citrus are exported to the United States, the Caribbean and France.

The population is represented almost equally between East Indians and Africans. There is a significant minority of mixed descent and small minorities of Europeans and Chinese. English is the official and predominant language. Sixty percent are Christian, 24 percent are Hindu, and 6 percent are Muslim. Port-of-Spain is the capital and chief city.

Columbus discovered the islands in 1498. Spanish colonists established plantations on Trinidad in the seventeenth century, importing African slaves to work them. In 1802 Trinidad was ceded to Britain, and in 1814 Tobago passed to the British crown. After the abolition of slavery in 1834, contract workers were imported from India. Trinidad and Tobago amalgamated into a single colony in 1889, and became independent in 1962. It is now the headquarters location of the 25-member Association of Caribbean States.

Did you know? Trinidad gave birth to calypso, a popular folk music of the Caribbean.

AREA: 1,980 sq mi (5,128 sq km)

■ **CLIMATE:** The tropical climate is marked by a rainy season from June to December.

■ **PEOPLE:** The population is represented almost equally between East Indians and Africans. There is a significant minority of mixed descent and small minorities of Europeans and Chinese.

POPULATION: 1,303,000

LIFE EXPECTANCY AT BIRTH (YEARS): male, 66.9; female, 71.8

LITERACY RATE: 94%

Tobago-Pigeon Point Beach

ETHNIC GROUPS: black 40%, East Indian 40%, mixed 18%

PRINCIPAL LANGUAGES: English (official), Hindi, French, Spanish, Chinese

CHIEF RELIGIONS: Roman Catholic 29%, Hindu 24%, Protestant 14%, Muslim 6%

■ **ECONOMY:** Petroleum and natural gas, chemicals, sugar, cocoa, coffee and citrus are exported to the United States, the Caribbean and France. Tourism is of growing importance.

MONETARY UNIT: Trinidad and Tobago dollar

GDP: $11.5 billion (2004 est.)

PER CAPITA GDP: $10,500

INDUSTRIES: petroleum products, chemicals, tourism, food processing, cement, beverage, cotton textiles

MINERALS: petroleum, natural gas, asphalt

CHIEF CROPS: cocoa, sugarcane, rice, citrus, coffee, vegetables

GOVERNMENT TYPE: parliamentary democracy

CAPITAL: Port-of-Spain (pop., 54,000)

INDEPENDENCE DATE: August 31, 1962

WEBSITE: www.gov.tt/about

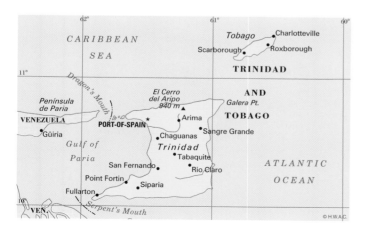

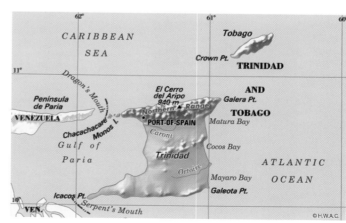

Facing on the Mediterranean Sea, the Republic of Tunisia in North Africa consists of a wooded fertile region in the north, a central coastal plain, and a southern region bordering the Sahara. Tunisia's climate is temperate in the north, with mild, rainy winters and hot, dry summers; desert conditions prevail in the south. Petroleum and phosphates are the chief natural resources; iron ore, lead, zinc and salt are also produced. Olives, dates, oranges and almonds are the chief cash crops; cereals, wine grapes and sugar beets are also grown. Mining, agricultural processing, textiles and footwear are major industries. Tourism is important. Exports, primarily petroleum and natural gas, agricultural products, phosphates and chemicals, go mainly to European Union countries. The population is 98 percent Arab and Berber, and 98 percent Muslim. There remains a small Jewish population in Tunis and other cities. Arabic is the official language; French is widely used. Tunis is the capital and largest city, Safāqis (Sfax) is second in size.

Seafaring Phoenicians settled Tunisia as far back as the twelfth century B.C. In the sixth century B.C., the city of Carthage was founded; it became the center of a powerful city-state that lasted until 146 B.C., when it was destroyed by Rome. Arabs conquered the region in the seventh century A.D. and during the Middle Ages transformed it into a major center of Arab power. In 1574 Tunisia came under the Ottoman Turks, but enjoyed virtual independence under its Turkish governors (beys). Tunisia became a French protectorate in 1881, and in 1956 won its independence. Tunisia is in the process of removing all duties and trade barriers with the European Union.

Did you know? Most of Tunisia was once part of the Roman province called Africa.

AREA: 63,170 sq mi (163,610 sq km)

■ **CLIMATE:** Tunisia's climate is temperate in the north, with mild, rainy winters and hot, dry summers; desert conditions prevail in the south.

■ **PEOPLE:** Tunisians are nearly all Arab. There remains a small Jewish population in Tunis and other cities.

POPULATION: 9,832,000

LIFE EXPECTANCY AT BIRTH (YEARS): male, 72.8; female, 76.2

LITERACY RATE: 67.8%

Tunis-Port de France (Sea Gate)

ETHNIC GROUPS: Arab 98%, European 1%, Jewish and other 1%

PRINCIPAL LANGUAGES: Arabic (official), French prevalent

CHIEF RELIGION: Muslim (official; mostly Sunni) 98%

■ **ECONOMY:** Exports, primarily petroleum and natural gas, agricultural products, phosphates and chemicals, go mainly to European Union countries. Tourism is important.

MONETARY UNIT: dinar

GDP: $64.5 billion (2001 est.)

PER CAPITA GDP: $6,600

INDUSTRIES: petroleum, mining, tourism, textiles, footwear, agribusiness, beverages

MINERALS: phosphates, limestone, marble

CHIEF CROPS: olives, olive oil, grain, tomatoes, citrus fruit, sugar beets, dates, almonds

GOVERNMENT TYPE: republic

CAPITAL: Tunis (pop., 1,927,000)

INDEPENDENCE DATE: March 20, 1956

WEBSITE: www.ministeres.tn/index.html

Turkey straddles two continents. A smaller part in Europe is separated by the Dardanelles, the Sea of Marmara and the Bosporus from the Asiatic part, which accounts for 97 percent of the total area. The Asian portion (Asia Minor) has a fertile coastal strip; the semiarid Anatolian plateau in the center is surrounded by hills and mountains. Turkey's chief rivers are the Kızılırmak and the Euphrates. The temperate climate has hot, dry summers and mild, wet winters; it is harsher in the interior. Turkey has large chrome ore deposits; coal, borate, iron ore, mercury, copper, gold and petroleum are also produced. Hydroelectric power is important. Tobacco, cotton, grain, olives, sugar beets, citrus fruits and livestock are the leading agricultural commodities. Turkey also has a dynamic automotive industry. Industrial products include textiles, processed food, electronics, steel and basic metals, paper products and petroleum. Exports of textiles and apparel, metal manufactures, motor vehicles, electronics, tobacco, foodstuffs and mining products go primarily to European Union and the United States. The tourist industry is an important growth sector.

Turks make up more than three fourths of the population while Kurds make up less than one fourth. The country is almost 100 percent Muslim. Turkish is the official language; some Kurdish and Arabic are spoken. Istanbul is the largest city, followed by Ankara, the capital.

Early cultures and civilizations flourished in Asia Minor, including the Hittite, Urartic, Phrygian, Trojan, Lydian and Armenian realms. In the seventh century B.C. the Greeks founded Byzantium on the site of present-day Istanbul. The Christian Roman emperor Constantine renamed the city Constantinople, which became the capital of the Byzantine Empire. In 1453 the city fell to the Islamic Ottoman Turks, who had conquered a large empire in Asia Minor and southeastern Europe. With the Ottoman collapse in 1918, modern Turkey was born. The successor to the Ottoman sultans was Kemal Atatürk, who founded the Turkish republic and westernized the country. Turkey was an early member of the North Atlantic Treaty Organization (NATO) in 1952. Turkey is currently a European Union candidate.

Did you know? Turkey is the site of Mt. Ararat, where Noah's ark was said to have come to rest.

Turkey is an important link in the East-West Energy Corridor bringing petroleum and natural gas from the Caspian Sea to European and world markets. The Baku-Tbilisi-Ceyhan pipeline, which began operation in 2006, delivers a million barrels of petroleum a day. The South Caucasus Pipeline (from Shah Deniz), which began operation in late 2006, delivers 16 billion cubic meters of natural gas from Azerbaijan to Turkey. Turkey is building an interconnector pipeline to Greece, an important step in bringing Caspian natural gas to Europe via Turkey.

Istanbul-Hagia Sophia

AREA: 301,383 sq mi (780,580 sq km)

CLIMATE: Generally Mediterranean, with hot, dry summers and mild wet winters; harsher in the interior and mountains.

PEOPLE: Turks make up more than three fourths of the population while Kurds make up less than one fourth.

POPULATION: 70,413,958

LIFE EXPECTANCY AT BIRTH (YEARS): male, 69.7; female, 74.6

LITERACY RATE: 85%

ETHNIC GROUPS: Turk 80%, Kurd 20%

PRINCIPAL LANGUAGES: Turkish (official), Kurdish, Arabic, Armenian, Greek

CHIEF RELIGION: Muslim 99.8% (mostly Sunni)

ECONOMY: Exports of textiles and apparel, metal manufactures, motor vehicles, electronics, tobacco, foodstuffs and mining products go primarily to European Union and the United States. The tourist industry is an important growth sector.

MONETARY UNIT: Turkish lira

GDP: $508.7 billion (2004 est.)

PER CAPITA GDP: $7,400

INDUSTRIES: textiles, food processing, autos, mining, steel, petroleum, construction, lumber, paper

MINERALS: antimony, coal, chromium, mercury, copper, borate, sulfur, iron ore

CHIEF CROPS: tobacco, cotton, grain, olives, sugar beets, pulse, citrus

GOVERNMENT TYPE: republic

CAPITAL: Ankara (pop., 3,428,000)

INDEPENDENCE DATE: October 29, 1923

WEBSITE: www.turkey.org

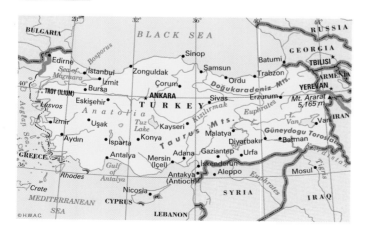

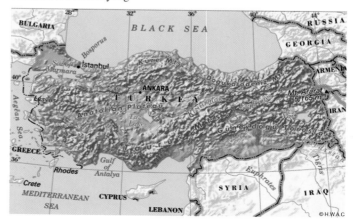

Turkmenistan, facing the Caspian Sea on the west, consists largely of a flat to rolling sandy desert that rises to mountains along the border with Iran in the south. The desert climate has warm summers and cold winters. Turkmenistan has major deposits of petroleum and natural gas. Sulfur and salt are also mined. It is a significant producer of cotton, which is grown on irrigated land. Livestock-raising includes the famous Karakul sheep. Fruits and grain are also grown. Industries include natural gas, oil, petroleum products, textiles and food processing. Turkmenistan is famous for its carpets. Natural gas, oil, petrochemicals, cotton and carpets are exported to the Ukraine, Iran, Italy, Turkey, Russia and the United States.

Turkmen make up more than three fourths of the population. There are small minorities of Russians and Uzbeks. The nation is 87 percent Muslim. Turkmen is the dominant language, but Russian and Uzbek are also spoken by minorities. Ashgabat is the capital and largest city.

Turkmenistan was settled by Turkic people who migrated from the Altai region in the east before 1000 A.D. At different times the area was controlled by Seljuk Turks, Mongols, Tatars - led by Timar (Tamerlane) - and Persians. The area was converted to Islam in the 700s. Tsarist Russia conquered Tajikistan between 1873 and 1881. Following the Bolshevik Revolution of 1917, the Turkmen Soviet Socialist Republic was created in 1924. Turkmenistan declared its independence in 1991.

> **Did you know?** The Kara Kum Desert occupies 80% of the area of Turkmenistan.

AREA: 188,456 sq mi (488,100 sq km)

CLIMATE: The desert climate has warm summers and cold winters.

PEOPLE: Turkmen make up more than three fourths of the population. There are small minorities of Russians and Uzbeks.

POPULATION: 5,042,920

LIFE EXPECTANCY AT BIRTH (YEARS): male, 57.9; female, 64.9

LITERACY RATE: 98%

ETHNIC GROUPS: Turkmen 77%, Uzbek 9%, Russian 7%, Kazakh 2%

PRINCIPAL LANGUAGES: Turkmen, Russian, Uzbek

Ashgabat-Presidential Palace

CHIEF RELIGIONS: Muslim 89%, Eastern Orthodox 9%

ECONOMY: Natural gas, oil, petrochemicals, cotton and carpets are exported to the Ukraine, Iran, Italy, Turkey, Russia and the United States.

MONETARY UNIT: manat

GDP: $27.6 billion (2004 est.)

PER CAPITA GDP: $5,700

INDUSTRIES: petroleum products, textiles, food processing

MINERALS: petroleum, natural gas, coal, sulfur, salt

CHIEF CROPS: cotton, grain

GOVERNMENT TYPE: republic with authoritarian rule

CAPITAL: Ashgabat (pop., 574,000)

INDEPENDENCE DATE: October 27, 1991

WEBSITE: www.turkmenistanembassy.org

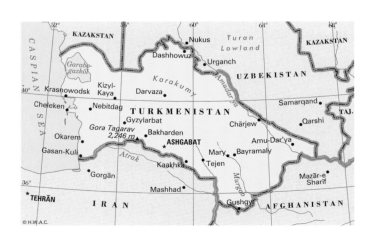

Tuvalu, whose nearest neighbors are Fiji and Kiribati, is composed of nine low-lying and narrow coral atolls in the South Pacific. The tropical climate is moderated by easterly tradewinds from March to November, and westerly gales and heavy rain from November to March. Tuvalu's income is dependent on worker remittances from abroad and the sale of postage stamps and coins to collectors. The country derives significant income from the lease of its ".tv" Internet country code. Exports of copra, fish and handicrafts go to Fiji, Australia and New Zealand.

The population is mostly Polynesian, with a small Micronesian minority. Ninety-seven percent of the people are members of the Church of Tuvalu (Congregationalist). Tuvuluan and English are the languages of the islands. The capital is on the island of Funafuti.

Tuvaluans consider Samoa as their ancestral home, with which they share a common Polynesian language and culture. The first European settlers, who were from the London Missionary Society, arrived in 1865 and soon converted the islanders to Protestantism. In 1892 Britain proclaimed a protectorate over the Ellice Islands, as Tuvalu was then called, and the neighboring Gilberts; the protectorate was reorganized as the Gilbert and Ellice Island Colony in 1915. In 1975 the islands were established as a separate dependency under the name Tuvalu, and independence was obtained in 1978. Tuvalu became a member of United Nations in 2000.

Did you know? These low-lying islands are threatened by rising sea levels.

Funafuti Atoll-beach

ETHNIC GROUPS: Polynesian 96%, Micronesian 4%

PRINCIPAL LANGUAGES: Tuvaluan, English, Samoan, Kiribati (on the island of Nui)

CHIEF RELIGION: Church of Tuvalu (Congregationalist) 97%

■ **ECONOMY:** Tuvalu's income is dependent on worker remittances from abroad, the lease of its ".tv" Internet country code, and the sale of postage stamps and coins to collectors. Exports of copra, fish and handicrafts go to Fiji, Australia and New Zealand.

MONETARY UNIT: Australian dollar

GDP: $12.2 million (2000 est.)

PER CAPITA GDP: $1,100

INDUSTRIES: fishing, tourism, copra

CHIEF CROPS: coconuts

GOVERNMENT TYPE: parliamentary democracy

CAPITAL: Funafuti (pop., 6,000)

INDEPENDENCE DATE: October 1, 1978

WEBSITE: www.timelesstuvalu.com

AREA: 10 sq mi (26 sq km)

■ **CLIMATE:** The tropical climate is moderated by easterly tradewinds from March to November, and westerly gales and heavy rain from November to March.

■ **PEOPLE:** The population is mostly Polynesian, with a small Micronesian minority.

POPULATION: 11,810

LIFE EXPECTANCY AT BIRTH (YEARS): male, 65.5; female, 70.0

LITERACY RATE: 55%

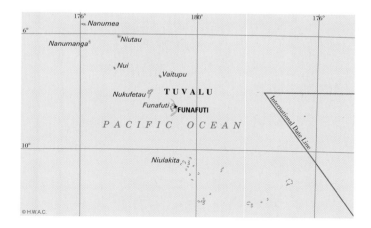

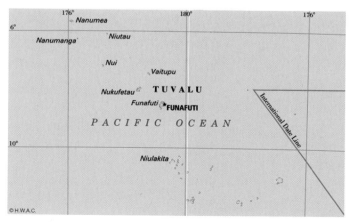

Landlocked Uganda in East Africa consists mostly of a plateau rimmed by mountains. Uganda borders several large lakes: Victoria, Albert, Edward and Kyoga. Thick forest covers parts of the south; the north is largely savanna. The Victoria Nile and the Albert Nile are the chief rivers. Uganda's tropical climate is generally rainy, but is semiarid in the northeast. Substantial deposits of copper and cobalt exist. Lake fishing and livestock raising is important. Uganda is a major coffee producer. Tea, cotton tobacco, sugar cane, cut flowers and vanilla are other cash crops which are exported to the European Union, Kenya and the United States.

Africans of three main ethnic groups are the Bantu, Nilotic and Nilo-Hamitic who comprise most of the population. Europeans, Asians and Arabs make up a small minority. The population is 33 percent Roman Catholic, 33 percent Protestant and 16 percent Muslim. English is the official language, but Bantu tongues are the languages of the people. Kampala is the capital and chief city.

Until the latter part of the nineteenth century, Uganda experienced a series of migrations over hundreds of years. Many kingdoms grew up, the chief of which was Buganda. Britain established a protectorate over Buganda in 1894 and subsequently extended it to the rest of Uganda. In 1962 Uganda gained independence. From 1971 to 1979, Uganda suffered under the dictatorship of Idi Amin, whose rule ended when Tanzanian troops joined by Ugandan rebels took the capital, Kampala, in 1979. After Amin's removal, the Uganda National Liberation Front formed an interim government. December 1980 elections returned the Ugandan People's Congress to power under the leadership of President Obote, who ruled until 1985, when an army brigade commanded by Lt. Gen. Olara-Okello, took Kampala and proclaimed a military government. Although agreeing in late 1985 to a cease-fire, Museveni's National Resistance Army continued fighting, seized Kampala in late January 1986, and assumed control of the country. In February 2006, the first multiparty elections since Museveni came to power were held. Ruling NRM candidate President Museveni was declared the winner.

Did you know? The tyrannical dictator Idi Amin expelled Uganda's Asians in 1972.

AREA: 91,140 sq mi (236,040 sq km)

CLIMATE: The tropical climate is generally rainy, with two dry seasons from December to February and June to July. It is semiarid in the northeast.

Murchison Falls

PEOPLE: Bantu, Nilotic and Nilo-Hamitic comprise most of the population. Europeans, Asians and Arabs make up a small minority.
POPULATION: 25,827,000
LIFE EXPECTANCY AT BIRTH (YEARS): male, 43.8; female, 46.8
LITERACY RATE: 62.7%
ETHNIC GROUPS: Baganda 17%, Ankole 8%, Basoga 8%, Iteso 8%, Bakiga 7%; many others.
PRINCIPAL LANGUAGES: English (official), Swahili, Ganda, many Bantu and Nilotic languages, Arabic
CHIEF RELIGIONS: Protestant 33%, Roman Catholic 33%, indigenous beliefs 18%, Muslim 16%

ECONOMY: Uganda is a major coffee producer. Tea, cotton tobacco, sugar cane, cut flowers and vanilla are other cash crops which are exported to the European Union, Kenya and the United States.
MONETARY UNIT: shilling
GDP: $29 billion (2001 est.)
PER CAPITA GDP: $1,200
INDUSTRIES: sugar, brewing, tobacco, cotton textiles, cement
MINERALS: copper, cobalt, limestone, salt
CHIEF CROPS: coffee, tea, cotton, tobacco, cassava, potatoes, corn, millet, pulses

GOVERNMENT TYPE: republic
CAPITAL: Kampala (pop., 1,274,000)
INDEPENDENCE DATE: October 9, 1962
WEBSITE: www.government.go.ug

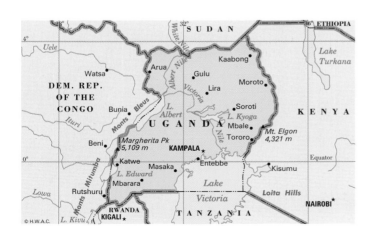

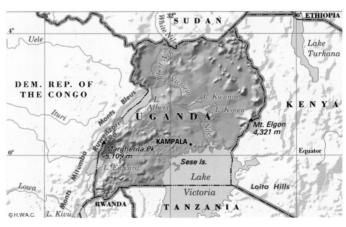

Ukraine is the second-most populous of the fifteen republics of the former Soviet Union and the third-largest in area. Bordering the Black Sea, most of Ukraine consists of fertile plains (steppes) and plateaus. Mountains are found only in the west and in the Crimean Peninsula. The climate is continental temperate, except in southern Crimea, which is sub-tropical. Precipitation is highest in the west and lowest in the east. While winters are cold in the interior, the climate is subtropical on the Crimean coast. Ukraine has huge deposits of coal, iron ore and manganese. Natural gas, oil, salt, sulphur and graphite are also present. Ukraine's hydroelectric facilities are important to industry. The fertile black soil generated more than one-quarter of the agricultural output of the former Soviet Union. Grain, vegetables, meat, milk, sugar beets and sunflower seeds are raised. Ferrous metals and products, oil and gas transport, coke, fertilizer, airplanes, turbines, metallurgical equipment, diesel locomotives and tractors are produced in Ukraine's many industrial plants. Ferrous and nonferrous metals, mineral products, chemicals, fuel and petroleum products, machinery, transport equipment and food products are exported to Russia, Germany, Turkey, Italy and the United States.

Ukraine's population is composed of Ukrainians (73 percent) and Russians (22 percent). The chief religions are the Ukrainian Orthodox faith and Roman Catholicism (Uniate); there are also Jewish and Protestant adherents. Ukrainian and Russian are the chief languages. Kiev is the capital and largest city, followed by Kharkiv, Dnipropetrovs'k, Odesa and Donets'k.

Did you know? Ukraine is a Slavic word meaning "borderlands."

An important principality arose at Kiev in the late 800s A.D., covering not only western Ukraine but also northern Russia. Most of Ukraine fell to Mongol invaders in the late 1200s. In the next century, Lithuania became ruler of Ukraine. Lithuania later united with Poland, which continued to dominate Ukraine until Poland's partition by Austria and Tsarist Russia. Ukraine briefly enjoyed independence at the end of World War I, but by 1921 most of Ukraine came under Communist rule, with the western portion passing to Poland. The Communist Ukraine Soviet Socialist Republic eventually absorbed the western part of Ukraine when Nazi Germany and the Communist Soviet Union divided Poland in 1939. In 1954 Soviet authorities transferred the Crimean Peninsula from Russia to the Ukraine. In 1991 Ukraine became independent.

AREA: 233,090 sq mi (603,700 sq km)

CLIMATE: The climate is continental temperate, except in southern Crimea, which is sub-tropical.

PEOPLE: Three fourths of Ukraine's population is Ukrainian; other groups include Russians, Belarusians, Moldovans, Hungarians and Bulgarians.

Crimea-Swallow's Nest

POPULATION: 46,710,816

LIFE EXPECTANCY AT BIRTH (YEARS): male, 61.4; female, 72.3

LITERACY RATE: 98%

ETHNIC GROUPS: Ukrainian 78%, Russian 17%

PRINCIPAL LANGUAGES: Ukrainian (official), Russian, Romanian, Polish, Hungarian

CHIEF RELIGIONS: Ukrainian Orthodox (Kiev patriarchate and Russian patriarchate), Autocephalous Orthodox, Ukrainian Greek Catholic

ECONOMY: Metals, mineral products, chemicals, fuel and petroleum products, machinery, transport equipment and food products are exported to Russia, Germany, Turkey, Italy and the United States.

MONETARY UNIT: hryvnia

GDP: $299.1 billion (2004 est.)

PER CAPITA GDP: $6,300

INDUSTRIES: mining, electric power, ferrous and nonferrous metals, machinery and transport equipment, chemicals, food processing

MINERALS: iron ore, coal, manganese, natural gas, oil, salt, sulfur, graphite, titanium, magnesium, kaolin, nickel, mercury

CHIEF CROPS: grain, sugar beets, sunflower seeds, vegetables

GOVERNMENT TYPE: constitutional republic

CAPITAL: Kiev (pop., 2,618,000)

INDEPENDENCE DATE: August 24, 1991

WEBSITES: www.ukraineinfo.us www.kmu.gov.ua/control/en

The United Arab Emirates are located on the Arabian Peninsula along the Persian Gulf between Oman and Saudi Arabia. A flat, broken, island-dotted coastal plain gives way to extensive sand dunes in the interior. Mountains form the eastern border. The climate is hot and dry, though cooler conditions can be found as the land rises in the east. The third largest oil producer in the Persian Gulf, the country possesses enormous petroleum reserves projected to last over one hundred years; natural gas reserves are also extensive. Some dates and vegetables are grown in the fertile Al Buraymī oasis. Some fishing and pearling contribute to the economy. Petroleum refining and petrochemical production are the chief industries. Petroleum and natural gas dominate exports, destined for Japan, Singapore, Korea, Iran and India. Tourism is important, with spectacular tourist resorts along the coast.

Over three fourths of the U.A.E.'s population is not Emirati. Half of this population are largely from south Asian and other Arab countries. Ninety-six percent of the population is Muslim. Arabic is the official language. Abu Dhabi is the capital; Dubayy is also important.

European and Arab pirates roamed the coastal area from the seventeenth to the nineteenth centuries, hence the former label, "Pirate Coast." During the first half of the nineteenth century, British expeditions successfully campaigned against the pirates. As a result, the sheiks signed treaties with the United Kingdom agreeing to a "perpetual maritime truce," thus the later label, "Trucial States." In 1971 Britain's protective treaty with the sheikdoms ended, and they became fully independent as the United Arab Emirates. Oil exploitation in the 1970s transformed the Emirates from an impoverished region of small desert principalities into a modern state with a high standard of living.

> **Did you know?**
> A hereditary ruler, or emir, governs each of the 7 emirates of this country.

AREA: 32,000 sq mi (82,880 sq km)

■ **CLIMATE:** The climate is hot and dry, though cooler conditions can be found as the land rises in the east.

■ **PEOPLE:** Over three fourths of the U.A.E.'s population is not Emirati. Half of this population are largely from south Asian and other Arab countries.

POPULATION: 2,602,713

ETHNIC GROUPS: Arab and Iranian 42%, Indian 50%

LIFE EXPECTANCY AT BIRTH (YEARS): male, 72.5; female, 77.6

LITERACY RATE: 79.2%

PRINCIPAL LANGUAGES: Arabic (official), Persian, English, Hindi, Urdu

CHIEF RELIGION: Muslim 96% (Shi'a 16%)

■ **ECONOMY:** Petroleum and natural gas dominate exports, destined for Japan, Singapore, Korea, Iran and India. Tourism is important, with spectacular tourist resorts along the coast.

MONETARY UNIT: dirham

GDP: $63.7 billion (2004 est.)

PER CAPITA GDP: $25,200

INDUSTRIES: petroleum, fishing, petrochemicals, construction materials, boatbuilding, handicrafts, pearling

MINERALS: petroleum, natural gas

CHIEF CROPS: dates, vegetables, watermelons

GOVERNMENT TYPE: federation of emirates

CAPITAL: Abu Dhabi (pop., 475,000)

INDEPENDENCE DATE: December 2, 1971

WEBSITES: www.government.ae/gov/en/index.jsp
www.uaeinteract.com

Dubai-Burj Al-Arab hotel

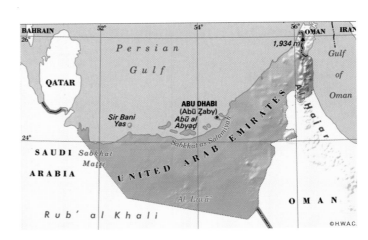

The United Kingdom of Great Britain and Northern Ireland, off the northwest coast of Europe and bordering the North Atlantic Ocean and the North Sea, lies between Ireland and France. Though not integral parts, offshore Guernsey, Jersey and the Isle of Man are British crown dependencies. The island of Great Britain contains England, Scotland and Wales. Great Britain consists mostly of rugged hills and low mountains, with level to rolling plains in the east and southeast. Northern Ireland contains mainly plateaus and hills. The Thames, Severn, Trent, Tyne, Clyde and Tees are the chief rivers. Britain's climate is temperate, moderated by prevailing southwest winds over the North Atlantic Current. Large coal, natural gas and North Sea oil reserves are the country's chief natural resources; some limestone, sand and gravel are mined. Highly mechanized and efficient farms produce a variety of crops including cereals, oilseed, potatoes and vegetables. Cattle, sheep and poultry are raised. The fishing industry contributes to the economy. The United Kingdom is one of the world's great trading powers and financial centers. Major industries include the manufacture of machinery, transport equipment and aircraft, space craft, electronics, metals, chemicals, textiles and other consumer goods. Such products are exported to European Union countries and the United States.

The population is mostly English, with a significant minority of Scottish. There are small groups of Irish, Welsh, West Indian and South Asian. Religious groups include 27 million Anglicans, 9 million Roman Catholics and 1 million Muslims. Nearly 2 million are non-Anglican Protestant; 300,000 are Jewish; 400,000 are Sikh, and 350,000 are Hindu. English is the predominant language, although 26 percent of the population of Wales speaks Welsh. London is the capital and greatest city; Birmingham, Glasgow, Liverpool, Manchester, Sheffield, Leeds, Edinburgh and Bristol are other large cities.

Did you know? The last successful invasion of England occurred in 1066.

The first-known settlers of Britain were Celts, who invaded the island from Northern Europe before 1000 B.C. Roman occupation began in the first century A.D. and lasted till early in the fifth century. Waves of Angles, Saxons and Jutes invaded Britain and gradually established a kingdom of their own. In 1066 William the Conqueror led his Norman army in the last successful invasion of England. The reign of Elizabeth I, 1558-1603, saw the rise of England as a leading European power. Her successor, James VI of Scotland, assumed the title of James I of England and ruled over both kingdoms. The eighteenth century saw the beginning of the Industrial Revolution and the gaining of a huge empire in Canada and India, and the loss of another in the American Revolution. Queen Victoria's reign, 1837-1901, witnessed Britain's rise to world leadership in commerce and industry. She ruled a world empire over which the sun never set.

The rise of other great industrial powers, the draining of Britain's wealth in both world wars, and the post-World War II loss of most of its overseas colonies have resulted in its gradual decline in primacy. The United Kingdom joined the European Union in January, 1973.

London-Parliament with Big Ben

AREA: 94,525 sq mi (244,820 sq km)

CLIMATE: The climate is temperate, moderated by prevailing southwest winds over the North Atlantic Current.

PEOPLE: The population is mostly English, with a significant minority of Scottish. There are small groups of Irish, Welsh, West Indian and South Asian.

POPULATION: 60,609,153

LIFE EXPECTANCY AT BIRTH (YEARS): male, 75.8; female, 80.8

LITERACY RATE: 99%

ETHNIC GROUPS: English 81.5%, Scottish 9.6%, Irish 2.4%, Welsh 1.9%, Ulster 1.9%; West Indian, Indo-Pakistani, and other 2.8%

PRINCIPAL LANGUAGES: English (official), Welsh and Scottish Gaelic

CHIEF RELIGIONS: Christian 72%, Muslim 3%, others

ECONOMY: Major industries include the manufacture of machinery, transport equipment and aircraft, space craft, electronics, metals, chemicals, textiles and other consumer goods, which are exported to European Union countries and the United States. Tourism is important.

MONETARY UNIT: pound

GDP: $1,782 billion (2004 est.)

PER CAPITA GDP: $29,600

INDUSTRIES: machine tools, electric power and automation equipment, rail, shipbuilding, aircraft, motor vehicles and parts, electronics and communication equipment, mining, chemicals, paper and paper products, food processing, clothing and other consumer goods

MINERALS: coal, petroleum, natural gas, tin, limestone, iron ore, salt, clay, chalk, gypsum, lead, silica

CHIEF CROPS: cereals, oilseed, potatoes, vegetables

GOVERNMENT TYPE: constitutional monarchy

CAPITAL: London (pop., 7,619,000)

INDEPENDENCE DATE: 1801

WEBSITE: www.britainusa.com

1. ENGLAND
2. SCOTLAND
3. WALES
4. NORTHERN IRELAND

The conterminous United States stretches across North America from the Atlantic Ocean on the east to the Pacific Ocean on the west, and from Canada on the north to Mexico and the Gulf of Mexico on the south. Alaska is to the northwest of Canada, and Hawaii is in the mid-Pacific Ocean. The country is centered on a vast central plain, with high mountains in the west and hills and low mountains in the east. Rugged mountains dominate Alaska; volcanic topography characterizes Hawaii. The climate is mostly temperate, but it is tropical in Hawaii and Florida and arctic in Alaska. Aridity prevails in the Great Basin area of the southwest. The Mississippi, Missouri, Yukon, Rio Grande, Arkansas, Colorado, Brazos, Ohio and Columbia are the major rivers. The country has substantial deposits of coal, petroleum, natural gas, iron ore, copper, gold, silver, lead and zinc. A favorable climate and fertile soils support a wide variety of crops and livestock. Fishing is a major industry. The nation is the world's largest producer of grain. A leading industrial power, the United States has one of the most technologically advanced economies. Highly diversified industries include steel, motor vehicles, aerospace, telecommunications, chemicals, electronics, food processing and consumer goods. Exports of industrial products, consumer goods and agricultural products go to the European Union, Canada, Mexico and Japan. The Hollywood film industry is world famous. Tourism is a major contributor to the economy.

Over three fourths of the population is white. Minorities include blacks of African descent, Hispanics, Asians and Native Americans. Protestants make up 56 percent of the population; 28 percent are Roman Catholic, and 2 percent are Jewish. English is the predominant language; Spanish is also spoken. New York is the largest city, followed by Los Angeles, Chicago, Houston and Philadelphia.

Did you know? Lake Michigan is the only one of the Great Lakes entirely within the United States.

Native Americans, the original inhabitants, formed many cultural and linguistic groups. Spain made the earliest European settlements in Florida and the southwest. English colonists settled along the Eastern seaboard along with short-lived Swedish and Dutch colonies. By 1763 the threat of French domination from the north had been removed, and the thirteen original colonies broke away from Britain, 1776-1783. After independence, the country grew by annexation and settlement until it reached the Pacific. The tragic Civil War (1861-1865) settled the vexing slavery question. Immigrants from Europe poured into the country throughout the nineteenth and twentieth centuries. During the twentieth century, the United States rose to become a world superpower. The same century was marked by the struggle for civil rights for minorities.

The opening of the 21st century was punctuated by the terrorist attacks on New York and Washington D.C. Reaction to this event led to war with Afghanistan and later Iraq.

Grand Canyon of the Colorado River

AREA: 3,718,709 sq mi (9,631,418 sq km)

CLIMATE: The climate is mostly temperate, but it is tropical in Hawaii and Florida and arctic in Alaska. Aridity prevails in the Great Basin area of the southwest.

PEOPLE: Over three fourths of the people are white. Minorities include blacks of African descent, Hispanics, Asians and Native Americans.

POPULATION: 301,139,947 (50 states and District of Columbia)

LIFE EXPECTANCY AT BIRTH (YEARS): male, 74.6; female, 80.4

LITERACY RATE: 97%

ETHNIC GROUPS: white 75.1%, black 12.3%, Asian 3.6%, Amerindian and Alaska native 0.9% (Hispanics of any race or group 12.5%)

PRINCIPAL LANGUAGES: English, Spanish

CHIEF RELIGIONS: Protestant 56%, Roman Catholic 28%, Jewish 2%

ECONOMY: Exports of industrial products, consumer goods and agricultural products go to the European Union, Canada, Mexico and Japan. The Hollywood film industry is world famous. Tourism is a major contributor to the economy.

GOVERNMENT TYPE: federal republic

CAPITAL: Washington, D.C. (pop., 4,098,000)

INDEPENDENCE DATE: July 4, 1776

MONETARY UNIT: U.S. dollar

GDP: $11,750 billion (2004 est.)

PER CAPITA GDP: $40,100

INDUSTRIES: petroleum, steel, motor vehicles, aerospace, telecommunications, chemicals, electronics, food processing, consumer goods, lumber, mining

MINERALS: coal, copper, lead, molybdenum, phosphates, uranium, bauxite, gold, iron, mercury, nickel, potash, silver, tungsten, zinc, petroleum, natural gas

CHIEF CROPS: wheat, other grains, corn, fruits, vegetables, cotton

WEBSITES: www.census.gov www.whitehouse.gov www.firstgov.gov

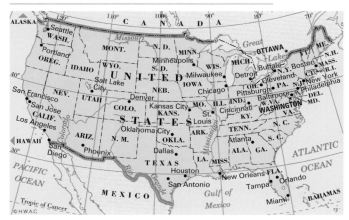

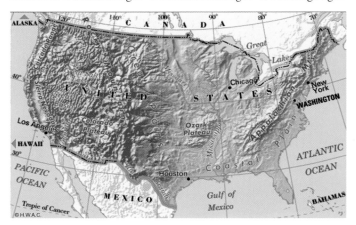

On the southeast coast of South America, Uruguay takes its name, the Oriental Republic of Uruguay, from the fact that it borders the east bank of the Uruguay river. The country consists of rolling, grassy plains and low hills. Its major rivers are the Uruguay, Negro and Río de la Plata. Uruguay enjoys a warm temperate climate. Hydropower is an important source of energy. Some granite and marble are mined. Rich soil supports cattle and sheep-raising. Fishing is important to the economy. Wheat, rice, corn and barley are also grown. Meat-packing, wool, textiles, leather goods, beverages, chemicals and petroleum refining are the leading industries. The service industry accounts for well over half of the GDP. Exports of meat, leather products, wool and wool products, rice, fish and dairy products go to the United States, Brazil, Argentina and Germany.

Most of the people are of European descent. There are small minorities of African descent and mestizo (Spanish-Indian). Roman Catholicism is the predominant religion. Spanish is the official and dominant language. Montevideo is the capital and chief city.

Originally occupied by the Charrúa Amerindians, the area was settled by Spain beginning in 1624. A war of independence supported by Argentina drove out the Spanish, 1810-1814. Brazil occupied the country beginning in 1820. A revolt threw off Brazilian rule, and in 1828, Uruguay was established as an independent buffer state between Brazil and Argentina. The country has enjoyed a high literacy rate and a large urban middle class. However, Uruguay has suffered from inflation and sluggish economic growth in the last decades of the twentieth century. An urban rebellion by the leftist Tupamaros guerrillas in the 1970s was quelled after military rule repressed all dissent. Civilian rule returned in 1985. Uruguay's current political and labor conditions are among the freest in South America.

Did you know? More than 90% of Uruguay's people are of European descent.

AREA: 68,039 sq mi (176,220 sq km)

CLIMATE: Uruguay enjoys a warm temperate climate.

PEOPLE: Most of the people are of European descent. There are small minorities of African descent and mestizo (Spanish-Indian).

POPULATION: 3,431,932

LIFE EXPECTANCY AT BIRTH (YEARS): male, 72.7; female, 79.2

Montevideo-Plaza Gomensoro

LITERACY RATE: 97.3%

ETHNIC GROUPS: white 88%, mestizo 8%, black 4%

PRINCIPAL LANGUAGES: Spanish (official), Portunol/Brazilero (Portuguese-Spanish)

CHIEF RELIGION: Roman Catholic 66%

ECONOMY: Exports of meat, leather products, wool and wool products, rice, fish and dairy products go to the United States, Brazil, Argentina and Germany. The service industry accounts for well over half of the GDP.

MONETARY UNIT: peso

GDP: $49.3 billion (2004 est.)

PER CAPITA GDP: $14,500

INDUSTRIES: food processing, electrical machinery, transport equipment, petroleum products, textiles, chemicals, beverages

CHIEF CROPS: rice, wheat, corn, barley

GOVERNMENT TYPE: republic

CAPITAL: Montevideo (pop., 1,341,000)

INDEPENDENCE DATE: August 25, 1825

WEBSITE: www.uruwashi.org

Uzbekistan is mostly level sandy desert. In the east is a mountainous area, and at the northwest is the southern end of the Aral Sea, which is shrinking in size. The Amudar'ya and the Syrdar'ya are the chief rivers. Uzbekistan's midlatitude desert climate has long, hot summers and mild winters. Uzbekistan is a major producer of natural gas, petroleum and coal. Gold, silver, copper, lead, zinc, tungsten, molybdenum and uranium are mined. The country is major world exporter of cotton, which is produced in the Fergana Valley and the irrigated strip along the Amudar'ya. Fruits and vegetables, grain and livestock are also raised. Textiles, food processing, machine building, metallurgy, natural gas and petrochemicals are the leading industries. Exports of cotton, gold, natural gas, mineral fertilizers, ferrous metals, textiles, food products and automobiles go to Russia, the European Union, China, Turkey and the Ukraine.

The population is made up mainly of Uzbeks. There are significant minorities of Russians and Tajiks as well as smaller groups of Kazakhs, Karakalpaks and Tatars. Eighty-eight percent are Muslim. Seventy-four percent speak Uzbek, 14 percent speak Russian. Tashkent is the capital and largest city.

Did you know? The tomb of the Mongol conqueror Tamerlane is in Samarkand.

The Uzbeks, a Turkic people, arose north of the Aral Sea about 1430 A.D. They settled in the oases and river valleys of the Amudar'ya and Syrdar'ya. The area was later a part of the Khanates of Bokhara and Khiva, which were made vassal states of Tsarist Russia in 1868 and 1873, respectively. Under the Communists, the Uzbek Soviet Socialist Republic was created in 1924. In 1991 Uzbekistan became independent.

AREA: 172,742 sq mi (447,400 sq km)

CLIMATE: Uzbekistan's midlatitude desert climate has long, hot summers and mild winters.

PEOPLE: The population is made up mainly of Uzbeks. There are significant minorities of Russians and Tajiks as well as smaller groups of Kazakhs, Karakalpaks and Tatars.

POPULATION: 27,307,134

LIFE EXPECTANCY AT BIRTH (YEARS): male, 60.7; female, 67.7

LITERACY RATE: 97.3%

ETHNIC GROUPS: Uzbek 80%, Russian 6%, Tajik 5%, Kazakh 3%, Karakalpak 3%, Tatar 2%

PRINCIPAL LANGUAGES: Uzbek (official), Russian, Tajik

CHIEF RELIGIONS: Muslim 88% (mostly Sunni), Eastern Orthodox 9%

GOVERNMENT TYPE: republic with authoritarian rule

CAPITAL: Tashkent (pop., 2,155,000)

INDEPENDENCE DATE: August 31, 1991

ECONOMY: Exports of cotton, gold, natural gas, mineral fertilizers, ferrous metals, textiles, food products and automobiles go to Russia, the European Union, China, Turkey and the Ukraine.

MONETARY UNIT: som

GDP: $47.6 billion (2004 est.)

PER CAPITA GDP: $1,800

INDUSTRIES: textiles, food processing, machine building, metallurgy, natural gas, chemicals

CHIEF CROPS: cotton, vegetables, fruits, grain

MINERALS: natural gas, petroleum, coal, gold, uranium, silver, copper, lead and zinc, tungsten, molybdenum

WEBSITES: www.uzbekistan.org
www.gov.uz

Samarkand-Tilla Kori Madrasah

Vanuatu, formerly the Anglo-French Condominium of the New Hebrides, lies in the South Pacific about three-quarters of the way between Hawaii and Australia. The main islands of Espiritu Santo, Malekula and Efate are composed mostly of mountains of volcanic origin. Vanuatu's climate is tropical with southeast tradewinds and occasional cyclones. Manganese deposits are the country's chief mineral resource. Forestry and fishing contribute to the economy. Agriculture is based primarily on subsistence farming, although copra, cocoa, coffee, cattle and timber are produced. Tourism and financial services are growing sectors of the economy. Exports of timber, coconut oil, copra, kava and beef go to Thailand, Malaysia, the European Union and Japan.

Indigenous ni-Vanuatu comprise most of the population. There are small minorities of Europeans, other Pacific Islanders and Asians. More than 77 percent of the population is Christian. English, French and Bislama, a pidgin tongue, are the official languages. Vila is the capital and chief town.

Melanesian settlement is thought to predate 400 B.C. Missionaries came in the 1820s and were followed by settlers from Britain and France. In 1906 the Anglo-French Condominium of the New Hebrides was established with dual administration for British and French citizens. Following much unrest during the 1970s, the independent nation of Vanuatu was proclaimed in 1980.

Did you know? Espiritu Santo, Vanuatu's largest island, was a key U.S. base during World War II.

AREA: 4,710 sq mi (12,200 sq km)

■ **CLIMATE:** The climate is tropical with southeast tradewinds and occasional cyclones.

■ **PEOPLE:** Indigenous ni-Vanuatu comprise most of the population. There are small minorities of Europeans, other Pacific Islanders and Asians.

POPULATION: 208,869

LIFE EXPECTANCY AT BIRTH (YEARS): male, 60.6; female, 63.6

LITERACY RATE: 53%

ETHNIC GROUPS: Melanesian 98%, French, Vietnamese, Chinese, other Pacific Islanders

PRINCIPAL LANGUAGES: Bislama, English, French (all official); more than 100 local languages

Tanna-Mount Yasur

CHIEF RELIGIONS: Presbyterian 37%, Anglican 15%, Roman Catholic 15%, other Christian 10%, indigenous beliefs 8%

■ **ECONOMY:** Manganese deposits are the country's chief mineral resource. Forestry and fishing contribute to the economy. Agriculture is based primarily on subsistence farming, although copra, cocoa, coffee, cattle and timber are produced. Tourism and financial services are growing sectors of the economy. Exports of timber, coconut oil, copra, kava and beef go to Thailand, Malaysia, the European Union and Japan.

MONETARY UNIT: vatu (VUV)

GDP: $580 million (2003 est.)

PER CAPITA GDP: $2,900

INDUSTRIES: food and fish freezing, wood processing, meat canning

MINERALS: manganese

CHIEF CROPS: copra, coconuts, cocoa, coffee, taro, yams, coconuts, fruits, vegetables

GOVERNMENT TYPE: republic

CAPITAL: Port-Vila (pop., 34,000)

INDEPENDENCE DATE: July 30, 1980

WEBSITE: www.vanuatugovernment.gov.vu

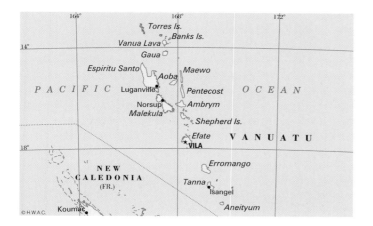

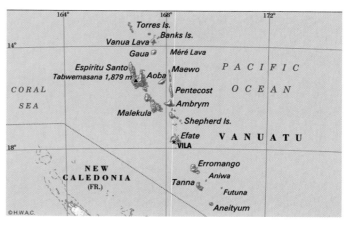

Vatican City, also called "The Holy See," is surrounded by the Italian capital city of Rome. As the center of the worldwide organization of the Roman Catholic Church and the seat of the Pope, the Vatican area includes St. Peter's Square; St. Peter's Basilica, the largest Christian church in the world; the Vatican Palace; the Papal Gardens and the museum, library and administrative buildings. Extraterritorial rights are exercised over twelve churches and palaces in or near Rome and at the Papal villa of Castel Gandolfo. The Vatican is supported by contributions from Roman Catholic dioceses throughout the world. Additional income is derived from the sale of stamps, coins, publications, medals and souvenirs, museum fees, investments and real estate.

The population is primarily Italian, with a significant minority of Swiss and a few other nationalities. Italian is the predominant language. Latin, French and various other languages are also spoken.

Vatican City is all that remains of the Papal States, which once included large areas of Italy, and which were annexed by Italy in 1870. The independence of the Vatican City enclave did not occur until the Lateran Treaty of 1929 with Italy. The current Head of State, Pope Benedict XVI, took office in April 2005.

Did you know? The Vatican's Swiss Guards wear a style of uniform that dates from the 1500s.

AREA: 0.17 sq mi (0.4 sq km)

CLIMATE: Vatican City, surrounded by theItalian capital city of Rome, enjoys a mediterranean climate.

PEOPLE: Mostly Italian with a significant minority of Swiss and a few other nationalities.

POPULATION: 921

ETHNIC GROUPS: Italian, Swiss, other

Saint Peters Basilica

PRINCIPAL LANGUAGES: Latin (official), Italian, French, Monastic Sign Language, various others

CHIEF RELIGION: Roman Catholic

ECONOMY: As the center of the worldwide organization of the Roman Catholic Church, the Vatican is supported by contributions from Roman Catholic dioceses throughout the world. Additional income is derived from the sale of stamps, coins, publications, medals and souvenirs, museum fees, investments and real estate.

GOVERNMENT TYPE: ecclesiastical state

INDEPENDENCE DATE: February 11, 1929

SOVEREIGN: Pope Benedict XVI

MONETARY UNIT: euro

WEBSITE: www.vatican.va/phome_en.htm

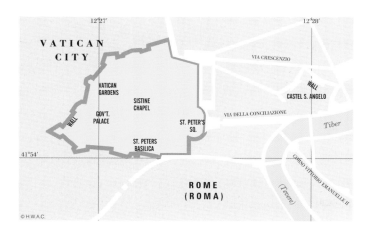

On the north coast of South America, Venezuela faces the Caribbean Sea on the north and the Atlantic Ocean on the northeast. In the northwest are coastal lowlands and the Andes Mountains. The plains, or llanos, stretch from the mountains south and east to the Orinoco river. South of the river are the Guiana Highlands, which consist of a high plateau and rolling plains. The Orinoco, Caroni, Caura and Apure are the chief rivers. The tropical climate is hot and humid, but more moderate in the highlands. Venezuela's vast reserves of petroleum are the backbone of its economy. There are also considerable deposits of natural gas, iron ore, gold, bauxite and diamonds. Hydropower is a major energy source. Corn, sorghum, sugarcane, rice, bananas, vegetables and coffee are the chief crops. Livestock products include beef, pork, milk and eggs. Fishing is important. Leading industrial products are iron, steel and aluminum, petrochemicals, paper products, textiles, transport equipment and consumer goods. Petroleum dominates exports, followed by aluminum, steel, iron ore, chemical products, plastics, fish, and paper products, which go mainly to the United States (including Puerto Rico), Mexico, the Netherlands Antilles, Colombia and the Dominican Republic.

Did you know? Angel falls, the world's highest waterfall, drops 3,212 ft (979 m).

Venezuela displays a homogeneous ethnic makeup. A credible breakdown would be two thirds mestizo, a fifth unmixed Caucasian and small minorities of Black Africans and Amerindians. Roman Catholicism is the religion of 96 percent of the population. Spanish is the official and universal language. Caracas is the capital and largest city, followed by Maracaibo.

Before the Spanish conquest in the sixteenth century A.D., two dominant ethnic groups, the Arawaks and the Caribs, inhabited Venezuela. Venezuela formed part of the Spanish Viceroyalty of New Granada until independence was declared in 1811. A bloody war did not end Spanish control until victory was gained in 1821. At that time, under the leadership of Simon Bolívar, Venezuela became part of Greater Colombia, which encompassed Venezuela, Colombia, Panama and Ecuador. In 1830, Venezuela broke away from Greater Colombia and became an independent republic. Venezuela became one of the world's leading oil producers after the opening of oil fields in the Lake Maracaibo area in 1917. The economy shifted after the first World War from primarily agricultural to one based on petroleum production and export. The overthrow of Gen. Marcos Perez Jimenez in 1958 and the military's withdrawal from national politics has given Venezuela unbroken civilian democratic rule. In December 1998, Hugo Chavez Frias won the presidency on a campaign for broad reform, constitutional change, and a crackdown on corruption.

AREA: 352,144 sq mi (912,050 sq km)

CLIMATE: The tropical climate is hot and humid, but more moderate in the highlands.

PEOPLE: Venezuela is about two thirds mestizo, a fifth unmixed Caucasian and small minorities of Black Africans and Amerindians.

POPULATION: 25,730,435

LIFE EXPECTANCY AT BIRTH (YEARS): male, 71.0; female, 77.3

LITERACY RATE: 91.1%

ETHNIC GROUPS: Spanish, Italian, Portuguese, Arab, German, black, indigenous

Caracas

PRINCIPAL LANGUAGES: Spanish (official), numerous indigenous dialects

CHIEF RELIGION: Roman Catholic 96%

ECONOMY: Petroleum dominates exports, followed by aluminum, steel, iron ore, chemical products, plastics, fish, and paper products, which go mainly to the United States (including Puerto Rico), Mexico, the Netherlands Antilles, Colombia and the Dominican Republic.

MONETARY UNIT: bolivar

GDP: $145.2 billion (2004 est.)

PER CAPITA GDP: $5,800

INDUSTRIES: petroleum, mining, construction materials, food processing, textiles, steel, aluminum, motor vehicle assembly

MINERALS: petroleum, natural gas, iron ore, gold, bauxite

CHIEF CROPS: corn, sorghum, sugarcane, rice, bananas, vegetables, coffee

GOVERNMENT TYPE: federal republic

CAPITAL: Caracas (pop., 3,226,000)

INDEPENDENCE DATE: July 5, 1811

WEBSITE: www.embavenez-us.org

Vietnam, in Southeast Asia, occupies the eastern part of the Indochinese peninsula. The long, narrow country fronts on the South China Sea. Two major rivers, the Red (Hong) in the north and the Mekong in the south, have created large, low, flat delta areas. Hilly mountainous land dominates the far north and northwest. Connecting the two delta areas are the central highlands. The climate is tropical in the south and monsoonal in the north with a hot rainy summer and a warm dry winter. Vietnam has significant deposits of coal, crude oil, manganese, iron, zinc, copper, silver, gold, bauxite and chrome ores. Forestry and hydropower are important. A major rice producer, Vietnam also grows coffee, rubber trees, cotton, tea, soybeans and bananas. Fisheries and livestock-raising contribute to the economy. Food processing and textile manufacturing are the chief industries. Others include mining and quarrying, electricity, gas, phosphates, machinery, and steel. Exports of garments and textiles, crude oil, footwear, rice (second-largest exporter in world), coffee, rubber, tea and fish are shipped to the United States, the European Union, Japan, China, Singapore and Australia. Tourism is of growing importance.

Most of the population is Vietnamese. There is a small group of Chinese descent as well as smaller groups of Khmer, Hmong, Thai, and Cham.

> **Did you know?** France took over Vietnam in 1854 and ruled there until 1954.

Buddhism is the dominant religion, followed by Roman Catholicism. Vietnamese is the official language. Ho Chi Minh City (Saigon) is the largest urban center. Hanoi, the capital, and Haiphong follow in size.

The Vietnamese migrated from China and settled in the Red River delta by the third century B.C. China ruled the region from the second century B.C. till 938 A.D., when independence was reestablished. The new state gradually expanded, occupying all of southern Vietnam. Beginning in 1858, France took control of Vietnam, establishing protectorates over Annam in the central area and Tonkin in the north. With Cambodia, the three parts were incorporated into the Indochinese Union (French Indochina) in 1887. During the Japanese occupation of Indochina in World War II, 1942-45, Communist and Nationalist forces organized for independence. For eight years, the Vietminh, led by the Communist leader, Ho Chi Minh, fought France until the French were defeated at Dien Bien Phu in 1954. The north went to the government of Ho Chi Minh in Hanoi, and the south was placed under control of a non-Communist regime in Saigon. In South Vietnam, Communist Viet Cong, waged war with North Vietnamese help against the Saigon regime after 1959. Massive United States military intervention began in 1965. Full-scale fighting dragged on until 1973, when, following the withdrawal of U.S. troops, a peace agreement was signed, formally ending the Vietnam Conflict. However, the North Vietnamese continued their hostilities against the South and in a massive offensive in 1975 occupied Saigon, ending the war and establishing Communist primacy throughout the country. Market-oriented economic reforms were initiated in the 1980s.

Mai Chau Valley

AREA: 127,244 sq mi (329,560 sq km)

■ **CLIMATE:** The climate is tropical in the south and monsoonal in the north with a hot rainy summer and a warm dry winter.

■ **PEOPLE:** Most of the population is Vietnamese. There is a small group of Chinese descent as well as smaller groups of Khmer, Hmong, Thai, and Cham.

POPULATION: 84,402,966

LIFE EXPECTANCY AT BIRTH (YEARS): male, 67.9; female, 73.0

LITERACY RATE: 93.7%

ETHNIC GROUPS: Vietnamese 85%-90%, Chinese, Hmong, Thai, Khmer, Cham

PRINCIPAL LANGUAGES: Vietnamese (official), English, French, Chinese, Khmer

CHIEF RELIGIONS: Buddhist, Roman Catholic

■ **ECONOMY:** Exports of garments and textiles, crude oil, footwear, rice, coffee, rubber, tea and fish are shipped to the United States, the European Union, Japan, China, Singapore and Australia. Tourism is growing.

MONETARY UNIT: dong

GDP: $227.2 billion (2004 est.)

PER CAPITA GDP: $2,700

INDUSTRIES: food processing, garments, shoes, machine building, mining, cement, chemical fertilizer, glass, tires, oil, coal, steel, paper

MINERALS: phosphates, coal, manganese, bauxite, chromate, offshore oil and gas

CHIEF CROPS: paddy rice, corn, potatoes, rubber, soybeans, coffee, tea, bananas

GOVERNMENT TYPE: Communist

CAPITAL: Hanoi (pop., 3,977,000)

INDEPENDENCE DATE: September 2, 1945

WEBSITE: www.vietnamembassy-usa.org

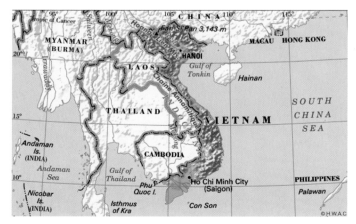

Yemen, in the Middle East, is located south of Saudi Arabia bordering the Red Sea and the Gulf of Aden. Flat-topped hills and rugged mountains back a narrow coastal plain. In the center, upland plains slope into the desert interior of the Arabian peninsula. The climate is temperate in the western mountain regions, extremely hot with minimal rainfall in the rest of the country, and humid on the coast. Oil, natural gas, rock salt, minor deposits of coal and copper are exploited. Grain, fruits and vegetables, coffee, cotton and qat (a shrub containing a natural amphetamine) are grown. Livestock and poultry are raised. Fishing is important. The chief industry is oil refining at the southern city of Aden. Other industries include mining, transportation, aluminum products, manufacturing, and construction. Remittances from Yemenis working abroad raise the national income. The chief exports are crude and refined oil, coffee, hides and dried fish, which go to China, Thailand, India, South Korea, Singapore and Saudi Arabia.

The people are predominantly Arab and almost entirely Muslim. There is a small South Asian minority. Arabic is the language of most of the population. Aden is the largest city, and Sanaa is the capital.

Did you know? The city of Aden is Yemen's principal port and commercial center.

Yemen formed part of what was Sheba (Saba) of biblical Old Testament fame. The Ottoman Turks exercised nominal sovereignty after 1517 A.D. North Yemen became independent in 1918. South Yemen came under British control in 1839 and gained its independence in 1967. Many years of conflict between the two Yemens ended in 1990, with the establishment of the unified Republic of Yemen. But civil war broke out again on May 5, 1994, when southern rebels declared an independent republic in Aden. Despite air and missile attacks against cities and major installations in the north, almost all of the actual fighting occurred in the south. Aden was captured in July, 1994. Resistance quickly collapsed and thousands of southern leaders and military went into exile. In the aftermath of civil war, leaders within Yemen reorganized and elected a new politburo. The country held its first direct presidential elections in September 1999, which were generally considered free and fair.

AREA: 203,850 sq mi (527,970 sq km)

CLIMATE: Temperate in the western mountain regions, extremely hot with minimal rainfall in the rest of the country. Humid on the coast.

PEOPLE: The population is mostly Arab, but also Afro-Arab. There is a small South Asian minority.

POPULATION: 21,456,188

LIFE EXPECTANCY AT BIRTH (YEARS): male, 59.5; female, 63.3

LITERACY RATE: 38%

ETHNIC GROUPS: Mainly Arab; Afro-Arab, South Asian, European

PRINCIPAL LANGUAGE: Arabic (official)

CHIEF RELIGION: Muslim (official; Sunni 60%, Shi'a 40%)

ECONOMY: The chief exports are crude and refined oil, coffee, hides and dried fish, which go to China, Thailand, India, South Korea, Singapore and Saudi Arabia. Remittances from Yemenis working abroad raise the national income.

Sanaa-clay houses

MONETARY UNIT: rial

GDP: $16.2 billion (2004 est.)

PER CAPITA GDP: $800

INDUSTRIES: oil, cotton textiles, leather goods, food processing, handicrafts, aluminum products, cement

MINERALS: petroleum, rock salt, marble, coal, gold, lead, nickel, copper

CHIEF CROPS: grain, fruits, vegetables, pulses, qat, coffee, cotton

GOVERNMENT TYPE: republic

CAPITAL: Sanaa (pop., 1,469,000)

INDEPENDENCE DATE: May 22, 1990

WEBSITE: www.nic.gov.ye

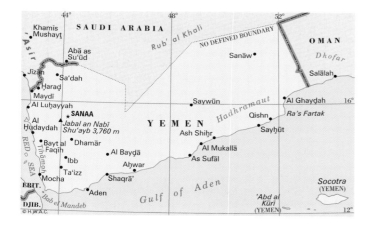

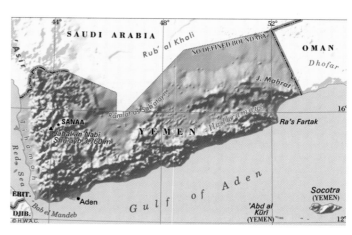

Most of landlocked Zambia is a high plateau; in the northeast are hills and mountains and three sizable lakes: Bengweulu, Mweru and the southern tip of Lake Tanganyika. The chief rivers are the Zambezi, Chambeshi, Luangwa and Kafue. Zambia's tropical climate is modified by altitude and has a rainy season from October to April. Zambia is a major producer of copper and cobalt. Lead, zinc, coal, emeralds, gold, silver and uranium are also mined. Hydroelectric power is important. The chief crops are rice, groundnuts, sunflower seeds, vegetables, flowers, tobacco, cotton, sugarcane and coffee. Livestock-raising is an important agricultural activity. Industries include mining, construction, food and beverages, chemicals, and textiles. Copper is the chief export, followed by cobalt, lead and zinc, tobacco, cotton and cut flowers which go to South Africa, the United Kingdom, Tanzania and Japan.

Nearly all of the population is African belonging to more than 70 ethnic groups. Christians form more than 70 percent of the population. English is the official language; there are about seventy indigenous languages. Lusaka, the capital, is the largest city, followed by Kitwe and Ndola.

In about 500 A.D. Bantu farmers entered the area, driving the Stone Age Bushmen far to the south. Following the explorations of David Livingstone between 1851 and 1873, the British South Africa Company developed local copper reserves. The Company took over administration of the territory in 1891, naming it Northern Rhodesia. In 1924 Northern Rhodesia became a British protectorate. From 1953 to 1963, Northern Rhodesia was part of the Federation of Rhodesia and Nyasaland. In 1964 the country became the independent Republic of Zambia.

Did you know? The beautiful Victoria waterfalls lie between Zimbabwe and Zambia.

AREA: 290,580 sq mi (752,610 sq km)

■ **CLIMATE:** Zambia's tropical climate is modified by altitude and has a rainy season from October to April.

■ **PEOPLE:** Nearly all of the population is African belonging to more than 70 ethnic groups.

POPULATION: 10,812,000

LIFE EXPECTANCY AT BIRTH (YEARS): male, 35.3; female, 35.3

LITERACY RATE: 78.9%

ETHNIC GROUPS: more than 70 groups; largest are Bemba, Tonga, Ngoni, and Lozi

PRINCIPAL LANGUAGES: English (official), Bemba, Kaonda, Lozi, Lunda, Luvale, Nyanja, Tonga, 70 others

CHIEF RELIGIONS: Christian 50-75%, Hindu and Muslim 24-49%

■ **ECONOMY:** Copper is the chief export, followed by cobalt, lead and zinc, tobacco, cotton and cut flowers which go to South Africa, the United Kingdom, Tanzania and Japan. Tourism is growing.

Victoria Falls

MONETARY UNIT: kwacha

GDP: $8.5 billion (2001 est.)

PER CAPITA GDP: $870

INDUSTRIES: mining, construction, foodstuffs, beverages, chemicals, textiles, fertilizer

MINERALS: copper, cobalt, zinc, lead, coal, emeralds, gold, silver, uranium

CHIEF CROPS: corn, sorghum, rice, peanuts, sunflower seed, vegetables, flowers, tobacco, cotton, sugarcane, cassava

GOVERNMENT TYPE: republic

CAPITAL: Lusaka (pop., 1,718,000)

INDEPENDENCE DATE: October 24, 1964

WEBSITE: www.zana.gov.zm

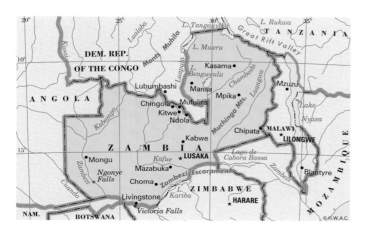

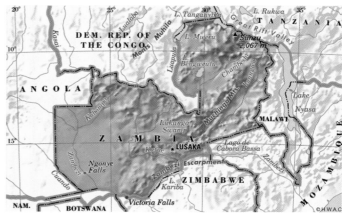

Zimbabwe, landlocked between Zambia, Botswana, South Africa and Mozambique, is situated on a high, rolling plateau, covered with grassland and savanna. Zimbabwe's rivers are the Zambezi, on which is found Victoria Falls, the Limpopo, Save, Lundi and the Guai. The climate is tropical, with a rainy season from November to March. Zimbabwe has deposits of coal, chrome ore, nickel, asbestos, copper and gold. Corn, cotton, tobacco, wheat, coffee, sugarcane, peanuts and livestock are raised. Manufacturing, mining, steel, wood products, chemicals, fertilizers, food and beverages are the chief industries. Exports of cotton, tobacco, gold, ferrochrome, clothing and textiles are shipped to the European Union, South Africa and China.

Shona comprise three fourths of the population; Ndebele are a significant minority. There are small minorities of other African descent. Nearly 50 percent of the people follow syncretic (part Christian, part indigenous) beliefs. Twenty-five percent are Christians. English is the official language; Shona and Sindebele are the chief spoken languages. Harare (formerly Salisbury), the capital, is the largest city, followed by Bulawayo.

Bantu farmers drove out the Bushmen after 500 A.D. In 1200 A.D. an impressive Shona monarchy, based on the export of gold to Arab traders, arose, with its capital at Great Zimbabwe. The British South Africa Company, formed by Cecil Rhodes, took over the area between 1889 and 1897. In 1923, as Southern Rhodesia, it became a self-governing colony within the British Commonwealth. In 1953 the area became part of the Federation of Rhodesia and Nyasaland, dominated by European settlers. In 1964 the British dissolved the Federation, but independence was refused to Southern Rhodesia unless representational government was assured. The white-dominated government declared its independence, a status unrecognized by Britain or the United Nations. African guerrilla groups carried on warfare against the white regime for over a decade. Finally an independent Republic of Zimbabwe, representing all ethnic groups, was established in 1980.

Did you know? The Great Zimbabwe Ruins is a World Heritage Site.

Prime Minister Robert Mugabe's National Union party won an absolute majority and was asked to form Zimbabwe's first government. Mugabe's policy of reconciliation was generally successful during the country's first two years of independence. However, by 2000 Mugabe's repressive government policies and chaotic land redistribution campaign caused an exodus of white farmers, crippled the economy and ushered in widespread shortages of basic commodities. As a result economic upheaval and runaway inflation has been a continuing problem.

Masvingo-Great Zimbabwe Ruins, Great Enclosure

AREA: 150,800 sq mi (390,580 sq km)

CLIMATE: The climate is tropical, with a rainy season from November to March.

PEOPLE: Shona comprise three fourths of the population; Ndebele are a significant minority. There are small minorities of other African descent.

POPULATION: 12,891,000

LIFE EXPECTANCY AT BIRTH (YEARS): male, 40.1; female, 37.9

LITERACY RATE: 85%

ETHNIC GROUPS: Shona 82%, Ndebele 14%

PRINCIPAL LANGUAGES: English (official), Shona, Sindebele, numerous dialects

CHIEF RELIGIONS: syncretic (Christian-indigenous mix) 50%, Christian 25%, indigenous beliefs 24%

ECONOMY: Exports of cotton, tobacco, gold, ferrochrome, clothing and textiles are shipped to the European Union, South Africa and China.

MONETARY UNIT: Zimbabwe dollar

GDP: $28 billion (2001 est.)

PER CAPITA GDP: $2,450

INDUSTRIES: mining, steel, wood products, cement, chemicals, fertilizer, clothing and footwear, foodstuffs, beverages

MINERALS: coal, chromium ore, asbestos, gold, nickel, copper, iron ore, vanadium, lithium, tin, platinum group metals

CHIEF CROPS: corn, cotton, tobacco, wheat, coffee, sugarcane, peanuts

GOVERNMENT TYPE: republic

CAPITAL: Harare (pop., 1,868,000)

INDEPENDENCE DATE: April 18, 1980

WEBSITE: www.gta.gov.zw   www.zimbabwe-embassy.us

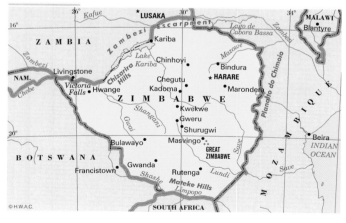

AZORES - PORTUGAL (EU)

Portuguese navigators discovered the Azores in 1427, and settlement began in 1432. Important Allied naval and air bases were maintained in the Azores during World War II. Many inhabitants of the Azores islands emigrated to the United States in the nineteenth and twentieth centuries, settling in Massachusetts, Rhode Island and New Jersey.

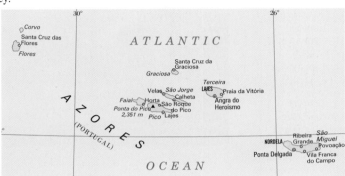

■ **POPULATION:** 241,762
ETHNIC GROUPS: Mostly Portuguese with some Flemish and Moorish minorities.
PRINCIPAL LANGUAGE: Portuguese
CHIEF RELIGION: Roman Catholic
■ **TOPOGRAPHY:** A group of nine volcanic islands, some still active, offering rocky terrain and some flat areas where most people live.
AREA: 902 sq mi (2,335 sq km)
CLIMATE: Temperate maritime, with high humidity and more rain in the winter.
■ **CAPITAL:** Ponta Delgada (pop., 65,000)
GOVERNMENT TYPE: autonomous region of Portugal
MONETARY UNIT: euro

■ **RESOURCES:** timber and fish
INDUSTRIES: fishing, boat construction and repair, fish processing, meat and dairy production
CHIEF CROPS: lumber, pineapples, passion fruit, tea, sugar beets, potatoes and tobacco
EXPORT PARTNERS: the U.S., Canada and the E.U.

CANARY ISLANDS - SPAIN (AF)

Portugal recognized Spanish control of the Canary Islands in the Treaty of Alcaçovas in 1479. The islands became an important base for voyages to the Americas. Their wealth invited frequent attacks by pirates and privateers. Spain granted political autonomy to the islands in 1982.

■ **POPULATION:** 1,694,477
ETHNIC GROUP: Mostly Spanish.
PRINCIPAL LANGUAGE: Spanish
CHIEF RELIGION: Roman Catholic
■ **TOPOGRAPHY:** The seven islands share a volcanic origin, tropical climate, and steep, mountainous terrain.
AREA: 2,808 sq mi (7,273 sq km)
CLIMATE: Tropical, mild and wet or very dry depending on the trade winds.
■ **CAPITAL:** Las Palmas de Gran Canaria (pop., 355,000)
GOVERNMENT TYPE: autonomous region of Spain
MONETARY UNIT: euro

■ **RESOURCES:** fish
INDUSTRIES: fish processing, wine, rum, oil refining, tourism
CHIEF CROPS: grapes, sugar cane, bananas, dates, tomatoes, oranges, lemons and figs
EXPORT PARTNERS: the U.S., Canada and the E.U.

ARUBA - NETHERLANDS (NA)

Acquired by the Dutch in 1636, the island's economy has been dominated by three main industries: a 19th century gold rush, an oil refinery which opened in 1924 and a recent tourist boom. Aruba gained autonomous status within the Netherlands in 1986.

■ **POPULATION:** 72,194
ETHNIC GROUPS: mostly mixed Black African, some Carib Amerindian, white European, East Asian
PRINCIPAL LANGUAGES: Dutch (official), Papiamento, English
CHIEF RELIGIONS: mainly Roman Catholic, some Protestant, Hindu, Muslim
■ **TOPOGRAPHY:** mainly flat with a few hills and scant vegetation
AREA: 75 sq mi (193 sq km)
CLIMATE: Tropical, moderated by northeast trade winds.
■ **CAPITAL:** Oranjestad (pop., 29,000)

GOVERNMENT TYPE: autonomous territory of the Netherlands
MONETARY UNIT: Aruban guilder/florin
■ **RESOURCES:** fish
INDUSTRIES: tourism, transshipment facilities, petroleum refining
CHIEF CROP: aloes
EXPORT PARTNERS: the U.S., the E.U., Venezuela, Panama and Colombia

MADEIRA - PORTUGAL (EU)

Portuguese navigators discovered Madeira in 1419 after being driven there by a storm. Settlement began around 1433. Sugarcane was a leading factor in the island's economy, but since the 18th century Madeira's most important product has been its wine. In 1976 Portugal granted political autonomy to Madeira. The region now has its own government and legislative assembly.

■ **POPULATION:** 245,012
ETHNIC GROUPS: Mostly Portuguese with some Flemish and other European minorities.
PRINCIPAL LANGUAGE: Portuguese
CHIEF RELIGION: Roman Catholic
■ **TOPOGRAPHY:** The Madeira Islands are of volcanic origin. Mountainous Madeira and Porto Santo with its magnificent sandy beach are inhabited. There are three small uninhabited islands called the Desertas, and three uninhabited islands called the Selvagens.
AREA: 307 sq mi (794 sq km)
CLIMATE: Subtropical, with moderate humidity tempered by the Gulf Stream.
■ **CAPITAL:** Funchal (pop., 110,000)
GOVERNMENT TYPE: autonomous region of Portugal
MONETARY UNIT: euro
■ **RESOURCES:** fish
INDUSTRIES: wine, embroidery and wicker- work, rum and sugar cane honey, tourism
CHIEF CROPS: grapes, sugar cane, willow, bananas, flowers
EXPORT PARTNERS: the U.S., and the E.U.

NETHERLANDS ANTILLES - (NA)

Once the center of the Caribbean slave trade, the island of Curaçao was hard hit by the abolition of slavery in the United States in 1863. In the 20th century, oil was discovered off the shores of Venezuela and a refinery was established. Curaçao became the seat of the Netherlands Antilles Government in 1954.

■ **POPULATION:** 223,472
ETHNIC GROUPS: mostly mixed Black African, some Carib Amerindian, white European, East Asian
PRINCIPAL LANGUAGES: Dutch (official), Papiamento, English
CHIEF RELIGIONS: mainly Roman Catholic, some Protestant, Jewish, Pentecosal, Seventh-day Adventist
■ **TOPOGRAPHY:** generally hilly with volcanic interiors, the Netherlands Antilles consists of the islands of Bonaire, Curacao, St. Maarten, Saba and St. Eustatius.
AREA: 371 sq mi (960 sq km)
CLIMATE: Tropical, moderated by northeast trade winds.
■ **CAPITAL:** Willemstad (pop., 123,000)
GOVERNMENT TYPE: autonomous territory of the Netherlands
MONETARY UNIT: Netherlands Antillean guilder
■ **INDUSTRIES:** tourism, offshore banking, transshipment facilities, petroleum refining
CHIEF CROPS: aloes, sorghum, peanuts, tropical fruit
EXPORT PARTNERS: the U.S., Venezuela, Guatemala and Singapore

CAYMAN ISLANDS - U.K. (NA)

Largely uninhabited until the 17th century, Great Britain took control of the Islands in 1670. The Islands have historically been popular as a tax-exempt destination. Initially a dependency of Jamaica, The Caymans became an independent colony in 1959. They are now a self-governing British Overseas Territory.

POPULATION: 46,600
ETHNIC GROUPS: Mostly mixed Afro-Europeans, Africans and Europeans.
PRINCIPAL LANGUAGE: English
CHIEF RELIGIONS: United Church, Anglican, other Protestant and Roman Catholic
TOPOGRAPHY:
A low-lying limestone base surrounded by coral reefs.
AREA: 100 sq mi (259 sq km)
CLIMATE: Tropical marine, with warm, rainy summers and cool relatively dry winters.
CAPITAL: George Town (pop., 21,000)
GOVERNMENT TYPE: overseas territory of UK
MONETARY UNIT: Caymanian dollar
RESOURCES: turtle farming and aquaculture
INDUSTRIES: tourism, offshore, banking, insurance, construction, and rum
CHIEF CROPS: vegetables
EXPORT PARTNER: the U.S.

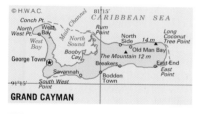

GRAND CAYMAN

MONTSERRAT - U.K. (NA)

Discovered by Columbus in 1493, Montserrat was colonized by Britain in 1632. It became an Overseas Territory of the United Kingdom in 1958. Severe volcanic activity in 1995 and 1997 has damaged the economy of this small island. Half of the island is expected to remain uninhabited for another decade.

POPULATION: 9,538
ETHNIC GROUPS: Mostly Africans & Europeans.
PRINCIPAL LANGUAGE: English
CHIEF RELIGIONS: Anglican, Methodist, Roman Catholic, Pentecostal
TOPOGRAPHY: Volcanic, mountainous terrain, with a small coastal lowland.
AREA: 39 sq mi (100 sq km)
CLIMATE: Tropical marine
CAPITAL: Plymouth (official) - abandoned due to volcanic activity
GOVERNMENT TYPE: overseas territory of UK
MONETARY UNIT: East Caribbean dollar
INDUSTRIES: rum, textiles and electronic appliances and limited tourism
CHIEF CROPS: cabbages, carrots, cucumbers, tomatoes, onions, peppers, livestock products
EXPORT PARTNERS:
the U.S., Antigua and Barbuda

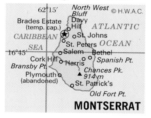

MONTSERRAT

ANGUILLA - U.K. (NA)

Colonized by English settlers from Saint Kitts in 1650, Anguilla was administered by Great Britain until the early 19th century. Anguilla was formally recognized as a separate British dependency in 1980.

POPULATION: 13,677
ETHNIC GROUPS: Mostly Africans. Some Mixed Afro-Europeans, and Europeans.
PRINCIPAL LANGUAGE: English
CHIEF RELIGIONS: Anglican, Methodist, Protestant and Roman Catholic
TOPOGRAPHY: A flat, low-lying island of limestone and coral reefs.
AREA: 35 sq mi (91 sq km)
CLIMATE: Tropical, moderated by northeast trade winds.
CAPITAL: The Valley (pop., 2,000)
GOVERNMENT TYPE: overseas territory of the United Kingdom
MONETARY UNIT: East Caribbean dollar
RESOURCES: salt, fish, lobster
INDUSTRIES: tourism, offshore banking, boat building, lobster fishing, rum
CHIEF CROPS: vegetables, tobacco
EXPORT PARTNERS: the U.S., the U.K.

TURKS AND CAICOS ISLANDS - U.K. (NA)

Part of the U.K.'s Jamaican colony until 1962, the islands assumed the status of a separate crown colony with Jamaica's independence. The governor of The Bahamas oversaw affairs from 1965 to 1973. With Bahamian independence, the islands received a separate governor in 1973. The islands remain a British overseas territory.

POPULATION: 21,746
ETHNIC GROUPS: Mostly Black African, small minorities of mixed and others.
PRINCIPAL LANGUAGE: English
CHIEF RELIGIONS: Baptist, Anglican, Methodist, Church of God
TOPOGRAPHY: Flat, low-lying islands of limestone, marshes and mangrove swamps.
AREA: 166 sq mi (430 sq km)
CLIMATE: Tropical marine, moderated by trade winds
CAPITAL: Grand Turk (pop., 4,000)
GOVERNMENT TYPE: overseas territory of the United Kingdom
MONETARY UNIT: U.S. dollar
RESOURCES: fish, spiny lobster and conch
INDUSTRIES:
tourism, recreational fishing, offshore banking
CHIEF CROPS: corn, beans, tapioca, citrus fruit
EXPORT PARTNERS:
the U.S., the U.K.

BERMUDA - U.K. (NA)

The Virginia Company first colonized Bermuda during the 1600s. Bermuda became a British Crown Colony in 1684. It is now an overseas territory of the United Kingdom. A referendum on independence from the United Kingdom was soundly defeated in 1995, however the debate has been reopened in recent times.

POPULATION: 66,163
ETHNIC GROUPS: Mostly Black African, a third of European descent, small minorities of mixed and others.
PRINCIPAL LANGUAGES: English, Portuguese
CHIEF RELIGIONS: Anglican, Roman Catholic, African Methodist Episcopal and other Protestant
TOPOGRAPHY: low, rocky hills separated by fertile valleys, lush vegetation
AREA: 19 sq mi (50 sq km)
CLIMATE: Subtropical, mild and humid with strong winds.
CAPITAL: Hamilton (pop., 1,000)
GOVERNMENT TYPE: overseas territory of UK
MONETARY UNIT: Bermudian dollar
RESOURCES: limestone
INDUSTRIES: offshore banking, international business, tourism
CHIEF CROPS: bananas, vegetables, citrus fruit and flowers
EXPORT PARTNERS: France, the U.K., Spain

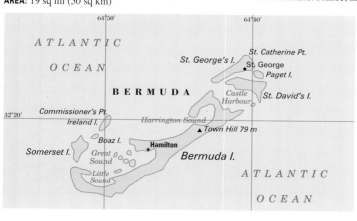

■ U.S. VIRGIN ISLANDS - U.S. (NA)

The archipelago was divided into two territorial units, one English and the other Danish during the 17th century. Sugarcane drove the islands' economy during the 18th and early 19th centuries. In 1917, the US purchased the Danish portion, which had been in economic decline since the abolition of slavery in 1848. Today, one of the world's largest oil refineries is located on St Croix.

■ **POPULATION:** St. Croix 53,234
St. John 4,197
St. Thomas 51,181

ETHNIC GROUPS: mostly mixed Black African, white European, East Asian

PRINCIPAL LANGUAGES: English, Spanish

CHIEF RELIGIONS: Baptist, Roman Catholic, Episcopalian

■ **TOPOGRAPHY:** The terrain is mostly hilly and mountainous, with little level land. St. Croix has a dense rain forest in the west and abundant vegetation in the north. Two-thirds of St. John is a national park. St. Thomas has a deep natural harbor.

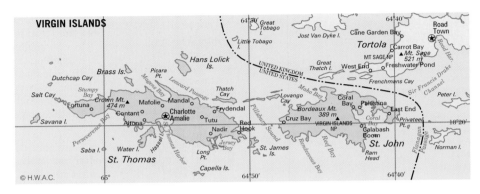

AREA: St. Croix 84 sq mi (218 sq km)
St. John 20 sq mi (52 sq km)
St. Thomas 32 sq mi (83 sq km)

CLIMATE: Subtropical, moderated by easterly trade winds

■ **CAPITAL:** Charlotte Amalie on the island of St. Thomas (pop., 11,000)

GOVERNMENT TYPE: United States territory

MONETARY UNIT: U.S. dollar

■ **INDUSTRIES:**
tourism, petroleum, rum distilling, sports fishing, manufacturing

CHIEF FARM PRODUCTS: fruit and vegetables,sorghum, Senepol cattle

EXPORT PARTNER: the U.S.

■ GALÁPAGOS ISLANDS - ECUADOR (SA)

The Galápagos Islands, an archipelago situated on the Equator off the coast of Ecuador, includes fifteen large islands and many smaller ones. All of the archipelago, famed for its unique animal and bird life, including giant tortoises, lizards, penguins and finches, is included in a national park.   In 1835 Charles Darwin studied the fauna of the Galápagos. His theory of evolution, presented in The Origin of the Species, derives from his work there. The Galápagos are a province of Ecuador, which annexed the islands in 1832.

■ **POPULATION:** 18,640

ETHNIC GROUPS: government employees, academic community, tourist service personnel

PRINCIPAL LANGUAGE: Spanish (official)

CHIEF RELIGION: Roman Catholic

■ **TOPOGRAPHY:** rough, largely desolate group of volcanic islands

AREA: 3,092 sq mi (8,010 sq km)

CLIMATE: Equatorial, cooled by the Humboldt current, with a wet season from January to April, and a cool, dry season from May to December.

■ **CAPITAL:** Puerto Baquerizo Moreno (pop., 5,000)

GOVERNMENT TYPE: province of Ecuador

MONETARY UNIT: U.S. dollar

■ **RESOURCES:** unique animal and bird life

INDUSTRY: eco-tourism

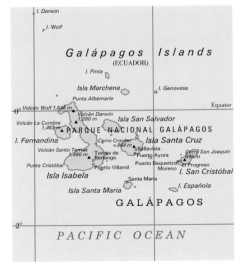

GUADELOUPE - FRANCE (NA)

Columbus discovered Guadeloupe in 1493. The French took possession of the island in 1635. It was annexed to France in 1674 but was seized several times by the British over the next century. French control of Guadeloupe was finally acknowledged in the Treaty of Vienna in 1815. Slavery was abolished on the islands in 1848. In 1946 Guadeloupe became an Overseas Department of France.

■ **POPULATION:** 456,698
ETHNIC GROUPS: Mostly Black African or mixed with a small European minority.
PRINCIPAL LANGUAGES: French, Creole patois
CHIEF RELIGIONS: Roman Catholic
■ **TOPOGRAPHY:** nine mostly volcanic islands
AREA: 687 sq mi (1,779 sq km)
CLIMATE: Subtropical, tempered by trade winds
■ **CAPITAL:** Basse-Terre (pop., 12,500)
GOVERNMENT TYPE: Overseas Department of France
MONETARY UNIT: euro
■ **INDUSTRIES:** construction, sugar processing, rum, food processing
CHIEF CROPS: bananas, sugarcane, tropical fruits, vegetables
EXPORT PARTNERS: France, the U.S.

FRENCH GUIANA - FRANCE (SA)

First settled by the French in 1604, the territory officially became a possession in 1817. The French government established penal colonies here, with the offshore Devil's Island being the most notorious, from 1852 to 1951. The possession became an Overseas Department of France in 1946. It is now the location of the European Space Agency (located in Kourou) which gives the economy a major boost.

■ **POPULATION:** 203,321
ETHNIC GROUPS: Two thirds African and mixed. Small groups of Europeans and others.
PRINCIPAL LANGUAGE: French
CHIEF RELIGION: Roman Catholic
■ **TOPOGRAPHY:** low-lying coastal plains rising hills and small mountains
AREA: 35,135 sq mi (91,000 sq km)
CLIMATE: Tropical, hot and humid with little seasonal temperature variation
■ **CAPITAL:** Cayenne (pop., 51,000)

GOVERNMENT TYPE: Overseas Department of France
MONETARY UNIT: euro

■ **RESOURCES:** bauxite, gold, kaolin, niobium, tantalum, clay, forestry, fish
INDUSTRIES: construction, shrimp processing, forestry, rum, mining
CHIEF CROPS: corn, rice, tapioca, sugar, cocoa, vegetables, bananas
EXPORT PARTNERS: France, Switzerland, the U.S.

MARTINIQUE - FRANCE (NA)

Columbus discovered Martinique in 1502. The French took possession of the island in 1635. Except for brief periods of British occupation, the island has remained under French control ever since. In March 1946 Martinique became an Overseas Department of France.

■ **POPULATION:** 439,202
ETHNIC GROUPS: Mostly Black African or mixed with a small European, East Indian and Chinese minorities.
PRINCIPAL LANGUAGES: French, Creole patois
CHIEF RELIGIONS: Roman Catholic, small numbers of Protestants, Muslims and Hindus
■ **TOPOGRAPHY:** mountainous volcanic terrain with indented coastline
AREA: 425 sq mi (1,100 sq km)
CLIMATE: Tropical, moderated by trade winds, with occasional severe hurricanes
■ **CAPITAL:** Fort-de-France (pop., 94,000)
GOVERNMENT TYPE: Overseas Department of France
MONETARY UNIT: euro
■ **INDUSTRIES:** tourism, construction, sugar processing, rum, oil refining
CHIEF CROPS: pineapples, avocados, bananas, flowers, sugarcane, vegetables
EXPORT PARTNER: France

NEW CALEDONIA - FRANCE (OC)

Settled by both Britain and France during the first half of the 19th century, the island became a French possession in 1853. It was a penal colony for four decades after 1864. The 1998 Noumea Accord, will transfer increasing governing responsibility from France to New Caledonia over a period of 15 to 20 years. The agreement also commits France to conduct as many as three referenda between 2013 and 2018, to decide whether New Caledonia should assume full sovereignty and independence.

■ **POPULATION:** 221,943
ETHNIC GROUPS: Two thirds African and mixed. Small groups of Europeans and others.
PRINCIPAL LANGUAGE: French
CHIEF RELIGION: Roman Catholic
■ **TOPOGRAPHY:** low-lying coastal plains rising hills and small mountains
AREA: 7,359 sq mi (19,060 sq km)
CLIMATE: Tropical, hot and humid, modified by southeast trade winds.
■ **CAPITAL:** Nouméa (pop., 77,000)
GOVERNMENT TYPE: Overseas Department of France

MONETARY UNIT: CFP franc
■ **RESOURCES:** nickel, copper, lead, gold, chrome, forestry, fish
INDUSTRIES: nickel mining, smelting
CHIEF CROPS: vegetables
EXPORT PARTNERS: Japan, France, Taiwan, South Korea

HONG KONG - CHINA (AS)

After the Chinese defeat in the First Opium War, Hong Kong island and the southern tip of the Kowloon peninsula were leased to the United Kingdom for 99 years in 1898. In July 1997, China resumed sovereignty over Hong Kong, ending more than 150 years of British colonial rule. As a Special Administrative Region of the People's Republic of China, Hong Kong has a degree of autonomy in all matters except foreign and defense affairs. According to the Sino-British Joint Declaration and the Basic Law, Hong Kong will retain its political, economic, and judicial systems and unique way of life for 50 years after reversion and continue to participate in international agreements and organizations under the name, "Hong Kong, China."

■ **POPULATION:** 6,980,412

ETHNIC GROUPS: almost entirely Chinese with small minorities of Europeans and others

PRINCIPAL LANGUAGES: Cantonese (a Chinese dialect) and English

CHIEF RELIGIONS: Buddhism, Taoism, various forms of Christianity and others

■ **TOPOGRAPHY:** hilly to mountainous with steep slopes and natural harbors

AREA: 402 sq mi (1,040 sq km)

CLIMATE: Subtropical monsoon, cool and humid in winter, hot and riny in spring and summer, warm and sunny in fall.

GOVERNMENT TYPE: special administrative region of China

MONETARY UNIT: Hong Kong dollar

■ **RESOURCES:** fish

INDUSTRIES: shipping, banking, tourism, textiles and clothing, electronics, plastics, toys, watches and clocks

CHIEF CROPS: vegetables

EXPORT PARTNERS: China, the U.S., Japan

GAZA STRIP (AS)

Gaza history dates to at least 1500 BC. Alexander the Great laid siege to the town in 332 BC. Later, the town was held by the Romans, the Crusaders, the Mamluks, the Ottomans and briefly even by Napoleon Bonaparte in 1799. The Turks took it back, then lost it to the British in World War I. The Egyptian army held it during the 1948 war that led to Israel's independence, opening camps for Palestinian refugees. The current political turmoil began when Israel occupied the Strip in 1967. Israel evacuated all settlements in August, and withdrew its troops in September 2005. Israel also gave up all its claims on the territory and regards the border with it as a frontier. The current status of the Gaza Strip is uncertain.

■ **POPULATION:** 1,482,405

ETHNIC GROUPS: almost entirely Palestinian Arab, small minority of Palestinian Jewish Principal languages: Arabic (official), Hebrew, English

PRINCIPAL LANGUAGES: Arabic, Hebrew, English

CHIEF RELIGIONS: Muslim (predominantly Sunni), Christian, Jewish

■ **TOPOGRAPHY:** flat to hilly, sand and dune covered coastal plain

AREA: 139 sq mi (360 sq km)

CLIMATE: Temperate, with mild winters and dry hot summers

■ **CHIEF CITY:** Gaza (pop., 480,000)

GOVERNMENT TYPE: in transition

MONETARY UNIT: new Israeli shekel

■ **RESOURCE:** natural gas

INDUSTRIES: small family businesses produce textiles, soap and souvenirs

CHIEF CROPS: olives, citrus, vegetables, flowers

EXPORT PARTNERS: Israel, Egypt, West Bank

WEST BANK (AS)

Direct negotiations over the status of the West Bank began in 1999, but were derailed a year later. In 2003 the U.S., E.U., UN, and Russia presented a roadmap for a settlement of the conflict based on reciprocal steps by the two parties leading to two states, Israel and a democratic Palestine. However, the proposed date for a permanent agreement was postponed indefinitely. In January 2005 the PA agreed to move the peace process forward. In September 2005, Israel withdrew all its settlers and soldiers and dismantled its military facilities in the four northern West Bank settlements. In January 2006, the Islamic Resistance Movement, HAMAS, won control of the Palestinian Legislative Council (PLC). Since then there has been little progress in the peace process.

■ **POPULATION:** 2,535,927

ETHNIC GROUPS: mostly Palestinian Arab, significant minority of Palestinian Jewish

PRINCIPAL LANGUAGES: Arabic, Hebrew, English

CHIEF RELIGIONS: Muslim (predominantly Sunni), Jewish, Christian

■ **TOPOGRAPHY:** mostly rugged uplands with sparse vegetation

AREA: 2,263 sq mi (5,860 sq km)

CLIMATE: Temperate, with mild winters and dry hot summers

GOVERNMENT TYPE: civilian control of the Palestinian Authority

MONETARY UNITS: new Israeli shekel, Jordanian dinar

■ **INDUSTRIES:** small family businesses produce cement, textiles, soap and souvenirs

CHIEF CROPS: olives, citrus, vegetables

EXPORT PARTNERS: Israel, Jordan, Gaza Strip

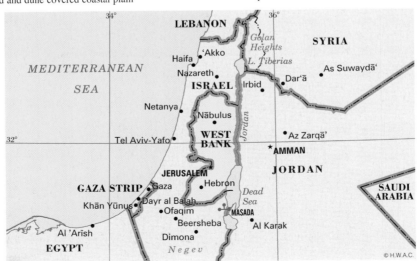

This index is a comprehensive listing of the places and geographic features found in the atlas. Names are arranged in strict alphabetical order, without regard to hyphens or spaces. Every name is followed by the country or area to which it belongs. Except for cities, towns, countries and cultural areas, all entries include a reference to feature type, such as river, island, peak and so on. The page number, appearing to the right of each listing, directs you to the map on which the name can be found. To conserve space and provide room for more entries, many abbreviations are used in this index. The primary abbreviations are listed below.

Index Abbreviations

A	Afg.	Afghanistan
	Afr.	Africa
	Alb.	Albania
	Alg.	Algeria
	And.	Andorra
	Ang.	Angola
	Angu.	Anguilla
	Anti.	Antigua and Barbuda
	Arch.	Archipelago
	Arg.	Argentina
	Arm.	Armenia
	Aru.	Aruba
	ASam.	American Samoa
	Aus.	Austria
	Austl.	Australia
	Azer.	Azerbaijan
	Azor.	Azores
B	Bahm.	Bahamas, The
	Bahr.	Bahrain
	Bang.	Bangladesh
	Bar.	Barbados
	Bela.	Belarus
	Belg.	Belgium
	Belz.	Belize
	Ben.	Benin
	Berm.	Bermuda
	Bhu.	Bhutan
	Bol.	Bolivia
	Bosn.	Bosnia and Herzegovina
	Bots.	Botswana
	Braz.	Brazil
	Bru.	Brunei
	Bul.	Bulgaria
	Burk.	Burkina Faso
	Buru.	Burundi
	BVI	British Virgin Islands
C	CAfr.	Central African Republic
	Camb.	Cambodia
	Camr.	Cameroon
	Can.	Canada
	Canl.	Canary Islands
	Cap.	Capital
	Cay.	Cayman Islands
	C.d'Iv.	Côte d'Ivoire
	Chl.	Channel Islands
	Col.	Colombia

	Com.	Comoros
	Cont.	Continent
	CpV.	Cape Verde Islands
	CR	Costa Rica
	Cro.	Croatia
	Ctry.	Country
	Cyp.	Cyprus
	Czh.	Czech Republic
D	Den.	Denmark
	Des.	Desert
	Djib.	Djibouti
	Dom.	Dominica
	Dpcy.	Dependency
	D.R.Congo	Democratic Republic of the Congo
	DRep.	Dominican Republic
E	Ecu.	Ecuador
	EqG.	Equatorial Guinea
	Erit.	Eritrea
	ESal.	El Salvador
	Est.	Estonia
	Eth.	Ethiopia
	ETim.	East Timor
	Eur.	Europe
F	Fin.	Finland
	Fr.	France
	FrG.	French Guiana
	FrPol.	French Polynesia
	FYROM	Former Yugoslav Rep. of Macedonia
G	Galp.	Galapagos Islands
	Gam.	Gambia, The
	Gaza	Gaza Strip
	GBis.	Guinea-Bissau
	Geo.	Georgia
	Ger.	Germany
	Gha.	Ghana
	Gib.	Gibraltar
	Gre.	Greece
	Grld.	Greenland
	Gren.	Grenada
	Guad.	Guadeloupe
	Guat.	Guatemala
	Gui.	Guinea
	Guy.	Guyana

H	Hon.	Honduras
	Hun.	Hungary
I	Ice.	Iceland
	Indo.	Indonesia
	Int'l	International
	Ire.	Ireland
	Isl., Isls.	Island, Islands
	Isr.	Israel
	It.	Italy
J	Jam.	Jamaica
	Jor.	Jordan
K	Kaz.	Kazakhstan
	Kiri.	Kiribati
	Kuw.	Kuwait
	Kyr.	Kyrgyzstan
L	Lat.	Latvia
	Lcht.	Liechtenstein
	Leb.	Lebanon
	Les.	Lesotho
	Libr.	Liberia
	Lith.	Lithuania
	Lux.	Luxembourg
M	Madg.	Madagascar
	Madr.	Madeira
	Malay.	Malaysia
	Mald.	Maldives
	Malw.	Malawi
	Mart.	Martinique
	May.	Mayotte
	Mex.	Mexico
	Micr.	Micronesia, Federated States of
	Mol.	Moldova
	Mona.	Monaco
	Mong.	Mongolia
	Mont.	Montenegro
	Monts.	Montserrat
	Mor.	Morocco
	Moz.	Mozambique
	Mrsh.	Marshall Islands
	Mrta.	Mauritania
	Mrts.	Mauritius
	Mt.	Mount
	Mtn., Mts.	Mountain, Mountains
	Myan.	Myanmar

N	NAm.	North America
	Namb.	Namibia
	NAnt.	Netherlands Antilles
	Nat'l	National
	NCal.	New Caledonia
	Neth.	Netherlands
	Nga.	Nigeria
	NI,UK	Northern Ireland
	Nic.	Nicaragua
	NKor.	North Korea
	NMar.	Northern Mariana Islands
	Nor.	Norway
	NZ	New Zealand
P	PacUS	Pacific Islands, U.S.
	Pak.	Pakistan
	Pan.	Panama
	Par.	Paraguay
	Pen.	Peninsula
	Phil.	Philippines
	Plat.	Plateau
	PNG	Papua New Guinea
	Pol.	Poland
	Port.	Portugal
	PR	Puerto Rico
	Pt.	Point
R	Reg.	Region
	Rep.	Republic
	Res.	Reservoir
	Reun.	Réunion
	Riv.	River
	Rom.	Romania
	Rus.	Russia
	Rwa.	Rwanda
S	SAfr.	South Africa
	Sam.	Samoa
	SAm.	South America
	SaoT.	São Tomé and Príncipe
	SAr.	Saudi Arabia
	Sen.	Senegal
	Serb.	Serbia
	Sey.	Seychelles
	Sing.	Singapore
	SKor.	South Korea
	SLeo.	Sierra Leone
	Slov.	Slovenia
	Slvk.	Slovakia

	SMar.	San Marino
	Sol.	Solomon Islands
	Som.	Somalia
	Sp.	Spain
	SrL.	Sri Lanka
	StH.	Saint Helena
	Str.	Strait
	StK.	Saint Kitts and Nevis
	StL.	Saint Lucia
	StP.	Saint Pierre and Miquelon
	StV.	Saint Vincent and the Grenadines
	Sur.	Suriname
	Swaz.	Swaziland
	Swe.	Sweden
	Swi.	Switzerland
T	Tai.	Taiwan
	Taj.	Tajikistan
	Tanz.	Tanzania
	Terr.	Territory
	Thai.	Thailand
	Trin.	Trinidad and Tobago
	Trkm.	Turkmenistan
	Trks.	Turks and Caicos Islands
	Tun.	Tunisia
	Turk.	Turkey
	Tuv.	Tuvalu
U	UAE	United Arab Emirates
	Ugan.	Uganda
	UK	United Kingdom
	Ukr.	Ukraine
	Uru.	Uruguay
	U.S.	United States
	USVI	U.S. Virgin Islands
	Uzb.	Uzbekistan
V	Van.	Vanuatu
	VatC.	Vatican City
	Ven.	Venezuela
	Viet.	Vietnam
	Vol.	Volcano
W	WBnk.	West Bank
	WSah.	Western Sahara
Y	Yem.	Yemen
Z	Zam.	Zambia
	Zim.	Zimbabwe

ACKNOWLEDGEMENTS

Publisher

Hammond World Atlas Corporation

Chairman	Andreas Langenscheidt
President	Marc Jennings
Vice President of Cartography	Vera Lorenz
Director Database Resources	Theophrastos E. Giouvanos
Cover Design	Marian Purcell
Design and Page Layout	Lee Goldstein
Photo Research	Lee Pierre-Charles

Layout and Composition	John A. DiGiorgio
	Maribel Lopez
Cartography	Walter H. Jones Jr.,
	Sharon Lightner
	Harry E. Morin
	James Padykula
	Thomas R. Rubino
	Thomas J. Scheffer

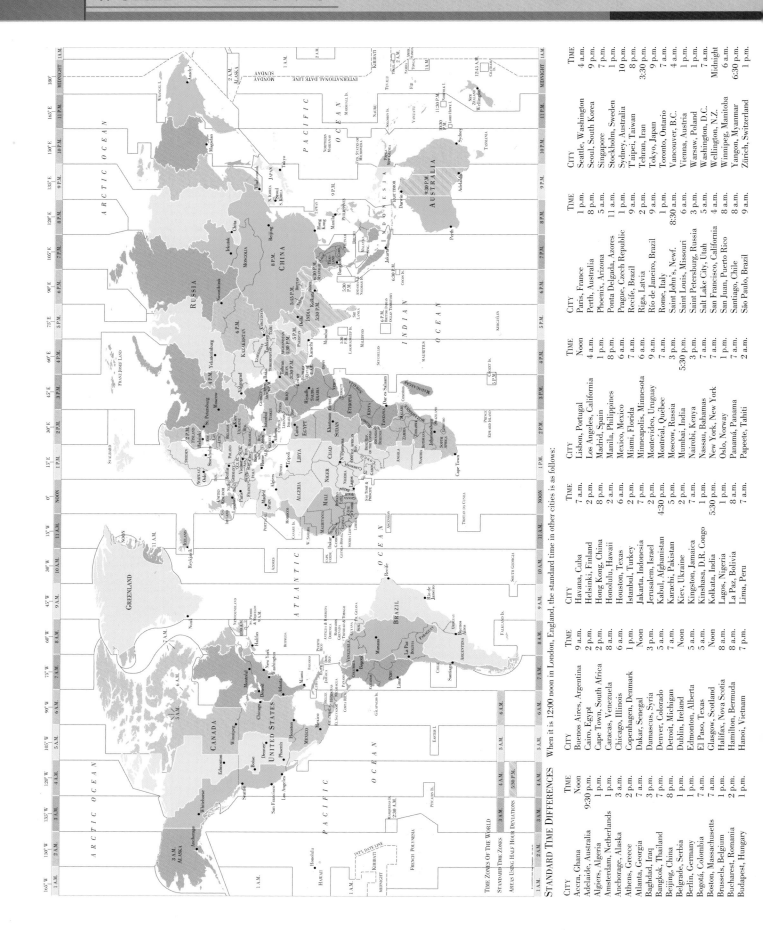

Time Zones of the World
Standard Time Zones
Areas Using Half Hour Deviations

STANDARD TIME DIFFERENCES   When it is 12:00 noon in London, England, the standard time in other cities is as follows:

CITY	TIME	CITY	TIME	CITY	TIME
Accra, Ghana	Noon	Buenos Aires, Argentina	9 a.m.	Havana, Cuba	7 a.m.
Adelaide, Australia	9:30 p.m.	Cairo, Egypt	2 p.m.	Helsinki, Finland	2 p.m.
Algiers, Algeria	1 p.m.	Cape Town, South Africa	2 p.m.	Hong Kong, China	8 p.m.
Amsterdam, Netherlands	1 p.m.	Caracas, Venezuela	8 a.m.	Honolulu, Hawaii	2 a.m.
Anchorage, Alaska	3 a.m.	Chicago, Illinois	6 a.m.	Houston, Texas	6 a.m.
Athens, Greece	2 p.m.	Copenhagen, Denmark	1 p.m.	Istanbul, Turkey	2 p.m.
Atlanta, Georgia	7 a.m.	Dakar, Senegal	Noon	Jakarta, Indonesia	7 p.m.
Baghdad, Iraq	3 p.m.	Damascus, Syria	3 p.m.	Jerusalem, Israel	2 p.m.
Bangkok, Thailand	7 p.m.	Denver, Colorado	5 a.m.	Kabul, Afghanistan	4:30 p.m.
Beijing, China	8 p.m.	Detroit, Michigan	7 a.m.	Karachi, Pakistan	5 p.m.
Belgrade, Serbia	1 p.m.	Dublin, Ireland	Noon	Kiev, Ukraine	2 p.m.
Berlin, Germany	1 p.m.	Edmonton, Alberta	5 a.m.	Kingston, Jamaica	7 a.m.
Bogotá, Colombia	7 a.m.	El Paso, Texas	5 a.m.	Kinshasa, D.R. Congo	1 p.m.
Boston, Massachusetts	7 a.m.	Glasgow, Scotland	Noon	Kolkata, India	5:30 p.m.
Brussels, Belgium	1 p.m.	Halifax, Nova Scotia	8 a.m.	Lagos, Nigeria	1 p.m.
Bucharest, Romania	2 p.m.	Hamilton, Bermuda	8 a.m.	La Paz, Bolivia	8 a.m.
Budapest, Hungary	1 p.m.	Hanoi, Vietnam	7 p.m.	Lima, Peru	7 a.m.

CITY	TIME	CITY	TIME	CITY	TIME
Lisbon, Portugal	Noon	Paris, France	1 p.m.	Seattle, Washington	4 a.m.
Los Angeles, California	4 a.m.	Perth, Australia	8 p.m.	Seoul, South Korea	9 p.m.
Madrid, Spain	1 p.m.	Phoenix, Arizona	5 a.m.	Singapore	7 p.m.
Manila, Philippines	8 p.m.	Ponta Delgada, Azores	11 a.m.	Stockholm, Sweden	1 p.m.
Mexico, Mexico	6 a.m.	Prague, Czech Republic	1 p.m.	Sydney, Australia	10 p.m.
Miami, Florida	7 a.m.	Recife, Brazil	9 a.m.	T'aipei, Taiwan	8 p.m.
Minneapolis, Minnesota	6 a.m.	Riga, Latvia	2 p.m.	Tehran, Iran	3:30 p.m.
Montevideo, Uruguay	9 a.m.	Río de Janeiro, Brazil	9 a.m.	Tokyo, Japan	9 p.m.
Montréal, Québec	7 a.m.	Rome, Italy	1 p.m.	Toronto, Ontario	7 a.m.
Moscow, Russia	3 p.m.	Saint John's, Newf.	8:30 a.m.	Vancouver, B.C.	4 a.m.
Mumbai, India	5:30 p.m.	Saint Louis, Missouri	6 a.m.	Vienna, Austria	1 p.m.
Nairobi, Kenya	3 p.m.	Saint Petersburg, Russia	3 p.m.	Warsaw, Poland	1 p.m.
Nassau, Bahamas	7 a.m.	Salt Lake City, Utah	5 a.m.	Washington, D.C.	7 a.m.
New York, New York	7 a.m.	San Francisco, California	4 a.m.	Wellington, N.Z.	Midnight
Oslo, Norway	1 p.m.	San Juan, Puerto Rico	8 a.m.	Winnipeg, Manitoba	6 a.m.
Panamá, Panama	7 a.m.	Santiago, Chile	8 a.m.	Yangon, Myanmar	6:30 p.m.
Papeete, Tahiti	2 a.m.	São Paulo, Brazil	9 a.m.	Zürich, Switzerland	1 p.m.